NELSON
THE COMMANDER

To the
PAST OVERSEERS SOCIETY OF
ST MARGARET AND ST JOHN, WESTMINSTER,
which had inherited from the erstwhile St Margaret's Vestry Club, the
tradition that, whilst enjoying a whitebait dinner at Greenwich in 1805,
its members received the news of Nelson's death and immediately rose
and in silence drank a toast to

THE IMMORTAL MEMORY

This tradition has since been honoured each year by the Society
at its annual dinner before the ceremony of transferring their unique and
famous Tobacco Box to its Custodians of the ensuing year, of which the
original component was acquired in 1713, and on which the year 1798 is
commemorated by a representation of the battle of the Nile and the year
1805 by a portrait of Lord Nelson

PEN & SWORD MILITARY CLASSICS

We hope you enjoy your Pen and Sword Military Classic. The series is designed to give readers quality military history at affordable prices. Pen and Sword Classics are available from all good bookshops. If you would like to keep in touch with further developments in the series,

Telephone: **01226 734555**,
email: **enquiries@pen-and-sword.co.uk**,
or visit our website at **www.pen-and-sword.co.uk**.

NELSON
THE COMMANDER

Geoffrey Bennett

PEN & SWORD MILITARY CLASSICS

By the same Author:
By Human Error
Coronel and the Falklands
Cowan's War, *British naval Operations in the Baltic 1918-1920*
The Battle of Jutland
Charlie B, *a biography of Admiral Lord Beresford*
Naval Battles of the First World War
Naval Battle of the Second World War

First published in Great Britain in 1972 by B. T. Batsford Ltd

Published in this format in 2005 by
Pen & Sword Military Classic
An imprint of
Pen & Sword Books Ltd
47 Church Street
Barnsley
South Yorkshire
S70 2AS

Printed and bound in England
By CPI UK

Pen & Sword Books Ltd incorporates the Imprints of Pen & Sword Aviation,
Pen & Sword Maritime, Pen & Sword Military, Wharncliffe Local history,
Pen & Sword Select, Pen & Sword Military Classics and Leo Cooper.

For a complete list of Pen & Sword titles please contact
PEN & SWORD BOOKS LIMITED
47 Church Street, Barnsley, South Yorkshire, S70 2AS, England
E-mail: enquiries@pen-and-sword.co.uk
Website: www.pen-and-sword.co.uk

Contents

Acknowledgements

To Her Majesty The Queen, for gracious permission to quote from papers in the Royal Archives, Windsor, the author submits his humble thanks.

My second debt is to my wife whose advice and help throughout the writing of this book have been of incalculable value. Without her wise guidance on Nelson's relations with his wife and with Emma Hamilton from the female viewpoint I should have been 'all at sea'.

My third is to Dr. J. E. de Courcy Ireland whose encyclopaedic knowledge and objective understanding of maritime history have done so much to enable me to deal with my subject 'warts and all'; and to Captain W. R. H. Lapper, Royal Navy, who by likewise reading this book in typescript, has steered me clear of many a shoal. Neither is, however, to be held responsible for any errors in my navigation.

My fourth, but by no means least, is to Admiral of the Fleet Sir Peter Hill-Norton, G.C.B. for allowing me to use the greater part of his speech delivered in Washington, D.C., on Trafalgar Day, 1970, as a singularly apposite Foreword.

Others to whom I am indebted include Mr. R. C. Mackworth-Young, Assistant Keeper of the Royal Archives and his staff at Windsor; Captain E. Borg, Royal Danish Navy, for an invaluable visit to Copenhagen; Commander L. T. Kúzmin, Assistant Naval Attaché to the Embassy of the U.S.S.R. in London, who enabled me to use the papers of Admiral Ushakóv; Mr. Douglas Robinson, M.D., of Pennington, New Jersey; Lieutenant-Commander W. E. Pearce, Royal Navy, Captain of HMS *Victory* (Ship) for a most illuminating visit to his command; the Director of the Central Maritime Museum, Leningrad; Mr. A. W. H. Pearsall and the staff of the National Maritime Museum, Greenwich; and the Librarians of the City of Westminster and the Royal Borough of Kensington and Chelsea and their staffs, in particular for the speed with which they obtained such books as I needed from abroad.

For permission to use copyright material I have to thank Miss Carola Oman for a short extract from her *Nelson*, and J. M. Dent & Son for a quotation from *The Mirror of the Sea* by Joseph Conrad.

ACKNOWLEDGEMENTS

I have also to thank Mr. P. S. Roland for translating Russian documents; Miss Mary Rundle for compiling the index; Mr Arthur Banks for drawing the admirable maps and diagrams, and Miss Adrienne Edye for untiringly typing and retyping my often illegible manuscript.

Lastly, I acknowledge my debt to all those who have 'charted the way', the authors and editors of the many books already published dealing directly and indirectly with Nelson's life and career which are listed in my Bibliography.

1970   GEOFFREY BENNETT

The Author and Publishers wish to thank the following for permission to reproduce the photographs appearing in this book: Her Majesty the Queen for figs. 15, 18, 36 and 38; Association of the Tourist Boards of the Eastern Caribbean for fig. 6; Trustees of the British Museum for figs. 19 and 23; Rector of Burnham Thorpe for figs. 2–4; Greater London Council for fig. 12; Ministry for the Environment (Crown copyright reserved) for fig. 43; Ministry of Defence (Navy) (Crown copyright reserved) for figs. 9 and 10; Trustees of the National Maritime Museum, Greenwich for figs. 5, 7, 8, 16, 17, 21, 25–8, 32, 37, 40 and 44; National Maritime Museum, Leningrad for fig. 30; Trustees of the National Portrait Gallery for figs. 14, 20 and 22; Mr. C. A. Prendergast for fig. 24; Radio Times Hulton Picture Library for figs. 34–5; Royal Library, Copenhagen for fig. 33; Committee of the United Service and Royal Aero Club for figs. 29 and 39; Dean and Chapter of Westminster Abbey for fig. 1; Westminster City Council for fig. 11; Mr. Leslie Wilcox, RI, RSMA, for fig. 45.

Acknowledgment is also due to the following for permission to reproduce line drawings: Blandford Press for p. 60 from E. H. Archibald's *The Wooden Fighting Ship*; Corrall Publicity Ltd., Portsmouth for p. 56 (top) drawn by Mr. Lawrence Bagley; Trustees of the National Maritime Museum, Greenwich for p. 83; The Captain, HMS *Victory* (Ship) for pp. 56 (bottom) and 58, drawn by Christine Warburton; Weidenfeld and Nicolson for p. 65 from Dudley Pope's *Guns*.

POSTSCRIPT

According to p. 2, 'the *Victory*, alone of all the great armada of warships which have flown the British ensign, is preserved in Portsmouth dockyard'. By a happy chance, this statement has been proved wrong whilst the book was with the printers; by the unexpected decision taken in the summer of 1971, to preserve for posterity in a Thames-side berth opposite the Tower of London, the last and largest of Britain's World War Two cruisers, HMS *Belfast*, 11,550 tons, completed in 1939 with twelve 6-inch guns.

Foreword

by

Admiral of the Fleet Sir Peter Hill-Norton, G.C.B.,
British Chief of the Defence Staff

*From a speech delivered in Washington, D.C.,
on Trafalgar Night, 21 October 1970*

Admiral Elmo Zumwalt, Gentlemen. . . . This is a unique occasion; the first time that any First Sea Lord has had the honour of entertaining the Chief of Naval Operations and his officers in their own capital city, to commemorate a British sailor who had his baptism of fire in the War of American Independence.

Your Navy shares with ours many traditions which have led to a mutual respect and understanding, and to a unique relationship of outstanding importance to the Free World. In 1782, when captain of the frigate *Albemarle*, Nelson captured an American fishing schooner, the *Harmony* of Massachussetts, whose skipper and owner, Nathaniel Carver, had almost reached port with a cargo representing all his worldly possessions. Ordered to pilot the *Albermarle* into Boston, Carver did so with such speed and skill that Nelson, saying that it was not the custom of English seamen to be ungrateful, returned his schooner to him and gave him a certificate of good conduct. Two months later, Carver by chance came across the *Albemarle* still on patrol, with her crew suffering badly from scurvy, and presented Nelson with four sheep, several crates of fowls and a large quantity of fresh vegetables. It would be difficult to find a better example of mutual respect and understanding.

We speak almost the same language, and our Services are governed in what they do and how they do it by long established tradition, which has its origin in professional integrity, courage, skill and diligence. And Lord Nelson had these qualities to a degree that no British sailor before or since has been able to equal: he is an example of what we should all like to be, and what from an early age we are taught to try and live up to.

Your Navy also has its heroes, and we admire the superb seamanship, courage and fighting qualities of the American captains in the classic single ship actions of the War of 1812. Bainbridge of the *Constitution*, Dekatur of the *United States*, Lawrence of the *Hornet* and the *Chesapeake*, all have an honoured place in both American and British naval history.

It is a widely held fallacy that to look back on the past is not only unprofitable but a sign of decadence. Nothing could be further from the truth; none of us should make the mistake of thinking that we have nothing to learn from history or its great men. The Royal Navy looks back with pride on what Nelson did for his country, but *not* because what we were doing at that time was necessarily right, nor because we are filled with nostalgia for our imperial past. We look back at the standards of conduct and the sense of purpose and duty of this small frail man, so that they may serve as an inspiration to us and our successors. These are sentiments which, in the context of your own great men, I am sure you share.

Today, it is the mode to denigrate the fighting Services, and with them the virtues of integrity and industry, skill and enterprise, courage and perseverance, without which we should have no purpose and could not hope to survive in a materialistic age. The remedy is in our own hands: it is for us to ensure that by our own conduct and example, the Profession of Arms, and particularly the Naval Service, continues to be recognized as an honourable, difficult and worthwhile vocation.

Nelson did it; let us, each in his own way, seek to rise to his standards. Gentlemen, I give you the toast: 'The Immortal Memory'.

NELSON

I

Dialectic

Horatio Nelson, Vice-Admiral of the White, Knight of the Bath, Baron and Viscount of the Nile and of Burnham Thorpe and Hilborough in the County of Norfolk, Duke of Brontë – plus the posthumous bestowal (on his elder brother, William) of an earldom and the viscountcy of Trafalgar and Merton. His death

> was felt in England as something more than a public calamity . . . [so] deeply we loved and revered him. . . . The country had lost . . . its great naval hero. . . . So perfectly had he performed his part, that the maritime war, after the battle of Trafalgar, was considered at an end: the fleets of the enemy were not merely defeated, but destroyed . . . through Nelson's surpassing genius. He could scarcely have departed in a brighter blaze of glory. He has left us . . . a name which is our pride, and an example which will continue to be our shield and strength.

Today, more than a hundred and fifty years after Robert Southey paid this tribute at the close of his classic biography, the British take a more realistic view. As one expression of the nation's feelings at the time of Nelson's death, Parliament voted an annuity of £5,000 ($12,000)* to his heirs in perpetuity; but the Labour Government which the Nation returned to power in 1945 discontinued this pension on the death of the 5th Earl, without compensation. Oliver Warner has written: 'Setback, reverse, disappointment, Nelson knew them quite as often as their opposite. . . . [But] his triumphs have so caught the general imagination

*Calculated here and henceforth at the 1971 rate of exchange of approx. £1.00 = $2.40.

that his failures are scarcely remembered.' Other historians have stressed the watch which a British fleet had to maintain over the French in the Mediterranean after Trafalgar, as part of a blockade that continued to occupy much of the Royal Navy's available strength. So much was this so that when the United States declared war in 1812, a sufficient force could not be spared to prevent their frigates and privateers operating as far afield as the English Channel, nor prevent them sinking and capturing more than 1,000 British warships and merchantmen.

Many consider Nelson's treatment of his wife inexcusable, especially the harshness of her final dismissal from his life. Others are at a loss to understand how a man who put his trust in God could have become the enslaved lover of a woman who had begun life in domestic service before becoming the mistress of Charles Greville and a model for George Romney. As Lord St Vincent wrote, when Nelson's letters to Lady Hamilton were published in 1814: 'It will reflect eternal disgrace upon [his] character ... which will ... be stripped of everything but animal courage.'

Yet Southey has been proved the truer prophet. The toast to 'The Immortal Memory', is drunk at more annual dinners than that of the Past Overseers of the parishes of St Margaret and St John, Westminster, who thus recall that their members chanced to be enjoying whitebait at Greenwich when they learned the news of Nelson's death. The *Victory*, alone of all the great armada of warships which have flown the British ensign, is preserved in Portsmouth dockyard, to hoist each year, on 21 October, Nelson's never-to-be-forgotten signal, 'England expects ...'. And it is only a couple of years since Field-Marshal Montgomery judged him *supreme* among captains of war.

Nor is praise confined to Britain: there is no naval academy, from the Tokyo of Admiral Togo to the Annapolis of Admiral Dewey, which has not sought to learn from the strategy and tactics with which Nelson countered and destroyed the fleets that challenged Britain's command of the sea. The finding of the board of inquiry held to investigate the circumstances in which six United States destroyers followed their leader on to the rocks off Honda Point, California, on the night of 8 September 1923 contained these words:

> Had Nelson at Cape St Vincent blindly followed the leader, John Jervis would not have gained the victory which he did. Had Nelson obeyed Parker, Copenhagen would not have been the monument to the British Navy which it is. Blindly following the leader, or unreasoning adherence

to set regulations, is more in accordance with the practice of those leaders of the past who hesitated to depart from the line ahead, even when advantages would accrue from a departure from such practice.

Even the French, for whom Nelson had such contempt, and whose Fleet he twice defeated so decisively, pay tacit tribute to his greatness; *coup de Trafalgar* is their expression for a sudden, decisive blow.

There is, however, another point of view. Moscow's pedagogues acknowledge that Nelson 'distinguished himself by his courage, decisiveness, and exceptional capacity for organization', and that 'his maritime victories had a substantial influence on the strategic position in Europe'. In the three volumes of Admiral Ushakóv's papers published in Moscow as recently as 1951–56, the only one of some 1,500 documents singled out for facsimile reproduction is a letter from Nelson. And the Soviet Navy has the same legend as the British, that the black neck silk which has been part of a seaman's uniform for more than a century, is worn in his perpetual memory. But the Nile and Trafalgar are ascribed to his use of Ushakóv's 'new original methods of waging war'; and they condemn his 'hostile attitude to the activities of Ushakóv's fleet [when Russia was Britain's ally] because he feared the strengthening of Russian influence in the Mediterranean'.*

Similarly, an Irish historian has written:

When an Englishman declares that 'no one questions' Nelson's right to look down on London from his Trafalgar Square column, it occurs to a mere Irishman that the many fine qualities of the English would be better symbolized by a statue of Samuel Plimsoll, the seaman's champion, or by William Hillary, founder of the Lifeboat Service, than by that of the jingo . . . who gloated over the executed body of a Republican admiral [Caracciolo] floating in the Bay of Naples. Nelson, who looked down on Ireland while living, no longer does so dead. We may deplore the loss of a Dublin monument, but not the explosion of another overgrown reputation.†

And another Irishman‡ has expressed a view of Nelson this side of idolatry:

Charles XII . . . Nelson [and] Joan of Arc . . . were . . . half-witted

---

*Articles on Nelson in the *Soviet Historical Encyclopaedia*, Vol. X (1967) and on Ushakóv in the *Large Soviet Encyclopaedia*, Vol. XLIV (1956).
†J. E. de Courcy Ireland in the *Irish Times*.
‡George Bernard Shaw in the preface to *Caesar and Cleopatra*.

geniuses, enjoying the worship accorded . . . to certain forms of insanity. . . . When [Nelson's] head was injured at the battle of the Nile, and his conduct became for some years openly scandalous, the difference was not important enough to be noticed.

So, where lies the truth? Though neither the Russians nor the Irish deny Nelson a niche in history's hall of fame, does he merit the supreme place that England accords him? Trafalgar was, after all, his only victory over an enemy fleet *at sea*: at Copenhagen and the Nile he destroyed ships at anchor. Did his strategy match his tactical skill? To what purpose did he pursue Villeneuve across the Atlantic to the West Indies – and back again? What were his qualities – not those that gained him the hearts as well as the huzzas of his countrymen, but as a sea commander in whom a disciplinarian so strict as Lord St Vincent discerned virtues that transcended all his shortcomings?

What was there in Nelson, in an age when the Royal Navy thrived on 'rum, sodomy and the lash',* that turned his captains into a 'Band of Brothers', and moved the roughest sailor to tears on hearing of his death? And has his example inspired Britain, especially her Navy, for good – or was it responsible for the complacency that imbued Queen Victoria's Fleet, from which Lord Fisher extricated it only just in time to avert defeat by Imperial Germany in the First World War? Is there something of lasting value to be learned from Nelson's career? Or, in an age in which the old military virtues – courage, self-sacrifice, comradeship and the rest – seem of questionable relevance,† should Nelson be struck from William Railton's column in London's Trafalgar Square, as he has been from William Wilkins' in Dublin's O'Connell Street?

Can an Englishman put aside the hero worship instilled into him in the nursery, when Britannia held undisputed sway over the oceans, and give objective answers to questions such as these? The present writer, who is proud to have served in the Royal Navy during the thirty years that covered a revolution comparable with the change from sail to steam – the replacement of the 'great gun' by the guided missile – can but try.

But guidelines first: if this study is to avoid being stranded on such domestic shoals as the insufferable conduct of Nelson's stepson, Josiah

---

*Sir Winston Churchill's phrase.
†The reader who is reluctant to accept the military virtues as relevant to the nuclear age is reminded of the Socialist George Orwell's words, in *My Country Right or Left*: 'The spiritual need for patriotism and the military virtues, for which however little the boiled rabbits of the Left may like them, *no substitute has yet been found*.'

Nisbet, or the possibility that his daughter Horatia had a twin sister;* if, too, it is to steer clear of such shallows as the theory, more appropriate to W. S. Gilbert's John Wellington Wells† than the serious historian, that Nelson so far courted death on 21 October 1805 as to be tantamount to suicide, the fairway must be buoyed. A naval commander's greatness is measured by more than the number and extent of his victories: one must assess the inborn qualities and acquired skills that enabled him to achieve results of such consequence to his country.

High on the list comes ambition: not for William Blake's 'strongest poison ever known', which is power; nor for riches, which Cicero condemned as 'so characteristic of a narrow and small mind'; but to do one's duty – to serve one's God, one's Sovereign and one's Country – to the best of one's ability, determined to do so better than other men and to get to the top. For no commander is born great and few have greatness thrust upon them; most must strive to reach the stars. A few are sufficiently inspired by the personal satisfaction of successful achievement. Wellington is a notable example: 'the great principle of his life was "duty". . . . He had but one object in view – to benefit the State . . . to the utmost of his ability and skill. . . . The desire to win applause . . . seems never to have moved him.'‡ Yet he became Prime Minister of England. But most men need public acclaim. They hunger for honour and glory for which the rewards counted for more in Nelson's day than in our own.

High, too, comes leadership, for no officer who lacks this talent is likely to command so much as a squadron, let alone a fleet. Nor, unless he be an outstanding leader, will he be able to make full use of his other gifts and skills. Its ingredients are many. The Royal Navy lists fifteen, headed by faith and knowledge. The Royal Air Force is content with seven, efficiency coming first and personality second. The United States Marine Corps counts fourteen, beginning with integrity and knowledge. The United States Army believes bearing and courage to be more important. And that well-proven leader, Field-Marshal Slim, rates courage highest and will-power next.

Such disparities between acknowledged authorities are understandable. Choose any two great leaders and their outstanding characteristics will seldom be the same. Compare a few examples from our own times; Jellicoe's brilliant brain with Beatty's dashing panache; Haig's taciturn strength with Montgomery's extrovert egotism. The essence of leadership

*Suggested by Winifred Gérin in her *Horatia Nelson*.
†In *The Sorcerer*.
‡Field-Marshal Lord Montgomery in *The Times*, 7 June 1969.

is, however, simply stated: it is the capacity to inspire men to give of their individual and corporate best in all circumstances, but especially when the odds against them are greatest.

A naval commander must be a strategist. This is not so evident today when radio has enabled this aspect of war to be directed from a nation's capital. But in Nelson's time, when communications were slow and uncertain, admirals, especially those serving overseas, had to have a clear understanding of how sea power should be used to further the conduct of a war so that the final victory might be gained on land; how best to employ their ships for the protection of their country's and its allies' maritime trade and in support of their armies, *and* to prevent the enemy from using the sea for either of these vital purposes.

A naval commander must be a skilled tactician. He must know not only how to manoeuvre and fight his fleet, but how to engage, or avoid action with, the enemy in circumstances that are most favourable to his own fleet. But there is more to naval tactics than applying rules formulated from the experience of others; more, too, than adapting them to suit new types of ship and new weapons. Naval tactics are an art as well as a science, far more so than on land where, to quote from a manual published in 1857,

it is almost a certainty that an order will produce certain results. The military commander moves his pieces with the precision of a chess-player. At the note of a bugle, columns form line, consolidate into masses, or deploy into fractions; an inevitable disaster is converted by successful generalship into an honourable retreat. But the seaman is dependent on two uncompromising agents, wind and wave; and over them he has no positive control; he must take them as they come and be ready with his resources. A shift of wind threw three ships out of the brunt of the battle of the Nile.... A gale scattered the hard-won trophies of Trafalgar.... And it was in the full conviction of the impossibility of adhering to fixed rules that Nelson threw himself on the bravery of his men and the undirected ability of his captains.

Napoleon is the classic example of a military commander who could not understand this essential difference between war on land and war at sea.* As Emperor of France he rebuked his admirals again and again for

---

*In sharp contrast to the great Duke of Marlborough who, having fought at sea as a young officer onboard the British flagship at the battle of Sole Bay (1672), was wise enough to rebuke those who would have him interfere with the conduct of naval operations in the War of the Spanish Succession, with these words: 'The Sea Service is not so easily arranged as that of land, there are many more precautions to take, and you and I are not capable of judging them.'

failing to carry out his orders to undertake operations against the British, when they were powerless to obey because adverse winds prevented their ships leaving harbour.

A naval commander should be a diplomatist. He has to do more than fight the enemy. He must work in harmony with kings and statesmen, governors and generals, of his own country and of its allies. He must negotiate with those of neutral powers; sometimes with those of the enemy. He should know when to threaten, when to plead, when to show the iron hand, when to wear a velvet glove, when to be tolerant of weakness, when to defy a bully's strength. And in all this he operates in waters more dangerous than those in which his flagship sails, a sea in which he is more likely to founder. For whilst the successful fleet commander is the man who follows Danton's advice, '*De l'audace, et encore de l'audace, et toujours l'audace*', the diplomatist must remember Talleyrand's counsel, '*N'ayez pas de zèle.*' To cite one example, Nelson's erstwhile second-in-command, Saumarez, made a significant contribution to Britain's ultimate victory over Napoleon when, from 1808 to 1812, he not only cleared the Baltic of a hostile Russian fleet, but maintained such amicable relations with Sweden that her ports remained open to British shipping, even though *force majeure* compelled her to join France's allies. In Nelson's own words, 'political courage . . . is in an officer abroad as highly necessary as battle courage'.

History records the names of many commanders – American, Dutch, Japanese, Spanish and Russian, as well as British and French – who have measured up to most of these requirements; who were therefore successful. But what of the few who achieved greatness; what *more* did they have to make them so? Genius? This is more easily recognized, especially after a man is dead, than defined. Of what value to say that it involves 'a transcendent capacity for taking trouble', or is an 'admixture of madness', even if both be true of Leonardo da Vinci? Moreover, genius may take many forms: Handel's is epitomized in the sublime matching of music to words in his *Messiah*, Einstein's in the harsh realities of $E = mc^2$. Both these men have, however, one thing in common; they needed no more than their own eyes and hands to transmit their inspiration to us. So, too, with most spheres of human activity. But not that of the naval or military commander: his eyes and hands are his officers and men: he depends on them for the execution of his strategy and tactics. And if they are to enable him to defeat the enemy, he needs a quality that is no more easily defined than genius.

It is well recognized in the theatre and concert hall. Pablo Casals, the

Spanish cellist, Lord Olivier, the British actor, Arturo Toscanini, the Italian conductor, and Galina Ulanova, Moscow's *ballerina assoluta*, are all world famous not only for exceptional talent but for that rare gift, star quality. But others besides great artists have this. 'If,' wrote Field-Marshal Lord Wavell* of the 27-year-old Napoleon's appointment to command the *Armée d'Italie*, 'you can discover how a young unknown man inspired a ragged, mutinous, half-starved army and made it fight . . . how he dominated and controlled generals older than himself, then you will have learned something beyond the study of rules and strategy.' Nor did the Emperor lose this quality in the hour of his final defeat: 'What an ineffable beauty there was in that smile . . . his mouth had a charm about it that I have never seen in any other human countenance,' noted a midshipman serving in HMS *Bellerophon* when Napoleon surrendered to Captain F. L. Maitland in 1815 for passage to Plymouth – where in the Sound he saw lying at their moorings the wooden walls that all his genius had been powerless to overcome. Star quality is, in short, one of the ingredients of true greatness in a naval or military commander.

It is, then, these gifts, talents, virtues, skills, call them what you will – ambition, leadership, strategist, tactician, diplomatist and star quality – which should guide our study of Nelson's career. It is with these in mind that we should judge his successes and failures, and give our verdict on his stature as a naval commander – and decide whether he is rightly numbered among the world's Great Captains whose victories are writ in letters of gold across the pages of history since Lysander of Sparta destroyed the Athenian fleet at Aegos-Potami in the year 405 BC – and whose courage even unto death is an inspiration to many more than those whose business is in the field of war.

*In *Soldiers and Soldiering*.

II

Neptune's Cradle

1758-1792

B orn within sound of the North Sea, in the parsonage house of Burnham Thorpe in the county of Norfolk on 29 September 1758, Nelson was the sixth child and fifth son of the rector, the Reverend Edmund Nelson, and his wife, *née* Catherine Suckling, a kinswoman of Sir Robert Walpole, fourth Earl of Orford.* He was baptized Horatio in the marble font that still serves this Christian purpose in his father's church, and was taught the virtues of discipline, and encouraged to stand on his own young feet, in the vigorous and frugal life of a staunch Protestant household. He first attended Norwich's Royal Grammar School, and then Sir John Paston's School, North Walsham, where the headmaster flogged enough Latin into his memory for him to be able to quote Cato more than thirty years later.

At the age of nine he suffered a traumatic experience which was to give him an Achilles heel: with the sudden death of his mother in 1767, at the age of 42, he was deprived of a woman's love and sympathy just when a boy needs them most. Horatio never forgot one lesson that she taught him, characteristic of an age in which France had superseded Spain and Holland as Britain's chief enemy: as she 'hated the French', so was he inspired 'to hate a Frenchman as you hate the devil'. But her brother, Captain Maurice Suckling, was of more immediate importance. He made his reputation in command of the 60-gun *Dreadnought* during the Seven Years War. In 1759, the 'year of victories' in a conflict that enabled Saunders to carry Wolfe up the St Lawrence to capture Quebec, and Clive to conquer India, the *Dreadnought* and two similar ships-of-the-line put Commodore

*The first Earl was the Admiral Russell who defeated the French at the battle of La Hogue in 1692.

de Kersaint's superior French West Indies squadron to flight. And towards the end of 1770 Horatio learned that Suckling was ordered to recommission the *Raisonnable*, a 64-gun vessel captured from the French, for a likely war with Spain. 'Do write to my father,' he urged his elder brother, William, 'and tell him I would like to go with my Uncle Maurice to sea.'

The need for a parson of small means to provide for the future of many motherless children spurred Edmund Nelson's pen. Suckling answered: 'What has poor little Horatio done that he, being so weak, should be sent to rough it at sea? But let him come, and if a cannon ball takes off his head he will . . . be provided for.' The boy might have a puny constitution as well as being physically small, but he was not being 'sent' to sea; he had chosen a naval career for himself. On 27 November 1770,* he was entered midshipman on the books of the *Raisonnable*.

Horatio joined her in the Medway in March 1771, 'thrown in at the deep end', into the privations and hardships of the midshipman's berth, when he was only twelve-and-a-half. But some boys went to sea even younger than this: almost within living memory in the case of Admiral of the Fleet Sir Provo Wallis who died in 1892; born 101 years earlier, he was first entered on the books of one of HM ships at the age of four, though he did not go to sea until he was thirteen. And except for a half-hearted experiment with a Naval Academy (opened in Portsmouth Dock-yard in 1733, and closed as a peacetime economy in 1837), the British Navy depended on this 'sink or swim' method for training its officers until the *Illustrious* (immediate forerunner of the *Britannia*) was commissioned as a harbour training ship in 1857. Until then they were expected to acquire the elements of the sea profession – the techniques of handling and fighting a ship-of-war, and of leading the men who manned her – from practical experience, and from such tutoring as their captains and lieutenants might be disposed to give them.

The trumpet call of war was muted when Spain withdrew her claim to the Falkland Islands, and the *Raisonnable* was paid off after a commission lasting only five months. But Suckling was fortunate in an age when few captains obtained employment in peace: he was transferred to HMS *Triumph*, 74, guardship in the Medway. And, realizing how little the boy would learn in a stationary vessel – characteristic, moreover, of the

---

*This is the date calculated by Mahan and accepted by Laughton. But Nicolas gives December 1770, and many other authorities 1 January 1771. Nelson himself gave the last date in an auto-biographical memorandum, but since this is inaccurate as to his date of birth it cannot be relied on.

irregular way in which many aspects of the Royal Navy were administered despite the reforms of Samuel Pepys – he arranged with an old shipmate, now employed by a West India trading house, to take his nephew aboard a merchant ship.

In the year that he spent in her Horatio studied the rudiments of navigation, visited the islands of the Caribbean, and had his first glimpse of Britain's mercantile marine. He 'returned a practical seaman with a horror of the Royal Navy, and with a saying, then constant with the seamen: "Aft the most honour, forward the better man." It was many weeks before I got the least reconciled to a man-of-war, so deep was the prejudice rooted . . . in a young mind,' by men to whom the sight of a British warship was small comfort, when it so often presaged boarding and the enforced transfer of some of their number into His Majesty's service. Yet, from this experience Horatio learned one invaluable lesson; that for success a commander depends as much on his men as upon his officers.

Back in the *Triumph*, Horatio spent the winter of 1772 handling her boats on the fifty-mile stretch of London's river between the Pool and the Swin, becoming, as he wrote later, 'a good pilot . . . confident of myself amongst rocks and sands, which has many times since been of great comfort to me'. Then, at the age of fourteen, he heard that the Royal Society was sending two vessels to explore a north-east polar route to the Pacific. The *Racehorse*, Captain the Hon. Constantine Phipps, and *Carcass*, commanded by 'that good man', Captain Skeffington Lutwidge, bomb-ships specially strengthened against ice, were not supposed to carry midshipmen who were no more than children: they needed able-bodied men for such an arduous voyage. But ambition, and the use of 'every interest', gained Horatio an unofficial berth in the *Carcass* as coxswain of her captain's gig.

The expedition sailed on 4 June 1773 to reach Spitzbergen three weeks later. A week more and the two ships were making uneasy progress through fog. By the end of July they were ice-bound north of Walden's Island. There, early one morning, (according to legend) Lutwidge chanced to see a small uniformed figure confronting a large polar bear some distance from the ship. When Horatio's musket misfired, and he prepared to club the animal with its butt, Lutwidge put the beast to flight with a shot from one of the *Carcass*'s guns. 'Sir, I wished to kill the bear that I might carry its skin to my father,' the boy explained when reprimanded for an exploit so foolhardy – yet characteristic of the physical courage he was to show when he became a man.

On 8 August Phipps judged that it would be necessary to abandon both ships, and for their crews to escape the onset of an Arctic winter by hauling their boats across the ice. However, preparations had no sooner been made for such a hazardous journey than a wind sprang up, dispersing the fog, and carving a clear passage through which the ships returned in safety to the Nore.

When the *Carcass* was paid off on 15 October, Suckling immediately obtained a berth for his nephew on board the *Seahorse*, a 20-gun frigate commanded by Captain George Farmer. In her Horatio voyaged to Basra, to Trincomalee which he thought 'the finest harbour in the world', on to Bengal, and 'made the islands of St Paul and Amsterdam before we hauled to the northward'. In her, too, he first heard the 'sound of the guns' when, off Malabar, Farmer attacked and captured an armed vessel belonging to Haidar Ali, the Muslim soldier-adventurer who, having made himself *de facto* ruler of Mysore, had become Britain's implacable enemy.

After eighteen months in the *Seahorse*, Horatio went down with malaria, which in those days 'baffled all power of medicine', and from which he was to suffer recurrent attacks all his life. As yet only seventeen, he had to be invalided home in the *Dolphin*, 'almost a skeleton', and despairing of his future. 'My mind was staggered with . . . the difficulties I had to surmount, and the little influence I possessed.' But, 'after a long and gloomy reverse in which I almost wished myself overboard, a sudden glow of patriotism was kindled within me, and presented my King and Country as my patron. "Well then," I exclaimed, "I will be a hero! and, confiding in Providence, I will brave every danger." '

In that crucial hour Nelson emerged from the chrysalis of childhood: the ambition that was to carry him to the peak of his profession was awakened. He was, however, wrong in supposing that he lacked the influence on which promotion in the Royal Navy largely depended for two generations after his own. By the time he returned to England in September 1776, Suckling had become Controller* of the Navy, which enabled him to secure for his nephew an immediate appointment to the *Worcester*, 64, Captain Mark Robinson, as an acting-lieutenant. Joining her at Portsmouth on 8 October, Horatio gained his first experience in charge of a watch at sea, escorting convoys to and from Gibraltar through the worst of that winter's weather. Then, on 8 April 1777, well short of his nineteenth birthday, he was formally examined for lieutenant's rank by officers of the Navy Board. This obstacle successfully surmounted, he

*Often spelt Comptroller. For the duties of this office see Chapter IV.

was appointed, again through Suckling's influence, second lieutenant in the 32-gun *Lowestoffe*.

In this 'fine frigate', in which he was 'left in [the] world to shift for myself, which I hope I shall do, so as to bring credit to myself and [my] friends', Horatio sailed for Jamaica.* King Louis XVI having decided to take advantage of the revolt by Britain's American colonies to seek revenge for his country's humiliating defeat in the Seven Years War, the *Lowestoffe* was required to protect British shipping in the Caribbean against both American and French privateers. Her captain, William Locker, an ardent disciple of Lord Hawke, encouraged his officers with such precepts as, 'Always lay a Frenchman close and you will beat him,' which Nelson later rephrased into his own immortal words: 'No captain can do very wrong if he places his ship alongside that of an enemy.' And he rewarded the determination with which Horatio boarded an American prize in a heavy sea with his first command, the schooner *Little Lucy*. More important, he spoke so well of him to the Commander-in-Chief, Rear-Admiral Sir Peter Parker, that he was transferred to his flagship, HMS *Bristol*, in which, by September 1778, he rose to be first lieutenant with the responsibilities of second-in-command of this 50-gun ship-of-the-line.

The next month brought the ill news that Uncle Maurice Suckling had died of a stroke. Horatio had, however, no need to despair at this loss of the man who had furthered his initial progress in the Navy. He had so proved himself by his own exertions that, in December, Parker chose him to be commander of the brig *Badger*. And six months in her, protecting the settlers of Nicaragua's Mosquito Shore and the north side of Jamaica from the depredations of privateers, were enough to remove any residual anxiety for his future in an age when patronage and 'interest' counted for so much. On 11 June 1779 Parker promoted him to command the 20-gun frigate *Hinchinbroke*. Since this was a captain's post his naval career was secure. Lieutenants and midshipmen could be passed over by their juniors: many, indeed, never gained promotion; there were midshipmen of forty. But post-captains were promoted by seniority: flag rank was certain if they lived for long enough, especially for those who survived 'a bloody war and a sickly season'.

It is often remarked that Nelson first hoisted his captain's pendant when he had yet to attain the regulation age of twenty-one. This is, however, of no special significance. The Admiralty's rules were so lightly observed that others achieved 'post' rank even younger; Barrington at eighteen, Keppel at nineteen, Howe at twenty, are three examples. A sufficient skill

*For a map of the Caribbean, see rear endpapers.

in handling a sailing frigate of 500 tons burthen could be acquired in adolescence. So, too, with leadership, when there was a wide gulf between the educated families from which the officers were drawn and the illiterate rustics who were the men. The *Hinchinbroke* might have a complement of 200, but in Nelson's day officers were born to command, the seamen to obey – and when this natural law failed, there was always 'the cat'.

It is, however, also true that many who became distinguished admirals were older than Nelson when they first achieved a 'post'. Rodney was twenty-four, St Vincent twenty-six, Hawke twenty-nine, Kempenfelt as much as thirty-nine. And Cuthbert Collingwood, another of Parker's protégés, who was destined to be second-in-command at Trafalgar, though born ten years earlier, and with fighting experience ashore at the battle of Bunker Hill (1775), was not chosen to be first lieutenant of the *Bristol*, and commander of the *Badger*, until after Nelson, so that he only achieved his 'post', likewise in the *Hinchinbroke*, at the age of thirty.*

In February 1780, six months after hoisting Nelson's pendant, the *Hinchinbroke* left Jamaica for Nicaragua. She was required only to escort 500 troops, who were to 'force a passage to the Pacific' across the narrow neck of Spanish territory joining North and South America, and 'bring about that grand object, a communication between sea and sea'. But such was the young Nelson's ardour for action that he insisted on leading the boats that carried the troops up the San Juan river; on being in the fore-front of their assault on San Bartolomeo Island; and on staying with them when they laid siege to Fort San Juan. 'He was the first on every service, whether by day or night,' wrote their commander, Captain John Polsen, 'and there was scarcely a gun fired, but was pointed by him.' He was not, however, destined to see the eventual failure of this ill-conceived and ill-equipped expedition: in mid-April Parker recalled him to Port Royal to take command of the larger frigate *Janus*.

Nelson's pendant flew in her for a very short time. In May he was stricken with 'Yellow Jack', the yellow fever that claimed so many victims in the Caribbean, and to which all but fifty of the *Hinchinbroke*'s crew had succumbed. His recovery was so slow and uncertain that he asked permission to return home. He reached England in the *Lion* shortly before Christmas, after an absence of nearly three years.

His health restored by six months in Bath and at Burnham Thorpe, Nelson was next appointed, in August 1781, to command the 28-gun

*Collingwood was handicapped by an adverse court martial verdict: in 1777 he was censured 'for want of cheerfulness in carrying on the duty of his sloop', HMS *Hornet*.

frigate *Albemarle*. He found her well manned, with an excellent master, good lieutenants and a crew largely composed of volunteers: but she suffered from being a converted French merchant ship; she was a poor sailer and a brute to handle; and in the two years that he spent in her Nelson had little but ill-luck. He began with a protracted visit to Elsinore, a bitterly cold anchorage in winter, collecting a Baltic convoy of 260 vessels. When he escorted them through the foulest of North Sea weather to Yarmouth and the 'horrid bad Downs', he added the disappointment of failing to catch a French privateer that attacked his charges to the seasickness that nearly sent him to his cot.

He was next ordered to join Rear-Admiral Sir Edward Hughes's squadron in the East Indies. But his high hopes of action with the redoubtable Suffren, (of whom Napoleon said, 'Had he been alive in my time, he would have been my Nelson': he died in 1788) were dashed in 1782, when a storeship dragged her anchor, fouled the *Albemarle*, and did so much damage to her that she had to go to Portsmouth for extensive repairs. These being finished, Nelson was detailed to escort an Atlantic convoy to St John's, Newfoundland. The two subsequent months, which he spent cruising between Cape Cod and Boston Bay, brought nothing more exciting than a fortunate escape. When the fog lifted on the morning of 14 August to reveal four French ships-of-the-line within gunshot, he eluded them by skilfully piloting the *Albemarle* among the shoals of St George's Bank where the larger enemy vessels could not venture.

The scurvy (which was the most serious ailment suffered by all seafarers until, in 1795, the Admiralty recognized the need to include in the sailor's rations items with anti-scorbutic properties, such as lemon juice), then struck Nelson and his ship's company, so that he had to proceed up the St Lawrence to Quebec, where there was a hospital and ample fresh provisions. There, too, he fell in love for the first time, with the sixteen-year-old Mary Simpson, daughter of the Provost-Marshal; and would have deserted his ship and the Service to marry this 'Diana of Quebec' had he not been dissuaded from such folly on the eve of sailing by a new found friend, who was to be a lifelong one, Alexander Davison.

In October the *Albemarle* escorted a convoy south to Sandy Hook. 'You are come upon a fine station for making prize money,' observed the complacent Commander-in-Chief, Rear-Admiral the Hon. Robert Digby, when they met at New York in the following month. Nelson's answer voiced his very different ambition: 'Yes, sir, but the West Indies is the station of honour.' He said as much to the energetic Rear-Admiral Lord Hood who had brought his squadron north to Sandy Hook after

playing a distinguished part in Rodney's defeat of de Grasse at The
Saints, off the island of Dominica. This recently created Irish peer had
no vacancy in his twelve ships-of-the-line, but he was sufficiently impressed with Nelson's knowledge of tactics, despite his lack of fighting
experience, to persuade Digby to allow the *Albemarle* to join his squadron
when he returned to the Caribbean at the end of the year, to counter the
Marquis de Vaudreuil's force of similar strength. But the French Admiral
gave Nelson no opportunity for winning the distinction for which he
craved. On the contrary, when in March 1783 the French landed 150
regular troops on Turk's Island in the Bahamas, his frustrated ambition
moved him to take two other frigates under his orders and attempt to
dislodge them by a bombardment and landing which were so hastily
organized as to justify this criticism by one who took part. It was a
'ridiculous expedition', wrote James Trevenen, 'undertaken by a young
man merely from the hope of seeing his name in the papers, ill depicted at
first, carried on without a plan afterwards, attempted to be carried into
execution rashly . . . and hastily abandoned for the . . . reason that it
ought not to have been undertaken at all'.

The War of American Independence was then ended by the Treaty of
Versailles, and Hood's squadron ordered home. The *Albemarle* reached
Portsmouth on 26 June, where she was paid off a week later. Never again
was Nelson to experience such a disappointing commission: 'I have
closed the war without a fortune [from prize money] but . . . true honour,
I hope, predominates in my mind far above riches.' He had two consola-
tions. 'The whole ship's company offered, if I could get a ship, to enter for
her immediately': in that day and age few captains inspired such devotion
among their crews. Secondly, and of greater consequence for his future,
Hood's displeasure at the Turk's Island fiasco did not diminish his belief
in Nelson's potential. 'His friendship' was akin to 'treating me as if I were
his son'. For the moment, however, Hood could do no more than present
him to King George III, who was interested to meet an officer described
by his third son, Prince William Henry (who had been a midshipman in
Hood's flagship), as 'the merest boy of a captain I ever beheld. . . . There
was something irresistibly pleasing in his address and conversation; and
an enthusiasm, when speaking on professional subjects, that showed he
was no common being' – an opinion so far shared by the King that he
invited Nelson to Windsor, no mean honour for an officer who had yet to
attain his twenty-fifth birthday.

Peace, with the consequent reduction of the greater part of the Fleet to 'ordinary' – hulls laid up in the Medway (Chatham), Fareham Creek (Portsmouth) and the Hamoaze (Plymouth), with yards lowered, topmasts struck, and sails stowed in lofts ashore – meant unemployment for all but a handful of officers. Nelson was no exception: uncertain of his future, he decided to visit France, intending to stay at St Omer until he had learned the language. But he spent most of his time paying court to Miss Andrews, daughter of an English clergyman and 'the most accomplished woman my eyes ever beheld'. And only uncertainty as to whether he could afford to support a wife deterred him from a proposal, until this romance and his linguistic studies were alike terminated in January 1784 by the news of the dissolution of Parliament. Seized with the idea of standing as a candidate at the general election to be held in March, he hurried back to London* – only to be quickly disillusioned. Within a month he 'had done with politics'. 'Let who will get in, I shall be left out,' expressed his disappointment at failing to find a seat. But by the time the electors went to the polls to confirm their faith in a Government led by the twenty-four-year-old William Pitt the Younger, he had been amply consoled: Hood, 'the greatest officer I ever knew', had used his influence with the First Lord, Lord Howe, to obtain for him command of one of the few ships which the Government thought necessary to retain in commission in peace. On 18 March Nelson was appointed to the 28-gun frigate *Boreas*.

Ordered to the Leeward Islands, so important to Britain for the riches of their sugar plantations, the *Boreas* reached Barbados towards the end of June, where Nelson found himself the senior captain and second-in-command to the Commander-in-Chief, Rear-Admiral Sir Richard Hughes. They were an ill-matched pair: Nelson's strong sense of duty was out of sympathy with a weak senior who showed little concern for it. When he realized that 'the Admiral and all about him are great ninnies', clashes were inevitable. The most serious was over Hughes' decision to waive the Navigation Acts for United States vessels. These reserved all trade by Britain and her colonies to vessels that were British built and British manned; but the West Indian islanders found every advantage in allowing ships built in, and manned by, Britain's former American colonies, to resume the trade in sugar, rum and molasses which they had carried on before the War of American Independence.

*Election to Parliament need not have curtailed Nelson's naval career. Officers, whether unemployed on half-pay or holding appointments on full pay, were allowed to take seats in the House of Commons until shortly before the First World War. Only in the present century has a parliamentary career been limited to officers on the retired or emergency lists.

Though ostracized by the merchants and planters who duped Hughes into sanctioning this illegality, Nelson was sufficiently sure that the Admiral was acting against Britain's real interests to send a memorial to the King – after he had parried the objection of the Governor, General Sir Thomas Shirley, that 'old generals were not accustomed to taking advice from young gentlemen', with the unanswerable reply: 'Sir, I am as old as the Prime Minister of England, and think myself as capable of commanding one of His Majesty's ships as that Minister is of governing the State.' Moreover, when the *Boreas* was away cruising, he turned back every American ship which he sighted, contrary to Hughes's orders. To put the issue as succinctly as Southey does: 'foreigners they had made themselves and as foreigners they were to be treated'. And when he found four of them lying in Nevis Roads, he gave them forty-eight hours warning to leave, or he would seize them.

Hughes considered court martialling Nelson for his disobedience, but was persuaded to ignore the incident, in part by his wife who had taken passage out from England in the *Boreas*, and believed her husband to be under an obligation to her young captain for his kindness to her – though Nelson thought of her and her entourage only as 'lumber' and 'an incredible expense'. The inhabitants of Nevis were less easily appeased: they persuaded the American ship owners to sue for £40,000 [$96,000] damages – but without success, the Admiralty recognizing the justice of Nelson's action and paying for his defence.

This affair throws considerable light on Nelson's developing character, showing how resolute he could be in pursuing a course he believed to be right, and the moral courage with which he could disobey a senior officer's orders when he believed this to be justified by the likely consequences.

It is difficult for the non-military mind to realize how great is the moral effort of disobeying a superior, whose order on the one hand covers all responsibility and on the other entails the most serious personal and professional injury; if violated without due cause, the burden of proving rests with the junior. . . . He has to show, not that he meant to do right, but that he actually did right in disobeying in the particular instance. Under no less vigorous exactions can due military subordination be maintained.*

In this instance Nelson argued: 'I must either disobey my orders or disobey Acts of Parliament. I determined upon the former, trusting to the uprightness of my intentions, and believing that my Country would not

*Mahan in his *Life of Nelson*.

allow me to be ruined for protecting her commerce.' He was supported by Collingwood, then in command of the frigate *Mediator*.

In 1787 Nelson displayed another facet of his potential worth. By the diplomatic skill with which he handled the 'difficult and disagreeable dispute' that developed between the 'volatile',* twenty-two-year-old Prince William Henry, now a post-captain and appointed to command HMS *Pegasus*, and his much wiser, thirty-four-year-old first lieutenant, Isaac Schomberg, Nelson contrived to save the latter from court martial without losing the royal favour. His singular zeal was likewise shown by the energy with which he worked to expose the peculations of government officials in the Leeward Islands, whom he was convinced had defrauded the Crown of more than £2 million [$4.8 million], though he failed to obtain evidence to allow those responsible to be brought to justice.

For relief from such worries, Nelson sought solace ashore, in a form to which more than passing reference must be made because of its eventual repercussions upon his career. The urge to fill the place in his heart that had been left empty by the sudden death of his mother, had grown stronger with the passing years. Having been dissuaded from eloping with Miss Simpson, and having hesitated to propose to Miss Andrews (either of whom, on the evidence of their later lives, would have made him an excellent wife), he now appeased his yearning for a female confidante with a platonic passion for the accomplished Mrs Moutray. She was the respectable young wife of the Resident Commissioner for the Admiralty dockyard on the south coast of Antigua, with whom Nelson was invited to stay when his ship was lying in English Harbour† during the hurricane months, notwithstanding his blunt refusal to agree that the Commissioner, being a civilian official, had any authority to issue orders to HM ships. 'Were it not for Mrs Moutray, who is *very*, *very* good to me,' he wrote, 'I should almost hang myself at this infernal hole. . . . Her equal I never saw in any country.'

But the 'heavy heart' with which he said farewell when 'my amiable

---

*Hood's adjective: RA. Add.15/750.

†Nelson's Dockyard, as it is now called, was first established in 1725. With officers' quarters and seamen's barracks, with capstan house, mast house, boat house and blacksmith's shop, with copper, canvas and timber stores, and with forts on nearby Shirley Heights and the Ridge guarding the entrance to a harbour that provided a safe refuge from hurricanes, it continued in use until the advent of steam-driven warships too large to negotiate the narrow entrance channel, compelled its abandonment in 1899, after which tropical decay and occasional hurricanes reduced much of it to ruins. Most fortunately, however, the Society of Friends of English Harbour was formed in 1950 and under their auspices the dockyard has been restored much as it was in Nelson's day, to serve anew as a yacht marina.

Mrs Moutray' sailed for England on 11 March 1785, was very soon requited. Within the week he met Mrs Frances Nisbet, *née* Woolward, a doctor's widow of his own age, who had recently returned to her birth-place to keep house for her widower uncle, Mr John Herbert, President of the Council of Nevis. And within the month Nelson was wooing her. He admired her 'personal accomplishments [which] I think equal to any two persons I ever saw, and her mental accomplishments [which] are superior to most people's of either sex'; he detected no disadvantage in her bird-like nervousness, which contrasted sharply with his quicksilver brain and his assertive self-confidence.

After Uncle William Suckling, a Collector of Customs, had promised financial help, they were engaged for eighteen months, for much of which they were parted by the exigencies of the Service. 'Duty is the great business of a sea officer: all private considerations must give way to it, however painful,' he wrote. For some 300 days in each year the *Boreas* was away cruising, watching over Britain's maritime rights in and around the Leeward Islands; in the words of a contemporary, 'always on the wing, and when it happened that any of the other ships were in company, he [Nelson] was always forming the line, exercising, chasing, etc.'

But these absences from Nevis did nothing to weaken his devotion; he filled them with letters to his, 'Dearest Fanny', that contained phrases as ardent as those of any lover who is not perchance a poet. 'All my happiness is centred with thee. . . . With my heart filled with the purest and most tender affection do I write this. . . . I daily thank God who ordained that I should be attached to you,' is one example. Mrs Nisbet's replies were less frequent, and did not evince the same rapture. On 23 April 1786 Nelson was impelled to write: 'I will not begin by scolding you although you really deserve it for sending me such a letter. Had I not known the warmth of your heart . . . I might have judged you had never seen me.' But with another letter he was sufficiently enraptured to reply, on 19 August in the same year: 'What I experience when I read such as I am sure are the pure sentiments of your heart, my poor pen cannot express. . . . My heart yearns to you. . . . It is you, my dearest Fanny, who are every-thing to me.' In short, and to quote Prince William Henry to Lord Hood, Captain Horatio Nelson and Mrs Fanny Nisbet, 'a pretty sensible woman', were 'head over ears in love'.

Just two years after their first meeting, on 11 March 1787, they were married in her uncle's home, Montpelier House,* Nevis, with the Prince

*On the evidence of the marriage certificate – *not* in the 'little church' of St John and St Thomas as is commonly stated. The site of the house is now occupied by a hotel.

as her sponsor. Nor was this exceptional honour the only favourable auspice for their future as man and wife. There was also Nelson's evident affection for his new stepson, the six-year-old Josiah who 'shall ever be considered by me as one of my own'. Moreover, as soon as June the *Boreas* was ordered home, whither Mrs Nelson followed her husband in a West Indiaman. Their hopes of settling down together suffered an initial setback. Rumours of a fresh war with France kept Nelson on board his ship at Sheerness, victualling and storing her for possible service in Home waters. But autumn proved the rumours false: the *Boreas* was paid off on 30 November, Nelson being placed on half-pay. He was free to join his wife ashore: as he had written on 19 August 1786:

> Absent from you, I feel no pleasure: it is you, my dearest Fanny, who are everything to me. Without you I care not for this world. . . . This you are well convinced are my present sentiments: God Almighty grant they may never change. Nor do I think they will: indeed, there is, as far as human knowledge can judge, a moral certainty they cannot: for it must be real affection that brings us together.

'The Navy,' wrote the *Boreas*'s first lieutenant, Thomas Wallis, 'lost its greatest ornament by Nelson's marriage. It's a national loss that such an officer should marry. Had it not been for that circumstance I foresee he would be the greatest officer in the Service.'

Nelson and Fanny made their first home together in the parsonage at Burnham Thorpe, from which his father moved out into a nearby cottage. And the five uninterrupted years that they lived there together should have laid the foundations of an enduring partnership. They proved to be the reverse: Nelson and Fanny were as fire and water; as a hawk mated to a dove. There might be love in the physical sense, but there was little intellectual companionship, no spiritual comradeship. His enormous vitality was at odds with her shy, retiring disposition. She was afflicted with such frequent colds and suffered so much from rheumatism and nervous debility, that she became more and more concerned with herself rather than for her husband.

More important, Nelson, having spent the greater part of sixteen years at sea, could not rest content with the quiet life of a country gentleman. The Navy proved to be his enduring passion; another ship was his chief ambition; and as time passed and none was vouchsafed him, he grew more and more restless. Above all, he and Fanny were unable to seal their marriage with a child. And it was he who suffered the greater disappoint-

ment when none was born; for all his devotion to him, Josiah was of
Fanny's blood: Nelson wanted a child of his own.

However, not too much, indeed little, should be made of Nelson's and
Fanny's incompatible temperaments at this stage of their lives. For after
they were parted he wrote (in August 1793): 'I shall rejoice to be with you
again. Indeed, I look back as to the happiest period of my life . . . being
united to such a good woman'; and a year later: 'All my joy is placed in
you, I have none separated from you.' The consequences, tragic for her,
near disastrous for his career, always a stain on his character, were nearly
a decade away. In 1792 their marriage seemed to be a satisfactory one,
except for Nelson's growing anxiety for another sea command. Hood, now
Second Naval Lord as well as a Member of Parliament for the City of
Westminster, from which he had unseated the redoubtable Charles James
Fox, assured him that 'a ship in peaceable times was not desirable; but
that should any hostilities take place, I need not fear having a good ship'.
But though a dispute with Spain over Nootka Sound, Vancouver Island,
so nearly threatened war that Howe was required to hoist his flag in
command of a fleet of thirty-one sail-of-the-line in Torbay in the summer
of 1790, this promise was not fulfilled.

'My not being appointed to a ship is so very mortifying that I cannot
find words to express what I feel,' Nelson told Prince William, now Duke
of Clarence. Hood did not conceal the reason: 'The King was impressed
with an unfavourable opinion of me,' which Nelson ascribed to 'a prejudice
at the Admiralty . . . against me, which I can neither guess at, nor in the
least account for.' His pride would not allow him to admit that the officious
zeal with which he had carried out his peacetime duties in the *Boreas*, had
spoiled the reputation he had gained for himself as a young captain of
exceptional promise up to and including his time in the *Albemarle*,
chiefly in war. Against such influential friends as the King (stricken with
his first attack of mental illness in 1788), the Duke of Clarence (preoccupied with the Regency crisis), and Lord Hood, he had to count more
opponents than the docile Hughes, and the dishonest government officials
in the Leeward Islands, in an age that placed little value on honesty in the
handling of public money; in which 'fiddling the books' was rife in the
highest places.

Whether Nelson would, nonetheless, have been given a command if a
war in 1790 had required more ships to be commissioned, is a question
that was rendered academic by the Nootka Sound Convention. But for
how much longer than this he would have had to wait before receiving a

further appointment, was answered sooner than anyone expected. Pitt's confident prophecy, made in 1791, that 'there never was a time when, from the situation of Europe, we might more reasonably expect fifteen years of peace', was proved false within a year. And 'when danger looms close at hand, the best men . . . are not left in the cold shade of official disfavour.'*

CHRONOLOGICAL SUMMARY FOR CHAPTER II

EVENTS IN NELSON'S LIFE	DATE	RELATED EVENTS
	1758	
Born at Burnham Thorpe.	*29 September*	George II on throne of England. Louis XV on throne of France. Seven Years War in progress (*since 1756*). Frances Woolward (the future Mrs Nelson) born at Nevis.
	1759	
		Keel of HMS *Victory* laid at Chatham.
	18 September	Saunders' operations in St Lawrence enable Wolfe to capture Quebec.
	21 October	Suckling's successful action against de Kersaint.
	20 November	Hawke defeats French at Quiberon Bay.
	1760	
		Death of George II. Accession of George III.
	1763	
	10 February	Peace of Paris ends Seven Years War.
	1765	
		Emily Lyon (the future Lady Hamilton) born.

*Mahan in his *Life of Nelson*.

EVENTS IN NELSON'S LIFE	DATE	RELATED EVENTS
	1767	
Mother dies.		
	1768	
Educated at Royal Grammar School, Norwich.		
	1769	
Transferred to Sir John Paston's School, North Walsham.		Arthur Wellesley (later 1st Duke of Wellington) born. Napoleone Buonaparte born.
	1770	
		Dispute between England and Spain over Falkland Islands.
Entered as Midshipman on books of *Raisonnable*, 64.	*27 November*	
	1771	
Joins *Raisonnable*.	*March*	
Transfers to *Triumph*, 74.	*August*	
Leaves in merchant ship for West Indies.		
	1772	
Returns to England and rejoins *Triumph*.	*September*	
	1773	
Takes part in abortive expedition to discover NE polar route to Pacific.	*June–September*	
Appointed midshipman in frigate *Seahorse*, and sails to East Indies.	*October*	
	1774	
In *Seahorse*.		Death of Louis XV. Accession of Louis XVI.
	1775	
Invalided from East Indies.		War of American Independence begins.

EVENTS IN NELSON'S LIFE	DATE	RELATED EVENTS
	1776	
Returns to England. Appointed acting-lieutenant in *Worcester*, 64, employed escorting Gibraltar convoys.	*October*	
	1777 *April*	
Promoted lieutenant and appointed to frigate *Lowestoffe*. Sails to West Indies.		
	1778	
		France allies herself with American Colonies against Britain.
	17 July	Keppel's action with French off Ushant. Suckling dies.
Appointed first Lieutenant in *Bristol*, 50.	*September*	
Appointed commander of sloop *Badger*.	*December*	
	1779	
		Spain joins with France against Britain.
Promoted Post-Captain in command of frigate *Hinchinbroke*.	*June*	
	6 July	Byron defeated by d'Estaing off Grenada.
	1780 *16 January*	Rodney defeats Spanish fleet off Cape St Vincent (The Moonlight Battle).
Takes part in abortive Honduras expedition.	*February–April*	
Appointed to command frigate *Janus*.	*April*	

EVENTS IN NELSON'S LIFE	DATE	RELATED EVENTS
	17 April	Rodney engages de Guichen off Martinique.
Ill-health compels return to England.	*Autumn*	
	1781	
		Hughes' first actions with Suffren in Indian Ocean.
Appointed to command frigate *Albemarle*.	*August*	
	5 September	Graves defeated by de Grasse off the Chesapeake.
Employed escorting Baltic convoy.	*Autumn*	
	18 October	Cornwallis surrenders to Washington at Yorktown.
	1782	
		Further actions between Hughes and Suffren.
Sails for North America.	*April*	
	12 April	Rodney's victory over de Grasse off The Saints.
Joins Hood's squadron in West Indies.	*October*	
	1783	
		The Younger Pitt becomes Prime Minister. Last action between Hughes and Suffren.
Abortive attempt to retake Turks Island.	*March*	
Returns to England.	*June*	Treaty of Versailles ends War of American Independence.
Appointed to command frigate *Boreas*, and sails for West Indies.	**1784** *March*	

EVENTS IN NELSON'S LIFE	DATE	RELATED EVENTS
	1787	
Marries Mrs Frances Nisbet at Nevis.	*11 March*	
Returns to England.	*July*	
Placed on half-pay.	*November*	
	1789	
		Outbreak of French Revolution.
		Dispute between Britain and Spain over Nootka Sound.
	1790	
		Nootka Sound Convention.

III

Ship-of-the-Line
1793-1796

B ritain's initial reaction to the French Revolution, begun by the storming
of the Bastille in July 1789, was one of sympathy for a nation that had
endured the absolute rule of a frivolous and extravagant monarchy,
epitomized in King Louis XIV, *le Roi Soleil*, ever since the States-General
had last been allowed to meet as long ago as 1614. But when '*liberté,
egalité, fraternité*' were enforced by atrocities that culminated in the
massacres of September 1792, this sympathy waned and, with the execution of Louis XVI in January 1793, evaporated altogether. Pitt, for whom
the Revolution had seemed a domestic upheaval without repercussions on
British policy, lost all hope of keeping the peace when the Convention not
only proclaimed France a republic, but offered help to any nation that
would throw off the shackles of monarchy. France's subsequent declara-
tions of war on Austria, Sardinia and Prussia, the first involving occupation of the Austrian Netherlands followed by a threat to invade Holland,
was Britain's 'moment of awakening'. As 'Peter Simple' has expressed it,

> Almost overnight the silly Lefties [headed by Charles James Fox] who
> had been fawning on the French Revolution, much as the silly Lefties
> of our own time fawned on the Russian Revolution [of 1917], were
> utterly discredited. Englishmen of every class suddenly realized that
> their ancient rights and liberties were in peril [as they did again in
> 1939]. Complacency and appeasement were sloughed off. Britain stood
> to arms. And a stunned French Ambassador [Chauvelin] reported to
> his Government that the English were scarcely recognizable.*

*Daily Telegraph, 11 April 1969.

France reacted with a declaration of war in February 1793, and in the same year Holland and Spain joined the First Coalition in a titanic struggle that, with one brief interval, engulfed Europe for more than two decades.

For Nelson, this new war with France came at a propitious time. He had reached the prime age of thirty-five, with fourteen years seniority as a post-captain, without achieving command of a ship-of-the-line; nor had Divine Providence favoured him with a chance to prove himself in battle. Now Britain must 'look to her moat': against an enemy with such a large Fleet, every available British warship would be needed.* On 7 January 1793 Nelson wrote jubilantly to Fanny: 'After clouds come sunshine. . . . Lord Chatham [the Prime Minister's elder brother, who had succeeded Howe as First Lord in 1788] yesterday made many apologies for not having given me a ship before this time, but that if I chose to take a 64-gun ship to begin with, I should as soon as in his power be removed into a 74.' Three weeks later he was appointed to the *Agamemnon*. Built at Buckler's Hard on the Hampshire Beaulieu river in 1781, she was 'without exception one of the finest 64s in the Service . . . with the character of sailing most remarkably well'. Chatham kept his promise in August, but by then Nelson was so satisfied with the *Agamemnon* that he rejected the offer of a larger vessel. 'I cannot give up my officers,' he wrote of a body whose lieutenants included his cousin, Maurice Suckling, and George Andrews, brother of the girl whom he had loved at St Omer, and whose gunroom messed his stepson, Josiah, now twelve years old. And the years which he spent in her

> hold a peculiar relation to Nelson's story. This was the period in which expectation passed into fulfilment, when development long arrested by unpropitious circumstances resumed its outward progress under the benign influence of a favouring environment, and the bud, whose rare promise had long been noted by a few discerning eyes, unfolded into the brilliant flower, destined in its maturity to draw the attention of the world.†

Leaving a disgruntled wife in lodgings in the Norfolk town of Swaffham, because she refused to stay at Burnham Thorpe alone, Nelson joined the *Agamemnon* at Chatham on 7 February. With a crew composed largely of volunteers, which his old friend Locker, now Commodore at Sheerness, did much to help him obtain, Nelson sailed from the Nore in mid-April

---

*The relative strengths of the two Fleets are discussed in Chapter IV.
†Mahan in his *Life of Nelson*.

to join Rear-Admiral William Hotham's division, with which he spent
the next two months off the Scillies, keeping the approaches to the
Channel open for a homebound convoy of East Indiamen, 'not having
seen a single Frenchman'. In June these five ships-of-the-line joined six
more under Hood, with his flag in the 100-gun *Victory*, and set course for
the Mediterranean, where Nelson's friend and patron assumed the
appointment of Commander-in-Chief of a fleet totalling twenty-two
sail-of-the-line.

Hood's first objective, before he could give seaborne support to the
Austrian army against the French in northern Italy, was the large French
fleet lying in Toulon, off which he arrived in the latter half of July, to be
reinforced some weeks later by a Spanish fleet under Admiral Don Juan
de Langara, of 'very fine ships [twenty-four of-the-line] but shockingly
manned'. Hood's problem, as Nelson noted, was how to induce 'these
red-hot [French] gentlemen' to come out and give battle. But a close
Anglo-Spanish blockade was of small consequence to the French commander, Rear-Admiral the Conte de Trogoff, when the task of commissioning thirty-one sail-of-the-line of a Navy that had sacrificed many
of its officers to the guillotine, proved insuperable. By 17 August the
faction which had seized power in Toulon had had enough of the Revolution; declaring for King Louis XVII and alliance with England, they
deposed Trogoff and surrendered both port and fleet.

Nelson chanced to be elsewhere when Hood's and de Langara's seamen
and marines occupied this 'strongest place in Europe'. The *Agamemnon*
had been detached to Naples with dispatches for Sir William Hamilton,
the sixty-three-year-old British Minister to the Kingdom of the Two
Sicilies,* whose enthusiasm for collecting Italian old masters and Etruscan
vases† was only rivalled by his esoteric interest in volcanoes. Neapolitan
troops were urgently required at Toulon as reinforcements against
advancing Republican forces. Judging the need to persuade the Court
to meet this requirement sufficient to override Hood's orders – that the
Agamemnon was to rejoin the fleet at its anchorage in Hyères Bay without
delay – Nelson accepted Hamilton's invitation to be his guest at the
Palazzo Sessa so that he could add his own persuasive words to those of
the Minister's negotiations with the singularly foolish King Ferdinand I,
and his Prime Minister, the ambitious Sir John Acton, a French-born

---

*All of Italy to the south of the Papal States and the island of Sicily.
†The British Museum is indirectly indebted to him for many treasures, the most famous being
the vase of Roman cameo glass, dating from the reign of Augustus, which he sold to the Dowager
Duchess of Portland for 1,800 guineas ($4,536).

NORTHERN ITALY AND CORSICA

KEY
⊗ Nelson's engagements.
✕ Military battles.

AUSTRIA

✕ Stockach
✕ Zurich

SWITZERLAND

P

S

Lake Maggiore

Lake Corno

LOMBARDY

Lake Garda

✕ Bassano

VENETIA

Trieste

A

MILAN

✕ Rivoli

Verona

Tipino

Po

Lodi

✕ Castiglione

✕ Arcola

Adige

Venice

TURIN

PIEDMONT

✕ Marengo

Mantua

✕ Piacenza

Legnago

Po

Dego

Novi

Trebbie

Parma

Montenotte

Genoa

MODENA

Modena

Adriatic Sea

Mondovi

Millesimo

Genoa

Spezia

Vado

Savona

Loano

Gulf of Genoa

Nice

Alassio

Oneglia

14. 3. 1795

Florence

St.Raphael

Leghorn

TUSCANY

Ancona

Toulon

Hyères Is.

C.Corse

Capraja

PAPAL STATES

13. 7. 1795

S.Fiorenzo

⊗ Bastia

Port Agra

Calvi

Elba

Castellana

10. 8. 1794

THE TWO SICILIES

Ajaccio

CORSICA

Civita Vecchia

4. 5. 1794

● ROME

Maddalena Is.

SARDINIA

Capua

Gaëta

Naples

Mediterranean Sea

San Pietro Bay

Cagliari

⊗ 22.10.1793

0   100

Miles

N

Englishman who owed his appointment to the machinations of the king's dominant partner, the forceful, cold-blooded Queen Maria Carolina, sister of the unfortunate Queen Marie Antoinette who was about to lose her head on the guillotine.

It was in this way that Nelson met for the first time Hamilton's second wife (his first had died in 1782), the twenty-eight-year-old former Emily Lyon, better known to the artist Romney as Emma Hart. Having been persuaded to take this amoral young country girl from the Paddington Green bed of his impecunious nephew, Charles Greville, into his own more sumptuous one, the British envoy had married her in 1791 so that she would be *persona grata* in a city which was then, after Paris, the largest on the European continent. Nelson was sufficiently impressed by her beauty and captivating personality to tell Fanny: 'Lady Hamilton has been wonderfully kind and good to Josiah. She is a young woman of amiable manners . . . who does honour to the station to which she is raised.' (Daughter of a Cheshire blacksmith, she had begun life as a nursemaid in Wales.) But there was no more between them than that: 'not a ripple disturbed the surface of his soul'.*

Nelson was too busy arranging the embarkation of 6,000 troops. Moreover, he had no sooner sealed his diplomacy by inviting the King, accompanied by the Hamiltons, on board the *Agamemnon* (the Queen was in purdah, pregnant with one of her seventeen children), than a French warship was reported off Sardinia, escorting a small convoy, and 'I had nothing left for the honour of our Country but to sail, which I did in two hours afterwards'. He showed this devotion to duty just *four days* after the *Agamemnon*'s arrival at Naples; and it was to be *five years* before he saw either Sir William or Emma again.

Nelson found his quarry, a 40-gun frigate, in Leghorn, but since she would not leave the safety of this neutral port for so long as a British ship-of-the-line lay to seaward, he moved on, to reach Toulon on 5 October. There Hood rewarded his initiative at Naples, and the success attending his diplomacy, of which the arrival of the much-needed troops was abundant proof, with a fresh mission. The *Agamemnon* was ordered to join Commodore Robert Linzee's squadron at Cagliari in Sardinia. *En route*, Nelson had his first brush with the enemy, here described in his own words. On the 22nd the *Agamemnon*

> fell in with five sail of French men-of-war, four frigates and a brig [in fact, three frigates, a corvette and a brig]. Brought one of the frigates

*Mahan in his *Life of Nelson*.

to action [for some three hours] but a calm prevented our capturing her. The other frigates . . . found enough to do to take care of their consort. . . . [and] declined bringing us again to battle although with such a superiority they ought to have taken us. . . . We lost only one man killed and six wounded, although my ship was cut to pieces, being obliged to receive the enemy's fire under every disadvantage, believing for a long time one of the enemy to have been [a ship]-of-the-line. . . .

We know now . . . that it was the *Melpomène*, 44 guns, 400 men, who got the dressing from us. She had 24 men killed, 50 wounded, and the ship so much damaged as to be laid up dismantled. . . . She would have struck long before we parted but for the gunner who opposed it, and the colours were ordered to be struck by general consent when we ran into a calm whilst the other [French] ships came up with a fresh breeze and joined their consort. She is allowed . . . to be the finest frigate out of France and the fastest sailer; we were unlucky to select her; the others we could outsize. Had she struck I don't think the others would have come down and I should have had great credit in taking her from such a superior force. . . .

I had every disadvantage but in the zeal and gallantry of my officers and ship's company. . . . Their force united was 170 guns, 1,600 men, to *Agamemnon* 64 guns, 345 men; the enemy superior to us, 1,255 men. Had they been English a 64 never could have got from them.

This spirited action is discussed further in Chapter IV. Here one comment will suffice: in Nelson's view *one* Englishman was a match for three Frenchmen.

On arrival at Cagliari 'we worked all night fishing our masts and yards and stopping shot holes, mending sails and splicing our rigging' so as to be ready to sail again next day, because Hood's orders required Linzee's squadron to proceed to Tunis as soon as it had been reinforced by the *Agamemnon*. 'You are to expostulate with . . . the Bey . . . on the impolicy of his giving . . . support to so heterogenous a government as the present one of France, composed of murderers and assassins, who have recently beheaded their Queen in a manner that would disgrace the most barbarous savages.' (Hood's, not Nelson's, strong words: the latter was far from being the only Englishman who 'hated the French'.) A French convoy, escorted by an 80-gun ship-of-the-line and a frigate, all lying in Tunis Bay, was proof of this support.

The Bey agreed that regicide was a heinous crime, but 'if historians told the truth, the English had once done the same'. Nelson wanted to treat this impertinent answer in one of two ways: arguing that the Bey was no better than a pirate, he pressed Linzee to seize the French ships without further ado; alternatively, if Linzee insisted on respecting Tunisian neutrality, he should offer the Bey a bribe of £50,000 ($120,000) to surrender the convoy, which was worth at least £300,000 ($720,000). But the Commodore refused to go beyond the letter of his instructions; and, to Nelson's disgust, when Hood was apprised of the position, the squadron was ordered to withdraw lest the Bey be driven to joining the war on the side of France.

Another paragraph in Hood's new orders was, however, some consolation: Nelson was rewarded for his near capture of the *Melpomène*.

> Thank God! Lord Hood has ordered me . . . to command a squadron of frigates off Corsica and the coast of Italy, to protect our trade, and that of our new ally, the Grand Duke of Tuscany, and to prevent any ship or vessels of whatever nation, from going into the port of Genoa. I consider the command as a very high compliment, there being five older captains in the fleet.

Now he would be on his own, able to use his initiative, unhindered by the pusillanimous attitude of a man such as Linzee. His likely opponents were two French frigates in San Fiorenzo Bay, another at Bastia, and the damaged *Melpomène* lying at Calvi. He spent a month in pursuit of them before calling at Leghorn for provisions and water towards the end of December, when he heard bad news from Toulon. Directed by an energetic, twenty-four-year-old Corsican major, who spelled his name Napoleone Buonaparte, and whose first choice of a career had been service in the French Navy rather than the Army, Revolutionary artillery had gained command of the roadstead. Thus compelled to relax their tenuous hold on Toulon, the allies had managed to wreck the arsenal, burn nine French ships-of-the-line, and carry off four more, including Trogoff's flagship, the 120-gun *Commerce de Marseille*, before withdrawing their troops. But the evacuation had been carried out in such haste, with consequent panic and confusion, especially among the Neapolitan and Spanish forces, that as many as eighteen French sail-of-the-line had escaped destruction.

This considerable reverse tempted Nelson into writing that 'our sea war is over in these seas', and into supposing that he would see more action if he could arrange a transfer to the West Indies. He had yet to appreciate the strategic importance of the Mediterranean in Britain's struggle against the French. He also underestimated his Commander-in-Chief, aged sixty-nine but 'as active as a man of forty'. If Hood was to keep an effective watch on the French fleet in Toulon, he needed a secure base nearer than Gibraltar to which to send his ships to replenish with provisions and water. Since Spain had retaken Minorca in 1782, and was now wavering in her loyalty to the First Coalition, he turned his eyes on Corsica, whose resistance leader, General Pasquale de Paoli, had offered to cede it to the British if they would help him expel the hated French, to whom Genoa had sold the island in 1768 against the wishes of its people. Having established a close blockade of the island, Hood ordered Nelson, whom he now recognized to be his most outstanding subordinate, to conduct a series of coastal raids – seizing one 'happy moment' to land sixty of the *Agamemnon*'s seamen and marines to burn Corsica's only mill and throw its store of flour into the sea, another to destroy four vessels loaded with wine – to divert the attentions of the garrison from San Fiorenzo Bay on the north coast the while General Sir David Dundas disembarked 4,000 troops there early in January 1794.

Although the Tower of Mortella had to be bombarded into submission,* the port of San Fiorenzo was occupied by mid-February. But Dundas insisted that he must await reinforcements from Gibraltar before he crossed the twelve-mile neck of the peninsula to tackle the walled town of Bastia. For Hood, now lying close off this port in the *Victory*, this meant an intolerable delay, a view which Nelson shared: 'Army go so slow that seamen think they never mean to go forward'; but, he conceded, 'I dare say they act on a surer principle.' That was on 28 February: a month later he wrote: 'The Army say we cannot attack Bastia, it is too strong and defended by too many French troops. Lord Hood and those in whom he is pleased to give confidence, are of opinion that Bastia may possibly be taken, but certainly ought to be attacked.' 'What would the immortal Wolfe have done?' Nelson argued, 'A thousand men would to a certainty take Bastia. With 500 and *Agamemnon*, I would attempt it. . . . My seamen are now what British seamen ought to be . . . almost invincible. They really mind shot no more than peas.' When Dundas's successor, Brigadier-General D'Aubant, described this as 'most visionary and rash', Nelson contended that to do otherwise would be 'a national disgrace'. Since he

---

*From the Tower's stout resistance came the Anglicized name Martello for the numerous circular forts soon to be built round Britain's coasts (*e.g.* seventy-four between Folkestone and Seaford) as a defence against a French invasion, many of which still stand (most in ruins but one, at Dymchurch, has been fully restored, complete with 24-pounder gun, and is open to the public).

was less than frank about the strength of the garrison – 'my own honour, Lord Hood's honour, and the honour of our Country, must have been sacrificed, had I mentioned what I know' – he won his point. Hood gave him 1,183 troops and marines under Lieutenant-Colonel Villettes and, with the addition of 250 seamen from the *Agamemnon*, authorized him to attack the town, whose defences mounted as many as seventy guns.

This puny force landed unmolested three miles north of Bastia during the night of 3–4 April. By noon next day it was encamped within 2,500 yards of the citadel, with eight of the *Agamemnon*'s 24-pounders augmented by 10-inch and 13-inch mortars which Nelson had asked Hamilton to send him from Naples. Six days were needed for the seamen to drag half these weapons up on to the heights overlooking the town, and to mount them in two batteries. On 11 April these opened a steady fire which was returned by the citadel. Two days later Nelson went forward to reconnoitre a ridge nearer the town and received his first wound, 'a sharp cut in the back'. But this did not deter him from establishing two more batteries as close as 1,000 yards from the citadel by the 21st.

The French were, nonetheless, able to continue such a heavy fire for day after day that Nelson began to have doubts whether he would succeed with his chosen task. Moreover, since D'Aubant, with his seven regiments at San Fiorenzo, still refused to 'entangle himself in any cooperation' until reinforcements arrived, Nelson foresaw the possibility that the General would be able to take all the credit for the eventual capture of Bastia, when his ambition demanded a full share of it. Fortunately the siege was not destined to last so long. On 18 May Hood learned that the garrison was not only short of food and ammunition, but terrified of falling into the hands of the Corsican patriots, so that it wished to surrender. This allowed Nelson to lead his force into the town on the 22nd, one day ahead of D'Aubant's Grenadiers. 'I am all astonishment when I reflect on what we have achieved: 1,000 regulars, 1,500 national guards, and a large party of Corsican troops, 4,000 in all, laying down their arms to 1,200 soldiers, marines and seamen. I always was of opinion . . . that *one Englishman* was equal to *three Frenchmen*.'

But the bubble of his pride in this vindication of his determination to triumph over superior odds – 'our Country will, I believe, sooner forgive an officer for attacking his enemy than for letting it down' – and a microcosm of so much that he achieved later in the war, was soon pricked. Hood's despatch credited him only with 'the command and direction of the seamen in landing guns, mortars and stores'. Captain Anthony Hunt was named as 'commander of the batteries'. Since, according to Com-

mander Walter Serocold, 'this young man . . . never was on a battery, or
even rendered any service during the siege', it is not surprising that
Nelson should write: 'There is nothing like kicking down the ladder a
man rises by.' But Hood was wiser than Nelson gave him credit for. Hunt
was an 'exceeding good young man, zealous for the Service' who had had
the misfortune to lose his ship through no fault of his own: his *ego* needed
a boost. Nelson's *ego* was so strong that his services were best acknowledged
in another way, if early success was not to go to his head and spoil his
chances of achieving greater things. As Nelson acknowledged after he had
discussed the despatch with the Admiral: 'Lord Hood and myself were
never better friends, *nor, although his letter does*, did he wish to put me
where I never was – in the rear.'

The Admiral was quick to demonstrate this faith. 'I [Nelson] may truly
say that [Bastia] has been a naval expedition': his next task presented the
greater challenge of a combined operation. He was appointed commander
of the naval component of a force with which General the Hon. Charles
Stuart intended to capture the strongly fortified port of Calvi at the north-
west corner of Corsica. Unlike the discord which has characterized relations between the naval and military commanders of so many similar
operations undertaken by British forces, right down to the Narvik campaign of 1940, Nelson and the enterprising Stuart quickly proved that
they could work as well together as Saunders and Wolfe. On 17 June 1784
the *Agamemnon*, with the smaller *Dolphin* and *Lutine*, escorted sixteen
transports, victuallers, and storeships to an anchorage three miles west of
Calvi. Covered by Hood's fleet against an attack by a force of nine French
ships-of-the-line which had recently slipped out of Toulon past Hotham's
blockading squadron, Nelson and Stuart began landing troops and seamen,
guns, ammunition and stores at Port Agra.

Despite a gale that required Nelson's ships to proceed to sea for five days
when this task was only half-completed, his seamen dragged their guns
over the intervening mountains, which the enemy supposed to be impas-
sable, to positions from which they commanded the town's outworks.
'By computation we may be supposed to have dragged one 26-pounder
with its ammunition and every requisite for making a battery upwards of
80 miles, 17 of which up a very steep mountain.' On 4 July the British
opened fire; and Nelson wrote to Fanny: 'I am so busy, but I own in all
my glory. Except with you, I would not be anywhere but where I am, for
any consideration.' He was to express this relish for action in much the
same words on many future occasions. With Hood's Bastia despatch in

mind, he added: 'I am well aware my poor services will not be noticed . . . but however service may be received, it is not right for an officer to slacken his zeal for his Country.' For all his personal ambition, Nelson put Country first:

> Corsica, in respect of prizes, produced nothing but honour, far above the consideration of wealth: not that I despise riches, quite the contrary, yet I would not sacrifice a good name to obtain them. Had I attended less than I have done to the service of my Country, I might have made some money, too: however, I trust my name will stand on record when the money-makers will be forgot.

Nor did he seek to steal the credit that was due to others: 'no officer ever deserved success more', was but one of his tributes to his partner in this operation, General Stuart.

A heavy price was, however, exacted for the physical courage that took him to the forefront of every engagement, first shown during the abortive Nicaraguan expedition. The enemy was not slow to reply to the British batteries, and whilst watching the bombardment from one of them on 12 July, Nelson was struck by splinters of stone which cut deep into his right brow, penetrating the eye, a wound of which more will be said shortly.

Calvi proved a tougher nut than Bastia. Though the besiegers continued their bombardment by day and night, they were unable to make a sufficient breach in the French defences for Stuart to attempt an assault. So he tried other tactics; on the 19th he 'sent a flag of truce to the town to know if they had any terms to propose. Their answer was . . . "*Civitas Calvis semper fidelis*".' Notwithstanding this defiant reply, Stuart kept his guns silent; on the one hand he hoped to starve the French into surrender; on the other he and Nelson needed a respite to prepare for a more vigorous assault, a task which led Stuart's chief of staff, the future General Sir John Moore of Corunna fame, to complain: 'Why don't Lord Hood land 500 men to work? Our soldiers are tired.' Nelson, who found Moore a difficult man to work with – as did others including the Viceroy, Sir Gilbert Elliot – answered for his own Service: 'We will fag ourselves to death before any blame shall lie at our doors.'

On 28 July the French Governor sent a letter 'to say that if no succour arrived in 25 days . . . they would enter upon terms for the surrender of the town'. But if by now the besieged faced a shortage of supplies, the besiegers faced a more deadly enemy. With, to quote Nelson, 'our troops and seamen getting sickly' with malaria, Stuart could not afford to wait for so long. 'He went onboard Lord Hood and it was determined to give

the garrison to 10 August when, if no succour arrived, we were to be put
in full possession of the town.' Unfortunately for this plan, 'in the night
four small vessels got in. The garrison gave three cheers which will probably end our negotiations.' And so they did: at 1.0 pm on the 30th the
French rejected Stuart's terms, and at 5.0 pm the guns of both sides
reopened fire.

This proved, however, to be no more than a last brave gesture. The
four vessels that had slipped through Hood's blockade had brought no
ammunition to replenish the garrison's near empty magazines. On 1
August they 'hung out a flag of truce and demanded the same time 10
August, which General Stuart thought proper to grant without consulting
Lord Hood . . . or even sending to Lord Hood to sign the capitulation',
an apparent criticism which is well explained by the next entry in Nelson's
Journal of the Siege: 'Every hour our troops and seamen falling ill and
dying.' By the 10th, 'not 400 soldiers were fit for duty'. But his fears that
malaria would deprive the besieging force of the success for which he had
striven so tirelessly, were groundless. On that day 'the garrison . . .
marched out with two pieces of cannon and the honours of war and laid
down their arms'. Whilst Stuart occupied the town, Nelson seized 'the
most beautiful frigate I ever saw', his old opponent, the *Melpomène*,
together with another, the 32-gun *Mignonne*.

But against this satisfaction, he had to set a disappointment. Stuart
took all the credit for the capture of Calvi: Nelson was not so much as
mentioned in his despatch.

> One hundred and ten days I have been actually engaged, at sea and on
> shore, against the enemy; three actions against ships, two against Bastia
> in my ship, four boat actions, and two villages taken, and twelve sail of
> vessels burnt. I do not know that any one has done more. I have had the
> comfort to be always applauded by my Commander-in-Chief, but
> never to be rewarded; and, what is more mortifying, for services in
> which I have been wounded, others have been praised who, at the same
> time, were actually in bed, far from the scene of action. They have not
> done me justice.

Nelson was, however, sufficiently consoled by Hood's assurance that he
would apprise the First Lord of the magnitude of Stuart's injustice, to
add the prophetic comment: 'But never mind, some day I'll have a gazette
of my own.'

Nelson's other problem was his wound. He had made light of this at the
time, describing it in his evening report to Hood as, 'a little hurt . . . not

much, as you may judge from my writing', and twenty-four hours later:
'My eye is better and I hope not entirely to lose my sight.' But by the time
the *Agamemnon* left Calvi for Leghorn, to refit and to restore the health of
her crew, Nelson knew that, far from regaining his sight, his eye had been
irreparably damaged. Never again would it do more than distinguish light
from dark. Because the retina retained this degree of sensitivity, he
suffered pain if it was exposed to bright sunlight. To protect it under such
conditions, he wore a green eye-shield. Hence the misconception that after
the siege of Calvi he wore a black shade over his right eye. (Careless artists
also make the mistake of portraying Nelson as blind in his left eye.)

Fortunately, this defect was not one which debarred an officer from
service afloat. But in a book whose aim is to assess Nelson's stature as a
naval commander, something more needs to be said of his injury than this.
First, the wound itself. He must have suffered excruciating pain; yet he
was able to ignore it as soon as the blood had been wiped away and the cut
dressed by a doctor. Such stoicism is indicative of exceptional strength of
will: without it Nelson could not have endured, in the years to come, not
only another crippling wound, but the recurring bouts of fever, the seasickness and the other afflictions he so often suffered. Secondly, and as at
the siege of Bastia, Nelson was wounded because he insisted on being in
the forefront of the attack. For the majority of men fear is a natural
emotion; courage is the ability to overcome it, which fighting men achieve
by discipline and by an instilled loyalty to their country, to their ship or
regiment, and to their comrades. There are, however, a fortunate few who
feel no fear, in whom physical courage is an inborn trait. And Nelson was
one of these who, like Shakespeare's Caesar, could say:

> It seems to me most strange that men should fear,
> Seeing that death, a necessary end,
> Will come when it will come.

As he wrote to Fanny, 'a brave man dies but once, a coward all his life
long'.*

The consequences were two-fold. He often risked his own person,
sometimes to a foolhardy extent; and it was this indifference to danger,
first shown in his boyhood encounter with a polar bear, which led him to
an untimely grave – albeit in St Paul's Cathedral. But it also gave him the
fighting spirit with which he placed his own ship to the fore in every

*Compare these words with Shakespeare's:
> Cowards die many time before their deaths;
> The valiant never taste of death but once.

action; and which, when he commanded a fleet, spurred him to seek not just *victory* over the enemy but *annihilation*.

In October the ageing Hood was granted leave to return to England to restore his health, leaving the worthy but uninspiring Hotham in command of the Mediterranean fleet. There was talk of Nelson going too, but both he and Fanny were disappointed. 'We must not repine . . .' he wrote on the 12th. 'The Service must ever supersede all private considerations. . . . Before spring I hope we shall have peace, when we must look out for some little cottage.' But with her fretful reply he showed less sympathy: 'Why you should be uneasy about me, so as to make yourself ill, I know not.' She would never understand her husband as well as Lord Radstock, one of Hotham's junior admirals, when he wrote that 'a perpetual thirst of glory was ever raging within him'. Nelson would not willingly miss the now growing possibilities of bringing the French Toulon fleet to battle, even though he doubted Hotham's capacity to gain a decisive result. 'If we are not completely victorious – I mean, able to remain at sea whilst the enemy must retire into port – if we only make a Lord Howe's victory [the Glorious First of June], take a part, and retire into port, Italy is lost.'

But Christmas and the winter gales passed without the fulfilment of his hopes. 'We have had three gales of wind in thirteen days. Neither sails, ships or men can stand it. In the Channel the fleet [blockading Brest] goes instantly into Torbay, here we always keep the sea.' 'There has been a most diabolical report . . . of our being captured and carried into Toulon (owing to my running into the harbour's mouth); I hope it has not reached England. . . . Rest assured that the *Agamemnon* is not to be taken easily.' And: 'I wish most devoutly Lord Hood may get me sent home; I am tired . . . of our present conduct and situation.' Not until March 1795 did Providence smile again on Nelson.

The 8th brought news that fifteen ships-of-the-line, under Rear-Admiral Pierre Martin, had left Toulon on a course for Corsica, which the French were planning to invade and regain. Hotham sailed at once from Leghorn with one less than this number, the *Agamemnon* being in his van squadron. British frigates were in touch with the enemy that evening, but the winds were too light and variable for Hotham's main body to sight their opponents before the morning of the 12th. Even so, they could not get closer than three miles before nightfall. Next morning, with the wind south-west and squally, Hotham ordered a general chase. The French ran for it in some confusion, and at 8.0 am the 84-gun *Ça Ira*, third from their rear, was in collision with her next ahead, losing her fore and main top-masts and dropping astern. This was Nelson's chance: the *Agamemnon* being one of the leading British ships, he headed for this more powerfully gunned lame duck. By the time he came up with her, she had been taken in tow by a French frigate, and two ships-of-the-line, the *Sans Culotte* and *Jean Bart*,* were closing her. Such opposition did not deter Nelson: 'Seeing plainly from the situation of the two fleets the impossibility of [my] being supported; and in case any accident happened to our masts, the certainty of being severely cut up, I resolved to fire as soon as I thought we had a certainty of hitting.'

This fearless decision paid him well: the *Sans Culotte* and *Jean Bart* hauled off and left the *Ça Ira* to her fate. For more than two hours 'scarcely a shot [from the *Agamemnon*] seemed to miss [her]: the instant all [guns of a broadside] were fired [I] braced up after yards, put the helm hard-a-port, and stood after [her] again . . . never allowing the *Ça Ira* to get a single gun from either [broad]side to fire on us'. (The diagram on p. 43 illustrates how Nelson thus contrived to use his own guns whilst avoiding all but the few at the stern of his stronger but unmanoeuvrable opponent.)†
By 1.0 pm the French battleship was 'a perfect wreck' and must soon have struck her colours. But the cautious Hotham delayed the kill: seeing the French Admiral turn his main body towards the *Ça Ira*, and fearing that his own van ships, especially the *Agamemnon*, might be cut off before he could come up with them, he hoisted the recall, which on this occasion Nelson did not hesitate to obey.

Next morning, 14 March, the *Ça Ira* was seen to be in tow of the 74-gun *Censeur*, both being much astern and to leeward of the rest of their fleet. Two British 74s, the *Captain* and the *Bedford*, stood down to attack them, but were roughly handled and eventually crippled. The French Admiral reversed course to support his separated ships before Hotham's main body could come up with them. But though the latter's centre and rear lagged behind in a tricky wind, the French lacked the resolution to prevent the British van passing between them and the *Ça Ira* in tow of the *Censeur*. 'The enemy's fleet kept this southerly wind,' wrote Nelson, 'which enabled them to keep their distance, which was very great. At 8.0 am they began to pass our line to windward, and the *Ça Ira* and *Censeur* were on our lee side; therefore the *Illustrious*, *Courageux*, *Princess Royal* and *Agamemnon*

---

*Not, as many historians have written, the *Jean Barras*, a mistake for which Nelson's better knowledge of the names of the members of the French Directory than of France's naval history, must be held responsible.
†Nelson's tactics in this action are discussed further in Chapter IV.

were obliged to fight on both sides of the ship' (see diagram below).

Though the leading British ships lost their main and mizzen masts, worse befell the French; the *Ça Ira* was completely dismasted, the *Censeur* lost her mainmast, and at 10.05 am, after a most gallant defence, both ships struck their colours.

As the rest of the enemy fleet turned off to the west, Nelson 'went onboard Admiral Hotham [whose flagship, the *Britannia*, was next astern of the *Agamemnon*] ... to propose to him leaving our two crippled ships, the two prizes, and four frigates, to themselves, and to pursue the enemy; but he is much cooler than myself and said, "We must be contented. We have done very well,"

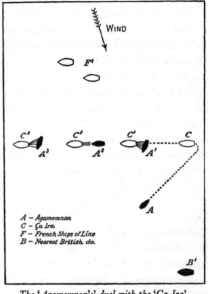

The 'Agamemnon's' duel with the 'Ca Ira', 13 March 1795

but had we taken ten sail, and allowed the eleventh to have escaped if possible to have been got at, I could never have called it well *done*.'

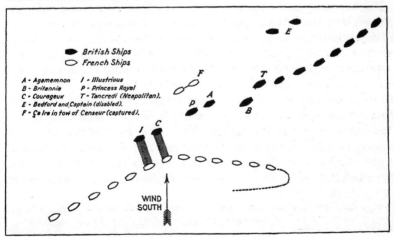

The battle of the Gulf of Genoa, 14 March 1795

In one sense, Hotham *had* 'done very well': Corsica was saved and two French sail-of-the-line had been captured. And Nelson was not blind to Hotham's difficulties when the wind was so tricky: 'Had we only a breeze, I have no doubt we should have given a destructive blow to the enemy's fleet.' But he also wrote: 'Had our good Admiral followed the blow, we should probably have done more, but the risk was thought too great.' And more forcibly: 'Sure I am that had I commanded our fleet on the 14th, that either the whole French fleet would have graced my triumph, or I should have been in a confounded scrape.' This was the spirit that was to win the Nile, Copenhagen and Trafalgar – but for the moment Nelson had to be content with the reflection that in this, his first fleet action, it was his *Agamemnon* that had so successfully engaged a larger and more powerful opponent; and that against 750 casualties in the *Ça Ira* and *Censeur*, his ship's company had suffered no more than thirteen wounded – a service for which he received his first official compliment, the honorary rank of Colonel of Marines.

Hotham was satisfied with writing that the enemy's 'intentions are for the present frustrated'. And Nelson was not insensitive to the Admiral's position: he 'had much to contend with, a fleet half-manned, and in every respect inferior to the enemy; Italy calling him to her defence, our newly acquired kingdom [Corsica] calling might and main, our reinforcements and convoy hourly expected; and all to be done without a force by any means adequate to it'. Yet, to quote Mahan's apt verdict, 'as one scans this list of troubles . . . it is scarcely possible not to see that each and every difficulty could have been solved by a crushing pursuit of the beaten French'.* In short, 'a man who . . . [failed] to realize that the destruction of the enemy's fleet is the one condition of permanent safety to his cause',* deserved the judgment which Hamilton expressed to Nelson: 'I can, *entre nous*, perceive that my old friend Hotham is not quite awake enough for such a command as that of the King's fleet in the Mediterranean.' The Minister at the Neopolitan Court understood that 'to destroy the French fleet was the one thing for which the British fleet was there, and the one thing by . . . which it could decisively affect the war,'* just as Nelson did when he boarded the *Britannia* immediately the *Ça Ira* and *Censeur* had struck – and as he was to express it to Lord St Vincent four years later: 'The best defence for his Sicilian Majesty's dominions is to place myself alongside the French.'

For the moment, however, Nelson had to rest content with being able to say: 'The enemy must now be satisfied (or we are ready to give them

*Mahan in his *Life of Nelson*.

further proof) that England yet reigns Mistress on the Seas.' The French were, indeed, sufficiently impressed with Nelson's conduct for their pamphleteers to give him a mistress, the goddess Bellona. And despite Hotham's preference for 'skulking in port', and the appointment of Lord Spencer to supersede Chatham as First Lord ('Now he is out, all hopes will be done away'), he determined to stay in the Mediterranean 'till the autumn, or another action takes place'.

June brought dismaying news. The French Toulon fleet having been strengthened by six sail-of-the-line from Brest in April, the British Mediterranean fleet needed reinforcement. The Admiralty sent nine ships-of-the-line, making a total of twenty-two. Hood, when about to return to his command, remonstrated so strongly that this was wholly insufficient to counter a French force numbering twenty when so many British ships were in need of large repair that he was ordered to strike his flag. 'Oh, miserable Board of the Admiralty,' wrote Nelson. 'They have forced the first officer in our Service from our command.' He could not foresee that in their Lordships' choice of a successor to Hood, Providence would smile on him again.

Before that he was again in action. Hotham's intelligence was so faulty that on the afternoon of 6 July the *Agamemnon*, accompanied by four frigates, fell in unexpectedly with an enemy fleet of seventeen ships-of-the-line, under Martin who was now a vice-admiral, midway between Nice and Genoa. The French immediately gave chase, and Nelson's force only just eluded disaster before next morning reaching the safety of San Fiorenzo Bay, where Hotham's fleet was watering. By the time that the British Admiral could leave this harbour early on the 8th with thirteen of his twenty-two sail-of-the-line, the enemy had gone; and it took him four days to find them again, by which time they were off Hyères, with Toulon in sight.

At 8.0 am on 13 July Hotham signalled a general chase in the hope of cutting the enemy off from their base. By noon the *Agamemnon* and half-a-dozen other British ships were in action with the rearmost three of the enemy. The 74-gunned *Alcide* soon struck her colours, then caught fire and blew up. Yet, to quote Nelson, 'thus ended our second meeting with these gentry. In the forenoon we had every prospect of taking every ship ... and at noon it was almost certain we should have had the six rear ships.' But, because such wind as there was then changed to the eastward, giving the weather gage to the French, it was 'impossible to close'. Moreover, Hotham, whose flagship had fallen eight miles astern, decided that 'those of our ships which were engaged had approached so near to the shore that I judged it proper to call them off'. He signalled his fleet to retire and, when he saw Captain Bartholomew Rowley in the *Cumberland* trying to join the *Agamemnon* in renewing the action, compelled compliance with this order. To quote the verdict of one of the *Victory*'s officers: 'Had the British fleet only put their heads the same way as the enemy's and stood inshore . . . the whole of the French line might have been cut off . . . taken or destroyed.'

Such was Nelson's second experience of a naval battle. If he did not acquit himself so spectacularly as in the Gulf of Genoa, he had again been in the van of the chase, and one of the few British ships actually engaged with the French. As noteworthy is another feature: neither on this occasion, nor in the Gulf of Genoa, did the enemy become engaged with more than a small part of the British fleet, whence Nelson learned that if the enemy was to be brought to decisive action, they must somehow be prevented from escaping – a lesson he was to demonstrate with considerable effect in less than a year. That, however, was after the consequences of Hotham's second failure to destroy the French fleet had become apparent; when the British fleet had been compelled to abandon the Mediterranean, and Spain had executed a *volte face* into the arms of France.

First, Nelson had another task. The Admiral selected him for command of a squadron ordered to Vado Bay, near Genoa, where the Austrians had their headquarters. From there he was to stop all enemy vessels, and all neutrals trading with the Genoese coast, so as to cut one of the main French supply routes, and facilitate an Austrian advance – not without result. To quote Buonaparte, 'by intercepting the coasters from Italy, it has suspended our commerce, stopped the arrival of provisions, and obliged us to supply Toulon from the interior of the Republic'. But dealing with neutral vessels gave Nelson an anxious time – one false step and he could be sued by their owners for heavy damages. Added to trouble with his good eye, this took such toll of his health that the doctors recommended a period of rest ashore. But a small action on 26 August made him 'feel better every way': descending upon Alassio, the *Agamemnon* and six frigates captured the corvette *Résolve*, two galleys, a gunboat and seven vessels carrying provisions and ammunition to this enemy occupied port.

Nelson spent the following months conducting similar inshore operations to help the Austrian army resist the French, but to little avail. 'Our admirals will have, I believe, much to answer for in not giving me that force which I so repeatedly called for . . . two 74-gun ships and eight or ten frigates and sloops to ensure safety to the army . . . and for . . . leaving me with *Agamemnon* alone . . . with only one frigate and a brig.' In truth, Hotham was no more capable of taking the offensive afloat than was the Austrian General de Vins willing to do so ashore: both were more concerned to avoid losses than with inflicting them on the enemy. The former allowed Rear-Admiral Joseph de Richery to slip out of Toulon on 14 September with six ships-of-the-line and three frigates to operate off Newfoundland, and Commodore Honoré Ganteaume to do likewise a fortnight later with seven sail to raise the British blockade of Smyrna. De Vins reaped the wild wind in December, the 4th bringing Nelson news of Masséna's victory at Loano.

> The French, half-naked, were determined to conquer or die. General de Vins, from ill-health, as he says, gave up the command in the middle of the battle, and from that moment not a soldier stayed at his post. . . . The Austrians ran eighteen miles without stopping. Since the campaign is finished by the defeat of the Austrians, and the French are in possession of Vado Bay . . . I am on my way to Leghorn to refit.

From this ignominious end of the Allies' attempt to frustrate French ambitions in northern Italy, Nelson was one of the few who emerged with credit. All with whom he came into contact gained a strong impression of unusual zeal and efficiency, coupled with the soundest of judgments, a willingness to cooperate with others, and a determination to overcome all difficulties. The Foreign Secretary, Lord Grenville, went so far as to write to the Admiralty: 'I esteem it an act of justice to that officer, to inform Your Lordships that His Majesty has been graciously pleased entirely to approve of the conduct of Commodore Nelson in all his transactions with the Republic of Genoa.'

Nelson was at Leghorn when Hood's successor, the sixty-three-year-old Admiral Sir John Jervis, reached Gibraltar, 'to the great joy of some, and sorrow to others'. The new Commander-in-Chief's record stood high, but the standards of discipline and efficiency that he demanded are epitomized in the rebuke, 'an officer who marries is damned to the Service'. Nelson had met him only once, a chance encounter many years before: they had never served together. Now they were not long in company before he realized that the British battle fleet would no longer spend much of its time at anchor in San Fiorenzo Bay. As soon did Jervis appreciate Nelson's worth. The *Agamemnon* was helping to maintain a close blockade of

Toulon in a blizzard in February 1796, when her captain wrote: 'Sir John . . . does not wish me to leave this station. He seems . . . to consider me as an assistant more than a subordinate. . . . He asked me if I had heard any more of my promotion. [Nelson was now very near the top of the captain's list.] I told him no. His answer was, "You must have a larger ship for we cannot spare you, either as admiral or captain." '

On the day that Buonaparte, having been appointed at the age of twenty-seven to command the *Armée d'Italie*, issued his first inspiring order ('Soldiers! you are naked, ill-nourished. . . . I will lead you into the most fertile plains in the world, where you shall find great towns, rich provinces, within your grasp.'), Midshipman William Hoste, who was himself to earn fame at the battle of Lissa in 1811,* noted:

> Our squadron . . . consists of two sail-of-the-line and four frigates, but is to be increased in the summer, when we shall not want for amusement . . . as our Commodore does not like to be idle. I suppose your curiosity is excited by the word Commodore Nelson. . . . Our good Captain has had this . . . distinction conferred upon him, which . . . his merit really deserves.

The British Mediterranean fleet still had more to do than watch Toulon: there was Corsica to be guarded, trade with the Levant to be protected and help given to the Austrians with their continued efforts to clear the French Army from the passes into Italy through the Maritime Alps. And Jervis was not slow to take advantage of Nelson's well-proven experience in the last of these tasks. On 30 May the Commodore captured Buonaparte's siege train from under the guns of Oneglia, when it was being carried in five transports, and escorted by two gunboats, to join him at Mantua, after his victories over the Austrians at Montenotte, Dego, and Lodi, and his triumphant entry into Milan.

Nelson's broad pendant did not, however, fly in the *Agamemnon* for long. June brought Admiralty orders that the ship-of-the-line most in need of overhaul was to escort a homebound convoy from the Mediterranean. Jervis was in no doubt about the wretched condition of Nelson's ship, and her Commodore would have gone in her but for the poor health of Captain J. S. Smith of HMS *Captain*, and Nelson's own wish, conveyed to his Commander-in-Chief: 'I cannot bear the thought of leaving your command.' On 11 June 1796, he was ordered to transfer to the *Captain*; and it was from the quarterdeck of this 74 – he had moved to a larger ship

---

*At which he led his squadron of four frigates into victorious action against a Franco-Venetian force of six frigates and four smaller vessels, flying the signal: 'Remember Nelson'.

at last – that he watched the *Agamemnon* – 'old and worn-out', he supposed, though he was to see her again on a very different occasion in nine years' time – make all sail and head for Gibraltar, just three years and three weeks since he had first conned her out of Spithead.

CHRONOLOGICAL SUMMARY FOR CHAPTER III

EVENTS IN NELSON'S LIFE	DATE	RELATED EVENTS
On half-pay.	**1792** *April*	France declares war on Austria.
	May	And on Sardinia.
	August	And on Prussia.
	1793 *21 January*	Execution of Louis XVI. Reign of Terror begins.
Appointed to command *Agamemnon*, 64.	*February*	France declares war on Britain, and subsequently on Holland and Spain (First Coalition).
Joins Hotham's division in Channel approaches.	*April*	
Sails with Hood's fleet to Mediterranean.	*June*	
Blockade of Toulon.	*July–August*	
	27 August	Surrender and occupation of Toulon.
Visits Naples and has first meeting with Sir William and Lady Hamilton.	*September*	
In action with squadron of French frigates.	*22 October*	
Takes part in abortive attempt to deter Bey of Tunis from being pro-French.		
	19 December	Toulon recaptured by French, with artillery commanded by Buonaparte. Execution of Queen Marie Antoinette.

EVENTS IN NELSON'S LIFE	DATE	RELATED EVENTS
	1794	
	January	British invasion of Corsica.
	February	Buonaparte given command of artillery of *Armée d'Italie*.
Takes part in siege and capture of Bastia.	*April–May*	
	1 June	Howe's victory over Villaret-Joyeuse on the Glorious First of June.
Naval commander at siege and capture of Calvi.	*June–August*	
	July	End of the Terror.
Wounded and loses right eye.	*12 July*	
	August	Corsica ceded to Britain.
Remains under Hotham's command when Hood recalled to England.	*October*	
	1795	
Takes part in battle of Gulf of Genoa.	*14 March*	
	April	France makes peace with Prussia.
	July	And with Spain.
Takes part in battle of Hyères.	*12 July*	
Conducts inshore operations along Genoese coast, notably at Alassio, in support of Austrian army.	*6 August*	
	November	Masséna defeats Austrians at Loano.
	December	Jervis succeeds Hood as Commander-in-Chief Mediterranean.
	1796	
Hoists broad pendant as Commodore.	*March*	
	2 March	Buonaparte appointed to command *Armée d'Italie*.

EVENTS IN NELSON'S LIFE	DATE	RELATED EVENTS
	12 April–10 May	Buonaparte defeats Austrians at Montenotte, Dego and Lodi.
	15 May	Buonaparte enters Milan.
Captures Buonaparte's siege train at Oneglia.	*30 May*	
Transfers broad pendant to *Captain*, 74.		

IV

The Fleet In Which He Served

This chapter is by way of being a necessary digression. Up to the age of thirty-eight Nelson was involved in three actions on the high seas in each of which he played a conspicuous part. But the first was no more than a fight between his own ship-of-the-line and several frigates; the others were partial engagements, without decisive results. Jervis's arrival in the Mediterranean brought more changes than the transfer of Nelson's broad pendant to HMS *Captain*: in his new flagship he was soon involved in a major action between two battle fleets. And if his outstanding conduct in this engagement is to be appreciated – more important, if his tactics in subsequent actions are to be properly assessed – something must be said of the state of the Royal Navy in the years 1793 to 1805. No man-at-arms can be judged without a knowledge of the weapons with which he fights.

This, then, is a survey of the Fleet in which Nelson served; of the ships with which Britain asserted her maritime supremacy against Napoleon and his allies, of the weapons with which they were armed, how they were manned, and how they were fought. A word must be said, too, of the enemy Fleets which Nelson engaged, for no naval commander is to be ranked among the Great Captains unless he has defeated a worthy opponent, an enemy whose ships, weapons, men and methods were akin to his own.*

*For example, Admiral Togo's claim to be counted among the Great Captains is open to question because, although he scored an annihilating victory at Tsushima in 1905, this was over a Russian fleet whose ships were ill-found, poorly manned and inadequately led, notwithstanding Admiral Rozhéstvensky's considerable feat in surmounting all the obstacles which stood between the Baltic and Vladivostock, except for the enemy fleet that awaited him in the Sea of Japan.

However, the reader to whom technical details are anathema, may pass to the next chapter without losing the thread of Nelson's meteoric progress to the summit of his career.

1 'His Majesty's Ships and Vessels'

The principle type of war vessel in Nelson's time was the full-rigged sailing *Ship*. Evolved by English shipwrights to mount King Henry VII's 'great guns', broad of beam with bluff bows, these proved their superiority over Spain's finer lined galleons and galleasses in the time of Queen Elizabeth I before being copied by the Dutch in the Stuart era, and improved by France's naval architects in the first half of the eighteenth century. HMS *Victory*, launched at Chatham in 1765 and forty years old when she led Nelson's line at Trafalgar, was no more than a sophisticated version of the 100-gunned *Sovereign of the Seas*, built by Phineas Pett for King Charles I back in 1637, except for the omission of the carved and gilded stern favoured by Stuart monarchs. With hulls of seasoned English oak (the largest class of ship required 3,000 loads of timber, as much as can be grown on 40 acres of land in 100 years*), copper sheathed below water as protection against the destructive teredo worm, and masts and yards of Scandinavian and Russian pine after the loss of Britain's American Colonies stopped that source of supply (hence the importance attached to Baltic convoys†), these Ships were classed according to their armament. The largest, mounting 100–120 guns, were *first rates*: those with 90–98 guns *second rates*: those with 64–84 guns *third rates*. In all three classes, equipped with 80 guns or more, these were distributed between three decks; hence the term *three-decker*. The rest, including third rates with 64 guns (such as Nelson's *Agamemnon*) and with 74 guns (such as Nelson's *Captain*) which were the most numerous class of Ship in service, were *two-deckers*. All were sufficiently well armed, and stout enough to withstand damage, as to be able to engage an enemy Ship of the largest size. (In the Franco-Spanish wars that stretched from 1689 to 1815 the French and Spaniards lost six three-deckers in action with British two-deckers.)

---

*Hence the importance attached to growing oak trees in England, and the eighteenth century wartime ban on using their wood for any purpose other than shipbuilding. When, for example, the Myddletons of Chirk, on the Welsh border, required new beams to repair Chirk Castle, they were obliged to 'make do' with discarded ships' timbers, despite the extent to which these had been shaped and bored to fit them for their original purpose. These 'second hand' beams are still *in situ* at Chirk.

†As many as 4,500 British ships passed through the Sound in a year, chiefly laden with naval stores, with more than 350 in a single convoy.

First, second and third rates formed the hard core of a navy, termed its *battle fleet*; and since, for reasons discussed in Section 5, this was required to fight in the formation known as line ahead, these were referred to as *ships-of-the-line* (or sometimes as sail-of-the-line, or line-of-battle ships, whence the term battleship when steel and steam replaced oak and sail).

Of Ships 'below the line', those with 50–60 guns were classed as *fourth rates*, those with 32–44 as *fifth rates*, and those with 20–28 as *sixth rates*. Fourth and fifth rates with 44 or more guns were *two-deckers*; the rest mounted all their armament on one deck, needing no gunports cut in their sides. Fifth and sixth rates included a design evolved by the French, and so termed *frigates* (such as Nelson's *Boreas*), whose lighter scantlings and finer lines enabled them to outsail other Ships, which improved their chances of avoiding an unequal fight with a ship-of-the-line. Ships 'below the line' were chiefly employed capturing enemy merchant vessels and escorting convoys, but some worked with the battle fleet, as scouts and for repeating signals.

How these six classes differed in size may be gathered from *Table A*, which also gives the building cost per ship, excluding armament, in 1789.

TABLE A

Dimensions, etc. of typical Ships

Class	Length (*in feet*)	Extreme breadth (*in feet*)	Draught (*in feet*)	Burthen (*in tons*)	Cost
Ships-of-the-Line					
First rate, e.g. *Victory*	186	52	21½	2,162	£67,600 ($162,240)
Second rate	170	48½	20½	1,730	£53,120 ($127,488)
Third rate	160	45	19⅜	1,414	£43,820 ($89,393)
Other Ships, including frigates					
Fourth rate	144	41	17	1,052	£21,400 ($52,360)
Fifth rate	133	37½	16	814	£15,080 ($36,192)
Sixth rate	113	32	11	508	£10,550 ($25,320)

Notes

(i) Some idea of the size of these Ships may be gathered by comparing them with a standard lawn tennis court, which is 78 feet long by 36 feet wide (for doubles). The length of the hull of a third rate, for example, was approximately double that of such a court with a breadth of only nine feet more.

(ii) Burthen = burden. Because warships were evolved out of merchant ships the tonnage of the former was calculated according to their *theoretical* cargo carrying capacity in tons (length of keel multiplied by greatest beam multiplied by draught, all measured in feet, and divided by 100), until the more realistic displacement (*i.e.* actual weight) method was introduced in the mid-nineteenth century. For a rough comparison the *Victory* of 2,162 tons burthen, displaced approx. 3,500 tons.

A description of one of these instruments of maritime power, which Ruskin classed as 'take it all in all . . . the most honourable thing that man, as a gregarious animal, has ever produced', would serve little purpose. Far better to visit HMS *Victory*, restored to her Trafalgar glory in Portsmouth (England) Dockyard, or the USS *Constitution*, which is likewise preserved in the Charlestown Navy Yard at Boston (Massachussetts), where she was built in 1797. (This 44-gunned frigate compelled the British *Guerrière* and *Java* to surrender during the War of 1812, in the worthy tradition established by John Paul Jones and the crew of the *Bonhomme Richard* in their action with HMS *Serapis* in 1779.) For those who can do neither, the drawings reproduced on p. 56 show the *Victory* under sail and illustrate Nelson's quarters.

Compared with HMS *Victory*, a 32-gun frigate had a slighter hull as well as a smaller armament. But her sails were common to all six rates: two flying jibs stayed to a jib-boom which in the *Victory* extended for 110 feet; spritsail and spritsail course (not shown in this picture) spread from spritsail yards on the bowsprit; course, topsail and topgallant sail, each set square from their own yards on the foremast; three similar but larger sails on the mainmast, whose cap or truck was 205 feet above the waterline in HMS *Victory*; driver, topsail and topgallantsail on the mizenmast. A Ship carrying this canvas was said to be 'under all plain sail'. When running before a fair wind, square studding sails, which gave wings to the fore and main courses and fore and main topsails, were also set from studding sail booms which extended the arms of the main and topsail yards. Contrariwise, in winds of force four and more, sail was progressively shortened, first by reefing, then by clewing up and furling to the yards, until in a full gale a Ship was reduce to topsails alone or, exceptionally, to bare poles.

H.M.S. 'Victory' under all plain sail

H.M.S. 'Victory' : the Admiral's quarters

Some idea of the complexity of the standing and running rigging needed for all these masts, yards and sails can be gathered from plate 9, to which may be added these telling facts: the *Victory*'s rigging required more than 90 tons of hemp ropes, of which the largest, the cables for the four-ton bower anchors, had a circumference of 24 inches, and 1,430 elm and lignum vitae blocks.*

The contemporary paintings reproduced in this book give a fair impression of how these Ships must have looked in this heyday of sail; a word picture, such as this one, is also needed to convey something of their beauty:

She had just tacked, and was close aboard on our lee quarter, within musket-shot at the farthest, bowling along upon a wind, with the green sea surging along her sides. The press of canvas laid her over, until her copper sheathing was high above the water. Above it rose the jet black bands and chrome yellow streaks of her sides, broken at regular intervals by ports from which cannon grinned, open-mouthed. Clean, well-stowed hammocks filled the nettings, from taffrail to cat-head. Aloft a cloud of white sail swelled to the breeze, bending the masts like willow-wands, straining shrouds and backstays as taut as the strings of a violin, and tearing her bows out of the long swell until ten yards of her keel were clear of the sea, into which she plunged again burying everything up to the hawse holes. We were so near that I could see the faces of the men at their quarters in their clean white frocks and trousers, the officers and the marines clearly distinguishable by their blue or red coats. High overhead, the red cross of St George blew out from the peak, like a sheet of flickering flame, while from the main truck her captain's pendant streamed into the azure heavens like a ray of silver light.†

This vivid description is well followed by one of a battle fleet:

England's oaken walls never looked stronger or grander than they did that evening, as the great ships came towards us. The low sunlight glowing upon the piled up canvas made them look like moving thunder-

*It was the British Navy's enormous appetite for wood blocks, 100,000 a year in 1800, that impelled Marc Isambard Brunel (a French naval officer who, to escape the Revolution, adopted American citizenship, and who was later to build the first tunnel under the Thames) to design and equip Portsmouth Dockyard with special steam-driven machine tools in 1803 for the speedy manufacture of such a large number of sleeves and pulleys. Some of these machines are still in use today; the rest are preserved in London's Science Museum as the world's first mass production plant. See *The Portsmouth Block-making Machinery*, by K. R. Gilbert.
†Abridged from *Tom Cringle's Log*, by Michael Scott.

clouds. Signals were rapidly exchanged from one to another until, in a moment, the heavy topsail yards came down to the caps of each mast, while flying jibs and wing after wing of studding sails fell in, and were folded away among the confused tangle of rigging, which in an instant swarmed with men reefing topsails, or stowing jibs; while the great topgallant sails, clewed up, belled out before the wind, ready to be reset over reefed topsails for the night. So, as the fleet went on its way to the westward, did the ships change from clouds of light into picturesque variety of line and form showing dark against the orange glow left by the sun.*

Under the best conditions of wind and sea a ship-of-the-line might make seven knots, a frigate two knots more. But in Nelson's time speed depended so much on the prevailing wind and sea that it had little of the tactical importance which it acquired after sail gave way to steam.† What mattered was a Ship's ability to sail as close as possible, about 50° to the wind, for this enabled her, or a fleet, to gain the weather gage, i.e. to get to windward of an enemy. Of second importance was the facility with which a Ship could tack (alter course head to wind) or wear (alter course stern to wind) since on this depended the rapidity with which she could bring her broadsides to bear. So it was with these features that eighteenth century warship designers were chiefly concerned.‡

Of other types of vessel – those armed with fewer than twenty guns, some with none – which were included in the Navies of Nelson's time, the *sloop* (such as Nelson's *Badger*) was the most common, some being large enough to be ship-rigged, the rest stepping two masts and brig-rigged. They were employed as 'cruisers', on such tasks as patrol and escort in areas where the risk of meeting larger enemy vessels was slight. A plethora of smaller vessels, some brig- or ketch-rigged, others stepping only a single mast, included shallow draught *gun vessels* and *bomb vessels* (usually

---

*Abridged from *A Sea-Painter's Log*, by R. C. Leslie.

†Nelson was, incidentally, sufficiently far-sighted to recognize the advantages of steam propulsion even though the first practicable steamboat was not built (by the American Robert Fulton) until two years before his death – nor the first seagoing steam vessel completed (by a Scot, Thomas Bell) until 1815. This contrasts sharply with the Admiralty attitude. In 1828 they (wrote the First Lord, Lord Melville) 'felt it their bounden duty to discourage, to the utmost of their ability, the employment of steam vessels, as they considered that the introduction of steam was calculated to strike a fatal blow at the naval supremacy of the Empire' – an attitude that was maintained until its patent absurdity was exposed in both the Baltic and the Black Seas during the Crimean War.

‡For merchant ships cargo-carrying capacity was more important. Hence the reason why Nelson's converted *Albemarle* was 'a poor sailer and a brute to handle'.

known as *bombs*) intended for inshore operations,* *cutters* for mundane tasks like the prevention of smuggling and carrying dispatches, and *transports* for men and stores. Two of these are sketched on p. 60.

Table B gives the total numbers of these 'Ships and Vessels' (a collective term still used by the Royal Navy†) in Britain's Fleet during Nelson's crowning years.

TABLE B

British Fleet Strengths

Type	Guns	1793	1797 (Cape St Vincent)	1799 (The Nile)	1801 (Copenhagen)	1805 (Trafalgar)
First rates	100 and more	7	9	11	11	10
Second rates	90–98	21	20	21	21	18
Third rates	64–84	113	132	144	148	147
Total Ships-of-the-line	—	*141*	*161*	*176*	*180*	*175*
Fourth rates	50–60	20	23	21	20	24
Fifth rates	32–44	103	142	151	162	176
Sixth rates	20–28	42	44	49	51	46
Total other Ships (including frigates)	—	*165*	*209*	*221*	*233*	*246*
Sloops	—	61	97	120	134	171
Gun and bomb vessels	—	56	56	107	127	146
Transports etc.	—	88	95	99	114	106
Other war vessels	—	75	73	80	76	105

Notes

(i) Out of the above numbers about two thirds were commissioned for war service at any one time; e.g. in 1800 Britain's fleets in Home waters and overseas contained a total of 103 (out of 178) ships-of-the-line. The rest were under repair, refitting, etc.

(ii) 'The . . . battle fleet is like the queen on the chess board; it . . . dominates the game. . . . It is the final arbiter at sea; to lose it is to lose the

*They were, however, sometimes used for other purposes. In particular, the *Carcass*, in which Midshipman Horatio Nelson visited the Arctic in 1773, was a bomb stripped of her mortars.
†Since sail gave way to steam, battleships, aircraft-carriers, cruisers, destroyers and other sizeable craft have been classed as Ships, inshore minesweepers and fast patrol boats, etc. as Vessels.

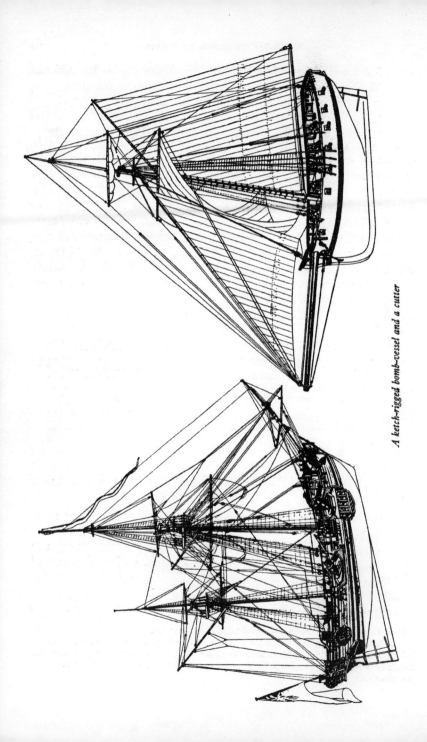

A ketch-rigged bomb-vessel and a cutter

game.'* Hence the use of *heavy type* for the total numbers of ships-of-the-line.

(iii) The majority of British Ships were either third or fifth rates. Most of the former were 74s and 64s: most of the latter were armed with 38, 36 or 32 guns.

In 1793 the French Fleet was about two thirds the size of the British, headed by ninety ships-of-the-line; but when Spain (with seventy-six ships-of-the-line), Holland and Denmark were, in turn, allied to France their combined Fleets would have exceeded the numerical strength of the Royal Navy but for the net increase in the latter during the period covered by *Table B*. This was due to the large number of enemy Ships and Vessels captured and taken into British service as well as to new construction, as against the small numbers lost, more to hazards of the sea than by enemy action.† The net reductions in the other Fleets were likewise due chiefly to the numbers captured or destroyed by the British, as *Table C* illustrates, in so far as figures are available.

TABLE C

Gains and Losses of Ships-of-the-Line (i.e. with 64 or more guns)

Period 1793–1805	Britain	France	Spain	Netherlands	Denmark
Lost by enemy action	5	59	20	18	3
Lost by hazards of the sea	19	8	Not known	Not known	Not known
Captured enemy vessels taken into service	55	5	—	—	—

Tables B and *C* may be usefully supplemented by the following figures for the British Navy:

Number of new Ships-of-the-Line under construction in 1801: 24 (including 17 74s)

Total number of Ships 'under the line', sloops and other war vessels built, captured and taken into service, purchased, and converted from merchantmen, between 1793 and 1801: 536 (including 151 fourth, fifth and sixth rates)

Total number of such Ships, etc. captured by the enemy, wrecked, sold

It Might Happen Again by Admiral of the Fleet Lord Chatfield.
†In 1780 mariners were warned of the proximity of the English coast by only twenty-five lights: today it is marked by as many hundred. As important, British naval strategy required her fleet to be constantly at sea when those of her enemies were as often as not secure in their own ports (see Section 5).

or otherwise disposed of between 1793 and 1801: 205 (including 72 fourth, fifth and sixth rates).

But although the British Fleet was not, until after Trafalgar, superior in quantitative terms to the Navies of Napoleon and his allies, mere numbers are seldom all. For one thing, both France and Spain built a larger number of first and second rates, i.e. more powerfully gunned ships. (The Spanish Fleet included a first rate armed with as many as 140 guns, the only four-decker in the world.) For another, French frigates were likewise larger and more heavily armed, often with as many as 44 guns (e.g. the *Melpomène* which engaged Nelson's *Agamemnon* on 21 October 1793), when the British favoured 32, 36 and 38. As important however, is the extent to which British ships were inferior in another respect. The French and Spanish were not, as is sometimes stated, better *built*; on the contrary, the *Commerce de Marseille*, captured at Toulon in 1793, was found to be so badly built, and of such poor material, that she was unfit to bear her 120 guns, and, after two voyages as a troopship, had to be scrapped. They were, however, of better *design*.

Gun for gun they were larger, broader in the beam and of deeper draught, which made them steadier gun platforms and placed their lower gunports higher above the waterline, as Admiral Mathews recognized in 1744: 'I have now but two ships of 90 and three of 80 that can make use of the lower tiers of guns if it blow a cap-full of wind.' In a sea that prevented most of his ships-of-the-line using their lower-deck batteries, the French experienced no such handicap, so that in the words of Admiral Knowles, 'one of their ships of 52 guns is near as good as ours of 70'. But the British were slow to recognize and remedy this deficiency. Not, for example, until 1798, when Nelson captured the new French 80-gun *Franklin* and she was taken into service as HMS *Canopus*, was it accepted that she was so admirably designed that British dockyards were ordered to build eight more on the same lines. As much is true of the Spanish Fleet; in 1740 three British 70-gun ships experienced the greatest difficulty in capturing a single Spanish vessel of the same armament because she was so much more strongly built. For contrast, the Dutch had to accept the handicap of lighter built ships so that they would have the shallower draught needed to enter the shoal waters off the coast of Holland.

2 *Guns and other Weapons*

The principal weapon in the navies of Nelson's time was the *gun*, or cannon, as it had been since the Tudor kings. Of iron – exceptionally of bronze – this was cast solid, then bored smooth; in Britain chiefly at the Government arsenal at Woolwich. The pressure of the propellent on firing required a greater circumference at the breech than at the muzzle. A trunnion on each side allowed for securing in an elm truck carriage which was fitted with four wheels so that the gun could recoil inboard. This was checked by a stout breeching-rope passed through a ring at the rear of the gun, tackles secured to the carriage serving to run the gun out again after reloading, an easy task for the lee battery of a heeling ship, a slow and uphill one for the weather battery.

All guns were muzzle-loading. (The advantages of breech-loading had been recognized as early as the fifteenth century, but attempts to produce satisfactory weapons of this type had been abandoned because no reliable method of closing the breech could be devised.) The maximum range was limited to 2,500 yards – one and a quarter nautical miles – by the inefficiency of the only available propellent, gunpowder, of which the *Victory* carried 35 tons in her magazine, sited for protection below the water-line. Solid round shot were normally used: a three-decker carried 120 tons of them in her shot locker. Being heavier than fused powder-filled shot, these had a longer range and struck with greater force, causing more damage to an enemy's hull: at 'point blank' range,* 400 yards, the heaviest could penetrate three feet of timber from which the splinters were lethal to any man in their path. Powder-filled shot were also believed to be too dangerous to be carried by ships-of-the-line – not without reason; their introduction by the French towards the end of the eighteenth century helped destroy their flagship at the Nile. Other types were sometimes employed: for example, chain shot (two half-balls) against rigging, and canister or grape shot against exposed personnel.

The fleet with which Lord Howard of Effingham drove the Spanish Armada to destruction was handicapped by the difficulty of providing the large variety of shot required for the numerous sizes of gun with which ships were then armed. In the sixteenth century, the cannon royal, cannon serpentine, culverin, basilisk, saker, minion, falcon, robinet, and many more, were replaced by a smaller range of standard sizes, known by the weight of the ball which they fired. By Nelson's time, these were the 6, 9, 12, 18, 24, 32 and 42-pounders; but the last, mounted only in first rates, were found to be too large to be fought effectively, and in ships armed with them, like the *Victory* when first built, they were replaced by 32-pounders.

Because of the limitation on the size and weight of naval guns – a 32-

---

*i.e. the maximum range at which the trajectory of the shot was believed, erroneously, to be a straight line.

pounder was $8\frac{1}{2}$ feet long, had a calibre of $6\frac{1}{2}$ inches, and weighed 2 tons – which were necessarily worked entirely by hand, a large number had to be mounted, the great majority on the broadside. The requirement to be able to fire at an enemy lying ahead could only be met by mounting guns on the forecastle where the available space restricted their number, and where for stability reasons they could only be small ones. For the latter reason also, the largest guns had to be mounted on the lower deck where, as mentioned above, they could not be fired if 'it blow a cap-full of wind'. The similar requirement, to be able to fire at an enemy lying astern, could likewise only be met by stern-chasers, in the *Victory* two 32-pounders firing through ports cut in her square stern.

Typical gun armaments in the various classes of Ship towards the end of the eighteenth century are given in *Table D*.

TABLE D

Typical gun armaments in 1800

Class of Ship, etc.	Lower deck No.	Pdrs.	Middle deck No.	Pdrs.	Upper deck No.	Pdrs.	Forecastle and quarterdeck (all small)
First rate (100 guns)	30	32	28	24	30	12	12
Second rate (90 guns)	26	32	26	18	26	12	12
Third rate (74 guns)	28	32	—	—	28	18	18
Third rate (64 guns)	26	24	—	—	26	18	12
Fourth rate (44 guns)	20	18	—	—	22	12	2
Fifth rate (32 guns)	—	—	—	—	26	12	6
Sixth rate (24 guns)	—	—	—	—	22	9	2
Sloop	—	—	—	—	18	6	—

A 32-pounder was manned by a crew of fifteen, including powder monkeys who brought the powder up from the main magazine to one of two hanging magazines, where they measured it into flannel cartridge bags, then carried these to the guns. To load, the run-in gun, held inboard by the train tackle, was first cleaned of the burning embers of the last shot with the sponge. Every tenth round or so it had also to be cleared with the worm. A cartridge was then placed in the muzzle, followed by the shot (at close range two, a practice known as double-shotting), each in turn being driven down to the breech end with the rammer, and a wad inserted to keep both in place. Meantime the gunner rimed the vent (or touch) hole with a vent bit, pierced the cartridge bag through the vent hole with a priming iron, and inserted a goose quill tube filled with fine powder. The

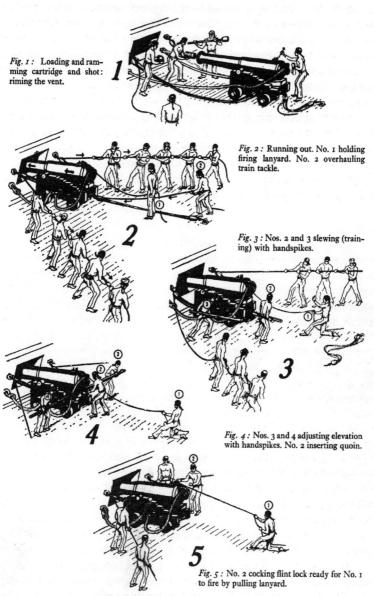

Fig. 1 : Loading and ramming cartridge and shot: riming the vent.

Fig. 2 : Running out. No. 1 holding firing lanyard. No. 2 overhauling train tackle.

Fig. 3 : Nos. 2 and 3 slewing (training) with handspikes.

Fig. 4 : Nos. 3 and 4 adjusting elevation with handspikes. No. 2 inserting quoin.

Fig. 5 : No. 2 cocking flint lock ready for No. 1 to fire by pulling lanyard.

Gun drill in an eighteenth-century man-of-war

gun was then run-out and slewed to the right or left by levering the rear wheels of the carriage across the deck with handspikes, a method so rough and ready, and limited to so small an arc, that a gun's training depended chiefly on the ship's heading, and the effect of her fire on the skill with which she was handled. Finally, the gun was elevated or depressed by handspikes inserted under the breech, the required elevation being kept by the quoin (a large wooden wedge).

The only sight was the dispart, a small raised portion of the muzzle ring which was aligned with a notch on the breech.* The range was adjusted by varying the weight of the charge – up to ten pounds with a 32-pounder – and by the point of aim, e.g. the main truck to hit the water-line at 1,200 yards, the main top to hit it at 800. The gunner had to wait until the ship's helm brought his gun on to the target for line, and until her roll brought it on for elevation. He then fired by igniting the powder in the quill, either by pulling on the lanyard attached to the flint lock,† or by applying a smouldering slow match held in a linstock.

All this sounds very clumsy and slow, as indeed it was. Nonetheless a good gun's crew could, in favourable conditions, fire three rounds in as little as two minutes. (With such efficiency did the British frigate *Shannon* compel the US frigate *Chesapeake* to strike in 1813 in an action that lasted for only twelve minutes.) But otherwise, as when using the weather battery of a heeling ship, or when it was necessary to wear, or 'bout ship, to bring the other broadside to bear, the interval was much longer. Even so, British guns' crews achieved a rate of fire three times faster than the French.

One point needs to be stressed. By comparison with the fused TNT-filled, cylindrical shell of a later age, solid round shot did little damage. It was virtually impossible to sink a ship by holing her below the water-line; the aperture was so small that the carpenter had no great difficulty in plugging it. It was as difficult to destroy an enemy by detonating the magazine. In sharp contrast to the turret-gunned ironclads of a later age, the Ships of Nelson's time were only destroyed in action when, exception-ally, enemy gunfire set them ablaze – always a possibility when slow matches had to be kept burning, and candle lanterns used to light the lower decks. A Ship might then burn down to the waterline, or the blaze might reach the magazine. This was, nonetheless, a rare event. At

*In 1801 Nelson rejected a proposal to introduce a better method of sighting guns with the comment that he hoped that 'our ships would be able, as usual, to get so close to our enemy's that our ships cannot miss the object'.
†Flint locks, the only significant improvement in gun design since the time of Henry VIII's *Mary Rose*, were introduced into the Royal Navy in 1755.

Trafalgar none were sunk and only one destroyed by gunfire. Normally, a Ship was only so far damaged – for example, by bringing down her masts and yards – that she could no longer be fought. Then – and contrary to the example set by Sir Richard Grenville, who scuttled his 'little *Revenge*' rather than let her fall into Spanish hands after she had been reduced to a wreck by the gunfire of fifty of their vessels – it was customary for a captain to avoid further bloodshed by hauling down his colours. Not until after the Napoleonic Wars was it realized how much the victor gained from this practice (see *Table C* on p. 61 for the large number of French warships captured and added to the British Fleet during the years 1793–1805), and surrender made an offence against naval discipline.

Battering a Ship into surrender by gunfire alone could take many hours. For this reason, whilst the French were content to rely on it, the British attempted to close and board, for which *small arms* were needed. The marines used smooth-bore muskets and hand grenades, whilst the seamen were armed with pistols, pikes and cutlasses for hand-to-hand fighting. As a defence against boarders the French stationed skilled marksmen with rifled muskets in fore-, main-, and mizen-tops, from where they could look down and pick off individuals on an enemy vessel's weather decks. Since Nelson had so little faith in this measure that he would not allow his own marines to be thus employed, there is a tragic irony in his untimely death from a wound inflicted by a French sharpshooter.

Guns of various calibres were supplemented by two special types. In 1774 General Robert Melville conceived, and Charles Gascoigne designed a light, short-barrelled, large bore weapon which could fire a ball as heavy as 68 pounds using a charge of only five-and-a-half pounds. Produced by the still extant Carron Ironworks, near Stirling (Scotland), *carronades*, which were of less than half the length and weight of a gun firing a ball of the same size, caused such devastating damage at close range – about 500 yards – that the Royal Navy welcomed them as supplementary to their Ships' normal armament. By 1800 most British ships-of-the-line mounted two or four of these 'smashers' on their forecastles. The illustration on p. 68 shows one of the *Victory*'s with its trainable mounting. The French Navy, with its preference for long range action, was slow to adopt them. The Spanish and Dutch Navies rejected them.

The other special type was the *mortar*, likewise short-barrelled and large-bored (12 or 18 inches), but given a sufficient elevation for the high trajectory needed when bombarding a shore target, against which they used time-fused, powder-filled shot. These formed the armament of bomb vessels in which, since size limited their number to two or three, these weapons were mounted on the centre-line on revolving platforms (as is shown in the sketch on p. 60).

One more very different type of weapon remains to be mentioned, the *fireship*, a vessel carrying a large quantity of tar and other combustible material. These were of use against an anchored enemy fleet, when the wind was favourable. But suitable opportunities arose so seldom that, despite their proven value against the Armada in Calais Roads, and against the French after the battle of Barfleur in 1692, there were only eighteen in the British Fleet in 1793, so that Nelson was unable to use them at the Nile or at Copenhagen.

To revert to the gun, which was the weapon of overriding importance in the naval warfare of Nelson's time, neither words, nor a visit to the preserved *Victory*, can convey any real idea of the monstrous inferno of a

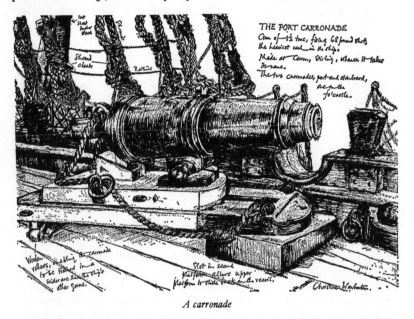

A carronade

Ship's gun deck in action. Some conception can, however, be gained by visiting Madame Tussaud's, in London, where a realistic representation of a part of Nelson's flagship at Trafalgar may be seen, complete with life-size wax figures and a cacophony of sound and light – but without the blood, the sweat, the confusion and the sickening stench of reality.*

*A similar one-third scale model has been installed in a building alongside HMS *Victory*.

3 *Officers and Men*

The number of officers and men required to man a Ship or Vessel depended chiefly on her armament – those needed to work her guns in action and to keep them supplied with ammunition. *Table E* gives figures for the various classes in the British Navy.

TABLE E

Typical Complements

Class	Total number of officers and men
First rate (100 guns)	837
Second rate (90 guns)	738
Third rate (74 guns)	590
Fourth rate (50 guns)	343
Fifth rate (32 guns)	215
Sixth rate (20 guns)	155
Large sloop	121

The composition of these complements may be illustrated by a closer look at the 837 officers and men borne in the *Victory* at Trafalgar. The admiral, being a commander-in-chief, was allowed a first captain (or captain of the fleet) – in effect a chief of staff, though Nelson had none at Trafalgar – a secretary and a clerk. The ship's own complement was headed by a (second, or flag) captain in command, and nine more commissioned 'sea officers' – a first lieutenant as second-in-command, and eight other lieutenants for such duties as watchkeeping and for charge of the gun decks in action. There were also twenty-two midshipmen, who were embryo lieutenants under training. Subordinate to these were four warrant officers; the master, who navigated the ship (anachronistic reminder of the sixteenth century when a warship's crew was sharply divided between the 'military' men who fought her and the 'mariners' who sailed her), the boatswain, the carpenter, and the gunner, whose titles are self-explanatory. There were, too, several 'civilian' officers, whose duties likewise need no amplification; the purser, the agent victualler and his assistant, the surgeon and his assistant, the captain's clerk, and the chaplain. A captain and three lieutenants of the Royal Marines (as they were styled in 1802 at the instigation of Lord St Vincent) brought the total number of officers up to forty-nine.

Not the least of Samuel Pepys' reforms was to establish the Navy as a career for its officers. He recognized the disadvantages of the jealous rivalry between 'tarpaulins', such as Admiral Benbow, and 'gentlemen captains', such as the mutinous Captain Kirkby, who were so admirably satirized when Commodore Flip and Captain Mizzen strutted the post-Restoration stage in Charles Shadwell's comedy, *The Fair Quaker of Deal.** Well before Nelson's time all had been replaced by true professionals of whom, by 1793, many had gained experience in the Seven Years War and the War of American Independence. Enough is said of Nelson's own career in other chapters to indicate how commissioned officers were recruited when very young from the upper and middle classes, to be trained at sea as midshipmen, and subsequently promoted to lieutenant, to commander, to post-captain and to flag rank. Warrant and civilian officers were a humbler breed without such opportunities, the former because they were concerned with material (a ship's rigging, hull and armament) rather than men – a form of ostracism preserved with the introduction of engineers in 1835 and only finally abolished after the Second World War – the latter because, to cite just one explanation for the social distinction, medical practitioners in England were required to call at the *back* (tradesman's) door until well into Victorian times.

The total numbers of sea officers entered into the Royal Navy and promoted to each rank were those required to man its ships and fleets in war. In peace, and when not otherwise needed, they were retained on half-pay, an acceptable system when they could augment inherited private incomes with considerable sums from prize money – and continued until the rapid technical developments of the second half of the nineteenth century made it impossible for an officer to keep up to date with his profession unless he was continuously employed. Not so satisfactory was their retention for life: there were no pensions except for those whose wounds rendered them unfit to serve. The inevitable consequence was that too many were past their prime. This was especially true of flag officers when their numbers were limited to twelve. This small figure was that required for the single fleet into which the Navy was at first organized. (Thus Admiral of the Fleet Sir John Norris achieved the doubtful distinction of being appointed to repel the expected French invasion of 1744 when he was as old as eighty-four.) But by Nelson's time the need for fleets and squadrons overseas as well as in Home waters had compelled a considerable increase, or he could not have hoisted his flag so young (though the principle of stepping into a dead man's shoes remained until its grave disadvantages were highlighted by half-a-century of peace after

*A minor classic which has not been played since 1773, except for a production in the BBC Third Programme in 1949 using a text edited by the present author. A revival is overdue.

1815, and the Treasury at last conceded the need to retire the older officers on pension). These comments on the state of the 'List of Sea Officers' must not, however, be allowed to obscure the fact that Nelson's Navy was officered by true professionals of outstanding ability and experience, whose admirals, though often in their sixties, gained many notable victories.

Turning to the *Victory*'s ship's company, her 135 sergeants, corporals and privates of the Royal Marines were also professionals of a trained, disciplined corps who had sworn an oath of allegiance to the Crown. But the 593 petty officers, (who included the master's, gunner's, boatswain's and carpenter's mates) and seamen, together with the 'idlers' (as they were then known, i.e. cooks, stewards, etc.), 653 in all, were very different. Some were not even British (or Irish), no fewer than eighty-five coming from more than a dozen other nations.* There was no need for a seafaring country to go to the expense of retaining in peace more than a tithe of the men it required in war, when the great majority of its ships could be kept 'in ordinary' without crews until war threatened, and when gunnery was so simple that 'raw material' could be turned into a good gun's crew in little more than a week. This is illustrated by the graph on p. 72 showing the annual totals of seamen and marines borne during the period 1750 to 1805.

Reasons ranging from an inbred love of the sea to inability to obtain any other form of employment produced a considerable number of volunteers – they made up a third of the *Victory*'s crew – but the majority had to be obtained by legal compulsion. Magistrates who shared Dr Johnson's opinion – 'No man will be a sailor who has contrivance enough to get him in jail; for being in a ship is being in a jail, with the chance of being drowned' – sentenced offenders to serve in the Navy as an alternative to imprisonment. But the more usual, and infamous method was the press gang. A captain sent a few trusted hands ashore by night in charge of a lieutenant to seize by force any able-bodied men they might find in the streets and taverns. And such a search of Britain's numerous ports could be fruitful: to quote Admiral Sir Charles Saunders in 1774: 'Give up the fishery, and you lose your breed of seamen.' A man so caught, who could prove that he was not a seaman, was entitled to be released; but necessity usually dictated that such proof should be ignored until too late – after the

*Moreover some ships' crews included women. For example, Nancy Perriam, who died in 1865 at the ripe age of ninety-eight, served onboard the *Orion* at the Nile. But this practice, tolerated but not officially recognized by the Admiralty, could involve complications: the shock of HMS *Elephant*'s first broadside at Copenhagen was enough to expedite the birth of a son to the sailmaker's mate.

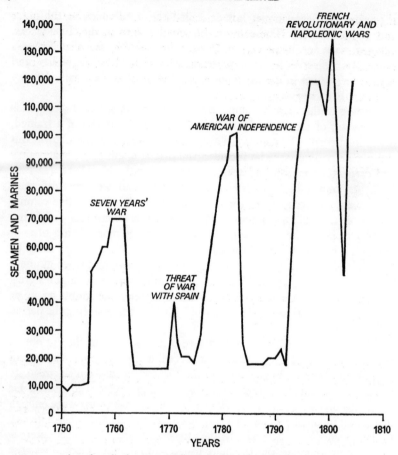

Annual totals of seamen and marines borne during period 1750–1805

ship had sailed. The evident hardships which this improvised form of conscription inflicted upon men – and upon their families – were, however, exceeded by an even more inconsiderate method, rightly pilloried by Herman Melville in his small masterpiece, *Billy Budd*. Since the best seamen were to be found in merchant ships, these were intercepted and boarded, often when approaching Britain on return from a long voyage overseas, and men from their crews seized for service under the Crown when they were almost in sight of their homes.

Nor was impressment the only hardship. For officers conditions afloat might be reasonable enough: they enjoyed cabins, of which the admiral's and captain's were large, almost luxuriously furnished, a wardroom, adequate food, and wine with it. But for the men life was very different, especially the inadequacy of their pay, of which *Table F* gives typical figures (expressed in decimal currency). The Spithead mutiny remedied no more than their worst grievances.

TABLE F

Monthly basic rates of pay in 1805

Vice-admiral	£74.50 ($180)
Post-captain	£28 ($75)
Lieutenant	£7 ($17)
Midshipman	£2.25 ($5.4)
Master	£9.10 ($21.4)
Carpenter ⎫ Gunner ⎬ Boatswain ⎭	£4 ($9.6)
Purser	£4 ($9.6) (plus 12 per cent commission on provisions issued and 5 per cent on slop clothing sold)
Chaplain	95p ($2.3) (plus 'groats' – 2p (5 cents) per head of t he ship's company)
Petty Officer	£1.75 ($4.2) – £2.50 ($6)
Seaman	£1.65½ ($4)

For an approximate comparison with the purchasing power of the pound sterling in 1970, these figures need to be multiplied by a factor of fifteen. But a more useful comparison is with wages paid ashore at the beginning of the nineteenth century. A skilled boat-builder on the Thames and Severn Canal earned £4 ($9.6) per month, a lockkeeper £2 ($4.8) plus the benefit of a tied cottage. But if there was no significant difference between these rates and those paid to their equivalents in the Royal Navy, carpenters and seamen, the latter suffered under the disadvantage of having to wait until their ships 'paid off' after a 'commission' (which might last two or more years) before they received much of what was due to them – a system which Nelson, with his characteristic interest in his men, roundly denounced for the hardships it inflicted on their families.* Moreover, unlike the officers, the men could not hope to make a fortune out of prize money: their shares were too small. After the capture of Havana in 1762 Admiral Sir George Pocock received £122,697 ($294,480), but each seaman a sum less than £4 ($9.6).

*According to an official estimate, in 1787 pay due to seamen was in *arrears* to the extent of the then very large sum of £1.5 million ($3.6 million).

The men's daily rations as set out in *Table G*, may seem sufficient. But they seldom received so much because of the peculations of the purser. Moreover, before canning and refrigeration, little could be done to rectify the almost uneatable quality of these victuals, especially the heavily salted meat (junk) and the rock-hard, weevil-infested ship's biscuit (hardtack). In harbour fresh meat might be issued in lieu of salted, but on only two days per week.

TABLE G

Daily allowance of provisions

	Gallons	Pounds			Pints		Ozs.	
	Beer	Biscuit	Beef	Pork	Peas	Oatmeal	Butter	Cheese
Sunday	1	1	–	1	$\frac{1}{2}$	–	–	–
Monday	1	1	2	–	–	1	2	4
Tuesday	1	1	–	–	–	–	–	–
Wednesday	1	1	–	1	$\frac{1}{2}$	–	–	–
Thursday	1	1	–	–	$\frac{1}{2}$	1	2	2
Friday	1	1	2	–	–	–	–	–
Saturday	–	–	–	1	–	–	–	–

The men were also denied shore leave because they might desert, for which their only compensation was the dubious privilege of having their wives and other women on board in harbour. Their only 'home' was a congested mess table rigged between a pair of guns, with a bare stool on each side, and a 20-inch space between the beams overhead in which to sling a hammock. And though much was done to keep the gun decks clean, aired and sanitary in fair weather, no words can describe their condition in a gale, with all ports and hatches closed, half the heads (lavatories) in the eyes of the ship unusable, and the decks swilling with more obnoxious fluids than sea water. (Since, for example, the *Victory* had only four heads to meet the natural needs of more than 800 men, many must have urinated elsewhere even in fair weather.) Nonetheless, such conditions were not so very different from the stews and hovels in which many lived ashore,* nor from those soon to be suffered by Durham miners and Lancashire cotton workers.

*Thirty-four years after Trafalgar one-third of the population of the Three Towns, Plymouth, Stonehouse and Devonport, which then totalled nearly 90,000, was still living in the crowded squalor of single-room homes, with no means of sewage disposal other than throwing it into the street.

The seaman was, however, much more likely to suffer – and die – from scurvy, typhus and yellow fever, as well as from smallpox, tuberculosis (especially virulent because of the dampness between decks where no fires could be allowed, except in the galley), typhoid and malaria, to none of which was the Admiralty particularly disposed to discover either prevention or cure until after Nelson's time. The seaman was also subject to naval discipline. This had to be strict if order was to be preserved in a necessarily congested vessel, with harsh punishments to enforce it when so many crews were composed of pressed men, including jail birds and other riff-raff. And there is no question but that some captains too readily evoked the 'cat' to assert their authority. But for every sadist, such as Captain Hugh Pigot of the 32-gun *Hermione* (whose tyranny impelled her crew to murder him and his officers in 1797, and then to carry their ship over to Spain), there were those, like Collingwood, who seldom resorted to flogging. Moreover, to set against every contemporary account of a 'flogging round the fleet' (the inhuman torture of 300 lashes of which a proportion was inflicted alongside each ship present), one can find a description of life afloat that is near idyllic; for example, in John Béchervaise's *Thirty Years of a Seafaring Life* or, more briefly, these words of one of Collingwood's men: 'A man who could not be happy under him could have been happy nowhere.' This was, after all, an age in which men and women were accustomed to bear such fearful pain as that inflicted by surgical amputation without anaesthetic, and in which women were stripped to the waist and whipped at the cart-tail from the Palace of Westminster to Temple Bar. It is, therefore, as unrealistic to suppose that life afloat was all 'rum, sodomy and the lash' as it is to see all life today through the eyes of London's *News of the World* or of the New York *Mirror*.

Be this as it may, conditions were better in the Danish and Dutch fleets. Both countries encouraged their seamen, as well as their officers, to make the Navy a career by such enlightened measures as the provision of married quarters ashore. (Those built in Copenhagen are still in use.) Since this enabled them to man their ships to a large extent with volunteers, and since the balance was provided by a regular form of conscription, neither Navy needed to enforce discipline with excessive punishment. Nonetheless, and despite their undoubted skill and courage, both Fleets were at a disadvantage when they fought against the British during the years 1793-1815. The Danes lacked experience of war at sea, except against the Swedes within the confined waters of the Baltic. The Dutch had no van Tromp nor de Ruyter to lead them.

Through maladministration in Madrid the Spanish Navy was chronic-ally short of both officers and men. To remedy these deficiencies they were compelled to use army officers who lacked the skill needed to sail and fight a ship of war, especially with crews largely composed of the sweepings of the streets and jails, with a stiffening of soldiers, all of whom were new to the sea. 'When ordered to go aloft, [they] fell on their knees, crying that they would rather be killed on the spot than meet certain death in trying so perilous a service.'* Nor did this state of affairs improve as the war progressed: in 1795 Nelson described the Spanish Fleet as 'ill-manned and worse officered'. Much more telling, however, is Napo-leon's order to Villeneuve in 1805, to the effect that, though the Spaniards sometimes fought like lions, two of their ships-of-the-line must be counted as equal to one French.

The French Fleet had won renown in the Seven Years War with experi-enced officers from the nobility and from the superior middle class, and with 10,000 trained seamen gunners to provide a sizeable proportion of its ships' complements. Admirals of the calibre of de Guichen, de Grasse and Suffren had tipped the scales against Britain in the more recent War of American Independence. But in 1789 much of this was sacrificed on the altar of revolution: anarchy superseded law and order afloat just as it did ashore. When Commodore D'Albert de Rions was ordered to commission a fleet of forty-five ships-of-the-line at the time of the Nootka Sound dispute, the National Assembly so far failed to support his attempts to restore discipline that he resigned his command in disgust and left his country for good. Many more French officers fled abroad during the Reign of Terror, including Admirals Kersaint and D'Estaing, while others fell victims of the guillotine.

The National Assembly made matters worse by refusing to believe that any special abilities were needed by those who manned their fleet. Fidelity to the new order of things was all. A lieutenant in 1791, Villaret Joyeuse was an admiral and Commander-in-Chief of the Brest fleet three years later. But 'patriotism alone cannot handle a ship', as Rear-Admiral Morard de Galles discovered a month after war broke out: 'The tone of the seamen is wholly ruined. If it does not change we can expect nothing but reverses in action, even though we be superior in force.'

Such warnings did not trouble men blinded by *egalité*. In 1792 the seamen gunners were replaced by less efficient marine artillerists. Two years later these were likewise seen to be a form of aristocracy, and abolished when Deputy Jean Bon Saint-André demanded of the Conven-

*J. de la Gravière in *Histoire de la Marine*.

tion, why 'these troops have the *exclusive privilege* of defending the republic upon the sea? Are we not *all* called upon to fight for liberty . . . to go upon our fleets to show [our] courage to Pitt and lower the flag of George?' He, nonetheless, found it necessary to accompany the fleet to sea himself in order to persuade its officers and men into doing their best for the Republic. And he was sufficiently purblind to blame the sharp rise in the number of accidents suffered by French warships, even in good weather, on King Louis XVI's 'system of ruining the Navy by carelessness and neglect'. The charge is an exaggeration. French naval administration after the Revolution was much inferior to what it had been before. The Fleet was constantly hampered by a shortage of timber, rigging, sails, provisions and clothing. And Admiral Ganteaume was not the only one to complain, as he wrote in 1801, of 'the frightful state . . . [of] the seamen, unpaid for fifteen months, naked or covered with rags, badly fed, discouraged; in a word, sunk under the weight of the deepest and most humiliating wretchedness'.

It must not, however, be supposed that, as a consequence of the Revolution, the French Navy ceased to be a fighting force, any more than the British Channel and North Sea fleets when they were riven by serious mutinies in 1797. Although the Comte de Trogoff was unable to get the Toulon fleet to sea in 1793, Admiral Martin not only managed to do so a year later, but in 1795 so harassed Hotham's fleet in two actions that, when Spain joined Britain's enemies, Pitt thought it wise to withdraw from that area. And, within weeks of writing his above-quoted complaint, Admiral Ganteaume took his fleet out of Brest and round to Toulon in midwinter. French admirals *had* to exaggerate the parlous state of their fleets in order to persuade their government to affect improvements. And French historians, understandably anxious to excuse the crushing defeats suffered by their Fleet during these years, have readily taken such critical reports at their face value. In truth, although much was wrong with the French Fleet at the outbreak of war, its officers were not devoid of skill, nor its men lacking in courage. Revolutionary fervour can overcome many obstacles, as the peoples of Russia have shown in our own century. And in so far as more than this is required for war at sea, so with each year that passed did the French Republican Navy gain in skill and experience.

Ill-clothed, poorly paid, too savagely punished, liable to desert and prone to mutiny – British seamen were all of these in 1793. Why then, were they superior to the Frenchmen of whom Ganteaume wrote a like description? The reputation which the British gained between 1793 and 1815, for being the finest seamen and the toughest fighters in the world (though sometimes deftly matched by the new-fledged United States Navy in the short, unnecessary War of 1812) is not to be denied. Nelson might write: 'Nothing can stop their courage', and Wellington say: 'I never found naval men at a loss. Tell them to do anything that is not impossible, and depend upon it, they will do it.' But it was Villeneuve's chief of staff, Captain Prigny, who voiced this damning comment after Trafalgar: 'We were all amazement, wondering what the English seaman could be made of. All ours were either drunk or disabled.' The most significant tribute was, however, paid by Captain Maitland of the *Bellerophon* after the Emperor's surrender in 1815:

> He seemed much struck with . . . the men, saying 'that our seamen were surely a different class of people from the French; and that it was owing to them we were always victorious at sea'. I answered, 'I must beg leave to differ with you; I do not wish to take from the merit of our men; but my opinion is that perhaps we owe our advantage to the superior experience of the officers; and I believe the French seamen, if taken as much pains with, would look as well as ours. As British ships are constantly at sea, the officers have nothing to divert their attention from them and their men; and in consequence . . . they are much better trained for the services they have to perform.'

Here lies the key to the superiority of British seamen. Both Fleets were largely manned by men culled from an ignorant, unskilled, unruly rabble: to turn them into an effective instrument of war required discipline, training and, above all, leaders. The Royal Navy had many officers who had learned this lesson: the French Republican Navy had all too few to turn their men into crews who could make proper use of their better designed, more powerfully gunned ships-of-the-line. Napoleon might be able to turn the French revolutionary mob into an all-conquering Army: there was no one to do as much for his Fleet.

4 *Command and Control*

Until the reforms of Sir James Graham, when First Lord in 1830-4, the affairs of the Royal Navy were managed at the centre – not without results despite the maladministration ruthlessly exposed by Lord St Vincent – by three autonomous bodies. Since 1628, policy, plans, operations and the appointment of officers (to use modern terms) had been directed by 'Commissioners for Executing the Office of Lord High Admiral'. This Board, which had its offices in Thomas Ripley's *Admiralty* building in Whitehall, comprised both Naval Lords and Civilian Lords (the latter drawn from Parliament), under the dominant chairmanship of the First Lord, (who had a seat in the Cabinet) who was sometimes a politician, at others a naval officer of distinction.* *Matériel*, in particular ship-building, repair and maintenance, including administration of the Royal Dockyards, and manning were the separate responsibility of the *Navy Board*, headed by a naval officer as Controller, with subordinate Victualling and Transport Boards, which had their offices in Somerset House. Guns and ammunition (for both the Navy and the Army) were provided by the *Board of Ordnance* which, in addition to such arsenals as that at Woolwich, maintained Gun Wharves adjacent to each dockyard.

With the exception of the handful of flag officers and captains on these Boards: of Port Admirals in home waters (at the Nore, Portsmouth and Plymouth); of Commissioners of H.M. Dockyards at home (Sheerness, Chatham, Portsmouth and Plymouth) and abroad (at various times, Lisbon, Gibraltar, Malta, Minorca, Corsica, Halifax, Nova Scotia and Antigua), such as Nelson's friend Captain John Moutray, no naval officers served ashore. In particular, all commanders-in-chief flew their flags afloat.

Time was when there were only three flag officers; a Lord Admiral who commanded the fleet from the centre, with a Vice-Admiral in charge of the van and a Rear-Admiral in charge of the rear. But the single large fleet (some hundred ships) into which the Royal Navy was organized during the Dutch Wars required more than these three: the admiral of the fleet was given a vice-admiral and a rear-admiral to help him command the centre division, now raised to the status of squadron, and the van and rear squadrons were each allowed an admiral in command, likewise with a vice-admiral and a rear-admiral to help them. To distinguish their respective ships, those of the centre squadron flew a red flag at the peak, those of the van squadron a white flag, and those of the rear squadron a blue flag – whence the names, *red, white* and *blue squadrons* – with (in order to avoid confusion with the white flag of the Bourbons flown by French ships) the cross of St George in the upper canton nearest the halyards, to which was added that of St Andrew in 1707. The union with Ireland in 1801 was similarly marked by the addition of the cross of St Patrick.

Flagships were further distinguished: the admiral of the fleet flew the Union Flag at the main masthead: others flew an additional flag of their squadron colour (the white having a St George's cross superimposed

*Middleton, First Lord, 1805-6, was the last naval officer to hold this office. The Naval Lords were co-equal subordinates until 1805, when the senior one became the First Lord's deputy, with prime responsibility for operations, and so First Naval (or Sea) Lord.

upon it), an admiral at the main, a vice-admiral at the fore, a rear-admiral at the mizen. In a commodore's flagship the captain's long, tri-coloured, swallow-tailed pendant was replaced by a broad red one.

When, at the turn of the eighteenth century, it became necessary to organize the British Navy into a number of fleets and squadrons for service overseas as well as in home waters, the elements of this system were retained. Although the largest of these forces no longer needed as many as nine flag officers, together they required a considerable increase in the flag list: by 1803 this totalled 166. The suffixes red, white and blue were retained only as an indication of relative seniority (e.g. a rear-admiral of the blue was junior to a rear-admiral of the white, and the latter junior to a rear-admiral of the red) when a fleet was no longer necessarily under the command of an admiral of the red. To cite two examples: Nelson had risen no higher than vice-admiral of the white when appointed Commander-in-Chief Mediterranean, at a time when the Commander-in-Chief in the Leeward Islands, the younger Samuel Hood, was only a commodore. The old system of distinguishing flagships was likewise retained; but for an ensign at the peak it became the custom for all ships in a fleet, even though organized into two or three divisions, to fly the colour of the flag officer in supreme command. Much of this was continued until it had become wholly outdated in 1864, when the *white ensign* was adopted for use by the whole of the Royal Navy, rather than the previously superior red, because the former had been flown by all of Nelson's ships in his finest hour (a tribute copied, perhaps unconsciously, by many other Navies, notably those of Imperial Germany, Imperial Russia, and the USSR); when for the same reason a white flag with the cross of St George superimposed, was adopted by all admirals, those of vice-admirals and rear-admirals being distinguished by the addition of one or two red balls in the cantons nearest the halyards (a far-sighted decision in a day when none could have envisaged flagships with less than three masts such as became a common feature of steam-driven battleships).

World-wide naval operations could be directed by such a small body as comprised the Admiralty at the turn of the nineteenth century – no more than those who sat around the table in the Board Room, aided by First and Second Secretaries and a mere score of clerks – because there was no strategic system of *communication* except by *letter*. These were subject to delays of upwards of twenty-four hours to ships lying in Torbay, a week to one in the Baltic, two weeks or more to one in the Mediterranean, and a month to one in the West Indies. Dispatches from Britain's fleets and squadrons were likewise delayed by days or months in transit to Whitehall. So the First Lord could do little more than issue *general* instructions, in accordance with the Government's intentions. There were, indeed, considerable advantages in leaving any closer control to the man-on-the-spot, as will be seen later in this book. Contrariwise it had its drawbacks. Pitt had every reason to regret the lack of a speedier methods of communication when, in 1806, Admiral Sir Home Popham exceeded instructions limited to capturing the Cape of Good Hope, to the extent of crossing the South Atlantic and attempting to do likewise with Buenos Aires, just when the British Government was determined on establishing friendly relations with Spain's colonies as they struggled for liberation.

Other European Navies were similarly directed and administered from their capitals, notably the French by a Ministry of Marine, whose fleets and squadrons were comparably organized, but without the complications of red, white and blue. France was, moreover, the first to evolve a method of communication which was a significant step towards the more effective method of controlling maritime operations that was later achieved by the invention of the electric telegraph and cable (brought into use during the Crimean War) and, after the turn of the twentieth century, by radio. Following up an idea suggested by Richard Edgeworth, the English author of such works as *Essays on the Construction of Roads and Railways*, Claude Chappe erected a chain of 116 'aerial *telegraph*' stations in 1794, linking Paris with Lyons, each comprising a tower surmounted by a mast to which were affixed a pair of rotating arms, given the name *semaphore*. This initial chain was subsequently extended to a network of over 500 stations serving 29 towns in more of Europe than France itself, because Napoleon found this speedy visual method of signalling messages of such value for controlling his armies when, as Emperor, he had sometimes to leave the field for Paris.

Two years later the British Admiralty, having previously ignored Edgeworth's idea, produced its own adaptation of Chappe's system, building chains of telegraph stations between Whitehall and the Downs, with a branch to the Nore; between Whitehall and Spithead; and later, between Whitehall and Torbay and Plymouth. These used an invention of the Reverend Lord George Murray, later Bishop of St Davids: six round holes in a large vertical board, which could be opened and closed by mechanically operated shutters in a sufficient number of combinations to cover both the letters of the alphabet and such standard phrases as: 'The fleet to weigh and proceed down Channel under easy sail.' (See plate 12.)

Chappe's and Murray's systems had serious limitations: they could not be used by night, nor in mist or fog. They were, nonetheless, a distinct advance: an order could be passed from the Admiralty to Spithead through eleven intermediate stations in as little as ten minutes; news of an approaching invasion force from the south coast to Whitehall in no more. The semaphore telegraph is, therefore, relevant to those brief periods of Nelson's career, to be covered in later chapters, in which he held commands in Home waters. Moreover, it so far proved its value that, except for the replacement of Murray's clumsy system by one similar to Chappe's in 1816 (see plate 11), both networks survived until the electric telegraph came into use some thirty years later, by which time the English chains had been augmented by commercial ones, notably from the City of London to Holyhead for transmitting intelligence and instructions to and from merchant ships inward and outward bound from Liverpool. Hence the numerous Telegraph Hills, Lanes, Inns and Farms which still remain as mute memorials to Chappe's and Murray's inventive brains (e.g. on London's Putney Common).

Turning to *tactical communications*, the need for a naval commander to issue orders to, and receive reports from his ships by *signal*, would seem so essential that nothing is, perhaps, more surprising than the failure to develop any method that was at all adequate before the last decade of the eighteenth century. For more than fifteen hundred years after centurions waved their cloaks to order their galleys to attack the enemies of Rome, navies were content to arrange for every ship (to quote a British instruction of 1558) to 'keep company with the Admiral and twice every day to speak with him', by 'speaking trumpet' or by boat, except for a very small range of intelligence which might have to be conveyed in an emergency – for example, to warn a ship against standing into danger – which was done by 'ringing bells, blowing horns, beating drums and firing guns'.

There was no real urge to provide anything more as long as naval battles were confused *mêlées*, such as those fought by Howard, Hawkins and Drake against Medina Sidonia's Armada. Not until the formal method of fighting in line was evolved in the First Dutch War, did Blake, Deane and Monk devise a code of signalling *by flags*. Even so, this comprised no more than five, but with different meanings according to the positions in which they were hoisted, at the fore, main or mizen. For example: 'When the Admiral would have the Rear-Admiral of the Red and his division tack and endeavour to gain the wind of the enemy, he will hoist a red flag at the mizen-top masthead.' Indeed, it was not possible to communicate more than such preconceived orders by signal for the better part of the subsequent century in which British tactics were confined to the *Permanent Fighting Instructions* of 1691. The only development was an increase in the number of flags, simple two or three colour designs being added to the initial single colour ones, to meet the requirements of the *Additional Fighting Instructions*.

The next major change was delayed until the second half of the eighteenth century, when Howe realized that, with the growth in the number of *Fighting Instructions*, it was not easy for his captains to find, from the one book, the meaning of a particular flag. In 1776, he issued to his ships in the West Indies a separate *Signal Book*, in which a page was allotted to each flag. Below a sketch of it was a list of the positions in which it might be hoisted, and against each a brief reference to the particular *Fighting Instruction* or other order with which the fleet was required to comply. A separation between tactical instructions and flag signals soon followed, as it had in the French Navy as early as 1693.

But the tactical innovations of Rodney and others of his age, required more *Fighting Instructions* than there were flags of a design simple enough

	Union Flag	
Where Hoisted	P A	*Signification*
Fore and Mizentopmastheads —	1 4 7 / 24 17	The whole Fleet to tack together
Foretopmasthead —	1 4 5	Weathermost & Headmost Ships
Mizentopmasthead —	1 4 6	Sternmost & Leewardmost Ships } to Tack first
Foretopmasthead —	1 22 9	Van of the Fleet
Mizentopmasthead —	1 22 10	Rear of the Fleet
Mizen Peak, with a Blue Flag under it —	1 22 7	Ships to Leeward to get into the Admiral's Wake
Foretopmasthead, w.th a Red Pendt. under it —	5 31	Ship that leads, to lead on the other Tack
Mizen Peak {a Pendant under it} —	1 21 1 / 1 21 2	To form the Line {a Head / a Breast}
Mizen Peak {a Blue Flag with a Red Cross / a Flag half Red half White under} —	9 4	To form the Line, a Head at {half a Cable / two Cables} distance
Mizen Peak, Same Flags & Pend.rs under —	1 9 4 / 1 16 1	To form the Line a Breast at the same distances / All Captains in the Fleet
Mizen Shrouds {a Wift with the Ensign — / & Blue & White flag at Miz.lith}	1 16 1 / 1 1 1	A Lieutenant from each Ship } to go on board the Admiral / Ditto, with Weekly Accounts
Jack Staff, in a Wift, and a Ship's Signal —	17 11	For that Ship's Tender to come under the Admiral's Stern
Mizentopmast Shr.s with Chacing flag for th.2.r	3 19	Apart Ship to chace in Order to look out
Jack Staff, in a Wift, by a Ship Engaged —	25 22	Distress
Maintopmasthead down the Backstay	2 5 12	Danger
Ditto —	many 5 12	Strikes and sticks fast
Jack Staff, & Ensign properly hoisted —	8 11	On seeing the Land

Page from an eighteenth-century signal book

to be distinguished at a distance. From Bourdé de Villehuet's *Le Manoeuvrier*, describing a signal code invented by Mahé de la Bourdonnais (who worsted Commodore Peyton off Negapatam in 1746), Rear-Admiral Richard Kempenfelt (before losing his life in the *Royal George* disaster) devised his *Primer of Speech for Fighting Ships*, which was adopted by Howe in 1782. Sixteen flags, hoisted in pairs, referred captains, first to one of the sixteen pages in the book, then to one of the sixteen articles on that page, giving a total of 256 pre-determined meanings. Eight years more and Howe issued his own *Signal Book for Ships of War*, which reduced the number of flags to ten, but numbered them from zero to nine and allowed as many as four to be deftly hitched to halyards in a single hoist, thereby increasing the number of meanings to 9,999.

Nelson took full advantage of this considerable step forward; but his

VOCABULARY.   67

C 3

2122	Cable.	I have lost a cable
2123		Can you spare a cable?
2124		I cannot spare a cable
2125		Take end of sheet cable in at stern port.
2126	Cadiz	
2127	Calais	
2128	Can you?	
2129		I think I can
2130		I am sure I can
2132	Cannot.	I am afraid I cannot
2133	Canvas.	Can you spare canvas?
2134		I can spare canvas
2135		I cannot spare canvas
2136	Cape of Good Hope	
2137	Cartridges.	I am short of musket cartridges
2138		I can spare some cartridges
2139		I cannot spare any cartridges
2140	Cattegate	

Part of page from Popham's signal book

tactical genius would not have blossomed to full flower, nor could his immortal signal have been hoisted at Trafalgar, if Popham had not written thus to Keith in 1801:

> My Lord, I take the liberty of sending you a vocabulary of marine telegraph. I have found it of particular use in receiving intelligence from detached ships, for every proper name and word not in the vocabulary can be spelt. I conceive the advantage to be not only a saving of time and trouble, but of boats. Instead of making signals for officers to be sent to the flagship to take down a message, it might be directly communicated.

First issued to ships-of-the-line in 1803, Popham's *Telegraphic Signals or Marine Vocabulary* was the final breakthrough to complete 'freedom of speech' by signal. In addition to a vocabulary of commonly used words, to each of which was allotted a number so that it could be signalled by a two- or three-flag hoist, this numbered the letters of the alphabet so that other words could be spelt in full.

To Nelson this new found freedom was so important that, before leaving England for the last time in September 1805, he twice visited the newly-appointed Second Secretary at the Admiralty, John Barrow, to ensure that Popham's code was supplied to *all* ships in his fleet.

This attention to detail allowed Captain Blackwood to write to his wife from the frigate *Euryalus* off Cape Trafalgar on 1 October 1805: 'At this moment we are within four miles of the enemy and talking to Lord Nelson by means of Sir Home Popham's signals.' So, too, did it allow Nelson to turn to his signal lieutenant three weeks later with these words: 'Now I'll amuse the fleet with a signal. Mr Pasco, I wish to say: "England confides that every man will do his duty." ' Popham's book in hand, Lieutenant Pasco answered: 'If your Lordship will permit me to substitute "expects" for "confides" it will be sooner completed, because "expects" is in the vocabulary, and "confides" will have to be spelt.' With Nelson's agreement, a series of flag hoists was run up to the *Victory*'s mastheads: 253 (England) – 269 (expects) – 863 (that) – and so on. Only 'duty' had to be spelt, using four hoists to the eight needed for 'confides', when Nelson was impatient to make one more signal before battle was joined – this last injunction to his captains for which a group was provided in Howe's *Signal Book*, flags 16 meaning: 'Engage the enemy more closely.'

5 *Strategy and Tactics*

How, in Nelson's time, were these sailing Ships, with their multi-gunned broadsides whose range was only 2,500 yards, which were officered by professionals but crewed by pressed men more than by volunteers, which could be controlled only by such restricted methods as by letter, 'councils of war' and flag signals – *how* were these Ships used in war?

Strategy first. Britain's was conditioned by her island structure and her consequent dependence on the sea. Bishop Adam de Moleyns spelled its essence as far back as 1436: 'Kepe then the sea that is the walle of England.' Bacon added the rest in 1625: 'He that commands the sea is at great liberty, and may take as much and as little of the war as he will.' The prime objective was the greatest danger, the enemy battle fleet. In the time of Queen Elizabeth I Spain's was opposed only when it came so close to England as the Channel. In the Dutch Wars, when the chief threat was to the North Sea and the Channel, the British waited in their own waters until the enemy was reported to have left harbour – usually only in the summer months. But something more was needed in the eighteenth century, when France's and Spain's geographical positions laid the Atlantic, the Mediterranean, and seas yet further afield, open to forays by their fleets, something which stronger ship construction made possible. The strategy of close blockade was then evolved by the elder Pitt and Lord Anson for use in the Seven Years War; neutralizing the enemy's fleets, until an opportunity arose to destroy them, by maintaining battle fleets of sufficient size off each of his principal ports, to ensure, so far as possible, that his ships did not put to sea without being brought to action. As already related in Chapter III, much of Britain's Mediterranean fleet was so employed under Hood and Hotham from 1793 to 1795. And thus did Britain's storm-tossed ships stand – off Brest, Rochefort, Ferrol and Cadiz, as well as Toulon – between Napoleon and his dream of French dominion of the world, throughout the ten years from 1796 to 1805 in which Nelson played a vital role, and in the ten subsequent years that ended at Waterloo.

Though close blockade was the keystone of Britain's defence against invasion, enabling Lord St Vincent to declare to Parliament in 1803: 'My Lords, I do not say the [French] cannot come. I only say they cannot come *by sea*', other stones completed the arch of maritime control. Seaborne trade, vital for the conduct of any war, in part for the raw materials which it brought (such as Baltic pine for ships' masts), in part for the wealth that it provided (sugar and its by-products from the West Indies were England's greatest source of wealth, wool not excepted, until the Industrial Revolution brought coal into its own), had to be protected against attack by enemy cruisers and privateers, which an Act of 1708 made the first charge on Britain's naval resources. Merchant vessels were sailed in escorted convoys, since, to quote Dryden: 'Your convoy makes the dangerous way secure.' Nelson was thus tediously employed during his first months in the *Albemarle*. For a like reason, enemy seaborne trade was curtailed by sending British cruisers to range the trade routes to capture his merchantmen wherever they might be found, as Nelson was employed during his first months in the *Agamemnon*. British squadrons were needed overseas, to find and destroy those of the enemy, as Rodney did in the West Indies just before the *Albemarle* joined Hood's force in those waters, and as Hughes tried so hard to do against Suffren in the Indian Ocean, highway for the rich treasures of the East. Britain's warships were required to support her Army and those of her allies, as Nelson did his best to support the Austrians in northern Italy – and, as Trafalgar made it possible, after his death, for Wellington to liberate Spain in a campaign that contributed so much to Napoleon's eventual downfall.

Britain also used her sea power to land military forces on enemy held territory. As Admiral of the Fleet Lord Fisher expressed it a century later: 'The British Army should be used as a projectile to be fired by the Navy', and thus did Hood and Nelson help the insurgent Corsican patriots to eject the French from their island. Finally, the British Fleet had to prevent the enemy from doing likewise or, if he managed to effect a landing, to ensure that he did not exploit it, as Nelson did when, as is related in Chapter VI, Napoleon tried to extend France's empire to the Middle-East.

France and her allies could pursue a different naval strategy in the eighteenth century because they were Continental powers, by no means dependent on the sea, except to sustain their colonies. Mahan coined one name for it, the 'fleet in being'; the French another, the *guerre de course*. Except for squadrons sent to East and West Indian waters to dispute Britain's command of these areas (as when Suffren went to the Indian Ocean and D'Estaing and de Grasse to the Caribbean), France, Spain and the Netherlands kept their battle fleets within such ports as Brest, Cadiz, the Texel and Toulon, where they were safe from attack but were a constant threat to Britain's interests in Home waters and in the Mediterranean. These were seldom sent to sea except for a specific operation, as when Villaret Joyeuse was ordered out of Brest in 1794 to meet and bring in a valuable homebound convoy (and suffered defeat by Howe at the Glorious First of June), as when Brueys was ordered to escort Buonaparte's *Armée d'Orient* from Toulon to Alexandria in 1798 (which doomed him to destruction at the Nile), and when Villeneuve and Gravina were ordered from Toulon and Cadiz to join with Ganteaume from Brest in 1805 to gain command of the Channel for the twelve hours that Napoleon needed for his invasion of England. Moreover, in all such cases, France's admirals were strictly enjoined to evade action, so far as possible, with any substantial enemy force, in sharp contrast to Britain's belief in engaging the enemy whenever opportunity offered.

This 'fleet in being' strategy may be termed defensive: not so the *guerre de course*. Against Britain's maritime trade French privateers roamed the oceans. Powerful frigate-size vessels, operating singly or in pairs, were a match for ships of their own size and could use their greater speed to escape if they chanced to meet an enemy ship-of-the-line. Britain's answer was the convoy system. Even so, many merchantmen sailed independently and were taken in prize. Indeed, such shipping was so vulnerable to attack in the Channel, where France could employ numerous privateers smaller than frigates, that the British went to the laborious extent of constructing a canal linking London with Portsmouth, so that goods, notably timber for ship building, might be sent this way instead of through the Straits of Dover.*

Now *Tactics*: and first the relative importance of being to windward or to leeward of the enemy since, as Drake expressed it: 'The advantage of time and place in all martial actions is half a victory, which being lost is irrecoverable.' Believing in the offensive, the British, from the day of Hubert de Burgh's encounter with Eustace the Monk in 1217, sought the weather position, from which they could best choose the time, direction and method for bearing down on the enemy; and achieving the faster rate of fire that was possible from a ship's lee-side battery; from which, too, they could most quickly close, first to point-blank range, then board in order to compel the enemy to surrender. They accepted the chief disadvantage that, once committed to battle, the fleet to windward could not easily withdraw if it was being worsted. The French, being usually on the defensive, preferred the leeward position from which a fleet could accept no more of the battle than it wished before retiring; in which, too, it might keep the range long, and aim to disable the enemy by destroying his masts and yards rather than battering his hull. It was these tactics

---

*Daniel Defoe noted in his *A Tour Through the Whole Island of Great Britain* that the roads were so bad that 'I have seen one tree on a carriage . . . drawn . . . by two and twenty oxen . . . carried so little a way . . . that sometimes it is two or three years before it gets [from the Surrey woods] to Chatham.' The roads were no better in the late eighteenth century. The canal was, nonetheless, begun too late; it was not finished until 1816, by which time it was again practicable to use the faster sea route between Spithead and the Nore (see *London's Lost Route to the Sea*, by P. A. L. Vine).

which allowed Nelson, in the 64-gun *Agamemnon* to bring the 44-gun *Melpomène* to action on 22 October 1793, and to damage her near to sinking, but prevented him completing her destruction when her consorts came to her rescue. The French had done so much damage to the British vessel's rigging that she was unable to pursue her victim.

The essence of a single ship action was a gun duel fought on parallel courses; if a British captain had his way, at point-blank range – 400 yards – at which solid shot inflicted most damage on the enemy's hull, followed, if this was still necessary to compel surrender, by boarding and hand-to-hand fighting; if a French captain had his way, at long range – 2,000 yards – in the hope that the enemy might be immobilized by dismasting, and so obliged to strike his colours. There was, however, one significant variation, not easily realized, but of which Nelson made good use in the *Agamemnon*'s duel with the more powerful *Ça Ira* on 13 March 1795. A ship's high square stern, from which she could bring very few guns to bear, was her most vulnerable part. To rake this with full broadsides, whilst avoiding those of the enemy, was every captain's desire. Nelson was able to do this time and again against the *Ça Ira* because, being dismasted and in tow of the *Censeur*, neither captain could thwart his design.

As much is true of actions between squadrons and fleets – but more than this needs to be said of the tactics which they employed. Blake, Deane and Monk (as did their Dutch opponents) saw the need to fight in *line ahead* (as opposed to the disorganized *mêlée* with which Howard, Hawkins and Drake disposed of the Armada), because this gave clear fire for their ships' broadside mounted guns. To impose such tactics on their captains, they issued written instructions; and since the Dutch were as determined on battle as the British, these proved sufficiently effective at the Gabbard and Scheveningen in 1653 to be printed as the *Fighting Instructions* of 1691, which went to the extent of forbidding any departure from a semi-rigid line 'till the main body [of the enemy] be disabled or run'. Moreover, although the battle fleet was divided into three squadrons, van, centre and rear, all were controlled by the admiral in the centre despite the already mentioned lack of signals to enable him to meet any unforeseen development. However, such battles as Barfleur in 1692 and Malaga in 1703 seemed to confirm the merit of this inflexible method, especially when it was amplified by *Additional Fighting Instructions*. By the beginning of the eighteenth century a naval battle was supposed always to be fought between fleets in line ahead on parallel courses, between sail-laden, heeling ships, each of which was wreathed with the smoke swirling from the thunder of a broadside, as illustrated in diagram (1) on p. 90. And many admirals

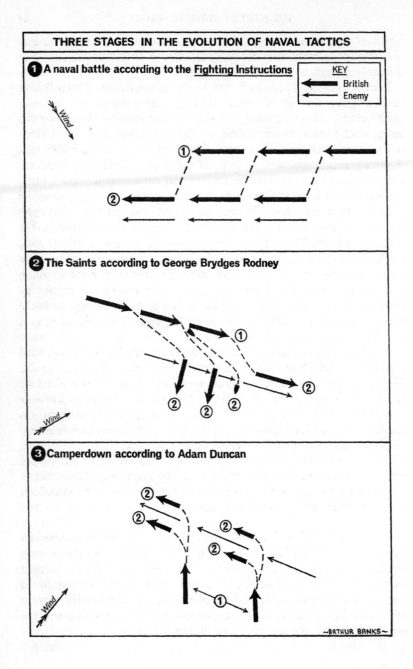

THREE STAGES IN THE EVOLUTION OF NAVAL TACTICS

1 A naval battle according to the <u>Fighting Instructions</u>

KEY

British

Enemy

Wind

① ②

2 The Saints according to George Brydges Rodney

① ② ② ②

Wind

3 Camperdown according to Adam Duncan

② ② ② ②

① Wind

~ARTHUR BANKS~

continued to believe in this until it not only cost Graves the opportunity to destroy de Grasse's fleet in Chesapeake Bay in 1781, but, in effect, lost Britain her American colonies.

These tactics were, however – as in the days of Rome's ram-bowed biremes – the concept of military minds, lacking experience of those uncontrollable elements, wind and weather, and so supposing that a sea battle could be successfully fought in rigid formation under firm control as was the proven method on land. Moreover, such tactics belied that important principle of war, concentration of force. There was, therefore, a growing realization of their futility especially when, unlike the Dutch, the French and Spanish fleets endeavoured to avoid action. Mathews off Toulon (1744) and Byng off Minorca (1756) attempted to mass their fleets against a part of the enemy's, and paid the price of failure. Anson at the First Battle of Finisterre (1747), Hawke at Quiberon Bay (1759), and Byron at Grenada (1779), ignored the *Fighting Instructions* when they realized that the French were intent on escaping: instead of forming line of battle, they ordered a general chase. And their success was capped by Rodney at The Saints: instead of ranging parallel to the enemy, he broke through their line, thereby dividing it and engaging it on both sides, as is shown in diagram (2) on p. 90.

These victories, together with Boscawen's off Lagos (1759) and Rodney's at the Moonlight Battle (1780), lifted the dead hand of the *Fighting Instructions*. With the advantage of the signal codes evolved by Howe and Kempenfelt, Howe broke the enemy's line at many points at the Glorious First of June in 1794, and in the same year Duncan approached the Dutch at Camperdown in two lines which divided the enemy into three parts, as illustrated in diagram (3) on p. 90.

The way was thus cleared for Nelson, especially when he gained the further freedom provided by Popham's signal book, to employ the tactics that gained such decisive results in the several major fleet actions in which he was engaged between 1796 and 1805.

This brief survey of the Royal Navy of Nelson's time will have served its purpose if it enables the reader to appreciate how these actions were fought – and won. And since the first falls within the span of the next chapter, it is time to rejoin HMS *Captain* with Commodore Nelson's broad pendant flying, where we left her at the end of Chapter III, serving under Admiral Sir John Jervis's command in the Mediterranean in the third year of Britain's war with Revolutionary France.

V

First Steps to Glory
1796-1798

Having hoisted his broad pendant in the 74-gun *Captain*, Nelson was first employed blockading Leghorn, after its capture by the French, 'in a manner I flatter myself unexampled', the while Jervis maintained a grip on Toulon. Next, he carried troops from Bastia for an unopposed occupation of Elba, to prevent this island being used as a stepping stone for the French to reconquer Corsica. In August 1796 his proven talents for independent command and responsibility, of which Jervis was making as much use as both Hood and Hotham had done,* were formerly acknowledged by his substantive promotion to commodore, a rank that brought him a welcome addition to his pay of the then considerable sum of ten shillings ($1.2) per day, and allowed him a captain (from December, Ralph Miller) to relieve him of the duties of commanding his own flagship. In September he occupied the island of Capraja, forty miles to the east of Corsica, as satisfaction for the Genoese Government's decision to sequester English property.

A month later Nelson learned that the speed with which Bonaparte (as he now spelled his name) had conquered northern Italy, had impelled Spain to change sides in the war. He was dismayed to hear that Pitt's Government was sufficiently alarmed by this breach in the bulwark of the First Coalition to order Jervis to abandon Corsica and withdraw from the Mediterranean, 'a measure which I cannot approve. At home they know not what this fleet is capable of performing, *any and everything*.' Our

*Or, as one jealous brother captain grumbled: 'You did as you pleased in Lord Hood's time, the same in Admiral Hotham's, and now again with Sir John Jervis. It makes no difference to you who is Commander-in-Chief' – to which speech Nelson returned 'a pretty strong answer'.

'object . . . in future is the defence of Portugal [Britain's staunchest ally] and keeping in the Mediterranean the combined fleets [of France and Spain]'. As one consequence Nelson was required – supreme irony – to conduct the evacuation of Bastia: he did it 'in a manner pleasant to my feelings: not a creature was left who wished to come off'.

Likewise, in December he was sent from Gibraltar to take off the troops which he had earlier landed on Elba. For this he transferred his broad pendant to the frigate *Minerve* in which, together with the *Blanche*, he had a sharp engagement with two similar Spanish ships off Cartagena, compelling the *Sabina*, captained by the renowned Don Jacobo Stuart (a descendant of King James II) to strike her colours. He found this a simpler task than the iron diplomacy needed to ensure that Corsican patriots, who now favoured France, did no damage to English lives and property, or the velvet style required to persuade General de Burgh to accept the validity of Jervis's instructions and agree to withdraw from Elba.

Not until the end of January 1797 could Nelson leave this island when he was all the time fearful that Jervis, who had taken the bulk of his fleet away to the Tagus, might engage the Spaniards before he could be there. Passing Cartagena, he discovered that the Spanish fleet, under Langara's successor, Admiral Don José de Cordova, had sailed on 1 February. Calling at Gibraltar on the 9th for water, he learned that the bulk of the enemy had passed through the Straits four days before. Two Spanish ships-of-the-line had, however, remained in Algeciras Bay and, when Nelson sailed again on the 11th, these came out and gave chase.

There followed an incident, of no great consequence, but revealing of Nelson's character. A British seaman chanced to fall overboard and the *Minerve*'s captain, George Cockburn, believing the enemy to be far enough astern, lowered a rescue boat in the charge of his first lieutenant, Thomas Masterman Hardy. But the search not only proved vain but took much longer than Cockburn expected, so that Hardy and his crew were in danger of being overtaken and captured. Seeing this, Nelson took a swift decision: exclaiming 'By God, I'll not lose Hardy', he ordered Cockburn to back the *Minerve*'s topsails. This checked the British frigate's way and allowed Hardy and his crew to be recovered. Most fortunately, it also confused the Spanish captains: uncertain of their opponent's intentions they, too, backed topsails when within a mile of bringing the *Minerve* to action, which enabled Cockburn to make good his escape.*

*This is a more likely version of how Hardy was rescued than that chronicled by Colonel Drinkwater, a passenger in the *Minerve*, which most historians have accepted without questioning its fallacies. According to this landsman, Hardy's boat was prevented from returning to the

So Hardy survived to be the *Victory*'s flag captain at Trafalgar. Nelson's impulsive order was, nonetheless, more humane than wise. He hazarded his flagship and her crew: they were within a few cables of being trapped by a much more powerful force. He could not have counted on the captains of two enemy ships-of-the-line reacting in a manner described as 'wholly inexcusable and only to be accounted for by that singular moral effect produced in many men by a sudden and unexpected occurrence'.* Nor was this all: Nelson also jeopardized his mission, the transmission of vital news to his Commander-in-Chief. But since Providence chose to smile upon his conduct, the incident may, perhaps, be closed with Jervis's verdict, albeit given on a different occasion; Nelson's 'zeal does now and then (not often) outrun his discretion'.

Pressing on to the west, Nelson next ran into fog; and when this began to lift he found that the *Minerve* had, by chance, sailed into the midst of the Spanish fleet. Fortunately his luck held; the visibility remained so poor that the British frigate avoided detection; and on the morning of 13 February Nelson located his own fleet 25 miles to the west of Cape St Vincent. There, before moving back into the *Captain*, he gave Jervis the vital news that Cordova was out of the Mediterranean. He was just in time: dawn next morning, St Valentine's Day, revealed the Spanish fleet in sight to the southward.

Nelson supposed their destination to be the West Indies, where Britain's interests, the islands and their seaborne trade, were vulnerable to enemy attack. In fact, with the final defeat of Austria in prospect, the French had decided to aim a direct and decisive blow at their most implacable foe. In December 1796, at the behest of Wolfe Tone, Admiral de Galles's Brest fleet attempted to land 18,000 troops in Bantry Bay to help the Irish patriots, an operation that was foiled more by bad weather and lack of skill in handling the French ships than by the inefficient Admiral Lord Bridport's lax blockade. (Bridport was formerly Alexander Hood, younger brother of Lord Hood.) In February 1797, 1,500 Frenchmen were landed by Commodore Jean Castignier's small squadron near Fishguard (Wales), under the command of 'Colonel' William Tate (an American who had been court martialled for fiddling the accounts of a

---

Minerve by the strong current flowing through the Straits – which ignores the natural phenomena that a current has as much effect upon a ship under way (as opposed to one at anchor) as it has upon any boat she may lower – and Nelson limited his order to Cockburn to, 'Back the *mizzen* topsail' – when more drastic action was clearly required to recover Hardy's boat as quickly as possible.

*Mahan in his *Life of Nelson*.

South Carolina artillery regiment), but these were quickly rounded up by Lord Cawdor's Welsh Yeomanry, Militia and Fencibles, long before they could comply with their ambitious orders, to destroy Bristol, then attack Chester and Liverpool. But such follies did not deter General Lazarre Hoche from planning to invade England. To pave the way for a Channel crossing, Cordova was to go north and join with de Galles, and with the Dutch fleet from the Texel, to form an allied force sufficient to gain command of the Narrow Seas. The Spanish fleet was, however, required to call first at Cadiz for provisions; and it would have been there on 14 February but for the chance of an easterly gale. This had blown it so far off course, that it was now running back to this port, 150 miles to the south-east, before a fair wind from the west.

Jervis's fleet numbered fifteen sail-of-the-line,* six of them, including his flagship, the *Victory*, being three-deckers of 90–100 guns, and eight being 74s, the *Captain* among them, plus four frigates. Cordova had nearly double this strength; twenty-seven sail-of-the-line and ten frigates, with many of his three-deckers armed with 112 guns, and his flagship, the enormous four-decker *Santísima Trinidad*, mounting as many as 136.

Despite the greater strength of the Spanish fleet, Jervis did not hesitate to engage. At 8.15 am he ordered his fleet to form in single line ahead in close order (which placed the *Captain* three from the rear) on a south-westerly course towards the enemy, and to prepare for battle. 'Confident in the skill, valour and discipline of the officers and men I had the happiness to command, and judging that the honour of His Majesty's arms, and the circumstances of the war in these seas required a considerable degree of enterprise', he accepted the calculated risk of pitting his ships against an enemy that had done little to support Hood at Toulon, and had given no better evidence of their fighting qualities since then.

Cordova's ships were, in truth, undermanned – in complements of up to 950 some had only 80 seamen, the rest being soldiers and fresh landsmen – and their officers so 'inexperienced that the appearance of the British took them completely by surprise'. Instead of sailing in good order, closed up, they were straggling in two groups, with six ships as much as seven miles ahead of the remainder, which were in a confused mass. And this gave Jervis his opening: he could minimize his own

---

*He would have had seven more but for Rear-Admiral Robert Man's 'desertion'. This officer, having been ordered to take his squadron to Gibraltar for stores in October, and then to rejoin Jervis's fleet (at that time still in the Mediterranean), decided that the threat presented by Cordova's fleet (then to the eastward of the Rock) justified a decision to forsake his Commander-in-Chief and return to the greater safety of English waters. The Admiralty showed their strong disapproval by ordering Man to strike his flag, nor was he again employed afloat.

THE OPPOSING BATTLE FLEETS AT CAPE ST VINCENT, 14 FEBRUARY 1797

BRITISH (in order of sailing)			SPANISH		
Ship	Guns	Commander	Ship	Guns	Notes
Culloden	74	Capt. Thomas Troubridge	Santísima Trinidad	130	Flagship of Admiral Don José de Cordova
Blenheim	98	Capt. T. L. Frederick			
Prince George	98	Capt. J. Irwin / Flagship of Rear-Admiral W. Parker	Concepción	112	
			Condé de Regla	112	
			Mexicano	112	
Orion	74	Capt. Sir James Saumarez	Príncipe de Asturias	112	
Colossus	74	Capt. G. Murray	Salvador del Mundo	112	Captured
Irresistible	74	Capt. G. Martin	San José	112	Captured
Victory	100	Captain (1st) R. Calder / Captain (2nd) G. Grey / Flagship of Admiral Sir J. Jervis	Neptuno	80	
			San Nicolas	80	Captured
Egmont	74	Capt. J. Sutton	Atlante	74	
Goliath	74	Capt. Sir Charles Knowles	Bahama	74	
Barfleur	98	Capt. J. R. Dacres / Flagship of Vice-Admiral W. Waldegrave	Conquistador	74	
			Firme	74	
			Glorioso	74	
Britannia	100	Capt. T. Foley / Flagship of Vice-Admiral C. Thompson	Oriente	74	
			Pelayo	74	
			San Antonio	74	
Namur	90	Capt. J. H. Whitshed	San Domingo	74	
Captain	74	Capt. R. W. Miller / Broad pendant of Commodore H. Nelson	San Firmin	74	
			San Francisco de Paula	74	
			San Genaro	74	
Diadem	64	Capt. G. H. Towry	San Ildefonso	74	
Excellent	74	Capt. C. Collingwood	San Juan Nepomuceno	74	
			San Pablo	74	
			San Ysidro	74	Captured
			Soberano	74	
			Terrible	74	

inferior numbers by dividing the enemy into two. At 9.30 am he ordered the *Culloden*, *Blenheim*, *Prince George*, *Irresistible*, *Colossus* and *Orion*, to put on all sail and head for the gap. Belatedly the leading Spanish division altered course to port in an attempt to fall back on their main body. Jervis responded at 11.0 am with the signal, 'Pass through the enemy line'.

This bold approach gained the success that it deserved. Deciding that it could not, after all, close the gap in time, the Spanish van, reinforced by three ships from the main body which managed to cross ahead of Jervis's approaching fleet, but weakened by one which made off alone to the south-east, turned to a northerly course to leeward of the British, leaving their main body, now reduced to eighteen sail-of-the-line – only three more than in Jervis's fleet – to windward. And at 11.30 am HMS *Culloden*, Captain Thomas Troubridge (whom, incidentally, Jervis believed to be more 'capable of commanding the fleet of England' than any of his other captains, Nelson not excluded), came within range of the leading Spanish ship and opened fire. When the *Culloden*'s consorts joined the action, the Spaniards altered to the north, so that the two fleets were passing each other on opposite courses. To counter this, Jervis ordered his ships to tack in succession. The *Culloden* was followed by the *Blenheim*, Captain Thomas Frederick, and by Rear-Admiral William Parker's flag-ship, the *Prince George*, Captain John Irwin.

The Spanish van, beating up from leeward, attempted to cut through the British line at the turning point, first between the *Orion*, Captain Sir James Saumarez, and the *Colossus*, Captain George Murray; next between the *Irresistible*, Captain George Martin, and Jervis's flagship, the *Victory*; finally, on each side of the *Egmont*, Captain John Sutton. But the British ships maintained such close station, and raked the enemy with such withering broadsides, that the Spanish van was driven off, except for the *Oriente* which, under cover of the smoke of battle, succeeded in joining her main body to windward.

The fight which, so far, had been no more than a series of brief engage-ments between passing ships, reached its crisis at 1.0 pm. Because Jervis tacked his ships in *succession* instead of *together*, his fleet had passed to the southward of both Spanish divisions before more than half the British vessels were round on to their new course. And since the Spaniards seized this chance to attempt a junction, Jervis was faced with the prospect of having to pursue a superior fleet which, except for the unlikely event of it deciding to fight, might well escape him into Cadiz.

This gave Nelson his golden moment. Ignoring the accepted dogma which required captains to maintain their allotted stations in a rigid line of battle unless otherwise ordered by the admiral, he wore the *Captain* out to port from her position near the rear of the British fleet and, having reversed course more than 180 degrees,* headed for the van of the Spanish main body. The speed with which Jervis realized and reacted to Nelson's initiative will always stand to his credit. Most admirals would have been shocked to the core of their souls by such a flagrant disregard of the *Fighting Instructions*, and signalled a peremptory order to the *Captain* to resume her station in the line. Jervis, at 1.19 pm signalled his rear ship, the *Excellent*, Captain Cuthbert Collingwood, (who had had the good fortune to command the *Barfleur* at the Glorious First of June) to leave the line and join the *Captain*. And by 1.30 pm these two ships were in close action with the *Santísima Trinidad*, which had the vital effect of slowing the Spanish fleet, still sailing in an unwieldy mass instead of in proper line of battle, for time enough to allow the *Culloden*, leading Jervis's line, followed by the *Blenheim* and *Prince George*, to engage them.

(Historians reluctant to allow Nelson full credit for his striking initiative on this occasion, have argued that it was both authorized and prompted by a signal which Jervis made to his ships at 12.51 pm 'to take suitable station for mutual support, and engage the enemy as coming up in succession'. But any such argument depends on more than a loose interpretation of Jervis's order; it involves total misunderstanding. There was, in truth, no evidence that Jervis intended his ships to do other than engage the enemy, each in turn after altering course to the northward, as from the van, the *Culloden* leading, they might manage to overhaul the Spanish main body. Nor is there any evidence that Nelson's decision to take the *Captain* out of the line was motivated by anything except his own clear understanding that there was no other way by which the Spanish fleet could be prevented from making good their escape.)

As certain, and far more important than this parenthetical comment were the consequences and eventual results of Nelson's brilliant manoeuvre.

At about 2 p.m. the *Culloden* had stretched so far ahead as to cover the *Captain* from the heavy fire poured upon her by the Spanish four-decker and her companions, as they hauled up and brought their broadsides to bear. The *Captain* took immediate advantage of this respite to replenish her lockers with shot, and repair her running rigging. Shortly afterwards the *Blenheim*, passing also to windward of the *Captain*, afforded her a second respite. The two more immediate

---

*It was much quicker to wear a ship round, stern to wind, even for a turn of more than 180-degrees, than to put her about, head to wind.

opponents of the *Captain* and *Culloden* had been the *San Ysidro* and *Salvador del Mundo*; these, having already lost their topmasts, and being in a crippled state, the *Blenheim*, by a few of her heavy broadsides, sent staggering astern, to be cannonaded afresh by the *Prince George*, *Orion* and other advancing ships. At 2.35 pm the *Excellent*, arriving abreast of the disabled *Salvador del Mundo*, engaged the latter for a few minutes; then passing on to the *San Ysidro*. This ship Collingwood engaged closely until 2.53 pm, when, after a gallant defence, she hauled down the Spanish, and hoisted the English flag. Very soon after the *Excellent* had quitted the much disabled *Salvador del Mundo*, the *Irresistible* and *Diadem* commenced an attack upon her, the 74 stationing herself upon her weather bow, and the 64 upon her lee quarter. Observing the *Victory* about to pass under her stern, and that the *Barfleur* was following close, the *Salvador del Mundo* hauled down her flag as soon as some of the *Victory*'s guns began to bear upon her. At about 3.15 pm the *Excellent* came to close action with the 80-gun ship *San Nicolas*, then with her foretopmast already gone in hot action with the *Captain*. Passing within ten feet of her starboard side, the *Excellent* poured in a destructive fire, and, in compliance with the signal then flying, to fill and stand on, made sail ahead.

In luffing up to avoid Collingwood's salute, the *San Nicolas* ran foul of the *San José*, whose mizen mast had been shot away, and which had received considerable other damage. As soon as the *Excellent* was sufficiently advanced to be clear of her, the *Captain* luffed up* as close to the wind as her shattered condition would admit, when her foretopmast, which had already been shot through, fell over the side. With the *San José* in an unmanageable state, with her wheel shot away, and all her sails, shrouds, and running rigging more or less cut, with the *Blenheim* ahead, and the *Culloden* crippled astern, the obvious course for Nelson was to board the Spanish two-decker.†

As a well-judged preparative, the *Captain* reopened, within less than twenty yards, her larboard broadside, whose heavy fire the *San Nicolas* returned with spirit for several minutes – when the *Captain* suddenly put her helm a-starboard, and, on coming to, hooked with her larboard cathead the starboard quarter-gallery of the *San Nicolas*, and, with her spritsail yard, the latter's main rigging. Nelson immediately called for boarders. In his own words:

*i.e. altered course towards the wind.
†*The Naval History of Great Britain*, by William James, Vol. II (abridged).

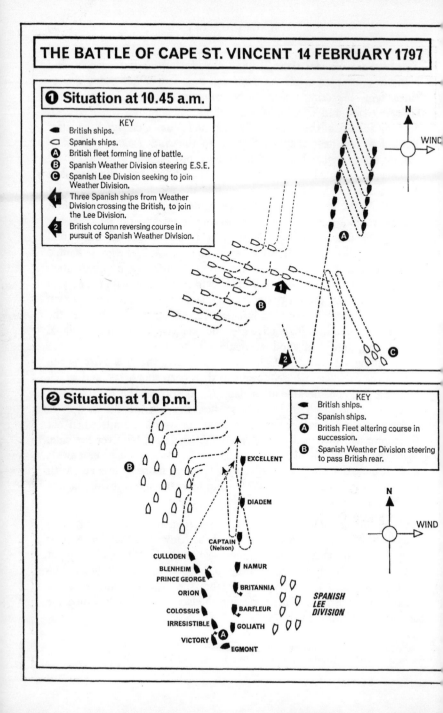

THE BATTLE OF CAPE ST. VINCENT 14 FEBRUARY 1797

❶ Situation at 10.45 a.m.

KEY
- British ships.
- Spanish ships.
- Ⓐ British fleet forming line of battle.
- Ⓑ Spanish Weather Division steering E.S.E.
- Ⓒ Spanish Lee Division seeking to join Weather Division.
- ◀1 Three Spanish ships from Weather Division crossing the British, to join the Lee Division.
- ◀2 British column reversing course in pursuit of Spanish Weather Division.

N
WIND

❷ Situation at 1.0 p.m.

KEY
- British ships.
- Spanish ships.
- Ⓐ British Fleet altering course in succession.
- Ⓑ Spanish Weather Division steering to pass British rear.

EXCELLENT
DIADEM
CAPTAIN (Nelson)
CULLODEN
BLENHEIM
PRINCE GEORGE
ORION
COLOSSUS
IRRESISTIBLE
VICTORY
NAMUR
BRITANNIA
BARFLEUR
GOLIATH
EGMONT
SPANISH LEE DIVISION

N
WIND

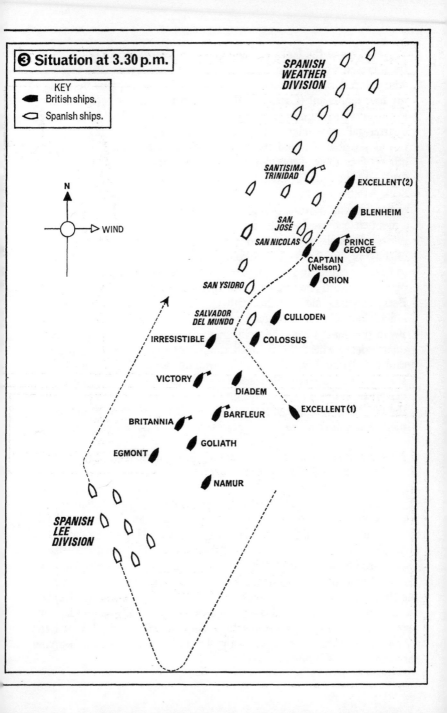

❸ Situation at 3.30 p.m.

KEY
British ships.
Spanish ships.

The soldiers of the 69th regiment, with an alacrity which will ever do them credit, were amongst the foremost on this service. The first man who jumped into the enemy's mizen chains was Captain Berry, late my first lieutenant (Captain Miller was in the very act of going also, but I directed him to remain). A soldier having broke the upper quarter-gallery window, jumped in followed by myself and others as fast as possible. I found the cabin doors fastened, and some Spanish officers fired their pistols; but having broke open the doors the soldiers fired, and the Spanish Commodore fell. Having pushed on the quarter-deck, I found Captain Berry in possession of the poop, and the Spanish ensign hauling down. I passed with my people to the forecastle, where I met two or three Spanish officers, and they delivered me their swords. A fire of pistols or muskets opening from the admiral's stern gallery of the *San José*, I directed the soldiers to fire into her stern; and calling to Captain Miller to send more men into the *San Nicolas*, directed my people to board the first-rate, which was done in an instant, Captain Berry assisting me into the main chains. At this moment a Spanish officer looked over the quarterdeck rail and said they surrendered. From this most welcome intelligence it was not long before I was on quarterdeck, where the Spanish captain presented me his sword and said the Admiral was dying of his wounds below. I asked him if the ship was surrendered. He declared she was; and on the quarterdeck of a Spanish first-rate, extravagant as the story may seem, did I receive the swords of vanquished Spaniards, which I gave to one of my barge-men, who put them with the greatest *sang froid* under his arm.

Nelson's impression that the *Captain*'s boarding parties compelled the *San Nicolas* and the *San José* to strike their colours is understandable. In truth, their surrender was as much due to the heavy fire poured into them by the other British ships. But this does not decry the gallantry with which, crying, 'Westminster Abbey, or glorious victory', Nelson led this fierce hand-to-hand fight, first aboard one Spanish ship-of-the-line, then aboard another, by a method which he subsequently described as 'Nelson's patent bridge for boarding first-rates'. 'Nothing in the world,' wrote Sir Gilbert Elliot, the late Viceroy of Corsica who witnessed the battle from the frigate *Lively*, 'was ever more noble than the transaction of the *Captain* from beginning to end, and the glorious group of your ship and her two prizes . . . was never surpassed and I dare say never will.' When the *Victory* passed the interlocked group, Jervis led her company in giving three cheers for Commodore Nelson.

This hotly contested battle, which lasted rather more than two hours, delayed the junction of the two Spanish divisions, but could not prevent it entirely. By 3.52 pm the Spanish van was near enough for Jervis to decide to break off the action rather than continue it against a much superior force. At 4.15 pm he ordered his frigates to take his four prizes in tow: at 4.39 pm he signalled his battleships to reform in single line ahead in the *Victory*'s wake. The last shots were fired shortly before 5 pm, when Nelson transferred his broad pendant to the nearest uninjured ship, HMS *Irresistible*.

Throughout the night the two fleets lay-to, repairing damage. Next morning they were in sight of each other, but the action was not renewed. The Spaniards had the wind and, after bearing down on the British fleet at 2.30 pm and hauling their wind as soon as Jervis hauled his, they disappeared, to take refuge in Cadiz, after nearly losing the damaged *Santísima Trinidad* to the 32-gun *Terpsichore*, Captain Richard Bowen, off Cape Spartel on 1 March.

This battle off Cape St Vincent was an undoubted British victory, even though Jervis was dissatisfied to the extent that he thought that his fleet should have secured two more prizes, 'the *Santísima Trinidad* and *Soberano*. . . . They only wanted some good fellow to get alongside them, and they were ours.' He lost no ships: only one, Nelson's *Captain*, lost a mast; and only the *Colossus*, *Culloden*, *Egmont* and *Blenheim* were otherwise significantly damaged. Their casualties were relatively light, too; 73 killed and some 400 wounded, the latter including Nelson who suffered 'a contusion of no consequence' from a splinter which, though superficial, caused him considerable pain for a week afterwards. The Spaniards, on the other hand, surrendered four ships, all of which lost masts, and suffered serious damage to ten more. And their casualties were high, numbering more than 400 killed and wounded in the *Santísima Trinidad* and the *San José* alone. But to ask why Jervis did not continue the action until dark on the 14th, or do more to renew it on the 15th, is being wise after the event. He was justified in engaging an enemy fleet numbering nearly twice as many ships more heavily gunned than his own, when they were divided; but to have fought the whole of it, even after four had struck, would have been more than a calculated risk. He might put his trust in the fighting skill and courage of his officers and men; but he could not know of the hopeless confusion which prevailed among the crews of Cordova's ships. So whilst hindsight may argue that Jervis *could* have scored a more decisive victory, no fair-minded student of naval warfare can suggest that he *should* have done so.

Nor did his countrymen think this of him. Whilst the Spanish 'Commander-in-Chief [was] sent to Madrid as a prisoner under an escort of horse, and the officers cannot come on shore for fear of the populace', Jervis was created Earl St Vincent and two of his admirals were made baronets. Nelson's part – his quickness in seeing opportunity and in seizing it, and his audacity in controlling it, which so brilliantly crowned the day – was specially recognized. When he went onboard the *Victory* at dark on 14 February, 'the Admiral received me on the quarterdeck and, having embraced me, said he could not sufficiently thank me, and used every expression to make me happy'. Nor was this all. When Jervis's first captain, Robert Calder, pointed out that Nelson's decision to wear out of the line was a breach of the *Fighting Instructions*, the Navy's strictest disciplinarian commented: 'It certainly was so, and if ever you commit such a breach ... I will forgive you also.' To the First Lord, Jervis wrote: 'Commodore Nelson, who was in the rear on the starboard tack, *took the lead on the larboard*, and contributed very much to the fortune of the day.' This and kindred tributes, including Elliot's enthusiastic eye-witness account when he reached England with news of the victory, gained the tangible reward for which Nelson had thirsted for so long.

'Chains and medals,' he told his brother, 'are what no fortune or connection in England can obtain; and I shall feel prouder of those than all the titles in the King's power to obtain.' Likewise, 'I do not want a baronetcy ...', the usual honour for a junior flag-officer in an important action, because he lacked the means to support a hereditary title. 'If these services have been of any value, let them be noticed ... by appointment to the Bath.'

And so they were. Commodore Sir Horatio Nelson, K.B.,* also received the Freedom of the City of London. But he was not promoted for his meritorious conduct – for a very good reason. On 1 April he received the delayed news that he had reached full flag rank in the ordinary course of seniority on 2 February. He was a rear-admiral of the blue before the battle of St Vincent was fought. But though he had achieved this at the age of thirty-nine, he was not exceptionally young for the times in which he lived. Christopher Parker (1762–1804) gained flag rank as early as thirty-three, and both Bartholomew Rowley (1763–1811) and Lord Hugh

---

*As an indication of the worth of this honour, when, shortly after the Napoleonic Wars this Order of Chivalry was divided into three classes, Knight Grand Cross (G.C.B.), Knight Commander (K.C.B.) and Commander (C.B.), all surviving holders of the K.B. became G.C.B.

Seymour (1759–1801) at thirty-six. On the other hand some post-captains were promoted when they were very much older: Thomas Hicks (1731–1801) at sixty-two, Edmund Dod (1734–1815) at sixty-three.

Two letters that Nelson received are worth quotation. Among many others Lady Parker, wife of his old Admiral, wrote in these encouraging terms: 'Your conduct on the memorable 14 February, a proud day for old England, is above all praise. . . . Long may you live, my dear Nelson, an ornament to your country and your profession.' But Lady Nelson could only write: 'Thank God, you are well. . . . My anxiety was far beyond my powers of expression. . . . Altogether, my dearest husband, my sufferings were great. . . . You have been most wonderfully protected; you have done desperate actions enough. Now may I . . . beg that you never board again.' And in her next: 'I sincerely hope . . . that all these wonderful and desperate actions – such as boarding ships – you will leave to others. With the protection of a Supreme Being, you have achieved a character and name which . . . cannot be greater; therefore rest satisfied.'

How little she understood her man. For what had this battle proved? That Nelson should have shown such physical courage was no new facet of his character; nor is it a *sine qua non* for a naval commander. The significance lies in his decision to turn the *Captain* out of the line, so as to prevent the Spaniards escaping. He had previously shown, notably in the *Boreas*, that he had the moral courage to disobey orders when he thought that the results would justify it – and as was in this instance abundantly proved. More important, he had now shown that he was not only a man of ambition, and a leader of a high order, but a commander with an exceptional understanding of the *essence* of the tactics of a naval action, as opposed to the time-hallowed instructions by which the Admiralty ordained that one should be fought, and in contrast to those of a single ship engagement of which he had previously proved himself a master.

After the battle the British fleet went first to Lagos Bay, then to the Tagus, whilst Nelson was sent into the Mediterranean with three ships-of-the-line to complete the evacuation of Elba in a convoy that was fortunate to avoid interception by a stronger French force. At Gibraltar, on his return, occurred an incident, small in itself, but confirmation of the wise diplomacy that Nelson had practised when working in support of the Austrians off Genoa.

The Consul of the [neutral] United States had to apply to him for the protection of twelve American merchant ships, then at Malaga, against the probable depredations of French privateers. . . . Nelson at once complied, ordering a British frigate to go to Malaga and escort the vessels to the Barbary coast, and even out of the Straits if necessary. In doing this he wrote courteously to the Consul: 'I am sure of fulfilling the wishes of my Sovereign, and I hope of strengthening the harmony which at present so happily subsists between the two nations.'*

– this less than twenty years after Britain's American colonies had fought so determinedly to secure their independence.

So that he could blockade the Spanish fleet in Cadiz, St Vincent received reinforcements from Home waters. Among these the 74-gun *Theseus* replaced the damaged *Captain*. Nelson's initial reaction to his new flagship, to which he transferred in May, was of two-fold dismay: she had come out destitute of stores of every kind, and her ship's company had played a prominent role in the 'breeze at Spithead' that disrupted the Channel fleet in April. Helped by Ralph Miller, Nelson met this challenge with all his vigour. Within a fortnight the *Theseus*'s material deficiencies had been remedied; and this note had been found, dropped on her quarter-deck:

> Success attend Admiral Nelson. God bless Captain Miller. We thank them for the officers they have placed over us. We are happy and comfortable, and will shed every drop of blood in our veins to support them, and the name of the *Theseus* shall be immortalized as high as the *Captain*.

It was signed, 'Ship's Company'. And even if one allows for the success of the Spithead mutiny in compelling the Admiralty to remedy the grosser injustices under which the Royal Navy had suffered for too long, and the men's sense of shame that this 'strike' had led on to something akin to a 'bloody revolution' in the North Sea fleet at the Nore, Nelson *must* have been something more than an exceptional leader to impress his personality so quickly upon the *Theseus*'s crew. He must have had 'star quality'.

For contrast, the captain of the *St George* had so much trouble with his ship's company that four of them were tried by court martial in July. Found guilty and sentenced to death, St Vincent ordered these men to be hanged at the yard-arm as soon as the fleet could be assembled to watch, which chanced to be on a Sunday. His second-in-command, Vice-Admiral Thompson, 'presumed to censure the execution on the Sabbath'. He was

*Mahan in his *Life of Nelson*.

immediately ordered to strike his flag. Nelson had a better understanding of his Commander-in-Chief's inflexible determination to ensure that the malaise that had afflicted the Fleet in Home waters did not infect his own: 'had it been Christmas Day instead of Sunday, I would have executed them. . . . Now your discipline is safe', was his terse comment.

Shortly before this episode, in June, St Vincent demonstrated his belief that in Nelson he had a young admiral of exceptional quality. Although the most junior of his flag officers, he entrusted him with command of an inshore squadron that included as many as half of his twenty ships-of-the-line. And with these, on the nights of 3 and 5 July, Nelson conducted vigorous bombardments of Cadiz.

> During this service the most perilous action occurred in which [Nelson] was ever engaged. Making a night attack upon the Spanish gunboats, his barge was attacked by an armed launch . . . carrying 26 men. Nelson had with him only ten . . . men, Captain Fremantle, and his coxswain . . . who twice saved the life of his Admiral by parrying the blows that were aimed at him, and at last actually interposed his own head to receive the blow of a Spanish sabre. . . . Notwithstanding the great disproportion of numbers, 18 of the enemy were killed, all the rest wounded, and their launch taken.*

But such heroisim did not, as was hoped, persuade the Spanish fleet to come out: their reaction was to withdraw from the outer harbour to the greater safety of the inner one.

Convinced by this that the enemy was unlikely to sortie for so long as a British fleet remained in the area, St Vincent decided that he could spare some of his ships to take the offensive elsewhere. Back in April Nelson had pressed to be employed on some more vigorous service than the tedious duty of maintaining the blockade. In particular, he had conceived a plan for an attack on Santa Cruz in the Canary Islands. Following the example of Drake and Hawkins, Blake had descended upon this port near the northern tip of Tenerife in 1657, and captured, burnt and sunk as many as sixteen Spanish vessels, including six laden with silver. He had, however, been lucky with the wind. The north-east Trade, which blew strongly all the summer, favoured a swift descent upon the harbour, but could not be depended upon to shift and come offshore in time to ensure a safe withdrawal. For this and other reasons, Nelson opposed a raid by ships alone. Remembering Bastia and Calvi, he suggested that General de Burgh's 3,700 troops, which had been unemployed

*Southey in his *Life of Nelson*.

since the evacuation of Elba, should be landed under cover of night. Since Santa Cruz was without protection, except for three forts, these should be able to enforce capitulation in three days at most. Moreover, Nelson argued, such a combined operation would require only 'a very small squadron'.

St Vincent could not authorize this operation because de Burgh refused to allow his troops to be employed on such a venture: nor would General Charles O'Hara, commanding the Gibraltar garrison, the only other British military force in the area, part with any of his men. June had, however, brought stimulating news: on 29 May the frigates *Lively* and *Minerve* descended on Santa Cruz, and their boats, directed by Lieutenant Hardy, managed to cut out the French frigate *Mutine* under heavy fire in broad daylight. And when this news was followed by a report that a richly laden treasure ship had reached Santa Cruz from Manila, St Vincent was persuaded to ask Nelson if he would attempt, not the combined operation he had suggested, but a naval attack such as he had advised against. And Nelson was likewise encouraged to answer that, given two hundred extra marines for a landing party, 'with "General Troubridge" ashore and myself afloat, I am confident of success'.

Such was the genesis of an expedition for which this squadron parted company with St Vincent's fleet on 15 July 1797:

Theseus, 74	Captain R. Miller
	Flagship of Rear-Admiral Sir Horatio Nelson
Culloden, 74	Captain T. Troubridge
Zealous, 74	Captain S. Hood*
Leander, 50	Captain T. Thompson
Seahorse, frigate, 38	Captain T. Fremantle
Emerald, frigate, 36	Captain T. Waller
Terpsichore, frigate, 32	Captain R. Bowen
Fox, cutter, 10	Lieutenant T. Gibson

St Vincent's orders to its commander were concise. Nelson was to proceed to Tenerife and capture Santa Cruz as expeditiously as possible; he was to seize the Spanish treasure ship and its cargo, and capture or destroy all other enemy vessels; 'and having performed your mission, you are to make the best of your way back to me'. 'Ten hours shall either make me a conqueror or defeat me', was Nelson's characteristic answer.

*This Samuel Hood (of whom we shall hear more) was a cousin of Nelson's 'patron', the Samuel (later Lord) Hood who was C-in-C Mediterranean before St Vincent (Jervis) was appointed to succeed him.

As the squadron neared the island, with its cloud-capped mountain peak, five days later, Nelson planned a surprise attack. His three frigates were to close Santa Cruz after nightfall. Their boats, with muffled oars, would land a force of marines and seamen soon after midnight on the beaches to the north-east of the town, from where they could gain the cover of Lion's Mouth Valley. As soon as they were assembled there, Troubridge would lead this force for an assault before daybreak, using special scaling ladders, starting with the most easterly fort. At dawn Nelson's 74s would close the port and support the attack with their broadsides. The two forts to the east having been taken, the Governor would be expected to surrender.

This plan went badly awry: the elements proved how little they could be trusted to play their part in ensuring success. As the *Theseus* and her consorts entered Santa Cruz shortly before sunrise, Nelson saw that Troubridge's boats were still as much as a mile from the chosen landing place: a strong offshore wind and current had delayed the arrival of the frigates until well into the middle watch, and had hindered even more the passage of the troop-laden boats to the beach. Troubridge boarded the flagship: should the attack continue now that surprise had been lost and the defenders alerted? (One notes here the difference in calibre between Nelson and Troubridge: for all the latter's merits, had Nelson been in the subordinate position he would never have wasted time in consulting his superior as to the wisdom of continuing the attack.) Nelson's answer was a determined yes. But the weather remained adverse, increasing to a full gale, so that neither that day nor during the ensuing night did Troubridge have any success. And before dawn on the 24th, the British squadron was compelled to stand away from the island, the 74s with their topmasts struck, the frigates with their boats rehoisted, and every seaman and marine re-embarked.

'Foiled in my original plan', by 'natural impediments' such as he had originally foreseen, many a man would have abandoned the attack. But it was not in Nelson to admit defeat: 'confident there is nothing which Englishmen are not equal to, and confident in the bravery of those who would be employed', he resolved to make a fresh attempt, this time a direct attack upon the town itself. And he would not leave this to Troubridge; he would lead it himself, 'a forlorn hope . . . I never expected to return'. But first he must mislead the enemy. At 5.30 pm on the evening of the 24 July he anchored his squadron two miles to the north-east of the port: supposing that the British intended to assault the two forts, the Spaniards hurriedly withdrew troops from the town to reinforce them. Darkness having fallen, some 700 seamen and marines were embarked in the squadron's boats, 180 more in the cutter *Fox*, and a further 80 in a captured Spanish vessel. Organized in six divisions, with Nelson leading the centre, these craft headed for the mole. All had orders to land and make for the town's principal square. Pitch darkness and a heavy sea veiled their approach from the enemy: Nelson's division was within half-gunshot of the mole before the alarm was given and they were met by a hail of grape and canister. Nonetheless, Captains Thomas Thompson, Thomas Fremantle and Richard Bowen landed their men, overwhelmed the mole's defenders, who numbered as many as 500, and spiked its six 24-pounder guns. But against such odds they could go no further; 'we were nearly all killed or wounded'.

One of these was Nelson. In the act of drawing his sword as he stepped out of his boat (according to one account; whilst pressing forward along the mole, according to another), grape shattered his right elbow, his fourth wound in as many years. Senseless, he was laid in the bottom of a boat where Josiah saved his step-father's life, first by applying a tourniquet, then by collecting a crew to take him back to his flagship. The boat was no sooner headed seawards than the cutter *Fox* was hit by cannon fire below water and seen to be sinking. Nelson, having recovered consciousness, insisted that Josiah should pick up survivors, so that the best part of an hour elapsed before the boat reached the anchored *Theseus*, where he showed stoic disregard for his wound.* Crying to those who would have helped him, 'Let me alone! I have got my legs left, and one arm,' he twisted a rope round his left arm and hauled himself inboard. His wounded arm was immediately amputated, 'very high, near the shoulder'. Almost unbelievably, when it be remembered that he had to suffer the pain and shock of this without benefit of anaesthetic, on top of what he had undergone for more than an hour from the wound itself without benefit of any painkiller, Nelson was able to give orders to his flag captain, 'as if nothing had happened', just half-an-hour later. Assuredly, he was no ordinary man.

A very different fate befell the rest of the landing force. Troubridge and Thomas Waller lost their way in the darkness and rain, their boats being driven into the surf pounding the rocks to the south of the town. Some escaped to seawards, but many struck, filled and sank: only a few were

---

*The story that the boat came first to the *Seahorse*, but that Nelson refused to board her, saying that he would die rather than alarm Captain Fremantle's bride, Betsy, who had been authorized to accompany the expedition, because he could give her no news of her husband's safety, is not supported by any reliable evidence, and is probably apocryphal.

safely beached, to land less than fifty men. But with these both captains fought their way to the town's central square. There, with the prisoners they had taken, they waited anxiously for reinforcements. After a little while came news that Captains Samuel Hood and Ralph Miller had landed even further to the south. But of Nelson, Thompson, Fremantle and Bowen there was no news, only the crack of cannon fire and the rattle of musketry concentrated on the mole.

At dawn Troubridge and Waller led their small party out from the square to join Hood and Miller. Together they had 340 seamen and marines, enough they supposed for an assault on the citadel. But as soon as they advanced, they were surrounded by as many as 8,000 Spanish troops, who were of tougher quality than the men who manned their Fleet. They faced, too, forty French-manned field pieces. A fight against such odds was out of the question – but so was unconditional surrender. Troubridge's solution was a magnificent gamble. At 7.0 am he sent Hood with a flag of truce to the Governor: unless he provided sufficient transport for the British force to re-embark from the mole, without opposition, and allowed them to return to their ships with colours flying, the town would be burned. Don Juan Antonio Gutierrez was so taken aback by this effrontery from an enemy who was clearly at his mercy, that he agreed – on condition that the British squadron ceased to bombard the town, as it was doing now under Nelson's direction – and undertook no further hostile action against any of the Canary Islands. At 9.0 am all gunfire ceased: by noon the embarkation had begun.

And here [wrote Nelson] it is right we should notice the noble and generous conduct of . . . the Spanish Governor. The moment the terms were agreed to, he directed our wounded men to be received into the hospitals, and all our people to be supplied with the best provisions that could be procured; and made it known that the ships were at liberty to send on shore and purchase whatever refreshments they were in want of, during the time they might be off the island.

Thanks to Troubridge, this was the not inglorious end to an operation which cost the lives of seven officers and 139 seamen and marines, with five officers and a hundred seamen and marines wounded; in all a quarter of the landing force; an operation which had been a total failure.* No one

*'In [this] action . . . several ensigns of the British boats were captured. Ever since [wrote Admiral Lord Charles Beresford in 1913], it has been a tradition in the [Royal] Navy that the flags ought to be recaptured. A party of bluejackets did once succeed in taking them from the Cathedral [of Santa Cruz] and carrying them aboard, but the Admiral ordered their restoration. They were then placed high up on the wall, out of reach, where I saw them [in 1863]. We held a

was more conscious of this than its commander: to quote from his letter to St Vincent, one of the first written with his left hand: 'I am become a burthen to my friends and useless to my country. . . . When I leave your command, I become dead to the world; "I go hence and am no more seen". . . . I hope you will be able to give me a frigate to convey the remains of my carcase to England.' Such despondency is partly explained by a postscript: 'I am in great pain.'

One may speculate whether the result would have been otherwise if Nelson had not been wounded. It is arguable that, under his vigorous leadership, the survivors from the two divisions that landed on the mole would have gained the town's central square. But it is impossible to accept Nelson's statement that, 'had I been with the first party, I have reason to believe complete success would have crowned our efforts'. His initial plan, a flank landing similar to those that he had made at Bastia and Calvi, *might* have surprised and overwhelmed the defenders. But when this was frustrated by the weather, a frontal attack by a force of no more than 1,000, which must be decimated in the initial assault, would have had small chance of capturing a town defended by so many seasoned troops; for like Rome's Legions, Madrid deployed her best ones overseas.

Nor is the failure to be blamed only on the weather: Nelson cannot be absolved from attempting a *naval* attack, without troops, since he had previously advised so strongly against one for the very reasons that foiled him of success. His more serious mistake was, however, the frontal assault which came so near to disaster. This was more than an error of judgment; it was as foolhardy as his youthful failure to retake Turks Island from the French in 1783.

Why, then, was Nelson so impetuous? Ambition was not this time the reason. Three words which he wrote after leaving Tenerife are a sufficient clue, 'My pride suffered'; and as Ruskin wrote later, 'Pride is at the bottom of all great mistakes.' The need to defeat the Spanish fleet off Cape St Vincent on 14 February justified the risks taken by Jervis – and by Nelson. But the assault on Santa Cruz was of small importance, attempted only to capture a treasure ship, – except to Rear-Admiral Sir

---

meeting in the gunroom of the *Defence* to consider the best method of taking the flags; but the Admiral, who . . . was aware that all junior officers cherished the hope of recovering the relics, issued orders that no such attempt was to be made.' Since then, other 'young gentlemen' from HM ships, imbued with more patriotic zest than diplomatic discretion, have no doubt attempted to recover them, but to no avail. These legitimate spoils of war can still be seen, preserved in Santa Cruz's parish church of Nuestra Señora de la Concepción, which is known locally as the Cathedral.

Horatio Nelson, K.B.: to his recently acquired self-esteem it mattered a great deal. To diagnose his fault more bluntly, he was suffering from a swollen head, the consequence of the belated satisfaction of his keen hunger for public recognition of his services. As he himself had written not long before this expedition: 'I have had flattery enough to make me vain,* and success enough to make me confident.' And there can be no more dangerous human emotion: it is all too easy for the man who strains to climb the mountain called success to fall into the crevasse that is labelled pride. Nelson must have realized this when, by way of excusing his failure, he could do no better than refer to it as 'a forlorn hope . . . yet the honour of our Country called for the attack'.

St Vincent did not, however, philosophize thus when the *Theseus* and her squadron rejoined the fleet off Cadiz on 16 August 1797. 'Mortals cannot command success', were the encouraging words with which he greeted Nelson. He was, too, wise enough to judge the true temper of the latter's words, 'a left-handed admiral will never again be considered as useful, therefore the sooner I get to a very humble cottage the better, and make room for a sounder man to serve the State'. Though he realized that Nelson would have to return to England to recover from his wound, he told the First Lord: 'I have very good ground of hope he will be restored to the service of his King and Country.'

Still suffering much from the amputated stump of his right arm, Nelson sailed for home in Fremantle's frigate, HMS *Seahorse*. According to a contemporary journal, 'he was received at . . . Portsmouth on the 1st [September] with a universal greeting [and] reached Bath on Sunday evening . . . to the great joy of his lady and venerable father, and gratification of every admirer of British valour'.

Two facets of this extract merit comment. First, its uncritical adulation, which was echoed by other newspapers. As has been mentioned already, Nelson's name had long been known in Paris, whilst in the Mediterranean 'a person sent me a letter . . . directed as follows, "Horatio Nelson, Genoa". On being asked how he could direct in such a manner, his answer was, "Sir, there is but one Horatio Nelson in the world." I am known throughout Italy; not a kingdom or state where my name will be forgotten.' But to gain recognition in England Nelson had had to wait until

---

Vanity, and its adjective *vain*, need definition. According to the *Concise Oxford Dictionary* *vanity* can mean 'futility, unsubstantiality, unreality, emptiness'. Nelson was none of these. It can also mean 'conceit, based on personal attainments' – and Nelson's attainments are indisputable.

early in this year of his return. And the emotional fervour with which public opinion then acclaimed his conduct off Cape St Vincent was not quenched by his subsequent failure to take Santa Cruz. His wound raised him above criticism. Pitt, Lord Dundas (Secretary for War) and St Vincent were blamed for the débâcle. Nelson remained 'the pride of the British Fleet and the terror of the enemy'.

Of second interest is the speed with which he joined his wife. Four years separation had not cooled his devotion to her, nor hers for him. Both had expressed this again and again in their frequent letters. He had penned stirring accounts of his manifold activities afloat and ashore, seldom forgetting to include news of Josiah. All began 'My dearest Fanny', and ended, 'Your most affectionate Horatio Nelson'. Many expressed such sentiments as, 'rest assured . . . of my most perfect love . . . and esteem for your person and character, which the more I see of the world the more I admire' (29 June 1797). She had written of her friends, especially those whom she made in Bath whose society was of as much benefit to her spirits as the waters were for her health; she had also told him the naval gossip of the day, and given him news of the family, in particular of his ageing father to whom she was as much attached as her husband was to his stepson. All began 'My dearest Husband', and ended, 'Your affectionate wife Frances Nelson'. And many expressed such sentiments as 'tomorrow is our wedding day, when it gave me a dear husband, and my child the best of fathers' (11 March 1797).

Indeed, the letters which Nelson and Fanny exchanged during these four long and eventful years (of which so many have survived), would call for no special comment were it not for later events which were now less than a year away. For this reason certain undercurrents are worth noting as evidence that theirs was not a marriage of 'twin souls'. Nelson too often expressed the ardent hope that he would soon return home and be able to retire with his wife to some cottage in the country – but in the next sentence made abundantly clear that the Navy was his mistress, that for so long as the war continued his Country had first claim upon him, and that he wanted nothing so much as immortal fame. And Fanny as often complained of her health, expressed acute anxiety for her husband's safety coupled with disappointment at his failure to return home, first with Hood, later in the *Agamemnon*, afterwards in the *Captain*, and showed too little pride in his achievements to satisfy his vanity.*

*Unfortunately for Nelson's heroic image, but not for his very human one, when the *Agamemnon* was refitting at Leghorn in 1794, he consorted with 'a dolly' – to use the euphemism of Captain Fremantle's *Diary* for one Adelaide Correglia – a lapse of which Emma Hamilton

Any shortcoming in their relationship were, however, far from their thoughts when they came together in September 1797. 'I found my domestic happiness perfect', Nelson told St Vincent, while Fanny was much concerned for her husband's wound. The ligature applied onboard the *Theseus* held fast to the artery and nerve, so that the stump was hot and swollen, the pain being sufficiently severe for him to have to take opium at night to ensure sleep: 'I have suffered great misery', he wrote. Ten days after Nelson's return, he and Fanny moved to London, to lodgings in fashionable Bond Street, so that the wound might be examined by the best surgeons. William Cruickshank, who had been a partner of the famous Dr Hunter of St George's Hospital, and Thomas Keate, surgeon to the Prince of Wales, rejected a further operation: they recommended the application of poultices, and advised that time and rest would be the best of healers.

But to persuade a man imbued with so much burning energy and spirit to rest was beyond Lady Nelson's powers. With their physical relationship impaired – for him by pain, for her by the repulsion which all but overwhelmed her sensitive nature when she daily dressed his wound – the Navy called him far more strongly than his wife could do. He was not to be satisfied with the honour of investiture with the Order of the Bath by King George III, and receiving the Freedom of the City of London in Guildhall, coupled with the security of a pension of £1,000 ($2,400) a year. He

had now attained the appearance made familiar by the most famous series of his portraits, for which the original sketches were made during the next few months. . . . The fixed dim right eye, the empty right sleeve, were painful novelties to his family, but that his old infective high spirits were untouched was . . . equally obvious. . . . He was . . . very slight,* far from handsome, unaffectedly simple in address, and of no great dignity, 'indeed, in appearance nothing remarkable either

---

learned enough to warn Nelson later, 'Pray . . . *do not go on shore at Leghorn*, there is no comfort for you there'; and St Vincent wrote, 'he [Nelson] is made of flesh and blood, and cannot resist [women's] temptations'. But this is not indicative of an unsatisfactory marriage: many a man has broken the seventh commandment when away from home without impairing a lasting union – especially, perhaps, those whose profession is the sea, because this imposes continence on some too often and for too long. [*Note :* At least one letter from Nelson to Adelaide Correglia, written in French, has been traced, and is preserved in the Huntington Library, in the USA.]

*He was in point of fact only 5 ft 5½ in high and his frame so spare that to an observer he appeared 'one of the most insignificant figures I ever saw. . . . His weight cannot be more than seventy pounds.' But, as another contemporary succinctly expressed it, 'when induced to talk about the things he knew he took on stature'.

way'. . . . The outstanding impression of those who encountered [him] . . . was of a man so active in person, so animated in countenance and so apposite and vehement in conversation that little else was recollected.*

And those who now 'encountered him' were not only old friends like Hood and Locker, both at Greenwich, but Pitt and others among the great. Above all, as the newspapers reported, he was 'daily at the Admiralty', keeping in touch with the progress of the war, and in a fever of anxiety lest there should be another decisive action before he might be fit enough to rehoist his flag. His satisfaction at the news of 'Admiral Duncan's total destruction of the Dutch fleet at Camperdown' on 11 October was tempered by a maddening regret: 'I would give this other arm to be with Duncan at this moment.'

However, in November, he found time to visit Suffolk. He went there to buy his first home, Roundwood Farm, Rushmere. It was to be a haven for his wife and his father – but he himself was not destined to live there. On the morning of 4 December he awoke free of pain for the first time. The surgeon, when he undid the bandaged arm, discovered that the ligature had come away at last. It would only be a matter of days before the wound was healed. And this news, conveyed to the First Lord on Nelson's next visit to the Admiralty, bore early fruit: St Vincent wanted no flag officer back under his command more than Nelson. So, said Spencer, he should rehoist his flag in the 80-gun *Foudroyant*, which was due to be launched in January and commissioned in February. But no sooner had Nelson chosen Edward Berry to be his flag captain, than he heard that the *Foudroyant*'s completion was delayed. On 8 December he told Berry:

> If you mean to marry, I would recommend your doing it speedily, or the to be Mrs Berry will have very little company; for I am well and you may expect to be called for every hour. We shall probably be at sea before the *Foudroyant* is launched. Our ship is at Chatham, a seventy-four, and she will be choicely manned.

In the event, Berry had ample time to marry his cousin, Louisa Forster. 'Our ship' was the 74-gun *Vanguard*, and her commissioning was also delayed: she was not ready for Nelson to hoist his flag at Spithead until 29 March 1798.

On his last night in London he and Fanny dined with the Spencers. 'A

*Carola Oman in her *Nelson*.

most uncouth creature', Lady Spencer thought him, but when he spoke, 'his wonderful mind broke forth'. And on this occasion 'his attentions to [Fanny] were those of a lover. He . . . sat by her; apologising to me by saying that he was so little with her, that he would not, voluntarily, lose an instant of her society.' Yet next day he left Fanny with instructions to move into Roundwood as soon as possible – 'it is right you should be in your own cottage' – without the sympathetic reflection that, since he had chosen to go abroad again so soon, she would have been happier in cosmopolitan Bath than in provincial Ipswich.

On 7 April, after a week's detention by contrary winds, HMS *Vanguard* sailed for Lisbon to join St Vincent's fleet off Cadiz.

CHRONOLOGICAL SUMMARY FOR CHAPTER V

EVENTS IN NELSON'S LIFE	DATE	RELATED EVENTS
	1796	
Commodore in *Captain*, 74.	*June*	
Blockade of Leghorn and Genoa.	*July*	
Occupation of Elba.		
	2–5 August	Bonaparte defeats Austrians at Legano and Castiglione.
Occupation of Capraja.	*September*	
Evacuation of Bastia.		
	8 September	Bonaparte defeats Austrians at Bassano.
	October	Spain rejoins war on side of France.
	Autumn	Britain decides to abandon Corsica and withdraw from Mediterranean.
	17 November	Bonaparte defeats Austrians at Arcola.
Transfers broad pendant to frigate *Minerve*. Action with two Spanish frigates.	*December*	Failure of French attempt to invade Ireland at Bantry Bay.
	1797	
Evacuation of Elba.	*January*	
	14–16 January	Bonaparte defeats Austrians at Rivoli and Mantua.

EVENTS IN NELSON'S LIFE	DATE	RELATED EVENTS
	February	Failure of French landing at Fishguard.
Leaves Mediterranean and rehoists broad pendant in *Captain*.	*13 February*	
Plays major role in Jervis' victory over Cordova's superior Spanish fleet at battle of Cape St Vincent, for which created K.B. Promoted Rear-Admiral of the Blue: hoists flag in *Theseus*, 74.	*14 February*	
	April–May	Mutinies in British fleets at Spithead and the Nore.
	May	Bonaparte occupies Venice.
Commands inshore squadron for bombardment of Cadiz.	*3–5 July*	
Attacks but fails to take Santa Cruz, Tenerife. Wounded and loses right arm. Invalided home.	*24 July*	
	11 October	Duncan destroys Dutch fleet at battle of Camperdown.
	October	Austria makes peace with France: end of First Coalition. Bonaparte appointed to command *Armée d'Angleterre*.
	1798	
Hoists flag in *Vanguard*, 74.	*March*	
Rejoin St Vincent's fleet off Cadiz.	*April*	

VI

Aboukir Bay
1798

O f Nelson's years in the *Agamemnon*, *Captain* and *Thesus*, Mahan aptly wrote, as was noted in Chapter III:

This was the period in which expectation passed into fulfilment, when development, long arrested by unpropitious circumstances, resumed its outward progress under the benign influence of a favouring environment, and the bud, whose rare promise had long been noted by a few discerning eyes, unfolded into the brilliant flower, destined in its maturity to draw the attention of the world.*

A change was now at hand.

We see the same man at the opening of a new career. . . . Before leaving England [in the *Vanguard*] he [was] a man of distinction only; prominent, possibly, among the many distinguished men of his own profession, but the steady upward course [had] as yet been gradual. . . . No present sign [had] so far [foretold] the . . . burst of meridian splendour with which the sun of his renown was soon to rise upon men's eyes.*

The *Vanguard* was in company with St Vincent's flagship for only forty-eight hours. As soon as 2 May 1798 she was ordered to quit the fleet that was blockading the Spaniards in Cadiz, and to join the 74-gun *Orion*, Captain Sir James Saumarez, and *Alexander*, Captain Alexander Ball, at Gibraltar. On the 9th these three ships-of-the-line, accompanied by three frigates, sailed into the Mediterranean and set course for the Gulf of Lions, because their admiral had brought with him from England

*Mahan in his *Life of Nelson*.

these words from the First Lord: 'I am very happy to send you Sir
Horatio Nelson again, not only because I believe I cannot send you a more
zealous, active and approved officer, but because I have reason to believe
that his being under your command will be agreeable to your wishes.'
Forgetting the failure of Santa Cruz, remembering who was chiefly
responsible for his St Valentine's Day victory, St Vincent answered: 'You
could not have gratified me more than in sending him. His presence in
the Mediterranean is so very essential that I mean to . . . send him away . . .
to endeavour to ascertain the real object of the preparations in the making
by the French.'

The Commander-in-Chief's choice of Nelson to lead this reconnaissance
of Toulon in a Mediterranean from which the British fleet had been
withdrawn eighteen months before, so angered his other flag officers, the
fifty-five-year-old Sir William Parker, Rear-Admiral of the Red, and the
nine years younger Sir John Orde, Rear-Admiral of the White, both of
whom were, therefore, senior to Nelson as well as older, that Orde
challenged St Vincent to a duel, for which offence he was, not surprisingly,
ordered home. Neither could know that Nelson was also the Admiralty's
choice, expressed in another letter from Spencer, which was already on
its way from Whitehall, to reach the Commander-in-Chief soon after the
Vanguard parted company:

> When you are apprised that the appearance of a British squadron in the
> Mediterranean is a condition on which the fate of Europe may at this
> moment . . . depend, you will not be surprised that we are disposed to
> strain every nerve, and incur considerable hazard in effecting it. . . . If
> you . . . send a detachment into the Mediterranean [instead of going in
> person with the fleet], I think it almost unnecessary to suggest . . . the
> propriety of putting it under the command of Sir H. Nelson, whose
> acquaintance with that part of the world, as well as his activity and
> disposition . . . qualify him in a peculiar manner for that service.

This letter went on to order more than a reconnaissance: Nelson's
squadron was to comprise not less than ten ships-of-the-line, to which end
St Vincent's fleet was to be speedily reinforced. The latter responded by
sailing ten of his best 74s, plus one 50, most of them veterans of The
Saints, the Glorious First of June, Cape St Vincent and Tenerife, all under
Troubridge in the *Culloden* since he had no flag officer junior to Nelson, to
join the three that reached the Gulf of Lions on 17 May, without awaiting
the arrival of a mere eight from home. Many months were to elapse, so
uncertain and slow were communications in those days, before St Vincent

learned whether the trust which he thus reposed in Nelson would be repaid.

To explain the British Government's – and their Commander-in-Chief's – anxiety at 'the preparations making by the French', it is necessary to go back to the autumn of the previous year, 1797. With the defeat of Austria (which she blamed on the British withdrawal from the Mediterranean), and the failure of Lord Malmesbury's attempts to negotiate a peace at Lille consequent on the death of the Anglophile Catherine of Russia, Britain stood alone against France's attempt to dominate Europe, except for one faithful ally, little Portugal, which allowed St Vincent's fleet to use the Tagus as a haven. To overcome their implacable foe, the French Directory in October appointed Bonaparte to command a new *Armée d'Angleterre*, which would achieve a more decisive result than their previous ineffective forays against Ireland and Wales: 'It is in London that the misfortunes of Europe are planned: it is in London that we must end them.' But the Corsican's initial ardour for a major expedition across the Channel soon cooled: in February 1798 he reported that no landing on the English coast was feasible: 'make what efforts we will [after Duncan's victory at Camperdown], we shall not for many years acquire the control of the seas. To make a descent upon England, without being master of the sea, is the boldest and most difficult operation ever attempted.' So the Directory looked elsewhere for employment for their ablest general.

Some months before this Bonaparte had written to Talleyrand:

Why do we not take possession of Malta? Vice-Admiral Brueys* might very well cast anchor there and make himself master of the place. Four hundred Knights and 500 soldiers are all that form the garrison of Valletta. The inhabitants, who number 100,000, are friendly to us and greatly disgusted with the Knights. . . . With the islands of Sardinia, Malta and Corfu, we shall be masters of the whole Mediterranean.

And also:

To go to Egypt, to establish myself there and found a French colony will require some months. But as soon as I have made England tremble for the safety of India, I shall return to Paris and give the enemy its

*Francois Paul Brueys, born 1753, served as lieutenant during War of American Independence, dismissed during Reign of Terror (1793), reinstated and promoted to flag rank in 1795, appointed to command Toulon fleet in 1797.

death-blow. . . . Turkey will welcome the expulsion of the Mamelukes
[the military order whose members were the *de facto* rulers of Egypt].

So in March Bonaparte was appointed to command an *Armée d'Orient*
with orders even more ambitious than he had himself suggested, and
which it was supposed could be safely executed because the British Fleet
had abandoned the Mediterranean. Having first seized the strategically
important island of Malta before it succumbed to the covetous blandish-
ments of Austria or Russia, he was to go on to conquer Egypt (ignoring
the embarrassing fact that this was a vassal state of France's ally, Turkey),
as a stepping-stone for an advance further east, whose aim would be the
destruction of Britain's growing power in India.

These objectives were, however, kept so secret that, from a vessel
which he intercepted in the Gulf of Lions, Nelson could only confirm
that the French were preparing a large overseas expedition at Toulon
and in nearby ports such as Marseilles and Genoa, 'probably [for] Sicily,
Malta and Sardinia and to finish the King of Naples at a blow', but
possibly 'to be landed at Malaga and march through Spain' to attack
Portugal. Nor was he watching Toulon on 19 May when the expedition,
comprising more than 30,000 troops, sailed in some 300 transports
escorted by thirteen sail-of-the-line and seven frigates, with Brueys' flag
in the 120-gun *Orient* in which the twenty-nine-year-old Bonaparte was
accommodated, expecting 'to be seasick the entire voyage'. The British
ships had been driven away from the French coast by a violent gale
which, on the night of the 20th, dismasted the *Vanguard* to the west of
Sardinia. Taken in tow by the *Alexander*, Berry's ship only reached the
safety of San Pietro Bay, instead of being wrecked on a lee shore, because
Ball rejected Nelson's order to ensure the *Alexander*'s safety by casting
off the tow, with words that were to turn them into enduring friends: 'I
feel confident that I can bring her [the *Vanguard*] in safe. I therefore
must not, and by the help of Almighty God, *will not* leave you.'

Four days under the eye of a Governor who readily admitted that he had
no power to enforce the British squadron's withdrawal from an island
allied to France, and the strenuous efforts of Ball's and Saumarez's men,
as well as Berry's, sufficed to fit the *Vanguard* with jury masts – days in
which Nelson confessed to his wife: 'I ought not to call what has happened
to the *Vanguard* by the cold name of accident. I believe firmly that it was
the Almighty's goodness to check my consummate vanity. I hope it has
made me a better officer, as I feel confident it has made me a better man.'
But Providence did more than this for Nelson when he sailed again on the

27th to rendezvous with his three frigates which had lost touch with his flag during the gale. Early on the 28th he fell in with a merchantman out of Marseilles which told him that Brueys had slipped out of Toulon. Since he could not search for the French armada with only three ships-of-the-line when he had no inkling of its destination, he continued to await his frigates. Instead, on 4 June, he fell in with the brig *Mutine*, Captain Thomas Hardy, who brought news of having sighted them *en route* for Gibraltar, their senior officer having decided on this course after receiving news of the *Vanguard*'s disabling accident. 'I thought [they] would have known me better', was Nelson's comment on a decision that was to hamper so seriously his search for Brueys.

But Hardy also brought good news, that Nelson could expect reinforcements. Three days later Troubridge joined his flag, increasing his strength to thirteen ships-of-the-line, plus the 50-gun *Leander*, a force that was a match for Brueys' fleet. This transformed his purpose: it had been limited to gaining intelligence of French intentions: now he was empowered 'to use his utmost endeavours to take, sink, burn or destroy the Armament preparing by the Enemy at Toulon'. But his joy at finding himself in command of so large a force was tempered by the knowledge that he had no secure base east of Gibraltar, that for supplies he must depend upon neutral states who would fear Bonaparte more than Britain – and by regret that Troubridge could not be his second-in-command. This went by seniority to the forty-one-year-old Saumarez, of whom Nelson was covertly jealous because he had already fought in four fleet actions including The Saints and Cape St Vincent. Saumarez, on the other hand, had openly criticized Nelson's unconcealed ambition for honour and glory, describing him in such terms as 'our desperate Commodore': he considered Nelson to be something of an upstart (just as many thought this of Field-Marshal Montgomery's egocentricity in the Second World War). However, no friction marred their relationship during the coming weeks – 'I have passed the day on board the *Vanguard* [Saumarez wrote on one occasion], having breakfasted and stayed to dinner with the Admiral' – even though Nelson could not feel for his second-in-command the affectionate trust which he placed in Troubridge, Berry and Ball.

Leaving the *Leander*, Captain Thomas Thompson, and the *Mutine* to wait for forty-eight hours, in the hope that the frigates might have thought better of returning to Gibraltar, Nelson delayed no longer in his pursuit of Brueys. Knowing only that the French had passed southwards between Corsica and the Italian mainland, he set course for Naples to gain news of their destination. As he rounded Cape Corse on the twelfth he made his intentions clear; first to St Vincent: 'You may be assured I will fight them [Brueys' fleet] the moment I can reach them, be they at anchor or under sail.' In the latter event he intended to divide his fleet into three squadrons; he himself would have six ships, Saumarez and Troubridge four each. 'Two of these squadrons were to attack the [enemy] ships of war,' wrote Berry, 'while the third was to pursue the transports and sink and destroy as many as it could.' This is of interest in showing that Nelson was willing to engage thirteen French ships-of-the-line with only ten of his own, so that the rest might wreak havoc among Bonaparte's troop transports. But of greater import Nelson also wrote to Sir William Hamilton: 'If their fleet is not moored in as strong a port as Toulon, nothing shall hinder me from attacking them.' For the moment, however, he could do no more than follow the course which he believed Brueys had taken.

The 14 June brought confirmation that he was on the right track:* a Tunisian cruiser reported having seen the French convoy off the western end of Sicily on the 4th, steering eastward. 'If they pass Sicily,' Nelson wrote next day to Spencer, who had suggested that the armada might be destined for Portugal, or even for Ireland,† 'I shall believe they are going on their scheme of possessing Alexandria, and getting troops to India.' Three days later the British fleet hove-to off Naples, so that Troubridge could bring replies to letters which Nelson had written to Hamilton and Acton, warning the Neapolitan Government that Sicily was threatened, and seeking supplies for his ships, frigates to act as lookouts, and pilots in Sicilian waters. He learned that he could expect no more than the first of these: the Kingdom of the Two Sicilies feared the French too much to breach their neutrality, nor would they give 'the smallest information of what was, or was likely to be, the future destination of the French Armament'. But Troubridge provided more helpful news: from private inquiries he gathered that the French were about to attack Malta.

*For the tracks followed by the two fleets during Nelson's search for Brueys see front end-papers.
†Ireland was in the throes of a rebellion, for which Wolfe Tone had obtained a promise of French support; but this was never Bonaparte's destination. 'I made one great mistake,' he told his secretary, when he was in exile on St Helena - 'my decision to invade Egypt.' The Directory sent no more than 1,150 troops under General Humbert whom Commodore Savary landed in Killálá Bay, Co. Mayo, on 22 August. These routed the Irish Militia at 'The Races of Castlebar', but were compelled to surrender to a much larger British army under General Cornwallis at Ballinamuck as soon as 8 September. And a second French force, numbering 3,000 troops, convoyed by Commodore Bompart's squadron, was intercepted by a stronger detachment from Bridport's fleet, under Commodore Sir John Warren, and defeated off Donegal Bay on 12 October. The British prizes included Bompart's flagship, from which Wolfe Tone was taken prisoner and sentenced to death.

Nelson immediately set course for the Straits of Messina which were passed on the 20th. On the 22nd, off Cape Passaro, two French frigates were seen, but Nelson could not spare any of his ships to chase them. A little later, he spoke with a Genoese brig which had left Malta the day before: the island had surrendered on the 15th, and next day the *Armée d'Orient* had sailed for Sicily. This intelligence was substantially but not wholly correct. The Knights Hospitallers of St John the Baptist, who had moved first from Jerusalem to Rhodes, then in 1522 to Malta, to build the great fortified cities of Valletta, Senglea and Floriana on both sides of Grand Harbour, had changed much since the Great Siege of 1565 when, for four long months, they successfully resisted a fierce attack by the Turks. Luxurious living, intrigues and quarrels had eroded the Christian fervour and military discipline upon which their strength depended. The people, who had once made them so welcome, now sought relief from rule by despotic Grand Masters.

When Bonaparte appeared off Malta on 9 June 1798, he asked only if his fleet might water in Valletta harbour, to which Grand Master Ferdinand von Hompesch answered: 'No more than four armed vessels should ever be admitted at once.' Bonaparte's irritation at this strictly neutral reply was fermented into anger by the interception of a small vessel found to be carrying a letter from Tsar Paul to the effect that Russia would be glad to take Malta under its protection. This determined him to lay siege to the island. But none was needed: the people were in no mood to resist the French troops when they landed on the 10th. And it needed only twenty-four hours for the effete von Hompesch to ask for an armistice rather than have the 'impregnable' fortress of Valletta bombarded into submission. Articles of capitulation having been signed on 12 June, Bonaparte set up his headquarters in the building that is now Malta's General Post Office, to stay for six busy days reorganizing the island's administration and economy as a French dependency, before he sailed again on 19 June, with his *Armée d'Orient* depleted by a garrison of 4,000 troops.

Nelson reacted to the news which he gleaned from the Genoese brig by calling Saumarez, Troubridge, Ball, and Captain Henry Darby of the *Bellerophon* to join him and Berry onboard the *Vanguard*. To all five captains he posed the question, do you think we had better stand for Malta, steer for Sicily or push on to Alexandria? Saumarez gave his opinion in writing, from which may be seen how one inaccuracy in the intercepted intelligence, that the French were bound for Sicily, was offset by another, that Bonaparte had left Malta as early as the 16th:

The French fleet having left Malta six days ago, had their destination been the island of Sicily, there is reason to presume we should have obtained information of it yesterday off Syracuse, or the day before coming through the Pharo of Messina. Under all circumstances I think it most conducive to the good of His Majesty's service to make the best of our way for Alexandria, as the only means of saving our possessions in India should the French Armament be destined for that country.

The others were in agreement. So was Nelson: no destination to the west of Malta was practicable for such a large armada when the prevailing wind was from that direction. The French must be heading to the east, perhaps intending to capture Corfu, perhaps to overthrow the Government of Turkey. But an attack on Egypt was the greatest menace to British interests: 'If they have concerted a plan with Tipu Sahib* to have vessels at Suez, three weeks at this season is a common passage to the Malabar coast, when our India possessions would be in great danger.'

Having thus decided Bonaparte's destination from the slenderest of clues, Nelson did not hesitate to follow his strategic insight: he ordered his fleet to crowd on all sail and steer for Alexandria.

The only objection I can fancy [being] started is, 'you should not have gone sail a long voyage without more certain information'. . . . My answer is ready, who was I to get it from? The Government of Naples or Sicily either knew not or chose to keep me in ignorance. Was I to wait patiently till I heard certain accounts if Egypt was their object? Before I could hear of them they would have been in India. To do nothing was I felt disgraceful; therefore I made use of my understanding and by it I ought to stand or fall.

With these words, and the resolution with which they were followed through, Nelson was to do much more than efface his failure at Santa Cruz, though the stump of his right arm would always remind him how rash he had been on that occasion.

Some days must now elapse [wrote Saumarez] before we can be relieved of our cruel suspense, and if at the end of our journey we find we are upon a wrong scent, our embarrassment will be great indeed. Fortunately, I only act here *en second*; but did the chief responsibility rest with me, I fear it would be more than my too irritable nerves could bear.

*Sultan of Mysore, who was seeking French help to expel the British, and against whom an expedition was already being organized in India, commanded by the future Duke of Wellington, who defeated and killed his enemy at Seringapatam in 1799.

Nelson carried this responsibility for the next five weeks. Brueys had a three-day start but, with a force so much larger than Nelson's, his progress was slower. On the night of 22 June the two fleets passed close to each other – but without making the contact that would have enabled Nelson to engage Brueys and prevent the *Armée d'Orient* reaching its destination. And when dawn came on the 23rd they were beyond sight of each other because they were steering diverging courses; Bonaparte had ordered Brueys to steer first for Crete instead of for Alexandria in order to mislead any merchantmen they passed.

For this reason Nelson reached the Egyptian port on 28 June to find that his insight had, seemingly, been wrong. Having started in pursuit of Brueys with a three weeks' handicap (counting from Bonaparte's departure from Toulon on 19 May to Troubridge's juncture on 7 June) and supposing that he had left the vicinity of Malta six days (instead of only three) after the French, he did not realize that he might have outstripped them. In part because the British Consul was absent from his post, leaving no one to negotiate with the Turkish Governor for the British fleet to be allowed to remain and take in supplies; in part because, according to Berry, Nelson's 'active and anxious mind would not permit him to rest a moment in the same place, he ... shaped his course to the northward, for the coast of [Turkey] to reach ... some quarter where information [of the French] could probably be obtained.' He was not, therefore, off Alexandria to hinder the arrival of the French just three days later, when the *Armée d'Orient* was disembarked at Marabout, four miles to the west.

By then Nelson was beating back to the southern shore of Crete, where he learned that the French were not at Corfu. Fearful that Sicily had been their destination after all, he took his fleet all the way back to Syracuse on 19 July, 'a round of near 600 leagues ... as ignorant of the situation of the enemy as I was 27 days ago', with, as he wrote to Hamilton, '*no frigates*, to which has been, and may be again, attributed the loss of the French fleet'. Nelson's anguish at the apparent failure of his pursuit was likewise expressed in a letter written to Troubridge several years later: 'Do not fret at anything. I wish I never had, but my return to Syracuse in 1798 broke my heart.' Yet, his resolution did not fail him: when he gained no news from the Two Sicilies, he was satisfied that the French must be somewhere in the Levant. As soon as he had persuaded the Governor to provision and water his ships, he sailed again to the east, on 24 July. 'Every moment I have to regret the frigates having left me,' he told St Vincent, '... but if they [Brueys' fleet] are above water, I will find them out, and if possible bring them to battle.'

By this time Bonaparte's army had marched south to Cairo, 150 miles across a waterless desert at the hottest season of the year. Attacked on 13 July by Murad Bey's Mameluke cavalry he defeated them at Shubrakhit. Within sight of the pyramids of Giza on the 21st, he routed a much larger Mameluke force. Two days later he entered the Egyptian capital in triumph. Nine more, and disaster struck – at sea. The news reached Bonaparte from an eye-witness, his Controller-General of Finances, E. Poussielgue, who chanced to be at Rosetta on the night of 1 August. Brueys had received no orders after Bonaparte's departure from Alexandria except that the French fleet should wait off Egypt, instead of returning to the security of Toulon. Considering the entrance to Alexandria harbour (the old eastern one, now silted up) too narrow for his larger ships-of-the-line, he had moved fifteen miles to the east, to Aboukir Bay. There he anchored on 8 July under the shelter of Aboukir Island. On hearing this, Bonaparte sent word that he should return to Alexandria, where he would be protected by the guns of the citadel. Although this order never reached the French Admiral, he was thinking of moving on his own initiative, when, on the 28th, three British frigates (sent by St Vincent to rejoin Nelson as soon as they returned to Gibraltar, but still seeking him) appeared to seaward. Even so, Brueys did not suppose that these presaged the arrival of a British battle fleet; he stayed at his chosen anchorage.

Nelson was, by this time, back off the Greek peninsula, and there, on 28 July, Troubridge gleaned the news his Admiral needed; that the French armada had been sighted four weeks before steering south-east. Confirmed by a passing vessel later in the day, this intelligence was enough for Nelson to head south under all sail. At 10.0 am on 1 August the *Alexander* and *Swiftsure*, which he had sent on ahead, sighted Alexandria and reported that the French flag was flying over the city but, to Nelson's disappointment, that the only ships in the harbour were Bonaparte's transports. Three hours later, however, all his anxieties were ended: at 1.0 pm the masthead lookout in the *Zealous*, which was leading the British force, sighted Brueys' fleet in Aboukir Bay. Nelson instantly hauled up to a brisk breeze from the north-north-west, and headed eastwards. Then, after many anxious days during which he never spared himself, seldom sleeping and eating little food, he sat down to a good dinner. As one eye-witness put it: 'The utmost joy seemed to animate every breast on board . . . and the pleasure which the Admiral himself felt was perhaps more heightened than that of any other man, as he had now a certainty by which he could regulate his future operations.'

Nelson had proved his strategic insight: could he now show as much tactical skill? Ambition and faith inspired this prophetic answer, as they had done off Cape St Vincent: 'Before this time tomorrow I shall have gained a peerage or Westminster Abbey.'

The two fleets are best tabulated to show their respective strengths, and the fate which befell Brueys' ships in the battle that was now imminent.

The table on p. 130 highlights two points. While both fleets counted the same number of ships-of-the-line, Brueys had the advantage of four which were more heavily armed; and to offset the 50-gunned *Leander*, a ship 'below the line', he had four frigates of which two carried as many as forty guns. Secondly, that Nelson all but annihilated his enemy, only two French ships-of-the-line and two frigates escaping capture or destruction, whereas no British ship was lost. How, then, did he gain such a resounding victory?

Aboukir Bay, whose sandy shore has changed little since Nelson's time, is a semi-circular indentation, some sixteen miles across, immediately to the west of the Rosetta mouth of the river that was to give its name to the coming battle. The small town near Aboukir Point at the western end of the bay, and Aboukir Island were both fortified and held by the French. The latter formed part of a chain of rocks and shoals that extended three miles to the north-east, forming a natural breakwater under whose lee Brueys berthed his ships. To afford the best defence against attack they were anchored in line of battle, slightly bowed to seawards, 160 yards apart. They were ordered to lay out an additional anchor to the south-south-east, as well as putting a spring in their main cable, so that they might readily bring their broadsides to bear. But for want of an accurate chart Brueys anchored the *Guerrier*, in the van (windward end) of his line, as much as 1,000 yards from the Aboukir shoals; and because he supposed that an enemy would have as much respect for this navigational hazard, he thought that the brunt of any attack would fall on his centre and rear, in which, therefore, he placed his more heavily armed ships.

Since there was no port in Egypt with fortifications comparable with those of Toulon, where a fleet could lie secure from attack, Nelson had already discussed with his captains how he would deal with Brueys' ships if, as seemed likely, he found them lying in some open anchorage. His fleet would concentrate first on a part of the French line, if possible engaging them on both sides. His ships must hold their fire until they were within point-blank range; and the sooner they closed to much less than 400 yards the better. For he would not be content if a few of the enemy struck their colours whilst the rest escaped.

THE OPPOSING FLEETS AT THE BATTLE OF THE NILE, 1 AUGUST 1798

BRITISH (in order of sailing)			FRENCH (in order of anchoring)			
Ship	Guns	Commander	Ship	Guns	Commander	Fate
Goliath	74	Capt. T. Foley	Guerrier	74	Capt. T. F. Trullet	Captured and later burnt
Zealous	74	Capt. S. Hood	Conquérant	74	Capt. S. Dalbarade	Captured
Orion	74	Capt. Sir J. Saumarez	Spartiate	74	Capt. M. J. Emeriau	Captured
Audacious	74	Capt. D. Gould	Aquilon	74	Capt. H. A. Therenard	Captured
Theseus	74	Capt. R. W. Miller	Peuple Souverain	74	Capt. P. P. Raccord	Captured
Vanguard	74	Capt. E. Berry	Franklin	80	Capt. M. Gilet	Captured
		Flagship of Rear–Admiral Sir H. Nelson			Flagship of Rear–Admiral A. S. M. Blanquet du Chayla	
Minotaur	74	Capt. T. Louis	Orient	120	Capt. H. Ganteaume (1st)	Destroyed by fire and
Defence	74	Capt. J. Peyton			Capt. L. de Casabianca (2nd)	explosion
Bellerophon	74	Capt. H. Darby			Flagship of Vice–Admiral F. P. Brueys	
Majestic	74	Capt. G. B. Westcott				
Leander	50	Capt. T. B. Thompson				
Alexander	74	Capt. A. J. Ball	Tonnant	80	Capt. A. A. Dupetit Thouars	Captured
Swiftsure	74	Capt. B. Hallowell	Heureux	74	Capt. J. P. Etienne	Captured and later burnt
Culloden	74	Capt. T. Troubridge	Mercure	74	Capt. Cambon	Captured and later burnt
			Guillaume Tell	80	Capt. Saulnier	Escaped
					Flagship of Rear–Admiral P. C. Villeneuve	
			Généreux	74	Capt. Le Joille	Escaped
			Timoléon	74	Capt. J. F. T. Trullet	Destroyed by fire
			Frigates:			
			Sérieuse	36	Capt. C. J. Martin	Sunk
			Artémise	40	Capt. P. J. Standelet	Destroyed by fire
			Diane	40	Capt. E. J. N. Solen	Escaped
					Flagship of Rear–Admiral D. Decrès	
			Justice	40	Capt. J. Villeneuve	Escaped

Note: The British battle fleet was accompanied only by the brig *Mutine*, the French by two brigs, three bombs and several gun vessels in addition to four frigates.

There was, therefore, no need for Nelson to call Saumarez, Troubridge and the others on board the *Vanguard* as the British fleet headed for Aboukir Bay. As he wrote afterwards to Lord Howe: 'By attacking the enemy's van and centre, the wind blowing directly along [their] line, I was enabled to throw what force I pleased on a few ships. This plan my friends readily conceived by the signals.' At 3.0 pm he hoisted, 'Prepare for battle'; at 4.0, 'Be ready to anchor by the stern', so that they could maintain a southerly heading instead of swinging round to the north-north-westerly wind; then, 'Form line of battle', ahead and astern of the *Vanguard*. Most important of all, Nelson signalled his intention to concentrate on the enemy's van and centre – because, in the prevailing wind, these could not easily be reinforced by their rear. By the time all this was done it was 5.30 and the British fleet was nearly abreast of Aboukir Island, approaching the bay from the north-west.

Brueys first sighted Nelson's ships at 2.0 pm. An hour later he ordered his own to prepare for battle. He also signalled his two brigs to lure the advancing enemy on to the Aboukir shoals. 'The bait,' says a French authority, 'was a clumsy one to put before a man like Nelson', whose van ignored it. At 4.0 the French Admiral showed symptoms of indecision: first he ordered his ships to cross topgallant yards, then concluded that the enemy would not risk an attack during the approaching hours of darkness and abandoned further preparations for getting under way.

Soon after 5.30 pm, Nelson hailed the *Zealous*, near the head of his line. No one in the British fleet knew Aboukir Bay, nor had they trustworthy charts. Did her captain, Samuel Hood think there was enough water to pass between the *Guerrier* and the nearest shoal? Hood answered: 'I don't know, sir, but with your permission I will stand in and try.' When Nelson readily agreed, the *Zealous*, supported to port by Thomas Foley's *Goliath*, bore up and, sounding all the way, successfully rounded the head of Brueys' line. So that he might watch this, Nelson ordered the *Vanguard* to heave to, with the result that several ships passed ahead of her: when the flagship stood on again at 6.0 pm, the British fleet was in the order given in the table on p. 130, except that the *Alexander* and *Swiftsure* had not yet rejoined from their reconnaissance of Alexandria, and the *Culloden*, with a prize in tow, was lying some distance astern of the remainder.

Twenty minutes later the battle began. (See diagram (1) on p. 136.) As soon as the *Goliath* and *Zealous* came within range of the *Conquérant* and *Guerrier*, the French ships opened fire. So, too, did the battery on Aboukir Island, but without effect. Foley held his broadside until the *Goliath* passed close across the *Guerrier*'s bows, when he raked her at point-blank range. He then tried to anchor on her port bow, but ran on too far, bringing up on the *Conquérant*'s port quarter, where he was in action with her and with the frigate *Sérieuse*. The *Guerrier* was not, however, left without an opponent: Hood anchored the *Zealous* off her port bow and, as the summer sun set over the wide bay, brought down her foremast with a well-directed broadside. Saumarez conned the *Orion* to starboard of the *Zealous* and *Goliath*; poured his starboard broadside into the *Sérieuse*, dismasting her, cutting her cable and reducing her to a sinking wreck; then anchored abeam of the *Peuple Souverain*, though at a greater distance than he intended. Davidge Gould cut between the *Guerrier* and *Conquérant*, to anchor the *Audacious* less than fifty yards from the latter's port bow. Ralph Miller took the *Theseus* between the *Zealous* and the *Guerrier*, then between the *Goliath* and *Conquérant*, to anchor his ship 300 yards on the *Spartiate*'s port beam.

Next came Nelson's *Vanguard*: seeing that five of his ships were in action to port of the enemy, he directed Berry to anchor within 100 yards of the *Spartiate*'s starboard beam at 6.40 pm. Thomas Louis followed his Admiral's example: steering the *Minotaur* to port of the *Vanguard*, he dropped anchor on the *Aquilon*'s starboard beam. John Peyton left the *Minotaur* to starboard and anchored the *Defence* on the *Peuple Souverain*'s starboard beam. By 7.0, the five ships in the French van were in close action with eight of the British, five to port, three to starboard. It was now so dark that the British ships, which had gone into action flying the white ensign instead of the blue of Nelson's rank, because the white could be more clearly distinguished from the *tricolor*, hoisted a horizontal row of four white lamps at the mizen peak so that they could also be distinguished from the enemy at night.

Meantime, the British fleet suffered a mishap. Lagging too far astern of the *Leander* to be guided by her wake, Troubridge, having slipped his prize, sailed the *Culloden* so close to the Aboukir shoals that she grounded and stuck fast. Thus denied any part in the fierce action that had already begun, Nelson's devoted disciple was nonetheless of service to him: his signals warned the *Alexander* and *Swiftsure*, as they came up from Alexandria, to keep well clear. The *Culloden* was not got off until around 2.0 am on 2 August, with the help of Hardy's *Mutine*, by which time she had lost her rudder and was so badly holed that she was making seven feet of water per hour.

Soon after 7.0 pm, the next ship in the British line after the *Defence*, Darby's *Bellerophon*, anchored by the stern abeam of Brueys' flagship. A few minutes later George Westcott's *Majestic* dropped anchor to starboard of the *Tonnant*, from where she shifted berth an hour later to one on the port bow of the *Heureux*. Despite the smoke and darkness, Benjamin Hallowell managed to let go the *Swiftsure*'s stern anchor abreast the gap between the *Franklin* and the *Orient*, 200 yards off the latter's starboard bow. With considerable skill and judgment, Thomas Thompson, after delaying to see if he could help the stranded *Culloden*, anchored the *Leander* across the bows of the *Franklin*, which he raked with his port broadside, then raked the *Aquilon* with his starboard one. Finally, the *Alexander* entered the bay, where, despite the darkness, smoke, and general confusion, Ball managed to cut through the French line astern of the *Orient* and anchor on her port quarter. (See diagram (2) on p. 137.)

So much for the way in which, between 6.30 and 8.30 pm on the night of 1 August 1798, all but one of Nelson's fourteen ships sailed into action in accordance with his plan to concentrate on Brueys' van and centre. How fared these eight French sail-of-the-line against this onslaught? The *Guerrier*, raked not only by the anchored *Zealous*, but by the *Goliath*, *Orion*, *Theseus* and *Audacious* as they passed, soon lost all her masts. Nonetheless, Captain T. Trullet and his men fought on with great gallantry until after 9.0 when they surrendered to the *Zealous*. The crew of the *Conquérant* were not so resolute: assailed by the *Goliath*, raked by the *Audacious*, and subjected to the passing fire of the *Orion* and *Theseus*, 'the slaughter became so dreadful . . . that the French officers declared it was impossible to make their men stand to their guns': after only twelve minutes Captain Dalbarade struck his colours. The *Spartiate*, engaged by the *Theseus* and *Vanguard*, backed up by the *Minotaur* and *Audacious*, was eventually dismasted despite some help from the *Aquilon*, when Captain Emeriau surrendered. The *Aquilon* suffered heavily from the *Theseus*'s carronades, losing all her masts, so that Captain Therenard hauled down her flag at 9.25. The *Peuple Souverain*, hotly assailed by the *Defence* and *Orion*, lost her fore- and mainmasts and had her cable shot away: by the time Captain Raccord could clear away another anchor, his ship had dropped down abreast of the *Orient* where she ceased firing. The *Franklin*, after initially having no opponent except for the distant *Orion*, was raked by the *Leander*, then engaged by the *Swiftsure*, followed by the *Defence* and *Minotaur*.

Captain Casabianca's *Orient* was first in action with the *Bellerophon*, but the odds were weighted against this British 74. By 8.20 she had lost all her masts to the French flagship's 120 double-shotted guns, and Darby was obliged to cut his cable and take his ship out of the battle. When an attempt to set her foretopsail brought down the foremast, he managed this under spritsail alone, in which condition she was engaged by the *Tonnant*, when, according to a French authority, her crew '*et principalment les officiers, jetèrent de grands cris, pour faire connaître qu'il était rendu*'. But there is no real evidence that Darby so much as considered surrender, only that he had an unusually noisy ship's company, whose voices incidentally saved their darkened ship from being mistaken for an enemy and engaged by the *Swiftsure* as she came in.

The attack on the *Orient* was continued by the *Alexander* and *Swiftsure*. Brueys was already dead; twice wounded early in the action, he was almost cut in two by a round shot at 8.0 pm while descending from poop to quarterdeck. When his men tried to take him below, he rebuked them proudly: '*Un amiral français doit mourir sur son banc de quart*.' He died before 9.0, when the *Orient*, already a wreck, with Casabianca mortally wounded, caught fire. Fanned by the wind, the flames spread along her decks and leaped up her rigging. Foreseeing a catastrophe, the British vessels near the doomed three-decker shifted berth or, closing all ports and hatches, held their men in readiness with buckets filled with water. At 10.0 pm the blaze reached the *Orient*'s magazine and shell lockers, when the darkness was rent by the brilliant flash and shattering roar of an explosion so violent as to injure ships lying some distance away, and throwing a hail of burning wreckage that set the *Alexander* and *Leander* on fire. The shock stupefied both fleets: Poussielgue told Bonaparte that the explosion was followed by 'the most profound silence for the space of almost ten minutes'. Almost all the *Orient*'s crew perished: her first captain, Ganteaume, and a few more managed to swim to the brig *Salamine*; seventy were saved by British boats. 'Throughout the Napoleonic wars it [was] a point of honour [with all maritime nations] to rescue from drowning those seamen whose ships had been taken or destroyed. . . . It was reserved for the twentieth century to witness . . . the deliberate jettisoning of all such obligations hitherto considered sacred.'* With the *Orient*'s destruction went the plate and bullion, valued at the best part of £1 million ($2.4 million), which Bonaparte had taken from the Knights of Malta.†

The French were the first to renew the action after this disaster, but to

---

*Sir Archibald Hurd in *History of the Great War, The Merchant Navy*.
†Not all of the *Orient* was lost. HMS *Swiftsure* picked up part of her mainmast out of which her carpenter fashioned a coffin for Hallowell to present to Nelson so that 'when you have finished your glorious course in this world, you may journey into the next in one of your trophies'. Nelson kept this bizarre gift in his day cabin, saying to curious visitors: 'You may look at it, gentlemen, as long as you please, but depend upon it, none of you shall have it.'

little avail. Broadsides from the *Defence* and *Swiftsure* soon brought down the *Franklin*'s main- and mizenmasts and reduced Admiral Blanquet du Chayla's flagship to such a shambles that Captain Gilet hauled down her flag. HMS *Majestic*, though likewise dismasted was, however, able to continue her duel with the *Tonnant*, supported at longer range by the *Swiftsure* and *Alexander*, for the further two hours needed to compel this 80-gun French vessel to cease fire. By then her gallant Captain Dupetit Thouars had lost both arms and a leg to British round shot. Instead of being taken below, he insisted on being placed in a tub of bran from which he continued to give orders until loss of blood rendered him unconscious. With his last heroic words, he implored his crew to sink their ship rather than surrender. They responded by veering sufficient cable to allow the *Tonnant* to drop astern out of range. And there she was allowed to stay, licking but unable to heal her wounds until the morning of 3 August, when such of her crew as had survived after putting up a more desperate defence than any of their consorts, finally struck to the *Theseus* and *Leander*.

Long before this, early in the middle watch on the 2nd, all the French ships ahead of the *Tonnant* had struck or been destroyed. Those next to the rear were engaged at long range by the *Majestic* and *Alexander* soon after daybreak. Simultaneously the *Theseus* and *Goliath* compelled the frigate *Artémise* to strike, but not until she had been set on fire so that she blew up before she could be taken, which Miller classed as a 'dishonourable action ... not out of character for a ... Frenchman: the devil is beyond blackening'. At 6.0 am Nelson signalled the *Zealous*, *Goliath* and *Theseus* to weigh, the first to chase the frigate *Justice*, which was threatening the disabled *Bellerophon*, the others, accompanied by the *Alexander* and *Leander*, to settle accounts with the *Heureux* and *Mercure*, whose captains had sought to avoid disaster by dropping sufficiently far to leeward to ground their ships in the bight of the bay. But this gave them no succour from their four opponents whose gunfire persuaded both to surrender as easily as Foley induced Captain Jean Villeneuve to abandon his designs on Darby's wounded vessel.

Directed by Rear-Admiral Pierre Charles Villeneuve, the remaining three French ships-of-the-line, and the frigate *Diane*, which was soon joined by the *Justice*, made belated sail shortly before noon and, with the advantage of being to leeward of Nelson's fleet, endeavoured to escape. The *Timoléon* was unlucky; embayed among shoals, Captain J. Trullet's ship ran ashore, where, rather than surrender, she was set on fire by her crew and eventually blew up. So, only the *Guillaume Tell* and the *Généreux*, accompanied by the two frigates, got away.

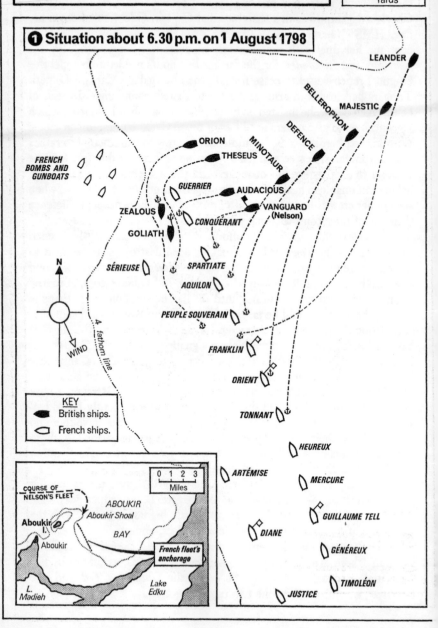

THE BATTLE OF THE NILE 1 AUGUST 1798

0   400
Yards

❶ Situation about 6.30 p.m. on 1 August 1798

LEANDER

BELLEROPHON

MAJESTIC

DEFENCE

ORION

THESEUS

MINOTAUR

FRENCH BOMBS AND GUNBOATS

GUERRIER

AUDACIOUS

VANGUARD (Nelson)

ZEALOUS

CONQUÉRANT

GOLIATH

N

SÉRIEUSE

SPARTIATE

AQUILON

WIND

4 fathom line

PEUPLE SOUVERAIN

FRANKLIN

ORIENT

KEY
◗ British ships.
◊ French ships.

TONNANT

HEUREUX

ARTÉMISE

MERCURE

GUILLAUME TELL

DIANE

GÉNÉREUX

TIMOLÉON

JUSTICE

Inset map

COURSE OF NELSON'S FLEET

0 1 2 3
Miles

Aboukir I.

ABOUKIR
Aboukir Shoal

Aboukir

BAY

French fleet's anchorage

L. Madieh

Lake Edku

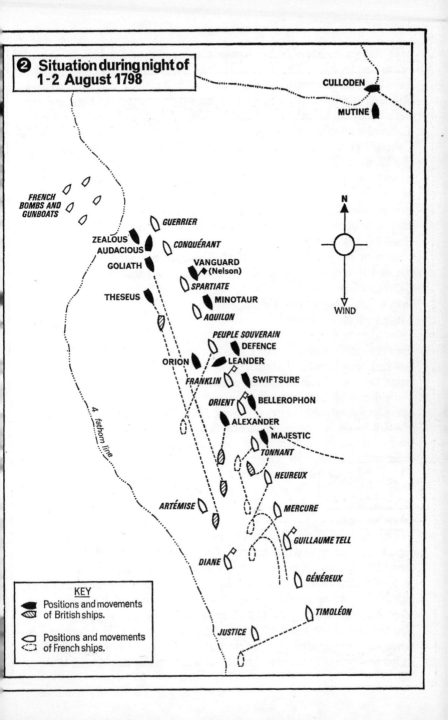

② Situation during night of 1-2 August 1798

CULLODEN

MUTINE

FRENCH BOMBS AND GUNBOATS

GUERRIER

ZEALOUS
AUDACIOUS
GOLIATH

CONQUÉRANT

VANGUARD (Nelson)

SPARTIATE

MINOTAUR

THESEUS

AQUILON

N

WIND

PEUPLE SOUVERAIN
DEFENCE

ORION

LEANDER

FRANKLIN

SWIFTSURE

ORIENT

BELLEROPHON

ALEXANDER

MAJESTIC

TONNANT

HEUREUX

4 fathom line

ARTÉMISE

MERCURE

GUILLAUME TELL

DIANE

GÉNÉREUX

KEY

Positions and movements of British ships.

Positions and movements of French ships.

TIMOLÉON

JUSTICE

By this time, none of Nelson's ships was in a fit condition to pursue these unharmed fugitives. The *Bellerophon* had lost all three masts, the *Majestic* two. Both these vessels and the *Vanguard* had serious hull damage; and although the rest had suffered less, all needed repairs to their rigging before they could make effective sail. Their casualties totalled 218 killed, and 678 wounded, mostly in the *Bellerophon* and *Majestic*, the latter's Captain Westcott being among those killed in her prolonged action with the *Tonnant*. The wounded included Ball, Darby, Saumarez, and Nelson himself. A splinter struck the Admiral above his blind eye early in the action, leaving pendant a strip of flesh. As at Santa Cruz ('I am shot through the arm: I am a dead man'), he at first supposed this his fifth wound to be mortal, crying out: 'I am killed: remember me to my wife.' But after a short delay in the cockpit because he insisted that he 'take his turn with his brave fellows' who had also been wounded, the surgeon stitched it and, with the same disregard for pain that he had shown at Calvi and Santa Cruz, he resumed command, and began writing a dispatch that began: 'Almighty God has blessed His Majesty's arms in the late battle by a great victory.'

This was no premature verdict. Out of thirteen French ships-of-the-line, two had been burnt and destroyed, nine had been captured. Seven of the latter had lost three masts, the others two; and all their hulls were so badly damaged that three had to be burnt, and it was several weeks before the *Conquérant*, *Spartiate*, *Tonnant*, *Peuple Souverain*, *Franklin* and *Aquilon* could be made sufficiently seaworthy to be sailed to the west (to be commissioned later under the British ensign, the first three under their own names, the others as the *Guerrier*, *Canopus* and *Aboukir*). The French casualties numbered 1,700 killed (including Brueys and Casabianca of the *Orient*, Thouars of the *Tonnant*, Therenard of the *Aquilon*, and Dalbarade of the *Conquérant*), 1,500 wounded and 3,000 taken prisoner.

The measure of this British victory was plain for all to see, 'the most signal that has graced the British Navy since the days of the Spanish Armada'. Nelson had redeemed his pledge, except, as he wrote afterwards to Sir Gilbert Elliot, now Lord Minto: 'I regret that one [enemy vessel] should have escaped, and I think if it had pleased God I had not been wounded, not a boat would have escaped to tell the tale.' Rodney, St Vincent and Howe had been content to take some six of their opponents when they brought them to battle and allow the rest to escape: Nelson in his first action in command of a fleet had virtually annihilated Brueys.

Much more important were the consequences of his victory: as yet only a junior rear-admiral and two months short of his fortieth birthday, he had, in one short night, regained command of the Mediterranean for Britain. He had also cut the only link between Bonaparte's *Armée d'Orient* and its homeland, shattering his dream of seizing British India. But, of more immediate import, Turkey was persuaded to declare war; so did her traditional enemy Imperial Russia; while Austria was encouraged to avenge her recent capitulation.

For a defeat of such consequence Brueys must bear the blame, both for having none of his frigates at sea to give him more warning of Nelson's approach, and for deciding to remain at anchor in an open bay instead of putting to sea where he should have been able to avoid such a devastating concentration on his van. But it is unreasonable to fault him, as some critics do, for anchoring his fleet in a line whose van could be turned, with his ships so far apart that an enemy could cut between them. Even if he had taken the soundings needed to berth the *Guerrier* as close to the Aboukir shoals as was possible without her stern grounding when the wind blew from the south, a seaman of Nelson's experience would know that there must be enough water for his ships to round her bows when she swung to a northerly wind. And 160 yards apart – two ships' lengths – was as close as the French vessels could be berthed in a tideless sea without the risk of collision when they swung idly at their anchors on a windless day.

So, too, with Admiral Villeneuve. It is contended that if he had ordered the French rear to weigh as soon as he saw Nelson's design, he might have prevented the *Alexander* and *Swiftsure* entering the bay, captured the *Culloden*, and brought succour to Brueys' hard-pressed van. But why should he, an inexperienced flag officer of thirty-five, be expected to show such extraordinary initiative? The more reasonable argument, that he should have issued such an order as soon as the *Orient* blew up and knew that Brueys could no longer control the battle, disregards the time the French rear must have taken to beat up to windward, in order to reach the *Culloden*, and that by then it was too late to save their van and centre. It is, however, fair to say that Villeneuve should have ordered the *Heureux* and all to leeward of her to weigh at dawn on the 2nd: five French ships-of-the-line might then have escaped instead of only two.

Such mistakes as were made by the French commanders cannot, however, belittle Nelson's achievement. He did not hesitate to bear down on the enemy as soon as he was sighted even though this entailed the confusion of a night action: 'I had the happiness to command a Band of

Brothers;* therefore night was to my advantage. Each knew his duty, and I was sure each would feel for a French ship.' He did not engage in accordance with the *Fighting Instructions*, which would have him range his fleet in a ship-for-ship gun duel all along the enemy's line. Instead, he concentrated on a part of it, risking the loss of a ship to test whether he could gain the advantage of turning the enemy's van. He also accepted the possibility that his ships might fire into each other, so that he could gain an effective strength of two ships against one. Saumarez, who thought one British ship a match for any Frenchman, would have criticized Nelson for this after the battle, despite the dismasting of the *Bellerophon*, but when he began to say, 'It is a pity that –', his Admiral cut him short with the fervent words, 'Thank God there was no order', i.e. that he had not followed the *Fighting Instructions*.

Soviet historians ascribe Nelson's victory to his 'use of the Russian Admiral F. F. Ushakóv's tactics, an attack from the landward side'.† In 1791 this able Russian commander led his fleet of eighteen ships inshore of a larger Turkish fleet whilst it was lying at anchor off Cape Kiliákra, near Varna in the Black Sea. But because the Turks at once cut their cables, Ushakóv achieved no more than an indecisive action in which neither side did much damage before nightfall and his enemy made good his escape. As well might a Dutch historian claim that Nelson was inspired by De Ruyter's destruction of Charles II's fleet in the Medway in 1667. How much more likely that he remembered the plan, aborted by bad weather, by which his erstwhile Commander-in-Chief, Lord Hood, proposed to attack the French Toulon fleet whilst it was at anchor in Gourjean Bay in 1794. What is certain is that Nelson's tactical skill at Cape St Vincent was no flash in the pan. The man capable of incurring the disaster of Santa Cruz possessed much more than the strategic insight needed to find Brueys' fleet: he had demonstrated his mastery of the whole art of tactics needed to destroy it.

Nelson's triumph placed him on the pinnacle which St Vincent believed he would achieve. He gained the crown which is worn only by that élite band, the sea kings of Britain. The hunger for honour and glory, which was his driving force, was largely appeased. Ordered to take Nelson's despatches home in the *Leander*, Berry was delayed by the ill-chance that

---

Cf. Shakespeare in *Henry V*, Act IV, Scene 3:

> We few, we happy few, we band of brothers:
> For he today that sheds his blood with me
> Shall be my brother.

†Article on Nelson in the *Soviet Historical Encyclopaedia*, Vol. X (1967).

this 50-gun vessel fell in with the 74-gun *Généreux* off Crete, and after a furious action lasting six and a half hours in which the British ship lost all her masts, was compelled to surrender, though the French gained little satisfaction from this aftermath of Brueys' defeat since the *Généreux*'s casualties numbered 288 against 92 in the *Leander*. But when Berry at last reached London in October many were the awards that Nelson received. He was created Baron of the Nile and of Burnham Thorpe, though he was disappointed not to receive a viscountcy for no better reason than that Spencer could find no precedent for the higher honour going to an officer who was not a commander-in-chief. He was no more satisfied when Parliament voted him a pension of £2,000 ($4,800): 'they cut me off £1,000 ($2,400) a year less than either St Vincent [for Cape St Vincent] or Duncan [for Camperdown]'. The Irish Parliament proposed, but did not agree, to give him another £1,000 ($2,400). The East India Company granted him £10,000 ($24,000).

The City of London presented him with a sword in return for the one surrendered by Blanquet du Chayla. The Porte of Turkey honoured him with the Order of the Crescent, created specially for non-Mohammedans, 'a superb *aigrette* . . . or plume of triumph . . . being a blaze of brilliants crowned with a vibrating plumage, and a radiant star in the middle'. Nor were his officers and men forgotten, those of whom he had written: 'It must strike every British seaman how superior their conduct is, *when in discipline and good order*, to the riotous behaviour of lawless Frenchmen.' Both Houses of Parliament accorded them their thanks. Nelson's friend, Alexander Davison, now his sole prize agent, struck commemorative medals at a personal cost of £2,000 ($4,800); in gold for admirals and captains (not excepting the luckless Troubridge), in silver for the only commander present, Hardy, and for lieutenants, in copper for warrant officers, and in bronze for the men. And Hardy and all the first lieutenants were promoted.

Unhappily there was soon to be another outcome of Nelson's victory at the Nile; a meeting that turned the whole course of his life, domestic and public, into a sea of troubles, which has written into the pages of history a romantic legend as immortal as that of Tristan and Isolde.

CHRONOLOGICAL SUMMARY FOR CHAPTER VI

EVENTS IN NELSON'S LIFE	DATE	RELATED EVENTS
	1798	
	23 February	Bonaparte reports invasion of Britain impracticable.
Hoists flag in *Vanguard*, 74.	*March*	
Rejoins St Vincent's fleet off Cadiz.	*April*	Bonaparte appointed to command *Armée d'Orient*.
With three ships-of-the-line enters Mediterranean and makes for Gulf of Lions.	*May*	
	19 May	*Armée d'Orient* sails from Toulon escorted by Brueys' fleet.
Vanguard dismasted in storm off Sardinia.	*20 May*	
Learns that French armada has sailed from Toulon.	*28 May*	
Reinforced to 13 ships-of-the-line, begins search for Brueys' fleet.	*7 June*	
	10–12 June	Bonaparte annexes Malta from Knights of St John.
Passes through Straits of Messina.	*20 June*	
Fails to find Brueys' fleet in Alexandria.	*28 June*	
	1 July	*Armée d'Orient* disembarks near Alexandria.
	8 July	Brueys' fleet anchors in Aboukir Bay.
	13 July	Bonaparte defeats the Mamelukes at Shubrakhit.
Returns to Syracuse.	*19–24 July*	
	21 July	Bonaparte defeats the Mamelukes at the Pyramids and occupies Cairo.
Finds Brueys' fleet in Aboukir Bay and destroys greater part of it at battle of the Nile.	*1 August*	

EVENTS IN NELSON'S LIFE	DATE	RELATED EVENTS
	September	Turkey and Russia declare war on France.
	May–October	Rebellion in Ireland.
	22 August	Savary lands Humbert's French expeditionary force in Killálá Bay.
	3 September	Humbert surrenders to Cornwallis at Ballinamuc.
	12 October	Warren intercepts and defeats Bompart's squadron off Donegal Bay before it can land a second French force.
Created Baron Nelson of the Nile and of Burnham Thorpe.	*6 November*	

VII

Emma
1798-1800

Having wiped out the greater part of the French battle fleet in the Mediterranean, Nelson could afford to divide his force. As soon as his six repairable prizes were seaworthy, on 14 August 1798, Saumarez took them to Gibraltar with an escort of seven sail-of-the-line: St Vincent might need them for the now practicable operation of retaking Minorca, which had proved of such value as a base for watching Toulon, whilst continuing his blockade of Cadiz. (In the event, Commodore John Duckworth needed only two ships-of-the-line to land troops commanded by Nelson's old companion of Corsican days, now Lieutenant-General Charles Stuart, on 7 November, to whom the garrison of 3,500 capitulated on the 15th.) Hood was left in the *Zealous*, together with the *Swiftsure*, *Goliath* and three frigates (which had at last rejoined their Admiral) to blockade the Egyptian coast so that Bonaparte's army received neither supplies nor reinforcements. The three ships most in need of refit, the *Vanguard* (into which Hardy had been promoted out of the *Mutine* in place of Berry), *Alexander* and *Culloden* sailed on the 19th for Naples. And Nelson went with them because he suffered so much from his head wound that he doubted his fitness to retain his command.

But this mood passed during a voyage that was delayed a week by the loss of the *Vanguard*'s jury foremast in a sudden squall. 'I shall not go home,' he wrote on 7 September, 'until [the *Armée d'Orient*'s] destruction is effected, and the islands of Malta, Corfu, etc. retaken' (which demolishes Bernard Shaw's facile contention, *vide* pp. 3–4 above, that what was now to happen was the consequence of Nelson's head wound).

When Ball and Troubridge reached Naples ahead of Nelson on 16

September, they brought word to Sir William Hamilton that their Admiral expected to stay for only four or five days because 'these times are not for idleness'. He was impatient to be off to Syracuse which would be his base for a blockade of Malta, whither Decrès and Villeneuve had taken their fugitive ships – and to which purpose he had already directed a Portuguese squadron of four 74s under Rear-Admiral the Marquess de Niza, following the French garrison's rejection of a surrender demand by Saumarez *en route* to Gibraltar. In the event, Nelson remained at Naples for the better part of a month. The magnet was Emma Hamilton. He had met the wife of the British envoy for only four days whilst serving in the *Agamemnon*, and had not seen her since 1793. They had, however, been in touch: that ugly virago, the forty-five-year-old Queen Maria Carolina, being the effective ruler of the Two Sicilies rather than her buffoon of a husband, King Ferdinand (Nelson was to call *her* 'a great king'), and etiquette denying Hamilton access to her so that he was obliged to employ Emma as a go-between, whereby she had gained considerable influence at the Neapolitan Court, Nelson had reinforced his formal appeals for help from the Two Sicilies with notes urging her to plead his cause. And she had warned him against the prostitutes of Leghorn, at least one of whose favours he had accepted in 1794. (See p. 114 n., above.)

Emma's effusive style impelled Nelson to respond with something of the same warmth. Thus, when to seaward of Naples seeking Brueys' fleet in June, he received this:

> God bless you, my dear Sir, I will not say how glad I shall be to see you. Indeed, I cannot describe to you my feelings on your being so near to us. Ever, ever dear Sir, your affectionate and grateful Emma Hamilton

to which he answered:

> My dear Lady Hamilton, I have kissed the Queen's letter [which Emma sent him]. Pray say I hope for the honour of kissing her hand when no fears will intervene, assure Her Majesty that no person has her felicity more at heart than myself, and that the sufferings of her family will be a tower of strength on the day of battle; fear not the event, God is with us. God bless you and Sir William. . . . Ever yours faithfully, Horatio Nelson.

This was no more than a pen-friendship, but out of it, from the day that the *Vanguard* entered Naples Bay to a hero's welcome, as '*Nostro Libera-tore*' – flags, gun salutes, bonfires, fireworks – there arose Dante's threatening personification of Love, '*E' m'ha percosso in terra . . .*'.

Emma's humble birth, and how she came to marry the dilettante Hamilton, have been mentioned in Chapter III. Now aged thirty-three, she had, according to William Beckford, 'beautiful hair and displayed it. Her countenance was agreeable – fine, hardly beautiful, but the outline excellent.' And to Lord Minto, now British Minister in Vienna, she was 'all Nature and yet all Art . . . excessively good-humoured and wishing to please and be admired. . . . One wonders at the . . . pains she has taken to make herself what she is.' But both men were also critical. Beckford described her as 'full in person, not fat, but *embonpoint* . . . ill-bred, often very affected, a devil in temper'. To Minto her manners were 'very easy . . . [as] of a barmaid. . . . With men her language and conversation are exaggerations of anything I ever heard anywhere.'

From these and other contemporary descriptions Emma emerges as a gifted woman of full-blooded charm, for all that she had lost the fresh beauty that inspired Romney's brush: but she remained a child of nature with a veneer of sophistication. She could be affectionate, amusing, brave and generous; she was also proud, impulsive, strong-willed and unscrupulous. Above all she was ambitious: not for her the passive role of consort to the British envoy to the Neapolitan Court; she must play an active part in the affairs of the Two Sicilies through her friendship with the Queen. Nor was she content with being wife to an amiable, but complacent husband more than twice her age whose chief interests were volcanoes and Etruscan vases: she was a Delilah seeking her Samson. And in Nelson she found him. On hearing the news of the Nile and of his expected arrival at Naples, she did more than prepare a room for him at the Palazzo Sessa; she dressed from head to foot '*alla* Nelson. . . . Even my shawl is blue with gold anchors all over. . . . Come soon.' And when she accompanied Sir William onboard the *Vanguard* on 23 September 1798, she displayed all the gifts of the born actress which she was accustomed to demonstrate in her celebrated 'Attitudes'. 'Up flew her Ladyship,' wrote Nelson, 'and exclaiming, "OH GOD, IS IT POSSIBLE?" fell into my arm more dead than alive.'

That this meant little to him at the time is clear from this tender comment to Fanny: 'If so affecting to those who were only united to me by the bonds of friendship, what must it be to my dearest wife, my friend, my everything which is most dear to me in this world?' and: 'May God bless you, my dearest Fanny, and give us in due time a happy meeting.' But, though great men be rare enough, those among them so fortunate as to love and be loved by a woman of the calibre of Sarah, first Duchess of Marlborough, are much rarer. And Emma was shrewd enough to know the key to the heart of a man who had a deep-seated longing for the devotion of a woman whose spirit matched his own. By appeasing his thirst for flattery, as the neurotic Fanny seldom attempted, she blinded him to her real worth; to his diamond brilliance she matched tinsel glitter.

'Lady Hamilton is an Angel,' wrote Nelson soon after his arrival at Naples; 'she has honoured me by being my ambassador to the Queen: therefore she has my implicit confidence and is worthy of it.' Beckford saw their relationship in a harder light: 'Nelson was infatuated. She [Emma] could make him believe anything. . . . He was her dupe.' One thing is certain, that Emma soon dominated all Nelson's thoughts and actions; and it is to explain his consequent mistakes, to use no harsher word, that so much has to be said about her in a book intended to study Nelson's naval career. The moral, ethical and psychological aspects of infidelity lie outside its scope.

To begin with, although Nelson sent the *Alexander* and *Culloden* to join de Niza's blockade early in October, the *Vanguard* did not arrive off Malta until the 24th. He believed that he delayed his departure from Naples to the good purpose of persuading the Two Sicilies to join the war against France, so that their handful of ships-of-the-line might strengthen his forces in Maltese and Egyptian waters. In his right mind he would have realized the consequences, that instead of helping his fleet this would impose an additional burden. As he wrote to St Vincent on 22 October:

> I shall, after having arranged the blockade of Malta, return to Naples, and endeavour to be useful in the movements of their army. In thus acquiescing in the desire of the King of Naples, I give up my plan, which was to have gone to Egypt and attended to the destruction of the French shipping in that quarter.

But he came nearer the truth when he told Emma: 'I feel my duty . . . is in the East, but who could resist such a Queen.' In plainer words, Nelson could not resist Emma: because of her he stayed off Malta for only a week, during which the smaller island of Gozo surrendered, then returned to Naples, entrusting to Ball and de Niza the tedious task of helping 10,000 insurgent Maltese to besiege General Vaubois' garrison of 3,000 within the fortress of Valletta. For the same reason he left Hood in charge of the Levant, and cancelled a plan to send Troubridge to evict the French from the Ionian Islands, which they had seized from the Venetians in 1796.

There is, however, another point of view; that other considerations justified Nelson's decision to keep a sizeable part of his fleet at Naples.

Admiralty orders issued on 3 October 1798, named first among his duties, 'the protection of the coasts of Sicily, Naples and the Adriatic, and . . . an active cooperation with the Austrian and Neapolitan armies' – though this anticipated the Emperor Francis II's decision to declare war by nearly six months. Secondly, his was not the only fleet now operating against the French in the Mediterranean: a Russo-Turkish force headed by twelve ships-of-the-line under Vice-Admiral F. F. Ushakóv, supported by Vice-Admiral Kadir Bey, passed through the Dardanelles on 1 October. And the fifty-four-year-old Ushakóv, whose considerable reputation rested on his victories over the Turks at the battles of Kerch, Tendra Island and Cape Kaliákra in 1790–1, wrote: 'I have the honour to congratulate you . . . on such a most perfect victory [the Nile] and hope that I shall soon have the pleasure of being in your vicinity, and, perhaps, of acting jointly with you against the enemy.'

Nelson suggested that Ushakóv and Kadir Bey should reinforce Hood, and also take the Ionian Islands. The Russian squadron was sufficient for the latter task; the Turkish was the proper one to help clear the French from Egypt. These Admirals would not, however, divide their force in this way; they feared to split their battle fleet lest another French fleet appear in the eastern Mediterranean; and Russian and Turk were alike determined that the Ionian Islands should be their country's prize. Two Turkish frigates and ten gunboats were all that Kadir Bey sent to Alexandria where they stayed only until mid-November. The Russo-Turkish battle fleet proceeded to capture Zante on 24 October 1798, Cephalonia on the 28th and Santa Maura on 13 November, then to blockade Corfu, where General Chabot held out with the help of the *Généreux* and the captured *Leander*.

Nelson was diplomatically critical. He hoped 'to hear soon about the destruction of French ships in Alexandria [which included ten armed transports under Ganteaume], as well as the entire French army in Egypt. . . . I nourish great hopes that Corfu will soon be taken thanks to your efforts, [but] Egypt is the first objective, Corfu the second.' How much better if he had gone to the Levant after visiting Malta, and discussed with Ushakóv and Kadir Bey a joint campaign against the French, instead of relying on letters which were inevitably a source of misunderstanding between men of very different races who had never met. As it was, Nelson not only returned to Naples but played a large part in a major strategic blunder. Accepting the Queen's assertion, derived from her daughter, the Empress, that Austria was about to open a campaign against the *Armée d'Italie*, he persuaded King Ferdinand to order his own army

The Illustrations

2 The old parsonage at Burnham Thorpe in which Nelson was born on 29 September 1758

3 Nelson's baptism recorded in the register of Burnham Thorpe Church

4 Burnham Thorpe Church of which Nelson's father was Rector

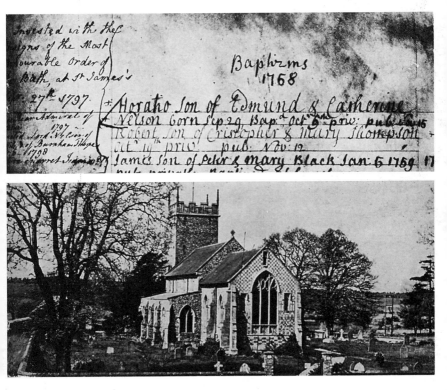

5 *Midshipman Nelson's first fight*

6 *Nelson's Dockyard, English Harbour, Antigua*

7 *Captain Horatio Nelson at the age of 23*

8 *Five of Nelson's ships drying sails at Spithead: from left to right, 'Agamemnon' (64), 'Vanguard' (74), 'Elephant' (74), 'Captain' (74), and 'Victory' (100)*

9 HMS 'Victory' as she lies today preserved in dry dock at Portsmouth

10 One of the 'Victory' gun decks. Note the centre gun on its wheeled carriage with breeching rope, train tackle, quoin and (overhead), sponge, rammer and crew's hammocks

11 *The Admiralty building in Whitehall, showing on the roof the new semaphore telegraph which replaced Murray's in 1816*

12 *Murray's semaphore telegraph, used for communication between the Admiralty and the Downs, Portsmouth, etc. from 1796*

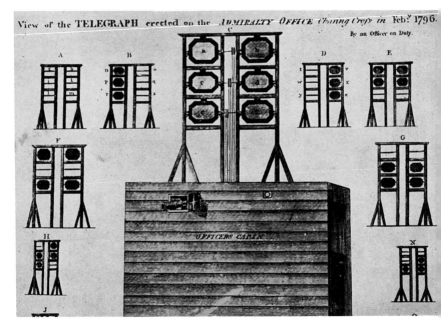

View of the TELEGRAPH erected on the *ADMIRALTY OFFICE Charing Cross* in Feb.ʸ 1796.

By an Officer on Duty.

OFFICERS CABIN

13 *The battle of Cape St Vincent, 14 February 1797: Nelson's 'Captain' (in foreground) in action with the 'Santísima Trinidad' to starboard and the 'San Nicolás' to port and, beyond her the 'San José'*

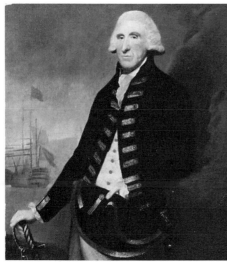

14 *Nelson's C-in-C in the Mediterranean, 1793-94: Admiral Lord Hood*

15 *Nelson's C-in-C in the Mediterranean, 1795-99: John Jervis, Admiral of the Fleet and 1st Earl St Vincent*

16 *The abortive attack on Santa Cruz: Nelson wounded in the right arm*

17 The battle of the Nile, 1 August 1798, about 6.0 p.m. HMS 'Zealous' in the van of Nelson's line, rounding the head of Bruey's fleet at anchor in Aboukir Bay

18 *The burning of the 'Orient' at the battle of the Nile, about 9.30 pm*

19 *A cartoonist's verdict on the Nile*

commander, the incompetent Austrian General Mack, to march into the neighbouring Papal States on 23 November.

In truth Francis II was far from decided whether to rejoin the war. And although Nelson landed 5,000 Neapolitan troops at Leghorn on 28 November 1798 to threaten the French from the north, these were no substitute for an Austrian army. Within a fortnight he had to admit the reality of the situation:

> The [Neapolitan] army is at Rome, Civita Vecchia is taken, but . . . [not] the Castle of St Angelo. . . . The French have 13,000 troops at . . . Castellana . . . Mack has gone against them with 20,000. The [outcome] . . . is doubtful, and on it hangs the . . . fate of Naples. If Mack is defeated, this country, in fourteen days, is lost; for the Emperor [of Austria] has not yet moved his army, and if the Emperor will not march, this country has not the power of resisting the French.

He justified himself in these words: 'It was not a case of choice, but necessity which forced the King of Naples to march . . . and not to wait until the French had collected a force sufficient to drive him . . . out of his kingdom.' In reality he had provided the French with a valid reason for an attack which they might otherwise have deferred. Ferdinand entered Rome in triumph on 29 November: eight days later he had to leave hurriedly to avoid being captured by the French. As soon as General Championnet ordered his men forward, the Neapolitan army – '*la plus belle Armée d'Europe*', according to Mack – showed how little it was worth: though nearly twice as strong, it broke and fled, with the French in hot pursuit to the outskirts of Naples itself.

Faced with this crisis, Nelson applied all his energy and skill to saving the King, not only from capitulation, but from the fury of his panic-stricken countrymen. With Emma's determined help he embarked the royal family onboard the *Vanguard*, and on 23 December 1798 sailed with them and the Hamiltons for Sicily. Three days later, he landed them at Palermo. This was well done: it was, nonetheless, a task which could have been entrusted to one of his captains; it did not merit the personal attention of an admiral whom Spencer and St Vincent had charged with the conduct of the naval war in all the Mediterranean to the east of Corsica and Sardinia. Moreover, in the light of subsequent events, Nelson would have been even wiser had he insisted on this task being carried out by Ferdinand's own ships.

For the next six months Nelson exercised his command from the Hamilton residence at Palermo more often than from the quarterdeck of the *Vanguard*.* Having entangled himself with a grotesque Neapolitan Court, he believed that he had a moral obligation to remain with them. The blunt truth is that he and Emma became lovers.† But this was only the half of it: many another man, Bonaparte for one, has taken a mistress without affecting his capacity for war. While Emma gloried in having a godlike hero, Nelson was obsessed by a passion such as he had never felt before, as just one of his letters to her shows:

> My Dearest Friend,
>
> I hope you will have seen Troubridge last night and he will probably tell you that he did not leave me perfectly at ease. . . . When I gave [him] a letter for you it rushed into my mind that in ten hours he would see you, and a flood of tears followed: it was too much for me to bear. . . . I am sure . . . that you will on no consideration be in company with that—‡ neither this day nor any other: he [the Prince Regent, who was supposed to be intent on seducing Emma] is a false lying scoundrel. . . . I have received your truly comforting letters. . . . I wish you in my heart for ever. I am all soul and sensibility. . . . I hope very soon to get a few days leave of absence. . . . I have been [asked] to dine ashore by the Admiral [and his] wife . . . but I will dine nowhere without your consent although with my present feelings I might be trusted with fifty virgins naked in a dark room. . . . I am, my Dear Friend, for ever and ever your faithful
>
>   Nelson and Brontë§

For all the affection in his many letters to his wife written before 1799, none is in such terms as this.

---

*There is no parallel between this and twentieth century practice. In Nelson's time letters could be sent and received by schooner and cutter as easily from a flagship at sea as from one in harbour. Admiral Sir Martyn Jerram, C.-in-C China in 1914, was the first to appreciate that an overseas commander could not take advantage of the speed and flexibility of radio communication (to control his ships during their search for von Spee's East Asiatic Squadron) from a flagship obliged, for her own security, to keep radio silence, and so to shift his flag ashore at Singapore. Although other overseas commanders were reluctant to follow his example, a further reason, the need for the closest cooperation with other forces, especially maritime air, compelled naval commanders overseas to establish headquarters ashore from the outbreak of the Second World War, although they sometimes hoisted their flags afloat for particular operations. For example, although Cunningham led his fleet in the *Warspite* at the battle of Matapan and for the raid on Taranto, he controlled the evacuation of Crete from Alexandria.

†One cannot be certain that Nelson and Emma consummated their love before April 1800 when their daughter, Horatia, was conceived, but there is ample circumstantial evidence that they must have done so during the early months of 1799.

‡Nelson omitted this word.

§R.A. Add 16/12.

The fact that it was penned in 1801, after Nelson's return to England, shows that theirs was no temporary infatuation, but a love that lasted until death. Hamilton was no cuckold: such was his admiration and liking for Nelson that he was not only a *mari complaisant*, but one who wished to avoid 'an explosion which would totally destroy the comfort of the best man and the best friend I have in the world'. He and Nelson lived with Emma in a *ménage à trois*, or, to use Hamilton's own description, a *tria juncta in uno*, whose luxuries Nelson financed to an extent he could ill afford – 'on my birthday night 80 people dined . . ., 1,740 came to a ball, 800 supped . . . in such a style of elegance as I never saw' – the while he penned mendacious answers to his wife's pleas to be allowed to join him: 'I could, if you had come, *only* have struck my flag, and carried you back again, for it would have been impossible to have set up an establishment at either Naples or Palermo. Nothing but the situation . . . in this country has kept me from England.' Hamilton might plead his age: Nelson was arrogant enough to suppose that the victor of the Nile could behave with scant regard for a scandal which soon spread much further than the corrupt Court of the Two Sicilies. Even his loyal subordinates – the captains such as Troubridge who were of his Band of Brothers – grew critical as the war continued.

Naples capitulated to Championnet on 23 January 1799. With a facile dismissal of his own part in this disaster, Nelson blamed the Austrian Emperor as readily as he criticized the commander of the Neapolitan fleet for staying to defend the city instead of getting it away to Palermo, so that he had to burn his ships-of-the-line to prevent them falling into enemy hands. In the same month the flamboyant thirty-four-year-old Commodore Sir William Sydney Smith, arrived in the 80-gun *Tigre* with Admiralty orders which not only appointed him senior officer in the Levant, but seemed to mean that this part of the station was to become an independent command. A slighted Nelson – 'never, never, was I so astonished' – sent Troubridge to Alexandria with instructions to ensure that Smith did not prise from his grasp any of the ships with which Hood was blockading Egypt. Simultaneously he wrote asking to be relieved: 'It is impossible for me to serve in these seas with the [Levant] squadron under a junior officer.' Fortunately St Vincent also protested: Spencer then realized that he had been trapped into an unfortunate gaffe by the Foreign Office's desire to appoint Smith as their envoy to Turkey. Fresh instructions were quickly sent making clear that Smith was under Nelson's orders. As quickly Nelson accepted Spencer's explanation and recalled Troubridge to Naples.

Meantime, although Ushakóv had a more than sufficient force for a strict blockade of Corfu, he failed to prevent the *Généreux* escaping to Ancona on the night of 5–6 February. His chagrin at this is one reason why, after the island capitulated on 1 March 1799 and the *Leander* fell into his hands, he refused to hand her over to Nelson until the Tsar ordered him to do so some six months later. But the mistrust between the two Admirals, which bedevilled effective cooperation between them, went deeper than this. Although he never visited Ireland, Nelson expressed nothing but contempt for its people, describing them as 'vagabonds'. He had the same insular dislike of all foreigners – with the singular exception of the Neapolitan Court. He wanted Ushakóv's help, but on his own terms. 'Surely I have a right to expect that the united Russo–Turkish fleets would have taken care of things east of [Crete]. I never wished to have them west of it', and, 'The Russians seem to be more intent on taking ports in the Mediterranean than destroying Bonaparte in Egypt.' 'Should any Russian ship . . . arrive off Malta,' he advised Ball after the Tsar was elected Grand Master of the Knights, 'you will convince [them] of the very unhandsome manner of treating the legitimate Sovereign [the King of the Two Sicilies] by wishing to see the Russian flag fly in Malta. . . . The Russians shall never take the island.' To ensure against this, he granted a petition from the Maltese Council to be allowed to hoist the British flag alongside the Sicilian, 'to show that the island was under the special protection of Great Britain'. Otherwise he thought of Malta as a 'useless and enormous expense' only to be incurred 'rather than let it remain in the hands of the French'.

With that acute suspicion of all foreigners which is so characteristic of the Russian people, Ushakóv paralleled Nelson's distrust. He rejected a further request to strengthen Smith's Levant force. 'I would willingly . . . fulfil your plan . . . but various circumstances prevent me.' His ships had 'absolutely no provisions': half of them suffered from storm damage; the Tsar had ordered the rest to the Gulf of Venice, etc. When Nelson pressed him 'to send as many ships and men as possible' to prevent Messina falling to the French and threatening Sicily, Ushakóv told Tomárov, Russian Ambassador in Constantinople:

I consider the demands of the English senior naval officers for the vain division of our fleet nothing but paltry friendship . . . to make us catch flies while they enter the places from which they are trying to keep us away. . . . They have always wanted to take Corfu for themselves and wished to send us away under various pretexts or, by splitting us up, reduce us to an incapable condition. . . . I am not going to be a pupil of Sydney Smith: it would not shame him to learn something from me.

A little later Ushakóv was 'extremely saddened' by the Tsar's order to send Rear-Admiral Pustóshkin's squadron to join Nelson: 'More than half my ships would have been taken from me and I would have remained here [Corfu] with the smaller and worse part needing great repairs. . . . My service and labours will be wasted in inactivity.' He hoped that 'our most merciful Sovereign Emperor . . . will magnanimously forgive me' for not obeying the order. One month more and he grumbled that it was impossible to link up with Nelson because 'there will be nowhere to get provisions and we will either die of hunger or possibly lose everything'.

Nelson, who achieved promotion to rear-admiral of the red on 14 February, was rightly concerned over the Levant: a prolonged bombardment of Alexandria by Troubridge and Hood did nothing to stop the French advancing into Syria where they first captured Jaffa, then, on 17 March, occupied Haifa, adding two new ports to be blockaded by the British squadron. Fortunately, when Bonaparte then laid siege to the Crusader fortress of Acre, Sydney Smith not only proved his metal, but showed the real significance of Nelson's triumph at the Nile. While taking HMS *Tigre* to support this town's Turkish defenders, he fell in with and captured the French convoy carrying the siege artillery which Bonaparte (despite his experience at Oneglia in 1796) had decided to send by sea to avoid the labour of dragging it across the Sinai desert. With this in Turkish hands, and by bombardments by the *Tigre* and the 74-gun *Theseus*, Bonaparte was prevented from doing more than breach the town's walls before 7 May, when fresh Turkish troops from Damascus threatened the French rear just as others arrived by sea from Rhodes. These, and marines from the British ships, did more than beat off Bonaparte's final assault; they lifted the French threat to Syria. On the specious excuse that Acre was contaminated by plague, Bonaparte raised the siege on the 19th and withdrew to Egypt, reaching Cairo on 14 June.

Bonaparte's retreat persuaded the Turks to send an expeditionary force to expel him from Egypt. On 15 July 1799 a fleet, headed by thirteen ships-of-the-line, landed 8,000 men at Aboukir. But instead of advancing into the hinterland to give this bridgehead depth, as Smith urged them to do, the Turks entrenched themselves within the town, with disastrous results. On 25 July the French launched a counter-attack and quickly drove them into the sea. But although this lifted the threat to their rear, and the Turkish fleet showed its old reluctance to share the blockade, preferring to withdraw to its own ports as speedily as it had arrived, it was the beginning of the end of Bonaparte's Egyptian venture. During an exchange of prisoners, Smith sent him copies of the latest newspapers which he had received from London. 'This man,' said Bonaparte, 'changed my destiny.' He referred to the capture of his siege train, but the comment could as well apply to Smith's courtesy, because these papers contained news from Europe that decided the future Emperor of France to make a drastic alteration to his plans, with immense consequences for the future.

The Austrian Emperor made up his mind to join the Second Coalition on 12 March 1799. One of his armies was immediately successful, defeating the French at Stockach* on 25 March and driving them back into central Switzerland. The other had to retreat after being defeated at Magnano* on 5 April, but it was then joined by a Russian army under the invincible Field-Marshal Prince Alexánder Suvórov. Although in his seventieth year, Suvórov had lost none of the skill, nor the resolution with which he had campaigned so successfully against the Turks and the Poles. When he turned the tide for the allies on the Adda towards the end of April, the *Armée d'Italie* faced eviction from the whole of the country which Bonaparte had conquered and occupied.

For Ushakóv the need to support Suvórov by bringing pressure to bear against the French from the sea transcended the importance which Nelson attached to the Levant. One Russo-Turkish squadron, under Commodore Sorókin, re-established Neapolitan authority in Brindisi on 4 May and in Bari on the 13th: another, under Rear-Admiral Pustóshkin, blockaded Ancona. For Nelson, Malta continued an intractable problem. Despite Ball's leadership of the insurgent Maltese, Vaubois held on to Valletta, whose blockade demanded as much of Nelson's ships as the piratical rulers of Tunis and Tripoli called for his diplomatic skill to dissuade them from seizing the Sicilian vessels carrying grain to the island. These and other negotiations wearied him. 'My public correspondence . . . is with Petersburg, Constantinople, the Consul at Smyrna, Egypt, the Turkish and Russian Admirals, Trieste, Vienna, Tuscany, Minorca, Earl St Vincent and Lord Spencer.' 'Believe me, my Dear Friend,' he told Davison in one of those fits of depression which are characteristic of men of creative talent when, as is inevitable from time to time, they are denied an opportunity to exercise it, 'my only wish is to sink with honour into the grave. . . . I am ready to quit this world of trouble, and envy none but those of the estate six feet by two.' Emma's consoling arms were not enough: 'This I like, active service or none.' Yet when opportunity

*See map on p. 31.

offered, he was slow to grasp it. Although he paralleled Ushakóv's activity by instituting a blockade of Naples with four ships-of-the-line including the *Vanguard*, he could not bring himself to leave the Palazzo Palagonia at Palermo: he transferred his flag to a transport, and charged his second-in-command with rousing the patriots.

Troubridge did this with such effect that Championnet's successor, Macdonald, evacuated the city on 22 April 1799, except for a garrison of 500 in the Castel St Elmo. But in the subsequent interregnum he was unable to unite the Neapolitans; although the countryside was held by an undisciplined army of loyal peasants, led by Fabrizio Ruffo, Cardinal of Calabria, and stiffened by a small Russian force from Ushakóv's fleet, the *lazzaroni* of Naples itself were not only infected with Jacobinism but enjoyed the support of a small naval force under Commodore Prince Caracciolo, who nurtured a bitter resentment against the King for his decision, when the capital was threatened in the previous autumn, to place his personal safety in the hands of a foreign admiral instead of his own fleet. Nelson urged Ferdinand to return at once to Naples to rally the dissidents; but his Queen was too frightened and obstinately opposed to risking failure. As Nelson told St Vincent, they would only 'cross the water when . . . Naples is entirely cleansed'; even so they would require 'British troops . . . [in] Naples to guard the person of Their Majesties'.

While thus preoccupied with Naples Nelson received news of grave import from the Atlantic. He had long realized that the French might transfer a sizeable part of their Brest fleet to regain control of the Mediterranean so that the *Armée d'Orient* could be reinforced and resupplied. The Minister of Marine, Vice-Admiral Eustache Bruix, hoisted his flag in command of some twenty-five ships-of-the-line and led them out of Brest on 25 April 1799. Though sighted by a patrolling British frigate, Bruix avoided further contact with the watching Channel fleet because Bridport mistakenly supposed his destination to be Ireland. St Vincent being away sick at Gibraltar, the blockade of Cadiz was being maintained by fifteen sail-of-the-line under Vice-Admiral Lord Keith, who sighted the French force on 4 May and prepared for battle. But in a gale which prevented the Spanish fleet leaving harbour to join their ally, Keith was unable to get within range before nightfall; nor could he overtake Bruix's ships next day before they slipped safely through the Straits.

St Vincent responded to this emergency by calling off the blockade of Cadiz; but Keith could not reach Gibraltar until 10 May, so that it was two days more before his Commander-in-Chief entered the Mediterranean with sixteen sail-of-the-line. Reinforced by Duckworth's four battleships, St Vincent anchored off Mahon in Minorca on the 20th, only to learn that Bruix had reached Toulon a week before – and that on the 14th the Spanish Admiral Massaredo had seized his chance to slip out of Cadiz with seventeen ships-of-the-line which were now at Cartagena.

As soon as he received news of Bruix's sortie, on 12 May, Nelson ordered Troubridge and Ball to take their ships to join Duckworth, now a rear-admiral, at Minorca. But he could not extricate himself from the tentacles of Palermo. 'Eight, nine, or ten sail-of-the-line shall in a few days be off Mahon . . .', he told St Vincent. 'I am only sorry that I cannot [myself] move to your help. . . . Nothing would console the Queen . . . but my promise not to leave them.' It was a decision that conflicted with his sense of duty and his thirst for action: 'My heart is breaking.'

Fortunately Nelson's dilemma was resolved in twenty-four hours by a report that Bruix had already passed Minorca: he had not only eluded St Vincent but might be steering for the eastern Mediterranean. Faced with this danger, Nelson hurried fresh orders to Troubridge and Ball to rendezvous off Maritimo Island, just to the west of Sicily, for which he himself sailed in the *Vanguard* on 20 May. There he collected ten ships-of-the-line, which 'if Duckworth reinforce me, will enable me to look the enemy in the face', fourteen ships to nineteen. 'Even if Duckworth . . . leave me to my fate, never mind. If I can get 11 sail together, [the French] shall not hurt me.' This, in sharp contrast to the man who had been 'inactive at a Foreign Court' for so long, was the true Nelson, a commander convinced of his own and his fleet's ability to deal effectively with a superior French force.

St Vincent had, meantime, left Mahon for a position south-west of Toulon to prevent a junction between Massaredo's and Bruix's fleets. On 30th May he learned that the latter had sailed from Toulon three days before. On the same day his own fleet was strengthened by a further five ships-of-the-line, bringing it up to twenty-five. This decided him to do something towards rectifying the weakness of Nelson's force: Duckworth was ordered to take his squadron to Palermo where he arrived on 6 June. He found that Nelson had returned on 25 May: believing Bruix's fleet to be a greater threat to the Two Sicilies than to the Levant, he had sent Ball to resume the blockade of Malta with two ships-of-the-line whilst keeping the rest of his fleet concentrated at Palermo.

Duckworth's squadron included the *Foudroyant*, which Spencer had first intended to be Nelson's flagship; to this larger, 80-gun vessel Nelson transferred his flag on 8 June, taking Hardy with him from the *Vanguard*. But any satisfaction which he derived from this accretion to his force was diluted by Duckworth's news of the sixty-five-year-old St Vincent's health. 'This distresses us most exceedingly and myself in particular . . .' Nelson wrote to the man who had so consistently supported him. 'For the sake of our Country, do not quit us at this serious moment. . . . We look up to you . . . as to our Father, under whose fostering care we have been led to fame.' His apprehension for the future was well-founded; although he wrote, 'I wish not to detract from the merit of whoever may be you successor', he knew that this was likely to be the fifty-two-year-old Keith for whom, as with the ineffective Hotham, he had scant regard, not least because he had reached such high rank without taking part in any action at sea. He owed his position to a life-long friendship with St Vincent, his unopposed capture of the Cape of Good Hope in 1795, and a talent for administration.

St Vincent did not immediately give up his command-in-chief: on 2 June 1799 he withdrew his flagship to Minorca, leaving Keith to search for Bruix along the Riviera. But his second-in-command was too late to prevent the French landing troops and stores in Vado Bay for the relief of Savona. He was about to follow them into the Gulf of Genoa when he received fresh orders: St Vincent required him to detach two ships-of-the-line to reinforce Nelson, then to steer for the north-east coast of Spain, to forestall a link-up between the French and Spanish fleets. The Commander-in-Chief's strategic insight was sounder than Keith's. Had the latter complied with these instructions, he might well have intercepted Bruix's twenty-two sail-of-the-line. He chose instead to cruise off Toulon, whereby Bruix reached Cartagena without impediment on 22 June. In the event, Keith's lapse had no significant consequences for the Mediterranean. Daunted by so much opposition – Keith with nineteen sail, Nelson with fifteen, another sixteen on their way from England, not to mention the Portuguese squadron, and the Russo-Turkish concentration at Corfu – Bruix and Massaredo decided that their combined fleets of forty ships-of-the-line would be better employed in the Atlantic after all. Leaving Cartagena on 24 June, while Keith was having another look in Vado Bay, they passed the Straits on 7 July, three weeks before Keith could reach Gibraltar in pursuit.

To his credit Keith pressed this with such energy that he all but over-took an enemy who delayed eleven days at Cadiz: when he arrived off Brest on 14 August 1799, he learned that Bruix and Massaredo had reached this haven only the day before, having again eluded Bridport's

Channel fleet. But since this had been reduced to a mere ten sail-of-the-line by the Admiralty's order to detach sixteen to the Mediterranean, prime responsibility for the British failure to prevent the combined Franco-Spanish force reaching Brest must lie with Keith, and justify Nelson's poor opinion of him. It is, however, as fair to comment that it was, perhaps, fortunate that he did not intercept Bruix and Massaredo, since it is very doubtful whether he had the qualities needed to fight a successful action, despite the advantage of a fleet nearly as strong numerically as the enemy, and indubitably more efficient.

Long before this Nelson made an ill-judged move. The Queen and Emma persuaded him to use his ships to reassert King Ferdinand's authority in Naples, despite the paramount need to keep them concentrated ready to intercept Bruix. He had no sooner sailed from Palermo on 12 June with Neapolitan troops embarked, than he was joined by the *Bellerophon* and *Powerful* with news that Bruix was on a course for Naples. 'The French force being 22 sail-of-the-line, four of which are first rates, the force with me being only 16 . . . not one of which was of three decks, three being Portuguese and one of the English being a 64 very short of men, I had no choice left but to return to Palermo', to disembark the troops before establishing a patrol to the west of Sicily. Having thus reproached Keith, a frustrated Nelson complained to St Vincent: 'I . . . regret that his Lordship [Keith] could not have sent me a force fit to face the enemy.' The Commander-in-Chief was too ill to reply that it was he who had ordered his second-in-command to detach only two ships-of-the-line: he was, indeed, about to sail for home. And his successor thought it best to react to such criticism from a subordinate with a dignified silence – but the first seeds of discord between Keith and Nelson had been sown.

There followed two related incidents which demonstrate more than any other the extent to which Nelson allowed not only his judgment but his humanity to be subordinated to his passion for an ambitious woman who was determined to maintain her favoured position with a vindictive Queen, married to a weak and irresponsible King. The need to concentrate his ships-of-the-line against Bruix obliged the Admiral to leave only small craft in Naples Bay to support the loyal Neapolitans' struggle to regain the three forts occupied by rebels with a hard core of French troops. On 20 June Ruffo persuaded the castles of Uovo and Nuovo to capitulate by offering their garrisons, numbering about 1,500, liberal terms, including the right to march out with military honours and the choice of remaining in Naples or of being evacuated to Toulon. Most were too fearful for their future safety to do other than choose the second alternative. Until the necessary transports could be made available, the rebels were to remain in the forts under flags of truce. The senior British naval officer present, Captain Edward Foote, consented to sign after a vain protest that the terms were too generous.

Such was the position when Nelson entered the bay with his fleet on 24 June 1799. Because he had left King Ferdinand and, even more so, Queen Carolina, seething with fury against those of their subjects who had allowed their loyalty to be traduced by Jacobinism – the Queen enjoined him to 'treat Naples as if it were an Irish town in a similar state of rebellion' – he signalled Foote that he intended to annul an 'infamous' truce, and attack the forts. Ruffo and Foote hurried onboard the *Foudroyant* to find Nelson supported by Hamilton and Emma. Foote expressed regret for having signed the treaty; Ruffo argued vigorously that, since some of its terms had been put into effect already – for example, the rebels had released their British prisoners – it must be scrupulously observed; but Nelson insisted that it had no validity because it had not been approved by the King. He was, however, eventually persuaded to abandon his attack, and to allow the garrisons to embark in fourteen transports on the 26th, provided that these stayed in the bay until the king could decide the rebels' future.

Having supposed that they were on their way to safety, these half-starved, disease-ravaged emigrants were kept prisoner under the guns of the British fleet until 10 July, when the King arrived and at his Queen's behest ordered many to be barbarously executed. But if their deaths stain Nelson's honour, how much more does that of Caracciolo, the Neapolitan Commodore who had fought with him at the battle of Genoa in 1795. This forty-seven-year-old rebel managed to escape from Castel Nuovo shortly before it surrendered. When Ruffo subsequently learned where he was in hiding, Nelson asked that he should be handed over to him, but the Cardinal not only demurred but issued orders that no rebel was to be arrested except on his personal authority.

Thinking only of the King's and Queen's wishes, Nelson then arranged for the Commodore to be privately seized and brought onboard the *Foudroyant*. Within an hour of his arrival in the flagship on the night of 28 June, Caracciolo was charged before a court martial, notably for firing upon a vessel which, though Sicilian, was acting under Foote's orders. Despite his request that the court should, therefore, be composed of British officers, Nelson insisted that they should be Neapolitan. The accused pleaded that he had served the rebels unwillingly and under a threat of death, but was not allowed to produce evidence to support this. When he was condemned by a majority of his judges who were headed by an old enemy, the Count Thurn, he asked for a second trial. Nelson refused this. He also rejected Hamilton's expressed wish, which even Thurn supported, that twenty-four hours should elapse before execution; and ignored Caracciolo's last request, that he be accorded the right of death by shooting. At 5.0 pm on 29 June, little more than twelve hours after his abduction, and before Ruffo could have a chance to intervene, Caracciolo was transferred to Thurn's ship, and hanged at the *Minerva*'s yardarm.

Nelson had no clear mandate to override Ruffo's authority ashore by arranging the arrest of any Neapolitan rebel. He had, however, this small justification for abducting Caracciolo: he had already written to the King to the effect that Ruffo had, by his negotiations with the rebel forts, shown himself to be disloyal, to which the King replied authorizing the Admiral, if necessary, to arrest the Cardinal – though Nelson did not receive this until 30 June. No such excuse can, however, be offered (even by those who believe Caracciolo to have been guilty) for his decision to order the Commodore's immediate execution after such a travesty of a trial, since he agreed to defer the fate of the other rebels for decision by the King – except that the stress of war has trapped other great leaders into committing a comparable injustice.

These two incidents were followed by another which, though of a very different kind, not only shows how Nelson's passion for Emma warped his judgment (to quote Lord Elgin: 'There never was a man turned so *vainglorious*. . . . He is completely managed by Lady Hamilton'), but the evil consequences which sometimes ensued from having no speedier means of communication between two senior officers than letters. On 13 July 1799, three days after the return of the King to Naples, two days after the last Jacobin-held stronghold in the city, the Castel St Elmo, surrendered, Nelson received this instruction from Keith:

> Events [the arrival of Bruix's fleet in the Mediterranean] . . . render it necessary that as great a force as can be collected should be assembled near . . . Minorca. . . . If your Lordship has no detachment of the French [fleet near] Sicily, nor information of their having sent any force towards Egypt or Syria, you are hereby . . . directed to send such ships as you can possibly spare . . . [to] Minorca to await my orders.

This was clearly an order to be complied with at once, Nelson's discretion being limited to the number of ships to be sent. But he answered in these uncompromising terms: 'As soon as the safety of His Sicilian Majesty's Kingdom is secured, I shall not lose one moment in making the detachment.... At present ... the safety of His Sicilian Majesty, and his speedy restoration to his kingdom, depends on [my] fleet.' And instead of sending any of his ships to join his new Commander-in-Chief's flag, he sailed them, under Troubridge, to lay siege to Capua, fifteen miles to the north of Naples.

Six days later, on 19 July, Nelson received an even clearer and more pressing order from Keith:

I judge it necessary that all, or the greater part of [your] force ... should quit ... Sicily and repair to Minorca ... [to protect] that island during the necessary absence of ... [the] squadron under my command [searching for Bruix], or for ... cooperating with me against the combined [Franco-Spanish] force of the enemy.

Nelson responded with an even blunter refusal:

Your Lordship ... was not informed of the change of affairs in the Kingdom of Naples, and that all our marines and a body of seamen are landed in order to drive the French ... out of the Kingdom.... Unless the French are at least drove from Capua, I think it right not to obey your Lordship's order ... I am perfectly aware of the consequence of disobeying the orders of my Commander-in-Chief.

To these offensive words he added this singular explanation, although he now knew that Bruix had reached Cartagena so that Keith had only thirty-one ships-of-the-line to oppose a Franco-Spanish fleet of forty: 'I have no scruple in deciding that it is better to save the Kingdom of Naples and risk Minorca, than to risk the Kingdom of Naples to save Minorca.' Finally, only three days later, Nelson received this third categorical order from Keith:

Your Lordship is ... directed to repair to Minorca, with the whole, or the greater part of the force under your command, for the protection of that island, as I shall, in all probability have left the Mediterranean.

This time Nelson complied, but only to the extent of sending Duckworth to Minorca with four ships-of-the-line: he neither went himself, nor sent 'the whole, or the greater part' of his force. This cannot be excused as the action of the man on the spot who believed he was in a better position to know what to do 'in the public interest' than his superior, such as achieved such spectacular results at Cape St Vincent and, later, at

Copenhagen. It was irresponsible and in defiance of a Commander-in-Chief for whom he had little respect, for which he cannot be exonerated either by the fact that, in the event, Bruix made no attack on Minorca, nor by the help which his fleet continued to give to the allied armies in Italy.

Capua capitulated to Troubridge's marines on 29 July 1799, Gaëta on the 31st. Civitavecchia surrendered on 29 September: next day Captain Louis of the *Minotaur* was rowed up the Tiber in his barge to hoist the British flag over the Capitol in Rome. Nelson was, therefore, fortunate to incur no more than this mild rebuke from an Admiralty who believed one of Britain's dominions to be of greater importance than those of the Kingdom of Naples:

> Their Lordships do not . . . see sufficient reason to justify your having disobeyed the orders you had received from your Commanding Officer, or having left Minorca exposed to the risk of being attacked without having any naval force to protect it. . . . Their Lordships by no means approve of the seamen being landed [in Italy] to form a part of the army . . . in operations at a distance from the coast where . . . they might be prevented from returning to the ships, and the squadron be thereby . . . no longer capable of performing the services required of it. . . . Your Lordship [is] not to employ the seamen in like manner in future.

But Nelson never admitted to being in the wrong:

> My conduct is measured by the Admiralty by the narrow rule of law when I think it should have been done by common sense. I restored a faithful ally by breach of orders; Lord Keith lost a fleet by obedience against his own sense. Yet, as one is censured the other must be approved.

To this travesty of the facts – as already mentioned Keith missed Bruix's fleet through ignoring St Vincent's instructions – Nelson subsequently added this explanation: 'I paid more attention to another Sovereign than my own. . . . I repine not. . . . I did my duty to the Sicilifying my own conscience, and I am easy.' And against the Admiralty's displeasure he could set King Ferdinand's reward; he was created Duke of Brontë, with estates in Sicily estimated to be worth £3,000 ($7,200) per annum.

Keith's absence in the Atlantic left Nelson as acting Commander-in-Chief Mediterranean for the remainder of the year – of six sail-of-the-line under Duckworth covering Gibraltar and Cadiz; of four protecting Minorca; of

Lord Nelsons signature on his being made a Lieutenant 11 April, 1777.

Horatio Nelson,

His ordinary writing before he lost his arm.

Horatio Nelson

*His Signature 1 Sept. 1797 after
the loss of his arm.*

Horatio Nelson

His Signature May 21, 1800.

Bronte Nelson of the Nile

His Signature in the latter years of his life.

Nelson Bronte

Nelson's signatures

three supporting the Portuguese squadron's blockade of Valletta; of Sydney Smith's division in the Levant; of Troubridge's force operating against Civitavecchia; and of a smaller one disrupting French communications in the Gulf of Genoa. All these he controlled, initially from the *Foudroyant* in Naples Bay, subsequently from the Palazzo Palagonia to which the Nelson-Hamilton *ménage* returned on 8 August 1799 because they could not persuade a frightened King Ferdinand to remain in his turbulent capital. And in Palermo Nelson now, for the first and only time, met Ushakóv.

When Bruix's fleet was nearing Toulon, the Russian Admiral recalled his squadrons from the Adriatic: 'I make haste to unite with Nelson', he wrote on 24 May but, on 6 June, 'I do not know how.' He sailed eventually on 24 July, to reach Palermo at the end of August. There is no evidence to support the Soviet historians who contend that Ushakóv seized this opportunity to rebuke Nelson for his preoccupation with Emma, but plenty to prove that their meeting was the reverse of fruitful. As Ushakóv told the Russian envoy at the Neapolitan Court:

> I did Nelson a signal honour by arriving with my combined squadrons in Palermo for discussions. . . . I first made suggestions about Malta but he had made his mind up in advance and immediately sent his ships . . . to Gibraltar and Mahon, and did not designate any common action with me. . . . It is very necessary to have frank cooperation, not what is taking place now . . . ministerial tricks and turns . . . under the cover of politeness.*

The abortive consequences were that while Nelson stayed anchored by Emma to Palermo, Ushakóv took his ships to Naples where they remained largely inactive for the next three months, while his Turkish colleague, whose crews were near to mutiny, returned to Constantinople.

August 1799 also witnessed an event of supreme importance in another part of the Mediterranean; the reaction of the man of whom Nelson had rashly written, on 1 September 1798, 'Bonaparte's career is finished', to the news of the serious defeats inflicted on the French armies in Europe contained in the newspapers given to him by Sydney Smith. *La Patrie en danger!* This was far more urgent than invading India, especially when Syria and Upper Egypt eluded his grasp. Accepting that his army had been cut off at its roots by the destruction of Brueys' fleet, Bonaparte turned over his command to General Kléber and left Cairo secretly for

---

Cf. Nelson's comment: 'The Russian Admiral has a polished outside, but the bear is close to the skin. . . . He is jealous of our influence.'

20 *Fanny (Lady Nelson)*

21 *Nelson out of uniform*

22 *Emma (Lady Hamilton) as seen by*
Romney

23 *Emma,* née *Emily Lyon, as seen by*
Gillray

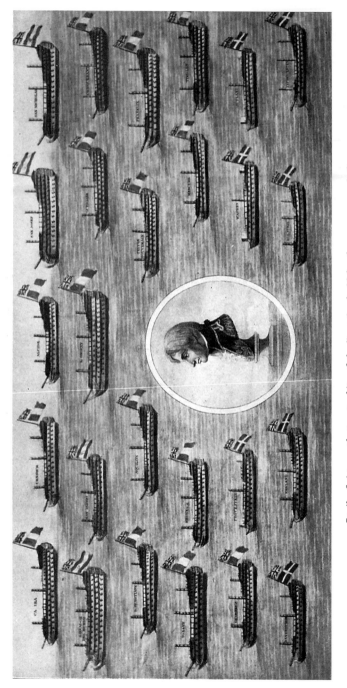

24 *Spoils of victory: the twenty ships-of-the-line taken by Nelson between 1795 and 1801*

25 *The battle of Copenhagen, 2 April 1801*

26 *Alexander Ball, (HMS 'Alexander')*   27 *Sir James Saumarez, Bt.*
                                          (HMS 'Orion')

BAND OF BROTHERS: FOUR OF NELSON'S CAPTAINS AT THE NILE

28 *Edward Berry, (HMS 'Vanguard')*   29 *Thomas Troubridge, (HMS 'Culloden')*

30 *Commander of the Russian fleet in the Mediterranean, 1798–1800: Vice-Admiral F. F. Ushakóv*

31 *Nelson's only meeting with the future Duke of Wellington, 13 September 1805*

32 Defeated at the Nile: Vice-Admiral François Brueys

33 Defeated at Copenhagen: Commodore Johan Fischer

NELSON'S OPPONENTS

34 Vanquished at Trafalgar: Vice-Admiral Pierre Villeneuve

35 Vanquished at Trafalgar: Admiral Don Federico Gravina

36 *Vice-Admiral Lord Nelson at the age of 43*

37 *Nelson's C-in-C in the Baltic, 1801 :*
Admiral Sir Hyde Parker

38 *Nelson's C-in-C in the Mediterranean*
1799-1800 : Vice-Admiral Lord Keith

39 *Nelson's Second-in-Command at*
Trafalgar : Vice-Admiral Cuthbert
Collingwood

40 *Nelson's Flag Captain at Trafalgar :*
Captain Thomas Masterman Hardy

41 *The battle of Trafalgar: 'The Approach'*

43 *(overleaf) HMS 'Victory' breaking the line at Trafalgar, engaged to starboard with the 'Redoubtable', with, on the latter's starboard hand, HMS 'Téméraire'*

42 *The battle of Trafalgar: 'The Engrace'*

41 *The battle of Trafalgar:* 'The Approach'

43 (*overleaf*) *HMS* 'Victory' *breaking the line at Trafalgar, engaged to starboard with the* 'Redoubtable', *with, on the latter's starboard hand, HMS* 'Téméraire'

42 *The battle of Trafalgar:* 'The Engrace'

Alexandria, sailing thence on 23 August onboard the frigate *Muiron*, with a small escort under Ganteaume's command. The need to beat back against the prevailing westerly winds by a route that would avoid patrolling British frigates so lengthened his voyage that forty-seven days elapsed before he landed at St Raphael on 9 October. His escape is not to be counted against Smith: his squadron was too small to maintain a continuous blockade: on the crucial date he had withdrawn to Cyprus for provisions and water. To suggest that it was a consequence of Nelson and Ushakóv giving such high priority to supporting the allied armies in their task of clearing the French out of Italy, not to mention Turkey's failure to use the greater part of her Fleet to any purpose, is nearer the mark. Be this as it may, the consequences were momentous.

After being defeated by Suvórov at battles on the Trebbia* on 17–19 June, and at Novi* on 15 August, the French were compelled to evacuate all of Italy except for a few small enclaves, notably around the ports of Genoa and Ancona, the fall of the latter being needlessly prolonged until 13 November by the failure of the local Austrian and Russian naval commanders to agree on how to prosecute an effective siege. The French retreat was, however, halted at Zurich where, at the end of September, Masséna was enabled to inflict a crushing defeat on the Allies because the Emperor Francis had withdrawn the larger part of his army from Suvórov's command in order to make a new and unimportant drive across the middle Rhine. Since this was followed in mid-October by the capitulation of the Duke of York's Anglo-Russian expedition to the Netherlands, a humiliated Tsar ordered his armies home on the 23rd. Thus, by the time Bonaparte reached Europe, the immediate threat to French territory had been lifted, leaving him free to rectify the political confusion and administrative chaos which he found in Paris. The Directory was overthrown on 9–10 November 1799 by the *coup d'état* of 18 Brumaire, its place being taken by three co-equal Consuls of whom Bonaparte was one. One month later the thirty-year-old Bonaparte established his pre-eminence as First Consul. Now was France's destiny in his hands alone.

During these eventful months none of the manifold problems with which Nelson had to deal troubled him more than Malta. Valletta's extensive underground granaries allowed Vaubois' garrison to keep their grip on the island's fortress despite a vigorous sea blockade, whilst for lack of grain 60,000 Maltese came near to starvation, the Sicilians being unwilling to meet more than a tithe of their needs when Nelson had too

*See map on p. 31.

few warships to protect their supply ships from seizure by Barbary pirates. He had to use all his tact to persuade de Niza to delay his departure, when Lisbon recalled the Portuguese squadron that had been the backbone of his blockading force for more than a year, the while he paid a brief visit to Minorca (where Berry, recovered from his wounds, resumed his post as flag captain in the *Foudroyant*) to press General Sir James Erskine to release British troops from Mahon or Messina to augment the 5,000 which Ushakóv hoped to bring from Naples for an assault on Valletta.

As de Niza left for home early in December, Troubridge landed the Messina garrison in Malta. But these 1,500 troops under Brigadier-General Graham were only enough to stiffen the resistance of the gallant islanders who owed so much to Ball's inspired leadership. Ushakóv's men never arrived. The Russian Admiral was about to leave Naples with seven ships-of-the-line and six transports carrying 2,000 troops to take a belated share in the siege and blockade when he received fresh instructions from St Petersburg. Having ordered Suvórov's army home, the Tsar also recalled his fleet from the Mediterranean. On 25 December 1799 a dejected Ushakóv wrote: 'I had hoped to take Malta, acting with . . . Rear-Admiral Nelson and Captain Ball . . . but all our actions depend on the will of the all-Highest.' In the hope that a capricious Tsar would reverse his decision, Ushakóv put into Corfu for 'the repair of ships damaged by a great storm'. He was still there on 23 April 1800, when Nelson wrote:

> The orders for the British squadron . . . are to seize the French army from Egypt under whatever protection they may be, and in consequence several have been taken under flags of truce granted by Sir Sydney Smith. I do not think that the French will send off any more . . . now they are informed of the determination of the Allies to prevent their return to Europe. I am this moment going to Malta where it would give me infinite pleasure to meet Your Excellency and . . . for us together to finish the famous expedition of Bonaparte and to tear from him his only remaining conquest.

But, when the Tsar remained adamant that Russia must withdraw from an alliance that included Austria, Ushakóv was left with no choice but to sail for Sevastópol on 17 July 1800.

The polite phrases of Nelson's letter veils a serious dispute with his subordinate commander in the Levant. A presumptuous Smith had no sooner arrived there in the spring of 1799 than he conceived a most unusual, perhaps unique, solution to the Egyptian problem. He offered to individual Frenchmen passports allowing them to return safely to Europe by sea, in the hopes of rapidly weakening the *Armée d'Orient* to the point which would enable the Turks to reconquer their dominion. Nelson's reaction was swift and certain: '*This is in direct opposition to my opinion* ... I must ... *strictly charge and command you* ... *not on any pretence to permit a single Frenchman to leave Egypt.*' 'Not on any pretence' included opposing '*by every means in your power, any permission which may be attempted to be given by any foreigner*, admiral, general, or other persons'.

For a time Smith obeyed this order; but when the Earl of Elgin, newly arrived as British Ambassador in Constantinople, encouraged the Sultan to negotiate with Kléber a treaty that would free the *Armée d'Orient* to return to Europe unmolested, Smith not only allowed it to be signed on 24 January 1800 onboard his ship, but in his presence. The fact that he refrained from adding his own signature to the Convention of El Arish did not save him from an angry rebuke: 'I did not give credit that it was possible for you to give any passport for a single Frenchman, much less the Army, after my positive order of 18 March 1799.' Nelson had, however, now lost the mandate which would have allowed him the irony of requiring implicit obedience when he himself had flagrantly disobeyed Keith's orders to protect Minorca. For Keith had returned to the Mediterranean early in 1800, bringing clear directions from London: 'I have positive orders,' he wrote to Kléber on 8 March, 'not to consent to any capitulation with the French troops ... unless they lay down their arms, surrender themselves prisoners of war, and deliver up all the ships and stores of ... Alexandria to the Allied Powers.' And this rendered the well-intentioned but ill-judged work of Elgin and Smith sterile.

Although the Admiralty told Nelson as early as 20 September 1799 that he would hold the supreme command only 'till the return of Lord Keith or some other superior officer', he continued to hope that he would be allowed to retain it. But the glory of the Nile had been too much tarnished by his subsequent conduct; the Board could not entrust the Mediterranean to an officer who allowed his judgement to be warped by a single-minded concern for the Neapolitan Court, especially when this went so far as flagrant disobedience of orders. Since Bruix made no further attempt to sortie despite his success in extracting Massaredo's fleet from Cadiz, which brought his strength up to forty-seven ships-of-the-line, Keith was ordered to leave the Brest blockade in the hands of Bridport's Channel fleet and to return to his own station. And his arrival at Gibraltar in the 100-gun *Queen Charlotte* ended Nelson's freedom to conduct his command from Palermo: he was ordered to meet Keith at Leghorn on 20 January. From there the two Admirals returned together to Palermo, but to stay for only eight days. Keith had no liking for the 'scene of fulsome vanity and absurdity' which he found there. On 15 February the *Queen Charlotte*, with the *Foudroyant* in close company, arrived off Malta, with 1,500 Neapolitan troops to hasten the end of the siege.

Nelson's reactions to this abrupt change in his fortunes can be judged from his letters to Emma: 'I feel all, and notwithstanding my desire to be as humble as the lowest midshipman, I am used to having attention paid me.' And: 'To say how much I miss your house and company would be saying little; but in truth you and Sir William have so spoiled me, that I am not happy anywhere else.' Yet to Keith he owed the opportunity to satisfy his hunger for battle which would not otherwise have come his way. The Commander-in-Chief was greeted off Valletta by the frigate *Success* bearing news of a French squadron to the west of Sicily. The *Généreux*, flying the flag of Rear-Admiral Perrée, accompanied by three smaller warships, was escorting three transports carrying 3,000 troops to reinforce Vaubois' garrison. Keith promptly ordered three 74s, the *Foudroyant*, *Audacious* and *Northumberland*, to chase to windward (i.e. to the west), whilst his own more powerful flagship guarded the entrance to Valletta's Grand Harbour.

Nelson was delayed by a heavy sea and thick fog so that he had not gone far from Malta when, at dawn on 18 February 1800, the *Alexander*, on patrol to the south-east of Malta, sighted Perrée's force to leeward of the island. On hearing this British 74's guns, Nelson turned to her support. 'Pray God we may get alongside them [the French]', he wrote in his journal, as his ships ran before the wind with studding sails set. 'The event I leave to Providence.' He had time to say more than this to Emma: 'I feel anxious to get up with these ships and shall be unhappy not to take them myself, for ... my greatest happiness is to serve ... my ... King and Country, and I am envious only of glory; for if it be a sin to covet glory, I am the most offending soul alive.'

At 8.0 am the *Alexander* forced the largest transport, the *Ville de Marseille*, to bring to. At 1.30 pm the French warships parted company and made good their escape. Not for another three hours did the *Foudroyant* and *Northumberland* overhaul the *Généreux*, whose attempted flight was impeded by the 32-gun *Success*, whose captain skilfully used her greater manoeuvrability to rake the stern of his more powerful opponent again and again. The *Foudroyant*'s first broadside injured Perrée's left eye; the *Northumberland*'s cut off his right leg at the thigh, a wound that was

mortal. Deprived of their leader, the French had no further heart for
battle against superior odds and struck their colours. 'I have got her – *le
Généreux* – thank God!' wrote Nelson that night. 'Twelve out of thirteen
[that were at the Nile], only the *Gillaume Tell* remaining.'

Keith did not hesitate to give Nelson generous credit for foiling this
French attempt to succour Valletta: 'on this occasion, as on all other, [he]
conducted himself with skill and great address, in comprehending my
signals'. But such was Nelson's anathema for his Commander-in-Chief that
he could not forbear to criticize him for ordering a pursuit to *windward*,
nor conceal the depth of his rancour at the Admiralty's reprimand of the
previous summer by contending that, in turning to support the *Alexander*
when she discovered the French force to *leeward*, he had deliberately
disobeyed orders. 'By leaving my Admiral without signal, for which *I may
be broke*, I took these French villains', he told Hamilton; whilst to the
First Lord he wrote: 'The *Généreux* was taken by me, and my plan . . .
my quitting Lord Keith, was at my own risk. . . . The way he went the
Généreux never could have been taken.'

One week later Keith sailed north to ensure an effective blockade of
Genoa which was now besieged by an Austrian army under General
Mélas. He left Nelson to 'prosecute the necessary measures for . . . the
complete reduction of Malta'. But the prospect of achieving this, brought
nearer by Perrée's failure to breach the blockade, had no appeal for a man
who had already told Keith: 'I . . . made a vow, if I took the *Généreux* by
myself, it was my intention to strike my flag.' Now he veiled the truth, his
passionate desire to be reunited with Emma, in a further letter: 'My Lord,
my state of health is such that it is impossible I can remain much longer
here. . . . I must . . . request your permission to go to my friends at
Palermo.'

Keith's unsympathetic response was an order forbidding the Malta
squadron to visit Palermo for supplies, and to use instead the nearer port
of Syracuse. Since this had been Nelson's own first choice for a base from
which to deal with the islands, he could not fail to understand that such
an instruction censured him for staying at Palermo for so long, and he
rebelled against it. Though Ball and Troubridge argued that he could not
leave the blockade without lasting discredit, he wrote to Emma on 4
March 1800: 'My health is in such a state, and to say the truth, an uneasy
mind at being taught my lesson like a schoolboy, that MY DETERMINA-
TION is made to leave Malta on the 15th.'

Most fortunately he not only advanced this date by five days but, on arrival at Palermo, transferred his flag to a transport, then ordered the *Foudroyant* to rejoin the blockade. For Berry returned to Malta only a few hours before Rear-Admiral Decrès decided to relieve the famished garrison of the need to feed the crew of the *Guillaume Tell* by running out of Valletta on the night of the 29th. 'If the *Foudroyant* had not arrived, nothing we have could have looked at her', wrote Troubridge: Nelson would have been blamed for her escape. As it was, the *Guillaume Tell* (although she lost her main- and mizen-topmasts to Captain Henry Blackwood's frigate *Penelope*, which repeated the tactics of the *Success*) managed to elude pursuit by the 64-gun *Lion* during the night. But the *Foudroyant* was able to come up with her at dawn, for Berry to write:

> At half-past six shot away the [*Guillaume Tell*'s] main and mizenmasts: saw a man nail the French ensign to the stump of the mizenmast. . . . Five minutes past eight, shot away the enemy's foremast. Ten minutes past eight, all the masts being gone by the board, the enemy struck his colours and ceased firing. . . . Performed Divine Service and returned thanks to Almighty God for the victory.

No ship-of-the-line was fought more gallantly than this, the last survivor from Aboukir Bay: the pity of it is that, although she surrendered to Nelson's ship, she did not do so to Nelson's flag. 'I would have given one thousand guineas your health had permitted your being in the *Foudroyant*', wrote Troubridge. But for Nelson there were no regrets. 'I am sensible of your kindness,' he told Berry, 'in wishing my presence at the finish of the Egyptian fleet, . . . the thing could not be better done, and I would not . . . rob you of . . . your well-earned laurels.'

Nor was this all: 'My task is done, my health is lost, and the orders of the great Earl St Vincent are completely fulfilled.' The man who had spo.ken so recently of 'my ambition to serve . . . my . . . King and Country . . envious only of glory', would not remain under Keith's command. 'I have wrote . . .,' he told Spencer, 'for permission to return to England, when you will see a broken-hearted man. My spirit cannot submit patiently.' But already the First Lord had expressed

> my extreme regret that your health should be such as to oblige you to quit your station off Malta, at a time when I should suppose there must be the finest prospect of its reduction. I should be very sorry that you did not accomplish that business in person, as the *Guillaume Tell* is your due, and that ship ought not to strike to any other. If . . . [an enemy fleet] should come into the Mediterranean . . . I should be much

concerned to hear that you learned of their arrival . . . either on shore or in a transport at Palermo.

And this rebuke, especially the sting in the last sentence, was followed by action: on 9 May 1800 Keith was told that, if Nelson's health rendered him unfit for duty, he was to be allowed to return to England, a decision which Spencer explained in these blunt words: Nelson's 'further stay in the Mediterranean cannot . . . contribute either to the public advantage or his own', while to Nelson he wrote:

It is by no means my wish . . . to call you away . . . but having observed that you have been under the necessity of quitting your station off Malta, on account of your health . . . it appeared . . . much more advisable for you to come home at once, than to . . . remain inactive at Palermo, while active service was going on in other parts of the station. . . . You will be more likely to recover your health and strength in England than . . . inactive . . . at a Foreign Court.

Others were less inhibited in their criticism, Lord Minto for one:

I have letters from Nelson and Lady Hamilton. It does not seem clear whether he will go home. I hope he will not for his own sake, and he will at least take Malta first. He does not seem at all conscious of the . . . discredit he has fallen into, or the cause of it, for he still writes, not wisely, about Lady H. . . . But it is hard to condemn . . . a hero . . . for being foolish about a woman who has art enough to make fools of many wiser than an admiral –

in Nelson's case one who 'is in many points a really great man, in others a baby'. The Foreign Office settled the matter: Hamilton had long been wanting leave but would not go without Nelson. Now he was superseded: on 22 April Hamilton presented his letters of recall. Free to quit the post he had served with credit for nearly forty years, he and Emma embarked two days later in the *Foudroyant*, and sailed with Nelson to visit Syracuse and Malta.

From off Valletta on 12 May 1800 a letter went to Keith saying that Nelson intended to withdraw the *Foudroyant* and the *Alexander* from the blockade in order to convey the Queen of Naples and her suite to Leghorn, so that she might visit her daughter in Vienna, after which he hoped that the *Foudroyant* might take him and the Hamiltons to England. Keith replied that no ships could be spared for such diversions – for one reason he had lost his flagship, the *Queen Charlotte*, with the greater part of her crew, by an accidental fire on 17 March. Before he could receive this

Nelson had not only taken both ships to Palermo, but sailed thence to Leghorn where he arrived on 14 June, with the naive explanation: 'I was obliged to bring the *Alexander* or the [Queen's] party never could have been accommodated.' Keith's comment was: 'Had not Nelson quitted the blockade . . . [Malta] might have fallen about this time.'

His own blockade had already triumphed: on 5 June Masséna, his army wasted by famine and disease, surrendered his hold on Genoa. But no success was more short-lived: on the day that Nelson reached Leghorn Bonaparte, once again at the head of an army, scored such a decisive victory over the Austrians at Marengo that Mélas was compelled to ask for an armistice. How, then, could Queen Maria Carolina continue her planned journey to Vienna? One thing was certain: Nelson would not abandon her. When Keith ordered him to take his ships to Spezia, he sent only the *Alexander*: the *Foudroyant* stayed at Leghorn 'to receive the Queen . . . should such an event be necessary'. Keith replied that no ships-of-the-line were to be so used when the Brest fleet might at any time reappear in the Mediterranean. Nelson answered tartly: 'I do not believe the Brest fleet will return to sea, and if they do the Lord have mercy on them, for our fleet will not.'

Keith sought to resolve the issue between them by proceeding to Leghorn on the 24th, 'to be bored by Lord Nelson for permission to take the Queen to Palermo and princes and princesses to all parts of the globe'. Although, according to Wyndham, British Minister to Tuscany,

> the Queen wept . . . [the Commander-in-Chief] remained unmoved and would grant nothing but a frigate. . . . He told her Lady Hamilton had had command of the fleet long enough. . . . Nelson . . . does not intend going home till he has escorted [the Queen] back to Palermo. His zeal for the public service seems entirely lost in his love and vanity.

Keith compromised to the extent of authorizing the *Alexander* to take the royal party round to Trieste, but by now Emma had had enough of the sea. She pressed the Queen to complete her journey by way of Florence and Ancona. And when Keith learned that the Hamiltons were to go with her, he seized his chance to be rid of his refractory subordinate: Nelson was allowed to strike his flag on 13 July 1800 and travel overland to England with them.

This chapter needs three footnotes. First, two ironic twists. To reach Venice from Ancona he and his fellow travellers were obliged to take passage not in a British ship but onboard the flagship of Rear-Admiral N.

Vóinovitch, who had refused to obey the Tsar's order to withdraw his frigates from the northern Adriatic (for which offence he was, not surprisingly, dismissed from the Imperial Russian Navy). And because Russia had abandoned the Second Coalition, the Treaty of Amiens, signed in 1802, established the Ionian Islands, not as a Russian colony, but as an independent republic to come again under French dominion in 1803, after which, from 1815 until 1864, they were under British rule.

Secondly, Malta. On 24 August 1800 the two surviving frigates from the Nile made their bid to escape from Valletta. The *Diane* was taken by the *Success*; the *Justice* outsailed the *Généreux* (now flying the British ensign) and *Northumberland*, eventually to reach Toulon. A fortnight later, Vaubois conceded defeat: on 5 September his garrison surrendered to Major-General Pigot who had arrived in April with a further 2,500 British and Neapolitan troops. The Treaty of Amiens restored the island to the Knights of St John, against the wishes of the islanders. Before this dispute could be resolved, the war against Napoleon was renewed, when Britain again took Malta under her protection whereby, eleven years later, the Treaty of Paris settled that 'the Islands . . . belong in full property and sovereignty to His Britannic Majesty', from one of whose successors they later, alone among his dominions, gained the George Cross for indomitable courage during World War Two.

Thirdly, Egypt. After Keith had annulled the Convention of El Arish, Kléber inflicted such a severe defeat on the Turks that the *Armée d'Orient* was able to remain in undisputed control of Egypt for more than a year in which they were helped by several frigates piercing the British blockade with supplies and reinforcements. But Keith's fleet and a squadron under Warren (now Rear-Admiral Sir John), foiled three attempts to reach Alexandria during the spring of 1801 by a sizeable fleet under Ganteaume, which managed to slip out of Brest. Characteristically Keith failed to bring the enemy to action. However, on 2 March he entered Aboukir Bay with a fleet of seventy sail to land an army of 16,000 troops under General Sir Ralph Abercromby, who decisively defeated the French near Alexandria on the 21st, at the cost of his own life. Six days later an Anglo-Turkish army occupied Cairo. General Menou continued to hold Alexandria with some 10,000 men until a bombardment compelled the final surrender of the *Armée d'Orient* on 2 September 1801, shortly before the end of hostilities in Europe, and the Treaty of Amiens which restored Egypt to its lawful sovereign, the Sultan of Turkey. How Egypt was later dominated, first by France and then by Britain, before achieving independence is another story.

To what extent did these two years during which Nelson, though only a rear-admiral, was entrusted with the conduct of the naval war in the eastern Mediterranean – for six months of which he was Commander-in-Chief Mediterranean Station in all but title – enhance his reputation as a naval commander? The answer must dismay all those to whom his is a peerless name. The true Nelson only brightened these sombre years as briefly as a flash of lightning splits the darkness of a summer night, as when he encountered the *Généreux*. For the most part all his actions and judgements were guided, not by his brain but by a heart gripped by merciless passion for a scheming woman who had no concern for her country's interests and, latterly, by a mind poisoned by intolerance of the Commander-in-Chief who succeeded his beloved St Vincent.

The ambition, which was his driving force, was largely quenched. His only action, with the *Généreux*, made no demands on his tactical genius. His diplomacy was marked by intolerance and a naive failure to understand the complex political situation in Naples. His whole approach was conditioned and circumscribed by his own and, through Emma, Queen Maria Carolina's, consuming hatred for the French, and a belief that King Ferdinand's rebellious subjects could be handled with the same crisp quarterdeck ease as mutinous seamen.

A vital component of leadership is example, not least in obedience and respect for a senior officer. Inspired disregard of an order by the man on the spot who is in a better position to judge the action required to further his superior's aim, may be instrumental in gaining success. Repeated disobedience of orders is a very different matter, Nelson's firm handling of Sydney Smith's intransigence being wholly offset by his arrogant contempt for Keith, but for whose forbearance he must have been tried by court martial.

His understanding of strategy, so clearly evinced immediately after the Nile, was undermined. But for Emma he would not have pressed King Ferdinand to make his disastrous march on Rome, nor believed that its débâcle required him to devote his energies to ensuring the safety of the Neapolitan Court and regaining their lost capital. But for her he would have done more to secure Ushakóv's active help, more to shorten the siege of Valletta, and more to end the *Armée d'Orient*'s grip on Egypt.

Probably a more perfectly beautiful being than Emma Lyon never existed. . . . We owe to Romney . . . a vivid presentation of that marvellous beauty which swept . . . all the better feelings of [Nelson's] nature before the passionate longing to possess this splendid work of nature;

which made him reckless of all moral restraint; and which has tarnished with an indelible stain an otherwise glorious career. Viewed in any light, one can but regret the fatality that threw Emma Hamilton in the path of Horatio Nelson, for not even the glorious close of his heroic life . . . can wash his memory clean of the infamy of his participation in the judicial murder of Caracciolo, or excuse his treatment of the Neapolitan political prisoners, whose lives . . . had [been] guaranteed, and whom he handed over to the tender mercies of Ferdinand and his sanguinary consort.*

A harsh verdict, yes, but one which is more honest than that of most of Nelson's biographers who have been bewitched into giving a false gloss to these two years of their hero's life;† and a verdict which is supported by the Admiralty's decision to recall him from the Mediterranean in 1800, discredited if not disgraced.

Fortunately for him, and for Britain, Nelson had five more years to live; time enough for him to reveal again amidst the shoals of Copenhagen his greatness as a naval commander, such as he had shown in Aboukir Bay on 1 August 1798, as those who served under him believed him still to be:

My Lord [wrote the Barge's crew of the *Foudroyant*], it is with extreme grief that we find you are about to leave us. We have been along with you . . . in every engagement your Lordship has been in . . . and most humbly beg . . . of your Lordship to permit us to go to England as your boat's crew . . . in any way that may seem most pleasing. . . . Pardon the rude style of seamen who are but little acquainted with writing.

Perhaps James Froude has the words for all this: 'Duty means justice, fidelity, manliness, loyalty, patriotism; truth in the heart and truth in the tongue.'

---

*Lord Ronald Sutherland Gower in *George Romney*.
†For one example, see the *Encyclopaedia Britannica* (1964 edition, volume XVI), where the relevant section makes this naive comment: 'Nelson's conduct at Naples is of course bound up with his friendship with Lady Hamilton . . . but that a private attachment seriously warped his judgment in public matters no one has yet shown, nor has anyone explained why it should.'

CHRONOLOGICAL SUMMARY FOR CHAPTER VII

EVENTS IN NELSON'S LIFE	DATE	RELATED EVENTS
	1798	
	August	Remnants of Brueys' fleet reach Malta.
Orders Saumarez to escort Nile prizes to Gibraltar. Orders Hood to blockade coast of Egypt.	*14 August*	
Leaves Aboukir Bay in *Vanguard*.	*19 August*	
	September	Turkey and Russia declare war on France.
Arrives Naples, to be greeted by Sir William and Lady Hamilton.	*22 September*	
	25 September	De Niza's Portuguese squadron blockades Malta.
	1 October	Russo–Turkish fleet under Ushakóv and Kadir Bey enters Mediterranean.
Orders Ball to reinforce blockade of Malta.	*12 October*	
	24 October	Ushakóv takes Zante.
	28 October	Ushakóv takes Cephalonia.
Visits Malta blockade. Gozo surrenders.	*24–30 October*	
Created Baron Nelson of the Nile and of Burnham Thorpe.	*6 November*	
	13 November	Ushakóv takes Santa Maura and blockades Corfu.
	15 November	Duckworth and Stuart take Minorca.
	26 November	Mack takes Rome.
Lands Neapolitan troops at Leghorn.	*28 November*	
	December	Championnet routs Mack.
Evacuates Neapolitan royal family and Hamiltons to Palermo.	*23–26 December*	

EVENTS IN NELSON'S LIFE	DATE	RELATED EVENTS
	1799	
	3 January	Britain, Portugal, Russia, Two Sicilies and Turkey form Second Coalition against France.
	23 January	French take Naples.
Places Malta under British protection.	*February*	Troubridge and Hood bombard Alexandria.
Promoted to Rear-Admiral of the Red.	*14 February*	
Orders Troubridge to blockade Naples.	*March*	Sydney Smith succeeds Hood in Levant.
	1 March	Ushakóv takes Corfu. Bonaparte invades Syria.
	12 March	Austria joins Second Coalition.
	17 March	Bonaparte takes Haifa and lays siege to Acre.
	25 March	One Austrian army defeats *Armée d'Italie* at Stockach.
	5 April	Another Austrian army defeated at Magnano.
	22 April	French evacuate Naples.
	25 April	French fleet under Bruix leaves Brest.
	4 May	Russian squadron compels French to evacuate Brindisi.
	5 May	Bruix enters Mediterranean.
Receives news of Bruix's sortie from Brest.	*12 May*	St Vincent lifts blockade of Cadiz and enters Mediterranean.
	13 May	Russian squadron compels French to evacuate Bari. Austro-Russian force blockades Ancona. Bruix arrives Toulon.
	14 May	Spanish fleet leaves Cadiz for Cartagena.
	19 May	Bonaparte lifts siege of Acre and retreats to Egypt.

EVENTS IN NELSON'S LIFE	DATE	RELATED EVENTS
Concentrates his fleet ready to intercept Bruix.	20 May	St Vincent arrives Minorca. Ushakóv concentrates his fleet at Corfu ready to intercept Bruix.
	June	Keith follows Bruix into Gulf of Genoa. Keith succeeds St Vincent as C-in-C Mediterranean.
Reinforced by Duckworth's squadron.	6 June	
Transfers flag to *Foudroyant*, 80.	8 June	
	17–19 June	Suvórov defeats French on the River Trebbia.
	22 June	Bruix joins with Spanish fleet at Cartagena.
Returns to Naples and rejects Ruffo's truce with rebel-held forts.	24 June	Bruix and Massaredo leave Cartagena.
Orders Caracciolo's execution.	29 June	
	7 July	Combined French and Spanish fleets leave Mediterranean.
Welcomes King Ferdinand back to Naples.	10 July	
	15 July	Turks seize Aboukir.
	25 July	French drive Turks out of Aboukir.
Disobeys Keith's orders to protect Minorca.	July	
Returns to Palermo.	8 August	
	13 August	Bruix evades Keith's pursuit and reaches Brest.
Acting C-in-C Mediterranean during Keith's absence in Atlantic. Created Duke of Brontë.	August–December	
	15 August	Suvórov defeats French at Novi.
	23 August	Bonaparte leaves Egypt.

EVENTS IN NELSON'S LIFE	DATE	RELATED EVENTS
	27 August	Duke of York's Anglo-Russian expeditionary force invades Netherlands.
Meets Ushakóv at Palermo.	*30 August*	
	September	Ushakóv proceeds to Naples. Kadir Bey returns to Constantinople.
	25–30 September	Suvórov defeated by Masséna at Zurich.
	30 September	French evacuate Rome.
Pays brief visit to Minorca to press Erskine to provide British troops to take Valletta.	*5–22 October*	
	9 October	Bonaparte lands in France.
	Mid-October	Capitulation of Duke of York's Anglo–Russian Netherlands expeditionary force.
	23 October	Suvórov's army ordered home.
	9–10 November	Bonaparte overthrows Directory.
	13 November	Surrender of Ancona.
	December	De Niza's squadron returns to Lisbon. Troubridge lands British troops in Malta. Ushakóv ordered to return to Black Sea, but remains inactive at Corfu.
	12 December	Bonaparte appointed First Consul.
	1800 *January*	Keith returns to Mediterranean.
Meets Keith at Leghorn and accompanies him back to Palermo.	*20 January*	
	24 January	Convention of El Arish signed; then repudiated by Keith.
Accompanies Keith to Malta.	*15 February*	
Captures *Généreux*.	*18 February*	

EVENTS IN NELSON'S LIFE	DATE	RELATED EVENTS
	March	Keith blockades Genoa.
Leaves Malta for Palermo.	*10 March*	
	20 March	French defeat Turks at Heliopolis.
	30 March	Berry captures *Guillaume Tell*.
	April	Mélas lays siege to Genoa.
Leaves Palermo with Hamiltons onboard *Foudroyant* for Syracuse and Malta.	*24 April*	
Admiralty authorizes return to England.	*9 May*	
	5 June	Masséna surrenders Genoa.
Arrives Leghorn with Queen of Naples and Court embarked.	*14 June*	Bonaparte defeats Mélas at Marengo. Austrians ask for an armistice. Kléber assassinated in Cairo.
Strikes flag and leaves Leghorn for home overland with the Hamiltons.	*13 July*	
	17 July	Ushakóv leaves Corfu for Sevastópol.
	24 August	Frigates *Diane* and *Justice* break out from Valletta. *Diane* taken: *Justice* escapes to Toulon.
	5 September	Vaubois surrenders Valletta to Pigot.
	1801 *Spring*	Keith and Warren foil Ganteaume's attempts to relieve *Armée d'Orient*.
	2–6 March	Keith lands Abercromby's expeditionary force in Aboukir Bay.
	21 March	Abercromby defeats French at Alexandria.
	27 March	Allies enter Cairo.
	2 September	*Armée d'Orient* surrenders Alexandria, subsequently evacuating Egypt.

VIII

To the Baltic

1800-1801

The First Lord might so far disapprove of Nelson's conduct as to recall him from his command; but to Britain's allies he was the victor of the Nile, the admiral who compelled the French fleet to relinquish its grip on the Mediterranean, the man who dispelled Bonaparte's Oriental dream, and helped to clear the Jacobins from Italy. His journey home across Europe with the Hamiltons was akin to a triumphal progress. They stayed for a month in Vienna where, wrote Lady Minto, 'the door of his house is always crowded with people, and even the street when his carriage is at the door; and when he went to the play he was applauded, a thing which rarely happens here'. The paeans of praise included a performance of 'Papa' Hadyn's D minor Mass, written two years before, with its flourish of trumpets and timpani accompanying the *Benedictus* inspired by the news from Aboukir Bay (now known as the *Nelson* Mass); and his forgotten cantata *The Battle of the Nile*, which Emma insisted on singing with the sixty-eight-year-old composer at the keyboard.

Lady Minto, who had known Nelson in Corsica, did not 'think him altered in the least. He has . . . the same honest simple manners; but he is devoted to Emma, he thinks her quite an *angel* . . . and she leads him about like a keeper with a bear.' Lord Fitzharris feared the consequences of this infatuation: 'Nelson . . . is not changed; open and honest, not the least vanity about him . . . [but he] told me he had no thoughts of serving again.' He had already said as much to others: 'Lord Nelson is not yet arrived in England,' wrote Troubridge in September, 'and between ourselves I do not think he will serve again.'

The trio followed the course of the Elbe by way of Prague and Dresden.

But for all its pleasures, their dilatory journey was not without worries. Fitzharris might admire Nelson, but 'Lady Hamilton is without exception the most coarse, ill-mannered, disagreeable woman I ever met', and the Electress of Saxony refused to receive her, which raised the spectre of whether she would be *persona grata* at the Court of St James. (She was not, in the event, received by any of the royal family, except for the Prince of Wales and Prince Augustus.) Eventually, on 31 October 1800, they reached Hamburg to embark for a stormy passage across the North Sea. Six days later, two years and eight months after sailing from Spithead, Nelson landed at Yarmouth for the hero's welcome that popular opinion believed he deserved: on 10 November he attended the Lord Mayor's Banquet in Guildhall to receive an elegant sword from the Corporation of London.

But he had also to face the moment of truth. Fanny had come from Roundwood to join her husband at Nerot's Hotel in King Street, St James's. (He had advised her not to meet him at Yarmouth.) For the past eighteen months she had forborne comment on the irregularity and brevity of his letters, for which he gave the mendacious excuse of pressure of work. She had ignored his repeated references to the Hamiltons – 'it is impossible for me to express the affectionate kindness Sir William and her Ladyship has [*sic*] shown me'. She had accepted his change of style, from, 'My dearest Fanny,' to, 'My dear Fanny', and from, 'Your most affectionate husband', to, 'Your affectionate'. Her lengthy replies, though filled, as always, with domestic gossip rather than praise for his achievements, ended with such sentiments as, 'God bless you, my dear husband, and grant us a happy meeting'. She vented her displeasure only at his supposed lack of consideration for her beloved son, ignoring the reality that Nelson had gained for Josiah command of the frigate *Thalia* when his reprobate conduct justified court martial.

But the resolution with which she hoped to retain her errant husband's affections was soon proved vain. With scant regard for her feelings, Nelson lost no time in taking her to dine with the Hamiltons; nor did he fail to give her other opportunities to see how real his devotion to Emma was. 'His conduct to Lady Nelson,' wrote Sir William Hotham, 'was the very extreme of unjustifiable weakness, for he should at least have attempted to conceal his infirmities, without publicly wounding the feelings of a woman whose own conduct he well knew was irreproachable.' He was as callous in Emma's absence. 'When,' wrote Lady Spencer, 'the Nelsons dined with the First Lord, he treated his wife with every mark of dislike and even of contempt.'

To gain relief from the quarrels which this conduct provoked, Nelson spent Christmas with the Hamiltons in William Beckford's folly at Fonthill. But although he subsequently rejoined Fanny at 17 Dover Street, a house which Davison had rented for him, their final parting was not long delayed. For reasons to be related, Nelson had to leave London for Torbay on 13 January. As he said goodbye he declared: 'I call God to witness, there is nothing in you or your conduct I wish otherwise' – but they never saw each other again. On 29 January Emma gave birth to a daughter, baptized Horatia, who must have been conceived during her cruise to Syracuse and Malta in the *Foudroyant*. A child of his own! Nelson had wanted one for so long, and Emma had succeeded where Fanny had failed. She had given him this 'clear pledge of love': henceforward – and Emma was as determined to ensure this as he was – there could be no woman in his life but her.

Horatia was quickly placed with a foster-mother, the highly recommended Mrs Gibson, both to conceal her existence from Hamilton and to avoid the inevitable consequence if Emma had brought her up at home, that Hamilton must have become her *de jure* father. Nelson wanted the child to be his, not another's. So, too, did he take elaborate steps designed to ensure that on his death much of his property would go to Horatia instead of to Josiah. And, early in March, Fanny received these heartless words in what she called her husband's letter of dismissal:

> . . . I have done *all* for him [Josiah] and he may again, as he has often done before, wish me to break my neck . . . but I have done my duty as an honest and generous man, and I neither want nor wish for anybody to care what become of me . . . seeing I have done all in my power for you. And if dead you will find I have done the same,* therefore my only wish is to be left to myself. . . .

Nonetheless, Fanny wrote to her husband a month later to express 'my thankfulness and happiness it hath pleased God to spare your life' in a 'victory . . . said to surpass Aboukir'. And although for reply she received no more than a further indication, through Davison, that Nelson wished 'to be left to myself, and without any enquiries from her', she wrote again in July to thank him for 'your generosity and tenderness . . . never more strongly shown than . . . the payment of your very handsome quarterly allowance'. But not until near the end of 1801 did she despair of recovering her husband: on 18 December she sent this pleading, forgiving letter:

*A bequest of £1,000 ($2,400) per annum in his will.

... The silence you have imposed is more than my affections will allow me, and in this instance I hope you will forgive me in not obeying you. ... I now have a ... comfortable warm house. Do, my dear husband, let us live together. I can never be happy till such an event takes place. I have but one wish in the world, to please you. Let everything be buried in oblivion, it will pass away like a dream. I can now only entreat you to believe I am most sincerely and affectionately your wife. ...

But the hour had already struck. With the same inhumanity that he had shown towards the unfortunate Caracciolo – and for the same reason, Emma – Nelson wrote *finis* to his union with Fanny. The letter was returned with this note by Davison appended: 'Opened by mistake by Lord Nelson, but not read.'

He could hardly have said anything more cruel. His ageing father could only help to relieve Fanny's unhappiness by continuing to live with her until he died some four months later. The sorry fact is that marriage between a man so warm-blooded and high-spirited and a woman so frigid and neurotic was ill-starred from the beginning; and it was foredoomed when they failed to consummate it with a child. But Nelson could no more expect her to divorce him than Hamilton would wish to lose both him and Emma: wedded in law, Nelson and Fanny remained unto the end, whilst to Emma he wrote:

Now, my dear wife, for such you are in my eyes and in the face of heaven, I can give full scope to my feelings. ... You know ... that there is nothing in this world that I would not do for us to live together, and to have our dear little child with us. My longing for you ... you may readily imagine. What must be my sensation at the idea of sleeping with you? It sets me on fire, even the thoughts, much more would be the reality. I am sure my love and desire are all for you. ... Kiss and bless our dear Horatia.

Nelson's determination to be rid of Fanny, Horatia's birth and the difficulty in ensuring for her future, and his continued passion for Emma, despite the King's strong disapproval and such public criticism as Gillray's fierce cartoons, not to mention his jealousy at Emma's delight in the attentions paid to her by the Prince of Wales – all this subjected him to much emotional stress. He wanted the private life of the victor of the Nile to be as far above criticism as his conduct of that battle, but though the world might not worry about a man's immoralities, it would not have them brandished in its face. 'They all hate me and treat me ill. I cannot . . . recall . . . one real act of kindness, but all of unkindness', he wrote. Such bitterness kindled his rebellious spirit, sometimes corrupting his driving ambition and self-reliance into a distasteful vanity and arrogance. Whether it had a significant effect – for good or ill – on his rôle as naval commander is a question which the remainder of this book must try to answer.

One thing is, however, certain. In his next command he would not be able to linger in port, enjoying the company of his mistress. Nor would he be tied by her ambition to a corrupt Court dominated by a tyrant Queen. Freed from the shackles which had bound him in the Mediterranean, he could go his own brilliant way, with the tremendous consequence that within three months he again climbed one of the high peaks of his unique career.

Despite his expressed intention not to serve again, Nelson had no sooner arrived in London, than he reported to the Admiralty that his health was restored and that he desired a further appointment. In two months this wish was granted: St Vincent, who had succeeded Bridport in the Channel fleet in April 1800, wanted none but Nelson as his second-in-command. And with Troubridge among the Naval Lords to prompt him, Spencer had no mind to reject the Commander-in-Chief's request now that a year had elapsed since Nelson's reprehensible conduct in the Mediterranean. On 1 January 1801 Nelson was promoted vice-admiral of the blue: twelve days later, as already mentioned, he left London for Devon to hoist his flag in the *San Josef* (as the name of the three-decker which he had boarded at Cape St Vincent was anglicized), with Hardy as his flag captain.

Nelson yielded to none in his admiration for St Vincent, who knew well how to handle and to use to best advantage his subordinate's special talents. Unfortunately, as soon as 5 February Destiny played an unexpected card. Because the King would not support Catholic emancipation, Pitt resigned; the new Prime Minister, Addington, appointed St Vincent to be his First Lord; and Admirals Cornwallis and Sir Hyde Parker were ordered to succeed him. This courted trouble. Nelson had seen how inadequately Parker handled his division in Hotham's actions in the Gulf of Genoa and off Hyères, and had had a disagreement with him in the short interregnum between Hotham's departure and the then John Jervis's arrival in the Mediterranean. ('Hotham kept my squadron too small for its duty; and the moment Sir Hyde took command, he reduced it to nothing.') He had, therefore, as little respect for Parker as he had had for Keith. Nor was it long before events justified this.

The Tsar had done more to disrupt the Second Coalition than withdraw Suvórov from the Alps and Ushakóv from the Mediterranean. Further angered, after Valletta's surrender in September 1800, by Britain's refusal to yield Malta to his sovereignty as Grand Master of the Knights, Paul had followed up the French defeats of Austria in the field, notably at Hohenlinden (near Munich) on 3 December, by persuading Denmark, Sweden and Prussia to agree with Bonaparte's suggestion that they should join with him in reviving the Armed Neutrality of 1780. The treaty which they signed in St Petersburg on 16 December might not be a declaration of war, even though it extended to seizing some 300 British merchantmen which were then in Russian ports, but it was a direct threat to Britain's ability to continue, again alone except for faithful Portugal, her mortal struggle with France. By insisting on protecting their own trade whilst denying Britain access to Baltic timber and hemp, these countries could reduce her sea power near to impotence. The British Government was, therefore, in no doubt of the need for swift decisive action: the small risk that the French fleet might sortie from Brest must be accepted: the greater part of the British fleet in Home waters must be sent to the Baltic. Backed by such a show of force negotiations might dissolve the Armed Neutrality; but if negotiations failed, the Fleets of these powers must be destroyed.

Parker and Nelson were ordered to go with this Baltic fleet, the former because he had been involved with planning a similar expedition in 1781 and because, as St Vincent put it, he was best fitted to do the talking, the latter because 'Nelson will act the fighting part very well'. In this respect the First Lord's judgement was to be proved sound, but there was another truth in Lady Malmesbury's comment: 'I feel very sorry for Sir Hyde . . . no man would ever have gone with Nelson, or over him, as he was sure to be [put] in the background.' Knowing that he must be destined for this shallow sea when he received orders to embark the 49th Regiment of Foot, under Lieutenant-Colonel the Hon. William Stewart, at Spithead, Nelson (after paying a hurried visit to London to see his newly born child) transferred his flag to the *St George* because this 98-gun ship drew less water than the *San Josef*. But on reaching Yarmouth on 6 March, he was dismayed to find his new Commander-in-Chief more interested in providing entertainment for the eighteen-year-old wife he had recently married than in his fleet and its mission. Without thought of how he himself had dallied with Emma at Naples and Palermo, Nelson promptly expressed his feelings in a note to St Vincent. Five days later he had the satisfaction of telling Troubridge: 'The signal is made to prepare to unmoor at 12 o'clock. Now he [Parker] can have no desire for staying; for her ladyship is gone, and the ball for Friday knocked up by yours and the Earl's [St Vincent's] unpoliteness to send gentlemen to sea instead of dancing with white gloves.'

Fifteen ships-of-the-line and two 50s, with nearly 1,000 troops embarked, accompanied by the usual frigates and smaller craft, sailed on 12 March. According to one of Nelson's letters: 'I know not that we are even going to the Baltic, except from the newspapers.'* Parker had been too 'sulky' to reveal his plans. According to another, 'Sir Hyde has not told me officially a thing': nonetheless, 'the *St George* is beginning to prepare for battle, and she shall be true to herself. . . . Nelson will be the first if he lives and . . . shall partake of all [the] glory.' For he had, in fact, gathered much of what was intended, since to Emma he boasted:

Reports say we are to anchor before we get to Kronborg . . . that our Minister at Copenhagen may negotiate. What nonsense! How much better could we negotiate was our fleet off Copenhagen, and the Danish Minister would seriously reflect how he brought the fire of England on his Master's fleet and capital; but to keep us out of sight is to seduce Denmark into a war. . . . If they are the plans of [our] Ministers, they are weak in the extreme. . . . If they originate with Sir Hyde, it makes him, in my mind as – but never mind, your Nelson's plans are bold and decisive – all on the grand scale. I hate your pen-and-ink men; a fleet of British ships of war are the best negotiators in Europe.

Parker, with his fleet augmented by three more ships-of-the-line, rounded the Skaw on 20 March 1801. Forty-eight hours later, he anchored in the Kattegat, eighteen miles from Kronborg, where the Sound (the channel between Sweden and Denmark) narrows to three miles to the north of Copenhagen. For one reason, Parker needed time to concentrate his force after it had been scattered by a North Sea gale. The other Nelson learned when he boarded Parker's flagship, the 98-gun *London*, even though 'there was not that degree of openness which I should have shown my second-in-command'. By virtue of her geography Denmark held the key to the Baltic. Addington hoped that she could be persuaded to allow the British fleet to pass Copenhagen without opposition, so that it might go on without loss and without substantial delay to deal with the Russian fleet. As Nelson put it, 'Paul was the enemy . . . of the greatest consequence for us to tumble.' He was also right in his belief that negotiations would

---

*A petulant exaggeration since, at St Vincent's suggestion, he had embarked in the *St George* Captain Sir Frederick Thesiger, an officer who had served in the Russian Navy, to be his adviser in the Baltic.

fail: the frigate *Blanche*, which carried the Hon. Nicholas Vansittart of the Foreign Office to Copenhagen for talks with the Danish Government, rejoined the fleet on 23 March with the news that the British Minister had been handed his passports.

But Vansittart also reported that the defences of Kronborg and Copenhagen were much stronger than the Admiralty supposed. To Nelson's dismay, Parker decided against forcing a way into the Baltic: he would 'stay in the Kattegat and there await the time when the whole naval force [i.e. the combined Danish, Russian and Swedish Fleets – the Prussian Fleet was of no consequence] might choose to come out and fight'. This being 'a measure, in my opinion, disgraceful to our Country' – 'I wanted to get at an enemy, as soon as possible to strike a *home* stroke': 'Go by the Sound, or by the [Great] Belt, or anyhow; only lose not an hour' – Nelson distilled all his strategic wisdom into a forceful letter to Parker of which this is the essence:

Not a moment should be lost in attacking the enemy: they will every hour be stronger: we never shall be so good a match for them as at this moment. The only consideration is how to get at them with the least risk to our ships. The Danes have taken every means to prevent our getting to Copenhagen by the Sound. Kronborg has been strengthened and very formidable batteries placed under the Citadel, supported by sail-of-the-line, floating batteries, etc., etc. The Government took for granted you would find no difficulty in getting off Copenhagen, and if negotiations failed, you might instantly attack; and that there would be scarcely a doubt that the Danish Fleet would be destroyed, and the capital made so hot that Denmark would listen to reason. But, by Mr Vansittart's account, their state of preparation exceeds this, and the Danish Government is hostile. Therefore, on your decision depends whether our Country shall be degraded in the eyes of Europe, or whether she shall rear her head higher than ever.

I begin with supposing you are determined to enter by the Sound, as if you leave that passage open, the Danish Fleet may sail and join the Dutch or French. I have no fears that, whilst their capital is menaced, 9,000 of her best men would be sent away. You are now above Kronborg: if you attack you must expect ships crippled, and one or two lost; for the wind which carries you in, will not bring out a cripple. This I call taking the bull by the horns. It will not, however, prevent the Reval ships, or the Swedes, from joining the Danes; and to prevent this is absolutely necessary – and still to attack Copenhagen.

One way is to pass Kronborg and down the deepest channel past the Middle Ground, and then up the King's Channel, to attack their floating batteries, etc. This must prevent a junction between the Russians, Swedes and Danes, and may allow us to bombard Copenhagen.

Should this be impracticable, the passage of the Belt could be accomplished in four or five days, and then the attack carried out and the junction of the Russians prevented.

Supposing us through the Belt, would it not be possible either to go with the fleet, or to detach ten ships to Reval [in the Gulf of Finland], to destroy the Russian squadron? I see no great risk in such a detachment, leaving the remainder to the business at Copenhagen.

The boldest measures are the safest; and our Country demands a most vigorous exertion of her force.

This advice tipped the scales. On the 26th Parker ordered his fleet to weigh: that evening he anchored his ships only six miles from Kronborg. Head winds and calms held them there until the 30th, when at 6.0 am Parker again headed for the Sound. One hour later the Danish batteries to the west of the narrow strait opened fire on the leading British ships; but, contrary to expectations, those on the other shore remained silent. This allowed Parker's fleet to keep within half-a-mile of the Swedish coast and so beyond range of the Danish guns. Before noon all his ships were safely anchored off the island of Hveen, fifteen miles to the north of Copenhagen. So much for the first obstacle which, but for Nelson, Parker would have refused.

The next one was, however, of a different order. When Parker, Nelson and Rear-Admiral Thomas Graves sailed south in a lugger to reconnoitre the defences of the Danish capital, they found that these were, indeed, formidable.* Guarding the entrance to Copenhagen harbour was the Trekroner fort,‡ built on piles and mounting sixty-six 36-pounders; and on the shore to the south of the walled city was the Strickers battery.† But the Danes had rightly appreciated that these were wholly insufficient:

*The reader is referred to the diagrams between pp. 196 and 197, for whose details the author is chiefly indebted to Danish historians who have been able to go more thoroughly into them, than most, if not all, British ones. Incidentally, the scene is today best visualized (rather than seen because parts of it have been reclaimed to construct a shipyard and an oil depot) from the top of the old mast crane, which is portrayed in several contemporary pictures, and is now preserved for posterity in the Royal Danish Navy's Copenhagen dockyard.

†Not two forts as is often stated. The adjacent Lynetten fort had no guns.

‡The other forts shown to the south of the city on most plans of the battle were no more than redoubts manned by infantry armed with muskets.

their Commander-in-Chief, Commodore Johan Fischer, had moored most of his ships, without their masts, in the channel immediately to seaward

THE FLOATING DEFENCES OF COPENHAGEN, 2 APRIL 1801*

Name	Description	Guns	Commander	Fate
Prövestenen	Three-decker, without masts	58	Capt. L. F. Lassen	Taken and burnt
Wagrien	Two-decker, without masts	52	Capt. F. C. Risbrich	Do.
Rendsborg	Transport	20	Cmdr. C. T. Egede	Do.
Nyborg	Do.	20	Cmdr. C. A. Rothe	Escaped but sank
Jylland	Two-decker, without masts	54	Capt. E. O. Branth	Taken and burnt
Svoerdfisken	Floating battery	18	2nd Lieut. S. S. Somerfeldt	Do.
Kronborg	Frigate, without masts	22	1st Lieut. J. E. Hauch	Do.
Hayen	Floating battery	18	2nd Lieut. J. N. Müller	Do.
Elven	Sloop	10	Cmdr. Baron H. Holsten	Escaped
Dannebrog	Two-decker, without masts	60	Capt. F. A. Braun *Broad Pendant of Commodore J. O. Fischer*	Blew up
Aggershus	Transport	20	1st Lieut T. Fasting	Escaped but sank
Gerner	Floating battery	20	2nd Lieut. P. Willemoes	Escaped
Sjaelland	Two-decker, unrigged	74	Capt. F. C. Harboe	Taken and burnt
Charlotte Amalia	Transport	26	Capt. H. H. Koefoed	Do.
Söhesten	Floating battery	18	1st Lieut. B. U. Middelboe	Do.
Holsteen	Ship-of-the-line	60	Capt. J. Arenfeldt	Taken and added to R.N.
Infödsretten	Two-decker, without masts	64	Capt. A. de Thurah	Taken and burnt
Hjaelperen	Frigate	16	1st Lieut. P. C. Lillienschiold	Escaped

*This table is compiled chiefly from Danish sources which the author accepts as more accurate than most, if not all, British ones.

of the city, and added a number of floating batteries, which were large rafts carrying guns but without protection for their crews. These are listed in their berthing order from south to north in the table on p. 190. The remainder of the Danish fleet, the *Elephanten*, 70, the *Mars*, 64, the *Danmark*, 74, the *Trekroner*, 74, the frigate *Iris*, 40, and two brigs, were likewise berthed in the harbour entrance.

Parker opposed an attack on these defences, partly because of their strength and because the Danes had removed the buoys marking the channels leading to Copenhagen harbour. Nelson held a very different view: 'The Danish line . . . looks formidable to those who are children at war, but to my judgement, with ten sail-of-the-line I think I can annihilate them.' And so strongly did he urge this that his weak-willed Commander-in-Chief reached the singular, if not unique, decision that, whilst he was unwilling to do so, his second-in-command should attack the enemy with the force listed in the table below; also seven bombs,

NELSON'S SQUADRON AT THE BATTLE OF COPENHAGEN

Ship	Guns	Commander
Elephant	74	Capt. T. Foley
		Flagship of Vice-Admiral Lord Nelson
Defiance	74	Capt. R. Retalick
		Flagship of Rear-Admiral T. Graves
Edgar	74	Capt. G. Murray
Monarch	74	Capt. J. R. Mosse
Bellona	74	Capt. Sir T. B. Thompson
Ganges	74	Capt. T. F. Fremantle
Russell	74	Capt. W. Cuming
Agamemnon	64	Capt. R. D. Fancourt
Ardent	64	Capt. T. Bertie
Polyphemus	64	Capt. J. Lawford
Glatton	54	Capt. W. Bligh*
Isis	50	Capt. J. Walker
Amazon	38	Capt. E. Riou
Désirée	40	Capt. H. Inman
Blanche	36	Capt. G. E. Hamond
Alcmène	32	Capt. S. Sutton
Jamaica	26	Capt. J. Rose
Arrow	30	Capt. W. Bolton
Dart	30	Capt. J. F. Devonshire
Cruiser	18	Cmdr. J. Brisbane
Harpy	18	Cmdr. W. Birchall

*Best known for his involvement in the mutiny in the *Bounty* in 1789.

six gun-brigs and two fireships. Nelson transferred his flag to the *Elephant* because the more heavily armed *St George* drew too much water for his purpose. He took Hardy with him, to advise and help, not to replace Thomas Foley in command, whereby Hardy gained the distinction of being the only captain to be present at the Nile, Copenhagen and Trafalgar.* Parker retained under his own direct command four 74s and two 64s in addition to his flagship and the *St George*.

On 31 March a council of war agreed the details of the plan which Nelson had outlined in the third paragraph of his letter quoted on pp. 188–9. Fischer had two advantages denied to Brueys; being in waters which he knew well, he had berthed his vessels very close to shoal water; and having no intention of getting under way, he had moored them by bow and stern so that the distance between them was much smaller than the swinging room required by ships anchored only by the bow. Nelson could not therefore repeat the concentration on one part of the enemy line which had proved so successful at the Nile: his ships would not be able to pass inside it, nor through it. Nor could he take the enemy by surprise: Parker had already lost him this benefit. Nor could he attempt an assault with fireships: he would have needed a dozen, instead of only two, for this to be effective. But, by sailing down the Outer Deep, round the Middle Ground and then up the King's Channel, he could begin his attack against the weaker, southern end of the enemy line – without coming within range of the Stricker's battery, and without first having to run the gauntlet of the Trekroner fort. To dissuade Fischer from attempting to reinforce his southern flank, Parker's eight ships would threaten an attack from the north.

Next morning, the wind being from the north, the Commander-in-Chief moved his whole fleet to a new anchorage only six miles from Copenhagen. From there his second-in-command made a swift reconnaissance in the frigate *Amazon*, chiefly to ensure that his instructions for buoying the Outer Deep had been properly executed. At 2.30 pm, soon after his return, he ordered his squadron to weigh. Piloted by the *Amazon*, his ships passed safely to a new anchorage close to the southern end of the Middle Ground at 8.0 pm.

Nelson spent much of that night preparing detailed instructions for his captains: most of them had been under his command for too short a time to be a band of brothers whom he could trust to act in accordance with a general plan. Edward Riou, in the *Amazon*, was ordered to lead four

*Four fought in two of these battles; Berry at the Nile and Trafalgar, Foley and Thompson at the Nile and Copenhagen, and Fremantle at Copenhagen and Trafalgar.

other frigates against the northern end of the enemy line. James Rose, in the frigate *Jamaica*, was to operate six gun-brigs against its southern flank. So, too, but independently, was Henry Inman's frigate *Désirée*. Nelson's ten ships-of-the-line, plus the *Glatton* and the *Isis*, were to sail down the enemy line, the leader anchoring by the stern abreast an allotted enemy vessel, the second passing on the disengaged side to anchor abreast another, the third then passing to starboard of the first two British ships and anchoring off a third Danish vessel, and so on until each British ship was in action with one of the enemy, as shown on the diagram on pages 196–7. As soon as any British vessel subdued her target, she was to weigh, pass to starboard of those ahead of her, and engage another of the enemy near the head of the Danish line. The seven bombs were to anchor to the east of the British line and throw their shells over it. The 49th Regiment, augmented by 500 sailors under Thomas Fremantle of the *Ganges*, was to be ready to seize the Trekroner fort as soon as its guns could be silenced.

As happens so often in war, these plans quickly went awry. Dawn on 2 April brought a fair south-easterly wind: Nelson could ask for no better. But the local pilots whom he had managed to engage decided against risking their lives in battle, so that the masters of the British ships had to feel their way into the King's Channel. George Murray's *Edgar*, which was in the lead, successfully rounded the Middle Ground after Nelson gave the order to weigh at 9.30 am. But the next to follow, his old flagship, Robert Fancourt's *Agamemnon*, was unable to weather this shoal, and had to anchor again. Without her support, Murray was so heavily engaged by Captain Lassen's *Prövestenen* at 10.5 that he was driven to berth the *Edgar* as much as 500 yards from Captain Branth's *Jylland* instead of Nelson's intended 250, which impelled the other British ships to engage their targets at this greater, and less immediately effective range – beyond instead of within point-blank range – as well as leaving less room for their consorts to pass on their disengaged sides.

Nelson rectified the *Agamemnon*'s failure by ordering John Lawford to berth the *Polyphemus* abreast the *Prövestenen*, instead of heading for the *Elephanten* in the harbour entrance. As successfully, James Walker dropped the *Isis*'s stern anchor abreast Captain Risbrich's *Wagrien*. But the *Bellona*, attempting to pass to starboard of these three British ships, went too close to the Middle Ground and stuck fast. So did the *Russell* following in her wake. Since Fancourt was no more able to warp the *Agamemnon* sufficiently far to windward to round the Middle Ground than Thomas Thompson and William Cuming were able to tow their ships off this shoal until after the battle, Nelson was, from the outset, deprived of three of his ten ships-of-the-line. Though much disturbed by this, he ordered Foley to keep to port of the stranded ships and anchor the *Elephant* in the *Bellona*'s berth, so that Captain Braun's *Dannebrog*, Fischer's flagship, would not be unopposed. And he then had the satisfaction of seeing Thomas Bertie and William Bligh take the *Ardent* and the *Glatton* to their berths between the *Elephant* and the *Edgar*, whilst the *Monarch*, Captain James Mosse, and Fremantle's *Ganges* reached theirs ahead of the *Elephant*, where they were so quickly in action that Morse was killed shortly after giving the order to anchor abreast Captain Koefoed's *Charlotte Amalia*. The last to reach a berth, abreast Captain Arenfeldt's *Holsteen*, was Graves' flagship, Captain Retalick's *Defiance* which, having been ordered to bring up the rear of the British line, was now at the head of it.

The bombs gained their station at 11.45, to open fire with their mortars, first on the enemy ships and subsequently on the town and dockyard. A strong current prevented Rose bringing his gun-brigs within range of the *Prövestenen*, but this failure was amply compensated by Inman's handling of the *Désirée* which helped the *Polyphemus* by raking this Danish three-decker again and again. The *Prövestenen* was, however, an exception: most of the ships in Nelson's shortened line had to deal with two targets even though many were of smaller size. Even so, the British brought some 420 guns into action against the enemy's 380, if one includes those in the Trekroner fort, but omits the *Elephanten* and the other ships berthed in the harbour mouth which, like Parker's squadron, were not to be involved in the battle. The Danes had, however, an important advantage denied to Nelson's ships: as soon as their guns crews were decimated by British fire, fresh men were brought off by boat from the shore. By 1.0 pm, when the fierce cannonade between the two lines of static vessels had lasted for more than ninety minutes, very few of the Danish weapons had been silenced.

Nelson was not the man to be discouraged by this: 'It is warm work,' he told Stewart as the soldier paced the deck beside him, 'and this day may be the last to us at any moment; but, mark you, I would not be elsewhere for thousands.' Parker's mood was very different. His squadron could make little progress against a head wind. At noon the *London* was still five miles from the head of the Danish line – but close enough to see the *Bellona* and *Russell* flying signals of distress, and the *Agamemnon*, unable to get within range of the enemy. To Parker this spelt potential disaster. Turning to his flag captain, he said: 'I will make the signal of recall for Nelson's sake. If he is in a condition to continue the action successfully, he will disregard it: if he is not, it will be an excuse for his retreat, and no blame can be imputed to him.' But the fleet was still limited to Howe's signal book: Popham's vocabulary code was four years away. As William Domett pointed out, Parker could only hoist the flags meaning, 'Discontinue the action', which was a positive order, allowing Nelson no latitude. Parker, therefore, sent his captain of the fleet, Robert Otway, to the *Elephant*, with a verbal message. But long before Otway's boat could reach Nelson's flagship, Parker's growing anxiety for the outcome of a battle for whose failure he would surely be held responsible, overruled Domett's advice. Shortly after 1.0 pm, when the *London* was still three miles or more from the *Elephant*, the latter's

> signal lieutenant called out that . . . the signal for discontinuing the action was . . . [hoisted] by the Commander-in-Chief. He [Nelson] . . . appeared to take no notice. . . . The signal officer . . . asked if he should repeat it. 'No,' he replied, 'acknowledge it.'* Presently he called . . . to know if [his own] signal for close action was still hoisted . . . [adding] . . . 'Mind you keep it so.' He now paced the deck, moving the stump of his lost arm in a manner which always indicated great emotion. 'Do you know,' said he . . . 'what is shown on board the Commander-in-Chief. . . . Why, to leave off action?' Then, shrugging up his shoulders . . . 'Leave off action? Now damn me if I do! You know, Foley . . . I have only one eye – I have a right to be blind sometimes', and then, putting the glass to his blind eye . . . he exclaimed, 'I really do not see the signal. . . . Keep mine for closer battle flying.'†

Parker's positive interference could have been as disastrous as the Admiralty's 'scatter' signal to Convoy PQ17 in the Second World War. To obey it, many of Nelson's ships would have had to run the gauntlet of the whole Danish fleet: to quote Graves, 'if we had discontinued the action before the enemy struck, we should all have gone aground and been destroyed'. As it was, Nelson lost the support of the *Amazon* and her accompanying frigates. These had been so badly mauled by the Trekroner fort that a reluctant Riou – 'What must Nelson think of us?' – whose bravery had been well established by his success in saving HMS *Guardian* after she had struck 'an island of ice' to the south-east of the Cape of Good

---

*In Nelson's time (and in contradistinction to British twentieth century practice), to 'acknowledge', a flag signal indicated no more than that it had been *seen*. To show that its meaning had been looked up in the signal book and was *understood*, the signal had to be repeated (*i.e.* hoisted) by the ship(s) for which it was intended.

†Southey in his *Life of Nelson*.

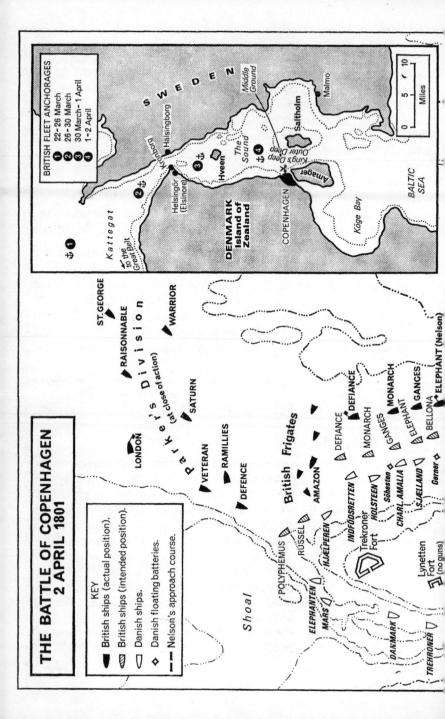

THE BATTLE OF COPENHAGEN
2 APRIL 1801

KEY

◆ British ships (actual position).
◢ British ships (intended position).
◁ Danish ships.
◇ Danish floating batteries.
— Nelson's approach course.

ST. GEORGE

RAISONNABLE

WARRIOR

Parker's Division

SATURN

LONDON

Parker's (at close of action)

VETERAN

RAMILLIES

DEFENCE

British Frigates

DEFIANCE

DEFIANCE

MONARCH

MONARCH

GANGES

ELEPHANT

GANGES

BELLONA

ELEPHANT (Nelson)

AMAZON

Gerner ◇

Shoal

POLYPHEMUS

RÜSSEL

HJÆLPEREN

INDFØDSRETTEN

Søhesten

HOLSTEEN

CHARL. AMALIA

S.SJÆLLAND

Trekroner Fort

ELEPHANTEN

MARS

Lynetten Fort
(no guns)

DANMARK

TREKRONER

BRITISH FLEET ANCHORAGES
❶ 22 - 26 March
❷ 26 - 30 March
❸ 30 March - 1 April
❹ 1 - 2 April

S W E D E N

Kronborg
Hälsingborg

Middle Ground

Malmo

Saltholm

The Sound

Kings Deep

Outer Deep

Hveen

Helsingör
(Elsinore)

DENMARK
Island of Zealand

COPENHAGEN

Amager

BALTIC
SEA

Köge Bay

Kattegat

to the
Great Belt

0   5   10
Miles

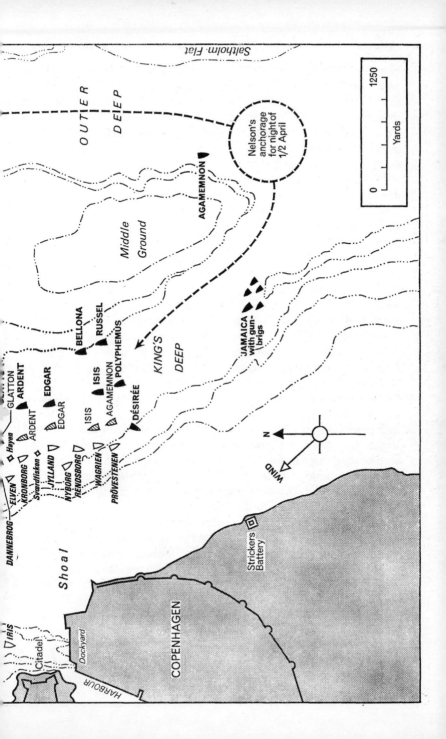

Saltholm Flat

OUTER DEEP

Nelson's anchorage for night of 1/2 April

Middle Ground

AGAMEMNON

1250

0

Yards

BELLONA

RUSSEL

GLATTON

ARDENT

EDGAR

ISIS

ISIS

POLYPHEMUS

Haven

KRONBORG

ARDENT

EDGAR

AGAMEMNON

KING'S DEEP

ELVEN

DANNEBROG

Sværdfisken

ISIS

DÉSIRÉE

JAMAICA with gun-brigs

JYLLAND

NYBORG

WAGRIEN

RENDSBORG

PRØVESTENEN

N

WIND

Shoal

Strickers Battery

COPENHAGEN

IRIS

Citadel

Dockyard

HARBOUR

Hope in 1789, thought it best to obey Parker's order. Unhappily, he had no sooner headed his ship away from the fort than he was killed by a ball from one of its guns. And had Nelson's Rear-Admiral been a lesser man than Graves, he would have lost the support of his division: the *Defiance* went so far as to repeat Parker's signal, but Graves ordered this to be done in a position inferior to Nelson's for close action, indicating that the latter was the one to be obeyed.

In the event, Nelson was no more called upon to justify his 'disobedience' on this occasion than he was after Cape St Vincent. His moral courage in rejecting Parker's order, on the clear grounds that he was in the best position to judge the progress of the battle, was rewarded soon after he put his blind eye to a use which will for all time stand as an epic example to others – and not only those whose profession is war. The British ships proved the superiority of their gunnery, especially their faster rate of fire: the stout-hearted resistance of the Danes began to weaken. Engaged by both the *Elephant* and *Glatton*, the *Dannebrog* caught fire, compelling Fischer to shift his broad pendant to the *Holsteen*. With as many as 270 killed and wounded, those who remained of Braun's crew were unable to control the flames: driven out of the line, she grounded near the Trekroner fort and later blew up. About 2.0 pm the transport *Rendsborg* broke from her moorings and was driven ashore, and the sloop *Elven* was so seriously damaged that she slipped her moorings and escaped into Copenhagen harbour. These casualties were quickly followed by the transports *Nyborg* and *Aggershus*, both of which sank, whilst the frigate *Hjaelperen*, was forced to slip her moorings and, like the *Elven*, seek safety in the harbour. Captain Harboe was likewise forced to cut the *Sjaelland*'s cables, while de Thurah's *Infödsretten* and Arenfeldt's *Holsteen* were reduced to wrecks, so that Fischer had to shift his broad pendant again, this time to the Trekroner fort.

By 2.30 pm the battle was virtually over. The floating defences of Copenhagen had been so battered that they could no longer offer effective resistance. 'The French fought bravely,' Nelson wrote later, 'but they could not have stood for one hour the fight which the Danes had supported for four.' By the time they struck their colours they had lost 1,700 officers and men killed and wounded, including Thurah of the *Infödsretten*, and Hauch of the *Kronborg*. For contrast the British casualties numbered 941, the worst sufferers being the considerably damaged *Monarch* and *Isis*.

The action was not, however, quite finished. When the British ships sent their boats away to take possession of their prizes, they were fired on, chiefly from the shore, but to some extent from the battered enemy ships.

Satisfied that he had completed the task which he had set himself, and averse to continuing a battle which could hazard Britain's ultimate purpose, the defeat of the Russian Fleet, an angry Nelson dispatched this note, under a flag of truce, to the Crown Prince of Denmark (later King Frederick VI) who was in overall command of Copenhagen's defences:

> Lord Nelson has instructions to spare Denmark when no longer resisting, but if the firing is continued on the part of Denmark Lord Nelson will be obliged to set on fire all the floating batteries he has taken without having the power of saving the brave Danes who have defended them.

It was addressed: 'To the Brothers of Englishmen, the Danes'.

Nelson has been unjustly criticized for this hastily written note. First, because he used the interlude following its despatch to make preparations for renewing the action, in particular for an assault on the Trekroner fort which the absence of the *Agamemnon*, *Bellona* and *Russell*, and Riou's compliance with Parker's recall, had prevented him taking earlier. Fremantle was right in saying that the note 'produced a cessation to the very severe battle, which was certainly as convenient for *us* as the enemy', but to say more than this is to confuse a flag of truce, which confers immunity only on its bearer and his escort, with an agreed general truce, or armistice, which Nelson could not be sure would be the outcome.

Those who criticize the wording of the note are, perhaps, on surer ground. On the evidence of Naples, Nelson's threat was no idle one, but the Crown Prince was so reluctant to believe that any British admiral would depart from the then accepted rules and courtesies of war, by renewing an attack on an enemy who had struck his colours, that he sent General Lindholm to ask for an explanation. And by the time Lindholm arrived onboard the *Elephant*, Hardy and Foley had cooled Nelson's temper: he was persuaded to give this reply:

> Lord Nelson's object in sending on shore a flag of truce is humanity; he therefore consents that hostilities shall cease till he can take his prisoners out of the prizes, and consents to land all the wounded Danes and to burn or remove his prizes. Lord Nelson, with humble duty to His Royal Highness, begs leave to say that he will ever esteem it the greatest victory he ever gained, if this flag of truce may be the happy forerunner of a lasting and happy union between my most gracious Sovereign and His Majesty the King of Denmark.

This was, however, a matter for negotiation with his Commander-in-Chief.

Nelson's more moderate tone sufficed to persuade the Crown Prince to accept the reality of his position, and to order a general cease fire. To quote one contemporary Danish authority: 'We cannot deny it, we are quite beaten. Our line of defence is destroyed. . . . The worst is the Trekroner battery can no longer be held.'

The cease fire did more than enable Nelson to take some 3,500 prisoners, to land the wounded, and to secure his prizes which, with the exception of Arenfeldt's 60-gunned *Holsteen*, proved to be beyond repair and had to be burnt. To quote Fremantle, Nelson

> was aware that our ships were cut to pieces, and it would be difficult . . .
> to get them out [of the King's Deep]. . . . [They] were so crippled, they
> would not steer. . . . We counted no less than six sail-of-the-line
> [including Nelson's and Graves's flagships], and the *Désirée* fast on
> shore. Luckily we had to contend with an enemy much beaten . . .
> otherwise all these ships must have been lost.

Hence Mahan's judgement: 'The battle was the severest and most doubtful he [Nelson] ever fought.'* None the less, for the second time in less than three years he had all but annihilated his enemy. As important, he had won a battle which, but for his insistence, would never have been fought, and which, but for his refusal to obey Parker's recall, might well have ended in disaster.

St Vincent (recently elevated from a viscountcy to an earldom) paid this just tribute:

> It is not given to us to command success: your Lordship and the
> gallant officers and men under your orders most certainly deserved it,
> and I cannot sufficiently express my admiration of the zeal and persever-
> ing courage with which this gallant enterprise was followed up,
> lamenting most sincerely the loss sustained in it. . . . The highest praise
> is due to your Lordship, and all under your command, who were
> actors in this glorious attempt.

How richly, then, did Nelson earn the viscountcy which was his tangible reward. But, unlike their generous reaction to the Nile, others at home, whose enmity was with the French, not the Danes, proved apathetic. Except for Graves, who was made a K.B., 'all under your command' received so little recognition that Nelson was moved to protest to the Lord Mayor that this was the first time that 'the smallest services rendered by either Navy, or Army had . . . [not been] noticed by the great City of

*Mahan's *Life of Nelson*.

London', to whom, after all, the reopening of trade with the Baltic was of prime importance.

Having rehoisted his flag in the *St George*, Nelson pressed Parker to go on into the Baltic to deal with the Russians and the Swedes. But his cautious Commander-in-Chief was determined first to ensure that, having forced open the door, it should remain so. The twenty-four hour truce must be extended into an armistice. Negotiations to achieve this were, as Nelson told Lindholm, Parker's responsibility; instead, just as he had left the fighting in Nelson's hands, so now did the Commander-in-Chief require him to do the talking. The velvet glove technique was of no avail. The Crown Prince feared the vengeance of Tsar Paul too much to yield to arguments that a restoration of friendly relations between Britain and Denmark were in the best interests of both countries. Nelson had to *demand* a sixteen weeks armistice – the time needed to act against the Reval squadron – sword in hand, a threat to bombard Copenhagen. The issue hung in the balance for six days, from 3 April when Nelson first landed in the capital, until the 9th.

For how much longer the Danish Crown Prince would have continued to resist; whether Parker would have authorized Nelson to bombard the capital; or whether Parker would have conceded Nelson's view that his fleet should go on to Reval without worrying so much about its means of exit from the Baltic – such questions were not destined to be answered. The scales were tipped by the news of a wholly unforeseen event that occurred on 24 March. A group of Russian officers, tired of Paul's wayward tyranny, had demanded his abdication and, when he refused, murdered him. With this removal of the keystone to the arch of the Armed Neutrality, the Crown Prince felt free to save his country from the consequence of a renewal of hostilities with Britain, whose eighteen ships-of-the-line still swung to their anchors within sight of his capital. He signed an armistice that was to last for fourteen weeks, after which hostilities would only be resumed 'upon giving fourteen days previous notice'. Throughout this time the Danish Navy's ships were to remain 'in their present . . . situation as to armament, equipment and hostile position, and the . . . Armed Neutrality shall, so far as it related to the cooperation of Denmark, be suspended'. And, in return for releasing all prisoners of war, Parker's ships were to be allowed to obtain supplies from any Danish port.

These terms having been conveyed speedily to London, St Vincent was required to send this grudging answer: 'Upon a consideration of all the circumstances, His Majesty has thought fit to approve.' Nelson, having

borne the brunt of talks which, but for his patient skill, must have broken
down before the arrival of the timely news from St Petersburg, could not
allow such thoughtless words to pass without protest: 'I am sorry that the
armistice is only approved under *all* considerations. . . . [I am] of opinion
that every part of *all* was to the advantage of our King and Country.' The
First Lord's reply gave honour where it was due: 'Your Lordship's whole
conduct, from your first appointment to this hour, is the subject of our
constant admiration. It does not become me to make comparisons: all
agree there is but one Nelson.'

Having been obliged to send the *Monarch*, and the *Isis* home for repairs,
Parker sailed on into the Baltic on 12 April with his fleet reduced to
seventeen sail-of-the-line. And one of these, Nelson's *St George*, was so
much delayed by the need to reduce her draught by removing some of
her guns before she could cross the shallows between Amager and Saltholm, that she was more than twenty miles from Parker's force when, off
Bornholm on the evening of the 15th, there came news of a Swedish
squadron being at sea. Nelson immediately ordered a boat alongside: to
quote an officer who went with him in it:

> His anxiety . . . lest the fleet should [engage the enemy] before he got
> onboard one of them . . . is beyond all conception. . . . It was [an]
> extremely cold [night], and I wished him to put on a great coat. . . .
> 'No, I am not cold; my anxiety for my country will keep me warm'. . . .
> The idea of going in a small boat, rowing six oars, without . . . anything
> to eat or drink, the distance about fifty leagues [*sic*] must convince the
> world that every other earthly consideration than that of serving his
> country was totally banished from his thoughts.

Since dawn on the 15th revealed no Swedish sail in sight, (numbering
only six sail-of-the-line, these had wisely returned to Karlskrona as soon
as they learned the strength of Parker's fleet) this incident would be
scarcely worth recording, but for its consequences. Nelson did not
manage to reach and rehoist his flag in the *Elephant* until midnight. As he
told Emma later,

> I rowed five hours in a bitter cold night. A cold struck me to the heart.
> On the 27th I had one of my terrible spasms of heart-stroke. . . . From
> that time to the end of May I brought up what everyone thought was
> my lungs, and I was emaciated more than you can conceive.

But ill-health attributable to his own carelessness was not Nelson's only
cross. He chaffed and fretted because Parker would not press on into the

Gulf of Finland, as the Government had ordered him to do, notwith-standing Paul's assassination. The ice which kept the Reval squadron in port must soon melt: nothing was more important than preventing these twelve ships-of-the-line from uniting with the rest of the Russian Fleet. When the spring allowed this to leave its winter quarters at Kronstádt, Parker would be powerless against a fleet more than twice the strength of his own.

But as with the Danes, the British Commander-in-Chief was chiefly concerned to ensure that his fleet would be able to withdraw safely from the Baltic. To him the small Swedish squadron in Karlskrona, was the greater danger. To neutralize it, he anchored his fleet off this port. And he was there when the 22nd brought news that the new Tsar, the liberal Alexander I, had ordered his ships to abstain from hostilities. With no concern for the larger issue, the need to obtain guarantees which would ensure an end to the Armed Neutrality, Parker promptly ordered his ships to weigh and return to Köje Bay, to the south of Copenhagen.

In this interlude the First Lord had time to study Parker's and Nelson's reports, and to appreciate the former's incapacity for his command. To quote from the diary of George Rose, Secretary of the Treasury:

> 22 April. Breakfasted with Lord St Vincent. . . . His Lordship entered in the late glorious victory at Copenhagen, and told me the merit of the attack rested solely with Lord Nelson, as Sir Hyde Parker had been decidedly adverse to the attempt being made . . . and that in the middle of the action Sir Hyde Parker had made the signal for discontinuing the engagement. . . . Lord St Vincent then added, 'For these and other courses . . . we have recalled Sir Hyde and Lord Nelson is to remain with the command.'

The First Lord's orders reached Köje Bay on 5 May. Parker sailed next day for England in the frigate *Blanche*, never to be employed again.

Freed from superior restraint, Nelson immediately sailed eastwards. 'My object,' he wrote, '*was* to get at Reval before the frost broke up at Kronstádt, that the twelve sail-of-the-line might be destroyed. I shall *now* go there as a friend, *but the two [Russian] fleets shall not form a junction*, if not already accomplished, unless my orders permit it.' On the 8th he detached Murray in the *Edgar*, with five other ships, to watch Karlskrona and ensure that the Swedish Admiral accepted his advice, that he would be wiser to remain in harbour than to risk a fight with a British squadron. Six days more and Nelson anchored the greater part of his fleet, eleven sail-of-the-line, off Reval. But he was too late – not of his own fault, but

Parker's. Just as he feared would happen, the ice had cleared on 29 April; the Reval squadron had sailed up the Gulf of Finland to Kron- stádt on 3 May.

The junction of the two Russian forces was, however, no longer significant. The new Tsar, having no wish to be a puppet manipulated to meet Bonaparte's ends, had already opened negotiations to end the Armed Neutrality. But, with characteristic Russian intransigence, Alexander and his Ministers would not have it supposed that they were submitting to a British fleet, even though its Admiral professed the friendliest intentions. Nelson had, after all, destroyed the fleet of their Danish ally. On 16 April Count Pahlen told him:

> The Tsar . . . does not consider [your arrival at Reval] compatible with the lively desire manifested by His Britannic Majesty to re-establish the good intelligence so long existing between the two Monarchies. The only guarantee of the loyalty of your intentions that His Majesty [the Tsar] can accept is the prompt withdrawal of the fleet under your command, and no negotiation . . . can take place so long as a naval force is in sight of his ports.

Nelson's self-control on receiving this threatening letter as the culmina- tion of his efforts to deal with the Reval squadron stands to his credit. According to Stewart,

> He appeared to be a good deal agitated by it but said little, and did not return an immediate reply. During dinner, however, he left the table, and in less than a quarter of an hour sent for his secretary to peruse a letter which . . . he had composed.

After pointing out that he had carefully refrained from bringing his whole fleet to Reval, Nelson wrote to Pahlen:

> My conduct . . . is so entirely different from what Your Excellency has expressed . . . that I have only to regret that my desire to pay a marked attention to His Imperial Majesty has been so entirely misunderstood. That being the case, I shall sail immediately into the Baltic.

In short, Nelson realized that it was better to swallow his own pride than risk turning an otherwise amenable Alexander against Britain; that unlike Copenhagen, this was not one of those occasions when a British battle fleet could ensure a favourable outcome to negotiations with a foreign power. To continue Stewart's words:

The signal for preparing to weigh was immediately made; the answer above-mentioned was sent onshore; and his Lordship caused the fleet . . . to stand as far to sea as was safe for that evening.

By the time Nelson returned to Köje Bay on 6 June he knew just how wise he had been to show such restraint: Russia and Sweden had dissolved the Armed Neutrality on 19 May.

Pitt's decision to order a British fleet back into the Mediterranean in May 1798, had quickly borne fruit: in less than three months Nelson destroyed France's maritime power in that sea and wrecked Bonaparte's plan to conquer India. The British Government's decision to send a fleet into the Baltic in March 1801, when coupled with Tsar Paul's assassination, garnered as rich a harvest: in as short a time Bonaparte's attempt to undermine Britain's only effective weapon against France's military power was set at nought. And, as in 1798, this triumph was Nelson's.

As a leader he had not only inspired his subordinates – 'What must Nelson think of us?'; he had dominated a superior whom he, fairly enough, criticized for 'his idleness . . . [there was] no criminality', without transgressing the tenets of naval discipline as he had done with Keith. He not only repeated his tactical skill, but proved that he could decisively defeat more determined fighters than the French. To quote Graves: 'Considering the disadvantages of navigation, the approach to the enemy, their vast numbers of guns and mortars on both land and sea, I do not think there ever was a bolder attack. . . . It was worthy of our gallant and enterprising little Hero of the Nile.' And unlike Naples, he displayed exceptional skill at the difficult art of diplomacy. In Addington's words: 'Lord Nelson has shown himself as wise as he is brave, and proved that there may be united in the same person the talents of the warrior and the statesman.' Above all, perhaps, his reiterated pleas to lose no time in reaching Reval, proved not only that he was a master of maritime strategy, but that he understood the significance of that vital principle of war, the maintenance of the aim.

Against these 'credits' must, however, be set the volatile temperament of his creative genius. The excitement of Copenhagen was followed by frustration at Parker's dilatory progress towards Reval. The exhilarating prospect of further action against the enemy was aborted by the likelihood that Paul's death would end Russia's hostility to Britain. It needed only the depression of ill-health after his night in the cold of an open boat, for Nelson's domestic worries to transcend all other thoughts. Parker's recall, and his own appointment as a commander-in-chief at the age of forty-two, gave him no satisfaction; it stopped him returning to England to take the sick leave which Parker had already approved.

Since Emma and Horatia were the magnets, not ambition and duty, Nelson applied to be relieved. It would have been very different, he told Troubridge, 'had the command been given me in February'; now 'any other man can as well look about him as Nelson'. 'The keen air of the North kills me.' 'I did not come to the Baltic with the design of dying a natural death.' To Emma he wrote: 'I am fixed to live a country life, and to have many (I hope) years of comfort, which, God knows, I never yet had – only moments of happiness. . . . I wish for happiness to be my reward, and not titles or money.' He wanted, too, to see his brother Maurice who was seriously ill and about to die.

St Vincent might be against giving Nelson the opportunity to return so soon to his scandalous life with the Hamiltons, but he could not be other than sympathetic to pleas that were reinforced by the testimony of the bearer of his letter, that Nelson was far from well. In mid-June Vice-Admiral Sir Charles Pole arrived in the Baltic, and on the 19th Nelson sailed for home. Six weeks later brought proof that his request to be relieved was ruled by logic as well as emotion; that after Reval there was no scope in the Baltic for a man of his exceptional talents. As soon as the end of July 1801 the Government agreed that a British fleet no longer served any useful purpose there, and Pole was ordered home.

CHRONOLOGICAL SUMMARY FOR CHAPTER VIII

EVENTS IN NELSON'S LIFE	DATE	RELATED EVENTS
	1800	
Leaves Leghorn for home with the Hamiltons, via Vienna, Prague and Dresden.	*13 July*	
Lands at Yarmouth.	*6 November*	
Reunited with Lady Nelson in London.	*8 November*	
	3 December	French defeat Austrians at Hohenlinden.
	5 December	Vaubois surrenders Valletta to Pigot.

EVENTS IN NELSON'S LIFE	DATE	RELATED EVENTS
	16 December	Denmark, Prussia, Russia and Sweden sign treaty reviving the Armed Neutrality.
	1801	
Promoted Vice-Admiral of the Blue.	*1 January*	
Leaves London – and Lady Nelson – for Torbay.	*13 January*	
Hoists flag in *San Josef*, 98, in Channel Fleet	*16 January*	
Nelson's and Emma's daughter Horatia born.	*29 January*	
	5 February	Addington succeeds Pitt as Prime Minister. St Vincent appointed First Lord. Cornwallis and Parker succeed St Vincent in Channel fleet.
Shifts flag to *St George*, 98.	*12 February*	
	2–6 March	Keith lands Abercromby's expeditionary force in Aboukir Bay.
Joins Parker at Yarmouth.	*6 March*	
Sails with Parker for the Baltic.	*12 March*	
Parker's fleet anchors off Kronborg.	*22 March*	
	24 March	Assassination of Tsar Paul: succeeded by Alexander I.
Parker's fleet passes into The Sound.	*30 March*	
Battle of Copenhagen.	*2 April*	
Signs armistice with Denmark.	*9 April*	
Parker's fleet leaves Copenhagen.	*12 April*	
Parker's fleet arrives Karlskrona.	*20 April*	
Parker's fleet returns to Köje Bay.	*25 April*	

EVENTS IN NELSON'S LIFE	DATE	RELATED EVENTS
	3 May	Russian squadron leaves Reval for Kronstádt.
Succeeds Parker as C-in-C.	*6 May*	
Leaves Köje Bay.	*7 May*	
Arrives Reval.	*14 May*	
Leaves Reval.	*16 May*	
	19 May	Armed Neutrality dissolved.
Created Viscount Nelson of the Nile and of Burnham Thorpe.	*22 May*	
Arrives Köje Bay.	*6 June*	
Relieved by Pole and sails for home.	*19 June*	
Lands at Yarmouth.	*1 July*	
British Baltic fleet sails for home.	*End of July*	
Lady Nelson writes last letter to her husband which is returned 'unread'.	*18 December*	

IX

Boulogne and Merton
1801-1803

Having landed at Yarmouth on 1 July 1801, Nelson hurried to join the Hamiltons at the Burford Bridge posting inn (today a flourishing hotel) near Dorking, twenty-five miles to the south of London. But he did not enjoy the peace of this beauty spot under Surrey's Box Hill for very long. His wish to 'live a country life' with Emma could not be granted: St Vincent – and England – had need of him. As soon as 20 July he was summoned to Whitehall.

Austria's defeat at Hohenlinden had left the Emperor Francis II with no alternative but to sue for peace. When the Treaty of Lunéville ended the Second Coalition on 9 February 1801, Bonaparte had subdued all France's enemies except for two. He dealt with one of these by pressing Spain to declare war on Portugal, which forced her to sign a peace treaty at Badajoz as soon as 6 June. But Britain presented a problem of a different order; her sea power, which had wrested Malta from France's grasp, played a major part in dissolving the Armed Neutrality of the North, and seemed likely to compel the *Armée d'Orient* to surrender its hold on Egypt, appeared to be an insurmountable obstacle. How then could Bonaparte persuade the British to negotiate the peace he needed in order to consolidate his position at home against those whom he had antagonized by his arbitrary seizure of power – the Royalists who wished to restore the Bourbons, and the Jacobins to whom his autocratic régime was the antithesis of their revolutionary principles?

France's resources were too strained for him to invade England, even if it were possible for his Fleet to escort an army across the Narrow Seas. The alternative was to *threaten* such an operation, in the hope of frightening the British into coming to terms. And to deceive them into supposing that he meant business, he moved troops into camps in northern France, and assembled a flotilla of small craft, supposedly to embark them, in Boulogne under Rear-Admiral Louis de Latouche-Tréville, among the ablest of his flag officers. News of these preparations soon reached London – Bonaparte saw to that – where the Government ordered urgent counter-measures. These included the formation of a Squadron on a Particular Service – a force of frigates, gun-vessels, bombs, floating batteries, and other small craft 'for the defence against invasion of the coast of England', from Orfordness to Beachy Head. And to allay public alarm, the First Lord chose for its commander the nation's hero, the certain victor of the Nile and Copenhagen.*

Nelson's reaction to this fresh call to duty was modest. 'I have seen Lord St Vincent,' he wrote to Addington, 'and submit to your and his partiality. Whilst my health will allow . . . every exertion of mine shall be used to merit the continuance of your esteem.' 'Exertion' was no idle word. On 25 July he completed a long memorandum from which these abridged extracts not only explain the task that faced him but illustrate his sure grasp of its solution:

The enemy's object *ought* to be getting on shore as speedily as possible. The dangers of a navigation of forty-eight hours appear to be an insur-mountable objection to rowing from Boulogne to the coast of Essex. It is therefore most probable the French are coming from Boulogne, Calais and even Le Havre to land in Sussex, or the lower ports of Flanders to land in Essex or Suffolk. The enemy will also create a diversion by sailing her Combined Fleet [from Brest, etc.]; and either sailing, or creating an appearance of sailing, of the Dutch Fleet.

Supposing that 40,000 men are destined for this attack; 20,000 will land on the west side of Dover, and the same number on the east side. Supposing 200 or even 250 craft are collected at Boulogne to carry them. In calm weather, they might row over in twelve hours. At the same instant, the same number of troops would be rowed out of Dunkirk, Ostend, etc. These are the great objects to attend to from Dover and the Downs. When the enemy row out, all our vessels and boats must meet them as soon as possible: if not strong enough for the attack, they must keep them company till a favourable opportunity offers. If a

*St Vincent's choice of a flag officer so senior for an appointment which would otherwise have been filled by a junior one, was also motivated by a desire to save Nelson's reputation from public scandal by removing him from the Hamilton household.

breeze springs up, our ships are to deal *destruction*; but should it remain calm, the moment the enemy touch our shore our flotilla must attack as much as they can. The bows of our flotilla will be opposed to their unarmed sterns, and British courage will never allow one Frenchman to leave the beach.

A great number of Deal and Dover boats should be off Boulogne, to give notice of the direction taken by the enemy. Vessels in the Channel can signal intelligence to our shores. A flotilla of gun-boats and flat-boats should be stationed between Orfordness and North Foreland; and a third in Hollesley Bay. The floating batteries are stationed in the proper positions for defending the different channels, and the smaller vessels will have the support of the stationed [guard] ships.

The moment of the enemy's movement from Boulogne is to be considered as the movement of the enemy from Dunkirk. Supposing it be calm, our flotillas are to be rowed, and the heavy craft towed, those near Margate three or four leagues to the north of North Foreland, those from Hollesley Bay a little approaching the centre division but keeping an eye towards Solebay, the centre division to advance half-way between the two. When the enemy's flotilla can be seen, our divisions to unite ready to execute such orders as may be necessary. For this purpose, men with confidence in each other should be looked for, that no jealousy may creep into any man's mind, but all be animated with the desire of preventing the descent of the enemy on our coasts.

Floating batteries are not to be moved, for the tide may prevent their resuming the stations assigned to them. They are on no account to be neglected, even should the enemy surround them; they must rely on support, and reflect that their gallant conduct may prevent the mischievous designs of the enemy. The moment the enemy touch our coast, they are to be attacked by every man afloat and on shore: this must be perfectly understood. *Never fear the event*.

These are the rude ideas of the moment for a sea plan of defence for London; but other parts may be menaced if the Brest fleet, and those from Rochefort and Holland put to sea. I feel confident that these will meet the same fate which has always attended them, yet their sailing will facilitate the passage of their flotilla as they will suppose our attention will be diverted to the fleets.

St Vincent approved this appreciation in time for Nelson to hoist his flag in the frigate *Unité* at Sheerness on the 27th. 'In the short time we were [there],' wrote Commander Edward Parker, 'he gave orders for thirty of the ships under his command, made everyone pleased, filled them with emulation, and set them all on the *qui vive*.' In forty-eight hours Nelson was on his way by road to Deal where in the Downs he hoisted his flag in the 32-gunned frigate *Medusa*. In her he was soon off Boulogne with some thirty bombs, reporting to St Vincent on 3 August:

> I was in hopes that the wind could have . . . enabled . . . the bombs [to] have a good knock at the mole and vessels outside it, but the wind falling nearly to a calm . . . I called the bombs off after they had fired ten or twelve shells . . . without any effect. . . . But we have ascertained that we can bombard the vessels at proper times of tide . . . and wind . . . with great facility. . . . I hope the wind will come westerly, when we can . . . try the effect of shells. If it does not . . ., on Captain Nichols' arrival I shall leave this business to . . . him . . . and get back to our own coast and arrange our . . . defence, or . . . be ready to assault the scoundrels should they dare to come over.

Next day Nelson added:

> The wind being at NE, the bombs anchored at half-past five abreast of the town. What damage has been done cannot be ascertained . . . inside the [mole]. On the outside two large floating batteries are sunk, and one large gun-brig cut her cables and run on shore where she lies abandoned. . . . Boulogne is certainly not a very pleasant place this morning, but it is not my wish to injure the poor inhabitants, and the town is spared as much as the nature of the service will admit. Very little damage has been done to our bombs. . . . P.S. One or two more gun-vessels are destroyed since I finished my letter.*

Nelson returned to Margate on 12 August well assured that his own force 'is perfect and possesses so much zeal that I only want to catch that Bonaparte on the water'. Since 'our first defence is close to the enemy's ports', and because 'no embarkation of troops can take place in Boulogne . . . the ports of Flushing and Flanders are more likely places to embark men than Calais, Boulogne or Dieppe', he proposed an assault on Flushing for which he would need 5,000 troops. But St Vincent hesitated to agree because of the difficulties of navigating this mouth of the Scheldt. So Nelson decided to make a fresh attack on the Boulogne flotilla, not this time by a bombardment with only limited results but (in accordance with the philosophy, 'it is annihilation that the country wants, not merely a splendid victory') one in which 'the business is not to be considered as

*RA.10332.

finished . . . until the whole flotilla be either taken or wholly annihilated, for there must not be the smallest cessation until their destruction is completely finished'.

Arriving off the port on 15 August, all the boats from Nelson's force were ordered to assemble round the *Medusa* at 10.30 pm. Forty-eight of them, manned by picked officers and men armed with cutlasses, axes, grapnels and 'combustibles', were divided into four divisions under Commanders Edward Parker, Isaac Colgrave, Philip Somerville and Richard Jones. Eleven more, under Commander John Conn, mounted mortars. One hour later, at a signal from the flagship, all headed shorewards under muffled oars, for what was designed to be a simultaneous surprise assault, under covering mortar fire, around 1.0 am, which would cut out, or destroy Latouche-Tréville's twenty-four gun-vessels which he had moored in line, secured bow to stern, to seaward of the mole and pier, and the flat-boats and other craft lying inside them.

Why, after his disastrous failure at Santa Cruz did Nelson plan such an operation? To recall the success of Rodney's comparable attack on Le Havre in 1759 is no answer. As at Tenerife, he ignored the obstacles of darkness and a strong current; he imagined that the enemy would be asleep; he underestimated their determination to resist. Moreover, he did not know that Latouche-Tréville had secured his vessels with chains instead of the usual ropes. To claim, as Nelson did, that it was all-important to seize any and every opportunity for attacking the enemy, is no excuse. In truth he was the victim of one of his great qualities. To be successful a naval commander must have confidence in himself and in his ships and men; he may, too, take calculated risks when a rich prize is at stake. But he must not fall into the traps of overconfidence, of discounting his enemy, of hazarding his force when, as in this case, the prize is known to be small since by now he realized that Bonaparte had no real intention of invading Britain. In all the circumstances it is, indeed, remarkable that Nelson did not, as at Santa Cruz, compound his errors by leading this assault on Boulogne himself, except that he may have felt that, with only one eye and one arm, he was no longer fitted for such a strenuous task.

In the event, Parker gave a premature alarm by attacking the brigs *Etna* and *Vulcan* as early as 12.30 am: both were so stoutly defended that he was compelled to retire after his division had suffered sixty-three casualties. By the time Colgrave made his attack an hour later, the enemy was fully alert: his division was repulsed with five killed and twenty-nine wounded despite the covering fire provided by Conn's mortars. Somerville's boats were swept so far to the east that it was near dawn before they attacked and carried a French brig, only to find that, for lack of any appliance to cut her securing chains, they could not remove her before a hail of enemy fire forced them to withdraw with as many as eighteen killed and fifty-five wounded. As for Jones's division, this failed to reach the enemy at all before daylight obliged him to retire, albeit without loss.

In addition to suffering forty-four killed and 126 wounded, the British lost twelve of their boats. No French craft was taken or sunk; they had, moreover, only ten killed and thirty wounded. In short, victory went to Latouche-Tréville: Nelson suffered a bloody defeat.

> I am sorry to tell you [St Vincent] that I have not succeeded in bringing out or destroying the enemy's flotilla moored in the . . . harbour of Boulogne. . . . The most astonishing bravery was evinced by many of our officers and men. . . . No person can be blamed for sending them to the attack but myself. . . . All behaved well, and it was their misfortune to be sent on a service which the precautions of the enemy rendered impossible.

In these words Nelson accepted full responsibility for his defeat, but he would have been more honest had he also admitted his failure to remember Tenerife which had, after all, lost him an arm, and all but cost him his life.

Fortunately this defeat was of no real significance for Britain; nor, had the action been successful, would it have achieved much beyond, perhaps, angering Bonaparte to an extent that might have deflected his desire to negotiate peace. Nelson, though grieved, was not discouraged: Boulogne was only a side-show; he had not lost a vital action with the enemy's battle fleet. He again considered an attack on Flushing, reconnoitering its approaches on 24 August to see for himself whether St Vincent's doubts were justified. His subsequent report was underscored by his experience at Boulogne: 'I cannot but admire Captain Owen's zeal . . . to get at the enemy, but I am afraid it has made him overleap sandbanks and tides. . . . We cannot do impossibilities . . . and I think I can discriminate between the impracticable and the fair prospect of success.'

By the end of August, Bonaparte's 'paper invasion' had achieved its purpose: Addington's envoys were negotiating peace. To avoid prejudicing the outcome Nelson could undertake no further offensive operations. From the crest of the wave of elation to which the prospects of action always carried him, inactivity now plunged him into the trough of depression. His thoughts were again dominated by Emma and his health: he asked to be relieved of his command. The First Lord replied that this was premature. Reluctant to think ill of St Vincent, Nelson supposed

Troubridge to be the evil influence who required him to stay in the Downs rather than allow him to rejoin the Hamiltons. 'I have been so *rebuffed*, that my spirits are gone, and the *great* Troubridge has . . . *cowed* . . . Nelson. . . . I shall never forget it.' He was, in truth, jealous of an officer who, from being under his command in the Mediterranean, was now, as a Member of the Board, his superior. Nor was the friendship which the two men had once enjoyed destined to be renewed: when Troubridge left the Admiralty, it was to hoist his flag as Commander-in-Chief East Indies – where tragedy ended his career: in February 1807 his flagship, the *Blenheim*, foundered with all her crew.

Since the Admiralty would not grant Nelson leave, the Hamiltons came to stay at an hotel in Deal. For the fortnight they were there in September he was happy: with Murray's chain of telegraph stations* to bring him speedy warning of any threatening move by the French, he could safely relax ashore. But when they left for London on the 20th he wrote: 'No Emma. . . . My heart will break. I am in silent distraction. . . . My dearest wife, how can I bear our separation. . . . I am so low I cannot hold up my head.' He showed much emotion, too, when his friend Parker died of the wound inflicted on him in the attack on Boulogne. But this time of trial lasted for little more than a month. On 1 October Addington's envoys signed an armistice. The news reached Nelson on the 4th: 'Thank God, it is peace!' he exclaimed – although St Vincent would not grant him leave until hostilities were formally ended on the 22nd.

That evening Nelson set out to join the Hamiltons at Merton, a village seven miles south of Charing Cross which has long since been absorbed into England's sprawling capital. For practical purposes this was the end of his command of a Squadron on a Particular Service, although his flag continued to fly until 10 April 1802, a fortnight after a winter's anxiety over Bonaparte's real intentions was ended by the Treaty of Amiens signed on 25 March.

This was 'a peace of which everyone was glad and nobody proud'. Of her hard-won conquests in a war that had lasted for all of eight years Britain retained only Trinidad and Ceylon: France kept the territory that is now Belgium, with the frontier of the Rhine. And Nelson was among those who had no illusions about the future:

> We have made peace with the French despotism, and we will, I hope, adhere to it whilst the French continue in due bounds; but whenever they overstep that and usurp a power that would degrade Europe, then

*Described on p. 81.

I trust we shall join Europe in crushing her ambition; then I would with pleasure go forth and risk my life to put down the detestable power of France.

He was to be allowed little more than a year after Amiens before being required to fulfil this pledge.

Since this book is a study of Nelson as a naval commander, not a biography of the man, little need be written of the period from October 1801 to May 1803, of which he spent the first six months on extended leave and the rest on half-pay. Except for a summer tour in 1802 of Wales by way of Oxford, where Nelson received the City's freedom and the University's Doctorate of Civil Law, the *tria juncta in uno* lived in Merton Place, 'the Farm' as Nelson called it, which Emma had found to satisfy his longing for a country home of his own, but within easy reach of London, and which Davison helped him to buy in September 1801 with the generous loan needed by a man who had become accustomed to living beyond his means. Like his birthplace at Burnham Thorpe, time has long since failed to preserve Merton Place for posterity, but several contemporary accounts of how Nelson lived there with the Hamiltons have survived. According to Lord Minto:

> The whole establishment and way of life are such as to make me angry, as well as melancholy; but ... I do not think myself obliged to quarrel with him for his weakness, though nothing shall ever induce me to give the smallest countenance to Lady Hamilton. She looks ultimately to the chances of marriage, as Sir William will not be long in her way, and she probably indulges a hope that she may survive Lady Nelson. . . . Meanwhile she and Sir William . . . are living with him at his expense. She is in high looks, but more immense than ever. The love she makes to Nelson is not only ridiculous but disgusting. . . . The whole house . . . [is] covered with nothing but pictures of her and him . . . and . . . of his naval actions, coats-of-arms, pieces of plate in his honour, the flag-staff of the *Orient*, etc. – an excess of vanity. . . . If it was Lady Hamilton's house there might be a pretence for it; to make his own house a mere looking glass to view himself all day is bad taste.

In sharp contrast, Nelson's nephew, George Matcham, without attempting to 'defend his one great error', described him as

> remarkable for a demeanour quiet, sedate and unobtrusive, anxious to give pleasure to anyone about him. . . . He delighted in quiet conver-

sation, through which occasionally ran an undercurrent of pleasantry,
not unmixed with caustic wit. At his table he was the least heard among
the company, and so far from being the hero of his own tale, I never
heard him voluntarily refer to any of [his] great actions. . . . A man of
more temperate habits could not . . . have been found. . . . He always
looked what he was – a gentleman. . . . He was, it is true, a sailor, and
one of a warm and generous disposition . . . [but] he was not 'a rude
and boisterous captain of the sea'.

And this favourable portrait is echoed by Miss Lancaster, the Vicar of
Merton's daughter:

I cannot refrain from informing you of his [Nelson's] unlimited charity
and goodness. . . . His frequently expressed desire was, that none . . .
should want or suffer affliction that he could alleviate; and this . . . he
did with a most liberal hand, always desiring that it should not be
known from whence it came. His residence at Merton was a continued
course of charity and goodness, setting such an example of propriety
and regularity that there are few who could not be benefited by following it.

Despite their contradictions both pictures are true. Minto was among
those who could never forgive 'the shocking injury done to Lady
Nelson': Miss Lancaster was of the pure to whom all things are pure.
And many a lesser man than Nelson, with religious convictions as strong,
has striven through charity to reconcile himself with God for his inability
to obey His most difficult commandment.

The reality was, perhaps, best expressed by Hamilton:

I have passed the last forty years of my life in the hurry and bustle . . .
attendant on a public character. I am arrived at the age when some
repose is . . . necessary and I promised myself a quiet home . . .
[sensibly admitting] when I married that I should be superannuated
when my wife would be in her full beauty and vigour. . . . That time is
arrived and we must make the best of it for the comfort of both parties.
Unfortunately our tastes . . . are very different. I by no means wish to
live in solitary retreat, but to have seldom less than twelve or fourteen at
table . . . is coming back to what was become so irksome to me in
Italy. . . . The whole attention of my wife is given to Lord N . . . but I
know how very uncomfortable it would make his Lordship, our best
friend, if a separation should take place and am therefore determined
to do all in my power to prevent such an extremity, which would be

essentially detrimental to all parties, but would be more sensibly felt by our dear friend than by us. . . . Therefore let us bear and forbear for God's sake.*

At Merton, on 26 April 1802, Nelson mourned the death of his ailing father, whose last months were saddened by his son's desertion of the neurotic Fanny – but declined to attend the funeral for fear of meeting her there. The ageing Hamilton died almost a year later, on 6 April 1803. 'The world never lost a more upright and accomplished gentleman', wrote Nelson – nor, be it added, one of more generous spirit, judged by this last codicil to his will: 'Madame Le Brun's picture of Emma† . . . I give to my dearest friend Lord Nelson . . . the most virtuous, loyal and truly great character I ever met with. God bless him, and shame fall on those who do not say Amen.' But Nelson was under no illusion that he deserved such a tribute: he expressed this note to his neighbour, Mr Perry, who was editor of the *Morning Chronicle*:

Our dear Sir William left this world at ten minutes past ten this morning in Lady Hamilton's and my arms. Her attentions to him to the last, and altogether for near twelve years, have been such as to call forth all our admiration for this excellent woman. *As I should wish neither to have too much nor too little said in your paper on this occasion, I entreat that I may see you as soon as possible.‡*

The italicized sentence reflects his concern that the newspapers would seize the occasion to rekindle criticism of his illicit passion. He had so far swallowed the unhappy truth, that no public figure can leave his wife and flaunt a mistress in her place without putting his entire reputation and career in jeopardy, to the extent of ensuring that his and Emma's visits to Mrs Gibson, to see his adored Horatia, were shrouded in secrecy. Such discretion stilled the waves of censure for so long as Hamilton lived; but whether he could have survived the fury of the storm that must have been unleashed had he continued to live with her after her husband's death is another matter. Fortunately, this situation did not arise: within the month he was given an appointment which took him away from Emma for all but one brief period two years later.

At Merton Nelson did much more than enjoy entertaining his many

---

*In this letter Hamilton also wrote: 'I well know the purity of Lord N's friendship for Emma', but it is impossible to accept that he really believed this.
†Now in the Wallace Collection.
‡RA. Add 21/14.

friends in some style amid the peace of the Surrey countryside. He remembered those who had fought with him at Copenhagen: in a prolonged correspondence with Addington, with St Vincent, and with the Lord Mayor of London, he contended that their services deserved to be rewarded with a special medal such as had been struck for those who were with him at the Nile. He argued in vain: a Copenhagen medal would have to be awarded to the Commander-in-Chief, and Parker had done nothing to deserve this honour. Nelson showed his anger at this decision by refusing to accept the thanks of the City of London in June 1802, for defending the country against invasion, and three months later declined an invitation to dinner with these words: 'Never, till the City of London think justly of the merits of my brave companions of 2 April, can I . . . receive any attention from the City of London.'

More important, Nelson did not drive into London, to spend a night or more in the Hamilton's town house in Piccadilly, only to visit Horatia. As early as 29 October 1801, he took his seat in the House of Lords, thereafter speaking whenever opportunity offered on both naval affairs and foreign policy. Under the first head he repaid Saumarez, now a rear-admiral, for his loyal support during the Nile campaign with a generous eulogy for his two hard won actions against Rear-Admiral the Comte de Linois' more powerful squadron off Algeciras on 6 and 12 July 1801. Under the latter head he seconded the Address from the Throne on 16 November 1802, with this clarion call:

I, my Lords, have in different countries, seen much of the miseries of war. I am, therefore, in my inmost soul, a man of peace. Yet I would not, for the sake of any peace, consent to sacrifice one jot of England's honour. Our honour is inseparably combined with our general interest. Hitherto there has been nothing greater known on the Continent than the faith, the untainted honour, the generous public sympathies, the high diplomatic influence, the commerce, the grandeur, the resistless power, the unconquerable valour of the British nation. . . . The advantages of such a reputation are not to be lightly brought into hazard. . . . As the nation was pleased with that sincere spirit of peace with which the late treaty [of Amiens] was negotiated, so, now that a restless and unjust ambition in those with whom we desired sincere amity has given a new alarm, the country will rather prompt the Government to assert its honour, than need to be roused by such measures of vigorous defence as the exigency of the times may require.

Churchillian in their eloquence, such sentiments are those of a great leader who had come to terms with his chief weakness, who was no longer 'aflame with passion'* for a woman who had so easily claimed a heart sickened by Fanny's complaining and reproach.

The Treaty of Amiens had gained for Bonaparte more than a peace that sealed France's dominant position in Europe: his personal prestige was so much enhanced that in August 1802 he was nominated Consul for life. But he was content with neither: two and a half years were to elapse before he satisfied his lust for personal power, before France, which had suffered so much to be rid of a king, acquired an emperor; but he showed his other ambition, to extend his country's control of other lands, as soon as August 1802 when he annexed the island of Elba. Nor was this all: in the next month he incorporated Piedmont into France without compensating the King of Sardinia; in October he ordered an invasion of Switzerland which brought that country under his domination in February 1803; and, a direct threat to Britain, he annexed the Netherlands.

Realizing that a Neapolitan garrison would provide no safeguard for the freedom of the Knights of St John, a prudent Pitt persuaded Addington to delay implementing the clause in the treaty that required British troops to be withdrawn from Malta. This impediment to his rapacity so incensed Bonaparte that, to quote Thiers, 'he was mastered by a patriotic and at the same time personal wrath, and from now on to conquer, humiliate, trample down and annihilate England became the passion of his life'. On 11 March 1803 he ordered the construction of an armada of landing craft to form invasion flotillas at Dunkirk and Cherbourg, and told Decrès, who was still his Minister of Marine: 'I want a memorandum on how we can inflict the greatest damage on British commerce in the event of a naval war now.' Two days later the French Fleet was ordered to make ready for sea. Two more uneasy months and the threat to Britain's continued existence as a sovereign independent state, and to her overseas trade and territories, was clear. On 12 May Lord Whitworth, British Ambassador in Paris, demanded the withdrawal of French troops from the Netherlands and Switzerland and claimed the right to garrison Malta for the next ten years. When Bonaparte replied that the island must be ceded to the Tsar, as titular Grand Master, Whitworth left France; and on 16 May 1803 Britain declared war. She was to stand alone for more than two years, until the autumn of 1805, with her fleet the only bastion against Bonaparte's ambition to gain dominion of the world.

Like France Britain had two months to plan for this renewal of hostilities. As early as 8 March Nelson heard the King ask Parliament to adopt

*One translation of the final words of I Corinthians, VII, 9.

measures to counter the military preparations which were reported from ports across the Narrow Seas. As of old he immediately answered the call of duty, with its chance for further glory; his doubts about his health and his yearning for a quiet country life with Emma were thrust aside. 'Whenever it is necessary, I am *your* Admiral', he scribbled to Addington. St Vincent chose him to succeed Rear-Admiral Sir Richard Bickerton in the Mediterranean. Since the Admiralty could make immediately available to Admiral the Hon. William Cornwallis commanding the Channel fleet, only ten ships-of-the-line to watch the thirty-four French sail in Brest and its neighbouring ports, there was no immediate possibility of reinforcing the nine British ships-of-the-line east of the Straits to counter the same number in Toulon, now under the redoubtable Latouche-Tréville, except by sending 'an officer of splendour', whose reputation was in itself worth at least two ships-of-the-line.

Nelson sought no greater honour. 'The Government cannot be more anxious for my departure than I am, if war, to go', he told St Vincent. His commission as Commander-in-Chief was, however, delayed until the actual declaration. He left immediately for Portsmouth where, on 18 May, Hood's old flagship, the 100-gunned *Victory* hoisted the blue ensign at her stern and broke Nelson's flag as Vice-Admiral of the Blue at the fore. Two days later Captain Samuel Sutton, 'a good man but not so active as Hardy', made all plain sail and, with Hardy's frigate *Amphion* in company, headed out of Spithead for a rendezvous with the Channel fleet, where Nelson was to transfer the *Victory* to Cornwallis's command. But off Ushant on the 22nd Nelson found no sign of his superior, who had been blown from his station by a gale. For twenty-four hours he waited fretting at the delay; then he transferred his flag to the *Amphion* and pressed on, leaving the *Victory* to await Cornwallis's return.

He reached Gibraltar on 3 June, to stay for only twenty-four hours before heading east for Malta where he arrived on the 15th. He expected to find his fleet in Valletta's Grand Harbour; he learned instead that Bickerton had 'very judiciously' sailed for Toulon. But though Nelson steered for the Straits of Messina as soon as the 17th, light and contrary winds delayed his meeting with Bickerton until 8 July. Not until then did he assume effective command of his fleet, the 80-gun *Gibraltar* and *Canopus*, the *Belleisle, Donegal, Kent, Renown, Superb* and *Triumph*, which were 74s, and the *Monmouth*, 64 – nine ships-of-the-line in all – plus a handful of frigates and other cruising vessels; and with this small force which was no stronger than Latouche-Tréville's, begin the most arduous task of his career.

CHRONOLOGICAL SUMMARY FOR CHAPTER IX

EVENTS IN NELSON'S LIFE	DATE	RELATED EVENTS
	1801	
	9 February	Treaty of Lunéville ends Second Coalition.
	2–6 March	Keith lands Abercromby's expedition in Egypt.
	6 June	Treaty of Badajoz suspends Portugal's alliance with Britain.
Lands at Yarmouth. Joins Hamiltons at Burford Bridge.	*1 July*	
	6–12 July	Saumarez in action with de Linois' squadron off Algeciras.
Hoists flag in command of Squadron on a Particular Service.	*27 July*	
Bombards Boulogne flotilla.	*3–4 August*	
Cutting-out attack on Boulogne flotilla.	*15–16 August*	
	2 September	*Armée d'Orient* surrenders Alexandria, subsequently evacuating Egypt.
Buys Merton Place.	*September*	
	1 October	Britain signs armistice with France.
Granted extended leave: joins Hamiltons at Merton.	*22 October*	End of hostilities between Britain and France.
Takes seat as Viscount in House of Lords.	*29 October*	
Returns Lady Nelson's last letter unread.	*18 December*	
	1802	
	25 March	Treaty of Amiens ends war between Britain and France.
Placed on half-pay after formally striking flag in command of Squadron on a Particular Service.	*10 April*	
Father dies.	*26 April*	

EVENTS IN NELSON'S LIFE	DATE	RELATED EVENTS
	2 August	Bonaparte proclaimed Consul for life.
	1803	
	11 March	Bonaparte denounces Britain's failure to evacuate Malta and orders formation of invasion flotillas.
Hamilton dies.	*6 April*	
Appointed Commander-in-Chief Mediterranean.	*16 May*	Britain declares war on France.
Hoists flag in *Victory*, 100.	*18 May*	
Sails from Spithead.	*20 May*	
Transfers flag to frigate *Amphion* off Ushant.	*23 May*	
Arrives Gibraltar.	*3 June*	
Arrives Malta.	*15 June*	
Joins fleet off Toulon.	*6 July*	

X

A Long Watch and a Long Chase
1803-1805

The British reader may suppose the Mediterranean* to have been a peaceful sea in which trade flowed unhindered during the period October 1801 to May 1803. The American reader will know otherwise. George Washington, and his successor John Adams, managed to steer the fledgling United States on a neutral course after the outbreak of war in Europe in 1793, except for a few months in 1798. Talleyrand's tactless treatment of Adams' envoys then provoked a series of naval actions in which a newborn United States Fleet was sufficiently successful to induce Bonaparte, on gaining supreme power as First Consul, to open negotiations to avert more general hostilities. But four smaller countries, Morocco, Algeria, Tunis and Tripoli, were not so tractable. Their rulers exacted 'presents' from nations trading in the Mediterranean in return for freedom from piracy by these Barbary States. But, as with other blackmailers, they could not rest content with their bargains; from time to time they demanded more.

The United States was so threatened by the Pasha of Tripoli in 1801. Failing to obtain satisfaction, this despot declared a war in which his neighbours joined. And this conflict in which America's powerful frigates won the spurs which the British Navy found so sharp in 1812, lasted until August 1805. Thus, for the whole of the time that Nelson was in the Mediterranean, the United States Navy did him the service of ensuring that he was not seriously distracted from his prime enemy, the French (unlike Hood's experience with the Bey of Tunis in 1793), by having also to deal with the Barbary States.

*See front endpapers for the area of operations covered by much of this chapter.

The Tsar's lack of enthusiasm for the war also eased Nelson's task. The greater part of the Russian fleet was kept within the Black Sea. The single frigate sent to guard the Ionian Islands in 1803 could be ignored. And when she was reinforced by several ships-of-the-line in July 1804, after Alexander I's delayed declaration of war on Britain, Nelson correctly appreciated that Rear-Admiral Sorókin would be no more active as an enemy than Ushakóv had been as an ally. He was not, therefore, tempted to weaken his battle fleet by sending a detachment into the eastern Mediterranean.

America and Russia thus coincidentally enabled Nelson to concentrate on his prime purpose, to thwart Bonaparte's insatiable appetite for conquest. He must safeguard Malta, now 'a most important outwork to India, that . . . will ever give us great influence in the Levant, and indeed all the southern parts of Italy. . . . I hope we shall never give it up', and Gibraltar, whose importance as a base was accentuated now that Portugal denied Britain use of the Tagus, especially against the day when Spain, reduced to virtual vassalage of France by the previous conflict, might drop her pretence of neutrality and join the war. He had to prevent a French army of 15,000 men which, in addition to occupying the northern half of Italy, had penetrated down the Adriatic coast as far as Brindisi and Taranto, from overruning the remainder of the Two Sicilies.

For two of these tasks Nelson's fleet supported existing British garrisons. For the third he asked for 10,000 British troops to help Neapolitan resistance in Calabria, 'though we must not risk Sicily too far in trying to save Naples'. But no such force was available: Abercromby's army had already returned from Egypt to England where every man was needed to protect the homeland against Bonaparte's threatened invasion. This left Nelson with the French fleet as his 'first objective . . . ever to be [kept] in check; and if they put to sea to have force enough to *annihilate them*. That would keep the Two Sicilies free from any attack by sea.' And since his fleet was no stronger than Latouche-Tréville's, he had to keep it together. He spared only one ship-of-the-line to lie in Naples Bay for King Ferdinand's protection. But this was never his own flagship; without the Hamiltons – without Emma (to whom he wrote, when passing '*dear* Naples', that 'the view of Vesuvius calls so many circumstances to my mind that it almost overpowers my feelings') – his judgement was not betrayed by a belief that he must *himself* ensure the safety of Queen Maria Carolina. Otherwise, for the protection of trade against privateers, and to guard the Straits of Messina and the entrance to the Adriatic, he deployed only cruisers based on Malta and Gibraltar.

Even so, the British fleet was at a serious disadvantage. The French lay in one of their principal ports, backed by all the resources of a dock-yard. The ships that Nelson inherited from Bickerton had been long away from home. 'As far as outside show goes,' he told St Vincent, '[they] look very well; but they complain of their bottoms and are very short of men' – by as many as a hundred in each ship-of-the-line. 'They are distressed for almost every article. They have entirely eaten up their stores. . . . I have applications . . . for surveys on most of their sails and running rigging, which cannot be complied with, as there is neither cordage nor sails to replace [them].' But though he pressed for fresh vessels to be sent from England, it was some time before enough could be manned for any to be spared for the Mediterranean; before he was joined by the *Canopus*, flying the flag of Rear-Admiral George Campbell, and the 100-gun *Royal Sovereign*. Nelson did, however, regain his proper flagship before this; as soon as 30 July he was able to return to the *Victory* (taking Hardy from the *Amphion* to be her captain), Sutton having learned that Corn-wallis did not require her.

As serious, if not more so observing the condition of his ships, Nelson had no base from which to keep a watch on the enemy. Genoa and Leg-horn were in enemy hands; Minorca had reverted to Spain; Naples and Palermo, not to mention Malta and Gibraltar, were too far from Toulon. He resolved this dilemma in a way that no admiral had attempted before. 'I have made up my mind never to go into port till after the battle, if they [the French] make me wait a year.' For so long, and if needs be more, he would keep his fleet continuously at sea so that Latouche-Tréville could be brought to action whenever he might sortie from Toulon. To achieve this, he organized storeships to bring supplies from Gibraltar and Malta, from the Two Sicilies and Sardinia whose rulers were benevolently neutral to Britain, and from ports in Spain where British gold spoke louder than Madrid's preoccupation with placating Bonaparte's demands.

Keeping the British fleet thus replenished at sea was an anxious task. As Nelson wrote to Davison in December 1803:

> My crazy fleet are [*sic*] getting in a very indifferent state. . . . I know well enough that if I was to go into Malta I should save [them] during this bad season; but if I am to watch the French, I must be at sea, and if at sea, must have bad weather; and if the ships are not fit to stand bad weather, they are useless.

He managed it, nevertheless, once he had allowed those most urgently in need of refit to go in turn to Gibraltar or Malta. By March 1804 he could write: 'The fleet put to sea on 18 May [1803], and is still at sea; not a ship has been refitted, or recruited, excepting what has been done at sea.' By comparison, Cornwallis's task of watching the Brest fleet was easier, except in so far as his ships were exposed to the fiercer gales and greater seas of the Atlantic. He, too, used storeships for replenishment at sea, but these could readily obtain supplies from the nearby ports of Cork and Plymouth. Nor was he wholly dependent upon them: when the wind blew from the west, preventing egress from Brest, he could avoid the hazard of a lee shore by taking his fleet to Torbay, a safer anchorage than Plymouth Sound until the breakwater was completed in 1820.

Nelson's storeships could not, however, keep his ships-of-the-line supplied with water. To obtain this vital commodity, he could have sent them in turn to some convenient roadstead, but with the consequence that his fleet would always be weaker than the enemy's. Since this was no way to *annihilate*, he adopted the alternative of withdrawing them all together, accepting the risk that the French might sortie in his absence. He chose the Maddalena Islands off the north-east end of Sardinia, whose King looked to a British victory to enable him to recover his lost dominion of Piedmont. Agincourt Bay provided a better anchorage for ships' boats to ferry casks filled from running streams than any in Corsica, or in Spain whom he did not wish to provoke by abusing the neutrality of her waters, which were likewise only 200 miles (a day's sail) from Toulon. His fears, that the French might seize Sardinia – 'the most important island as a naval and military station in the Mediterranean ... if I lose Sardinia, I lose the French fleet' – when the Government failed to respond to his suggestion that they should buy the island, proved groundless.

Nelson did more than replenish his ships with provisions, stores and water; as important, he kept his officers and men 'in good humour'. With his fleet undermanned, he had to ensure that it lost no more men. As early as 27 September 1803 he told Addington: 'We are at this moment the healthiest squadron I ever served in, for the fact is we have no sick.' By unceasing concern for the health of his crews, by providing them with 'onions ... good mutton ... cattle ... plenty of fresh water ... [and] half the allowance of grog instead of all wine', for 'it is easier for an officer to keep men healthy than for a physician to cure them,' he kept them fit throughout his command in an age in which sickness often claimed a greater toll than any enemy.

How apt, then, is this judgement:

It was the carrying out of this decision, with ships in such condition, in a region where wind and seas were of exceptional violence and supplies of food and water most difficult to ... [obtain], because surrounded ... by countries either directly hostile, or under the overmastering influence of Bonaparte, that made ... Nelson's command during this period a triumph of naval administration and prevision. It does not necessarily follow that an officer ... distinguished for ... handling a force in the face of the enemy, will possess also the faculty which foresees and provides for the many contingencies, upon which depend ... [its] constant efficiency and readiness. ... For twenty-two months Nelson's fleet never went into port, other than an open roadstead on a neutral coast, destitute of supplies: at the end of that time, when the need arose to pursue an enemy for four thousand miles, it was found massed, and in all respects perfectly prepared for so distant and sudden a call.*

Self-reliance, resource, fearless responsibility and initiative, were attributes which enabled Nelson to achieve so much. But 'a triumph of administration and prevision' would not of itself have ensured that, after twenty-two months, his fleet was in *all* respects ready to deal with the enemy. To surmount that obstacle required a leader of star quality, who by this gift welded his captains into a Band of Brothers, and raised the morale of officers and men to a height that is never likely to be surpassed.

Nelson's fertile imagination did not rest content with the novel concept of keeping his fleet continuously at sea. Although his strategy remained the well-established one of using his battle fleet to neutralize the enemy's, he applied it in a new way. As an officer in his fleet expressed it: 'Lord Nelson pursues a very different plan from Sir Richard Bickerton. The latter kept close to the harbour, but Nelson is scarce ever in sight of the land.' Latouche-Tréville could be prevented from leaving Toulon by a close blockade; this was the safe way, but it was not Nelson's. For so long as he had to counter a French battle fleet, his own could be put to no other purpose. But once he had annihilated the enemy, he would be free to conduct offensive operations – to harass the *Armée d'Italie*, to capture Minorca, to free the Ionian Islands. 'It is not my intention to close-watch Toulon', he wrote. 'My system is the very contrary of blockading. Every opportunity has been offered the enemy to put to sea, for it is there we hope to realize the ... expectations of our country.' To gain an opportunity to destroy the enemy outweighed the risk that 'my system' might

*Mahan in his *Life of Nelson*.

enable Latouche-Tréville to elude him altogether. Wherever his opponent went – to Sicily, to the eastern Mediterranean, or out into the Atlantic – Nelson was confident that he could find and destroy him, as he had found and destroyed Brueys in 1798. And 'my system' had the further advantage that Latouche-Tréville could not know when the British fleet was away watering in the Maddalenas.

For his normal station Nelson chose a position 150 miles south-west of Toulon and twenty miles to the south of Cape San Sebastian on the Costa Brava, where the highlands of Spain afforded shelter from the gales that were funnelled down between the Pyrenees and the Alps into the Gulf of Lions.

> There are [he wrote] three days of severe blowing weather out of seven, which frequently comes on suddenly, and thereby exposes the topmasts, topsail yards and sails to great hazard . . . and there are no topmasts or topsail yards in store, either at Gibraltar or Malta. [But] by the great care and attention of every captain, we have suffered much less than could have been expected: after twenty-one months we have not carried away a single spar.

And if Spain joined the war, this position would be the best 'to prevent the junction of a Spanish fleet from the westward'. Nelson did not, however, keep to this area: sometimes he cruised south to the Balearics, sometimes to the east round Corsica and Sardinia. Occasionally, too, he sought shelter under the lee of the Hyères Islands. With this exception, only his frigates, sometimes singly, sometimes a pair, stayed just over the horizon from Toulon, where they could not be seen by Latouche-Tréville whilst he remained in harbour, but must see him if he should put to sea.

But the winter of 1803–4 passed without the enemy making a move: Bonaparte was concerned only with preparing for a cross-Channel invasion: only for that would Latouche-Tréville be required to sail. Nelson could not know this: he was perplexed by news of other French intentions.

> Ball [Civil Commissioner at Malta] is sure they are going to Egypt; the Turks are sure they are going to the Morea [Greece]; Mr Elliot [British Minister at Naples] to Sicily; and the King of Sardinia to his only spot . . . but . . . I trust, and with confidence, they are destined for *Spithead* . . . [though] circumstances may make it necessary [for Bonaparte] to alter its destination . . . [to] Egypt or Ireland, and I rather lean to the latter.

There was even a time when he thought the French intended to bring their fleet from Brest into the Mediterranean, 'in which event I shall try to fight one part or the other before they form a junction'. Not until the spring of 1804 could he write: 'Monsieur Latouche sometimes plays bo-peep [sic] out of Toulon, like a mouse at the edge of his hole. Last week, at different times, two sail-of-the-line put their heads out . . . and on Thursday [5 April] . . . they all came out.' Latouche-Tréville was only exercising his ships, but for Nelson, 'if they go on playing this game, some day we shall lay salt upon their tails, and so end the campaign'.

He sent one division of his fleet inshore as bait. 'I think [the French] will be ordered out to fight close to Toulon, that they may get their crippled ships in again; and that we must then quit the coast to repair our damage, and thus leave the coast clear; but my mind is fixed not to fight them, unless . . . outside Hyères . . . [or] to the westward of [Cape] Sicis', from where his other division would join the battle with decisive effect. But only once did this 'method of making Mr Latouche-Tréville angry' come near to success. On 13 June, two months after Nelson's promotion to vice-admiral of the white in April 1804, when his own division of five ships-of-the-line was baiting this trap, two French frigates and a brig were reported near the Hyères Islands. Two British frigates were sent to deal with these vessels, but light winds prevented them from coming up with their quarry until the next day. Since the Frenchmen were then close under the islands' batteries, Nelson ordered the *Excellent*, 74, to support his frigates, then bore up with the rest of his division.

This move had the desired effect: Latouche-Tréville came out of Toulon at 5 pm with eight sail-of-the-line. Nelson reacted by recalling the *Excellent* and forming his division into line of battle. He then hove-to, waiting to be attacked in a position from which he could lead the enemy towards Bickerton's division, lying some fifty miles over the horizon. But 'Monsieur Latouche came out . . . cut a caper . . . and went in again. I brought-to for his attack, although I did not believe anything was meant serious, but merely a gasconade. On the morning of the 15th we chased him into Toulon.' In truth, eight French ships declined action with five British. But according to Latouche-Tréville's dispatch: '*J'ai poursuivi jusqu'a la nuit: il courait au sud-est*' which helped to gain him the highest rank in the Legion of Honour – and raised Nelson's ire. 'I do assure you,' he told the Admiralty when he read his opponent's report, 'I know not what to say, except by a flat contradiction; for if my character is not established by this time for not being apt to run away, it is not worth my time to attempt to put the world right.' His vanity had, nonetheless, to be appeased by letters to his friends in which he called his enemy a 'poltroon', a 'liar' and a 'miscreant': 'You will have seen [his letter] of how he chased me and how I ran,' he wrote, 'I keep it; and, by G—d, if I take him, he shall *eat* it.'

But this was not to be. In a further attempt to bring the French out, Nelson persuaded the Government to sanction a blockade of Genoese ports. 'Nothing,' he said, 'could distress France more: it will force Latouche out.' But the latter part of August brought news that ended his chances of avenging his defeat at Boulogne. By Latouche-Tréville's sudden death on the 20th on board his new, recently completed flagship, the 80-gunned *Bucentaure*, France lost her ablest admiral, and the British fleet an opponent worthy of its steel. 'He has given me the slip', wrote Nelson. 'The French papers say he died of walking so often up to the signal-post . . . to watch us.' To succeed him Decrès appointed Villeneuve, now a vice-admiral, the man who had held command of the French rear at the Nile, and whose flagship, the *Guillaume Tell*, had been one of the small handful of vessels to escape from Aboukir Bay.

For all this time – for half of 1803 and for all of 1804 – Nelson had much to do onboard the *Victory*, between turning out at his customary hour of 6 am and turning in at 9.0 pm, besides maintaining his watch on Toulon. Advised by his captain of the fleet, Rear-Admiral George Murray, and by Hardy, and helped by two secretaries, the Rev. A. J. Scott (who was also his chaplain and was usually known as Dr Scott) and the unrelated John Scott, he had to direct the manifold affairs of the Mediterranean station, by correspondence with the Prime Minister (Addington until Pitt regained his old office in May 1804); with the First Lord (St Vincent until the change in the Government brought Viscount Melville to the Admiralty); with the Kings of Sardinia and of the Two Sicilies and with the heads of other Mediterranean states, and with the British envoys at their Courts; with Ball at Malta; with the Dockyard Commissioners at Malta and Gibraltar; with the commanders of his cruisers employed protecting trade; and with many more. He had to find time, too, for his personal affairs, to write letters to such men as Davison (who suffered the misfortune of a year's imprisonment for dubious involvement in the conduct of a parliamentary election at Ilchester) – and, above all, to Emma.

Space precludes more than a brief mention of the problems which troubled him. For lack of ships 'to chastise these pirates', he had to depend on diplomacy to induce the Bey of Algiers to stop plundering Maltese traders, and to receive back the British Consul whom he had expelled. He was 'distressed for frigates. From Cape St Vincent to the head of the Adriatic, I have only eight which . . . are absolutely not one half enough'; and, 'Frigates are the eyes of the fleet. I want ten more th an I have in order to watch that the French do not escape me.' He had too few cruisers to deal with enemy privateers: 'I wrote to the Admiralty for more . . . until I was tired and they left off answering those parts of my letters.' And because neither he, nor the Admiralty, had any quicker method of transmitting orders than by letter, their arrangements for escorting convoys to and from the Mediterranean seldom dovetailed. 'If the *Maidstone* takes the convoy, and, when *Agincourt* arrives, there is none for *Thisbe*, it puzzles me to know what orders to give them. If they chase the convoy to Gibraltar, the *Maidstone* may have gone on to England and, in that case, two ships . . . will either go home without convoy, or they must return [to Malta] in contradiction to the Admiralty's order to send them home.'

These convoys needed a strong escort because the treaty of friendship between France and Spain, signed on 9 October 1803, allowed the French 74-gunned *Aigle* to operate from Cadiz, when Nelson could spare no more than three frigates for his Gibraltar force, whose commander, Captain Gore, was advised: 'Your intentions of attacking that ship are . . . very laudable, but I do not consider your force by any means equal to it.' And only a Nelson would read such instructions with a blind eye when it was generally held, by Hawke and Howe among others, that no force of frigates could measure up to a ship-of-the-line. (So, too, more than a century later, did a court martial decide that Rear-Admiral Ernest Troubridge, in command of four armoured cruisers 'was justified in considering the [German battlecruiser] *Goeben* a superior force . . . and in abandoning the chase'. Not until 1939 was this thesis disproved by Commodore Harwood's three cruisers' successful engagement with the pocket-battleship *Graf Spee*.)

Emma, having given birth to Nelson's second child early in 1804 – a daughter who only survived for a few weeks – pressed to be allowed to join her lover in the Mediterranean. But no woman could now deflect Nelson from his duty; Emma had to accept much the same answer as Fanny had received. His place was off Toulon, not in a harbour such as Naples or Malta; nor would he have her onboard the *Victory*:

We have a hard gale every week. . . . It would kill you, and myself to see you. . . . And I, that have given orders to carry no women to sea . . . to be the first to break them! I know, my own dear Emma, if she will let her reason have fair play, will say I am right. . . . Your Nelson is called upon . . . to defend his country. Absence to us is equally painful, but if I had stayed at home, or neglected my duty abroad, would not my Emma have blushed for me?

How marked the contrast between this attitude and that which Nelson adopted towards her in 1798–1800, when, in particular, he had taken her for a cruise in the *Foudroyant*. His devotion remained, but he was no longer obsessed; the naval commander had triumphed over the lover: his Achilles heel had been cured.

Nor was this the only contrast between the present and the past, between Nelson as commander-in-chief and Nelson as a post-captain and junior flag officer. As striking is the difference between the few floggings recorded in the logs of his previous ships and the appreciable number noted in the *Victory*'s. As a captain his personality was enough to maintain discipline: only in exceptional circumstances did he order this brutal punishment as a sharp lesson to all, much as Jervis ordered the immediate execution of the mutineers off Cadiz in 1797. So was it, too, in the years when the benevolent Berry was his flag captain. But the later Nelson who, because of Emma, had Caracciolo so speedily executed, whose vanity was so much disturbed by criticism when he expected nothing but adulation, and who dismissed Fanny so cruelly from his life, was not troubled by Hardy's belief in the need for punishment to maintain discipline, especially in a ship that was required to remain at sea without respite for so long.

Nelson's physical health, always so robust in the past, remained (according to a contemporary authority) 'uniformly good. . . . The only bodily pain . . . was a slight rheumatic affection of the stump of his amputated arm on any sudden variation in the weather.' Otherwise he was afflicted only with seasickness, to which he was so accustomed that he did not allow it to trouble him. In particular, he did not lose a vital quality lacking in many another great commander, his sense of humour ('Nelson was the man to *love*', said an officer who also knew the future Duke of Wellington). Having advised two of his frigate captains not to engage both ships of a similar enemy force, but to 'endeavour together to take one frigate; if successful chase the other; [for] if you do not take the second, still you have won a victory', he bade them farewell with the smiling comment: 'I daresay you consider yourselves a couple of fine fellows, and when you get away from me you will do nothing of the sort, but think yourself wiser than I am.'

But it was otherwise with Nelson's mental state. The mercurial temperament of the creative genius, which throve on action and withered when there was none, rebelled against the tedium of waiting and watching. 'If that [French] Admiral were to cheat me out of my hopes of meeting him, it would kill me much easier than one of his balls.' Debilitated by a year's suspense and anxiety, he wrote to Melville in August 1804: 'The state of my health [is] such as to make it absolutely necessary that I should return to England. . . . Another winter such as the last I feel myself unable to stand against. A few months of quiet may enable me to serve again next spring.' Bickerton was well able to command the Mediterranean in his absence. The First Lord agreed, but before his reply, written on 6 October, reached the *Victory* in December (an example of how long communications dependent on letters alone could be delayed, with significant consequences) events combined to change Nelson's mood.

In October, having managed (after nearly eighteen months of war) to find the men to commission some eighty ships-of-the-line, out of an available force of nearly 120, the Admiralty decided to spare five to blockade Cadiz, both to counter the *Aigle* and against the likelihood of Spain joining the war. Nelson should have welcomed this reinforcement when he had 'but four [ships-of-the-line] fit to keep the sea'. The rest needed docking, but he could spare none for this when he had no margin over Villeneuve. But the Admiralty accompanied their decision with a tactless one: to command this new squadron they chose an admiral senior to Nelson. Sir John Orde, now a vice-admiral of the red, had languished on half-pay since his quarrel with St Vincent over his choice of Nelson to command the squadron sent into the Mediterranean in the spring of 1798. Melville, having no such aversion to Orde, decided to re-employ him, and to overcome the problem of his seniority, removed from Nelson's command that part of the Mediterranean station which lay to the west of Gibraltar, extending to Cape Finisterre, which was the richest for prize-money. This, because of his prodigal expenditure, Nelson could no longer afford to scorn in favour of honour. He resented Melville's decision:

He [Orde] is sent off Cadiz to reap the golden harvest. . . . It is very odd [two Admiralties] to treat me so: surely I have dreamed that I have done the State some service. But never mind: I am superior to those who could treat me so. I believe I attach more to the French fleet than making captures. . . . This thought is far better than prize-money – not that I despise money – quite the contrary, I wish I had £100,000 [$240,000] this moment.

He protested to the Admiralty at the consequences; Orde was issuing instructions to *his* frigates; Orde was denuding Gibraltar dockyard of *his* stores. And when Gore received direct orders to intercept a Spanish treasure fleet expected at Cadiz from South America, he went much further than complaining that this was not the way to treat the Commander-in-Chief Mediterranean; he countermanded Gore's orders.

For this drastic action, Nelson had, however, another reason: he disagreed with the Government's decision to counter Spain's frequent breaches of neutrality (the *Aigle*'s use of Cadiz being one of many) by ordering the seizure of the treasure ships on which her economy largely depended. For this must finally provoke a war which would give his fleet the additional task of preventing the five Spanish ships-of-the-line which were lying in Cartagena from joining with Villeneuve's to form a fleet superior to his own. This prospect became a reality on 14 December shortly after Campbell suffered a nervous breakdown and had to be invalided home. Since Bickerton could not be left without the support of another flag officer, Nelson wrote on the 30th: 'I shall avail myself of Their Lordships' permission to return home on leave the moment another admiral . . . joins the fleet, unless the enemy . . . should be at sea, when I shall not think of quitting my command until after the battle.'

He was, indeed, so determined not to miss 'the battle', that, when he heard that Orde might relieve him, he compounded vanity with magnanimity. Having complained that Orde's 'general conduct towards me is not such as I had a right to expect', 'I shall show my superiority . . . by offering to serve under him, and the world will see what a sacrifice I am ready to make for my King and Country'. Orde's appointment to the Mediterranean command was, however, *only* rumour. Nelson's flag still flew in the *Victory* when his ships closed Toulon at the beginning of January 1805. He had heard, 'from various sources . . . that the French were assembling troops near Toulon. . . . On the 16th the *Active* spoke a vessel from Marseilles who reported that 7,000 troops had embarked on board the French fleet.' But a week close off Toulon produced no other evidence that Villeneuve was about to sortie, by which time Nelson's ships needed water. On 11 January his fleet anchored in the Maddalenas. One week later, in the afternoon of the 19th, his two look-out frigates hove in sight: the reason they had left their station to seaward of Toulon was clear as soon as their signal flags could be distinguished against the darkening sky of a north-westerly gale. Villeneuve was at sea.

Would Nelson's strategy now be proven? His first aim, to encourage the French fleet to come out had succeeded; but would he be able to *find* Villeneuve and bring him to battle? First, however, a look 'over the hill' for the answer to another question, why the French fleet had left the security of Toulon. Bonaparte had evolved his initial plan for invading England in the summer of 1803. Four army corps (150,000 officers and men) were assembled, Marmont's at Utrecht, Davout's at Bruges, Soult's at St Omer, and Ney's at Montreuil, with a fifth (20,000 strong) under Augerau at Brest for a landing in Ireland. And to carry them more than 2,000 transports, schooners, brigs and landing craft were assembled, chiefly at Boulogne and Étaples, under Bruix, with another flotilla of 400 provided by the Dutch at Flushing and the Texel. But the operation could not be launched for so long as Keith's squadron, based on the Downs, and Cornwallis' fleet ruled the Narrow Seas and its western approaches. This much Bonaparte understood – but little more. Accustomed to ordering armies to march, and to be sure that they would adhere to his time-table, he was frustrated by his admirals' reluctance to face their enemies. In his growing impatience at the delays imposed on his plans, he issued orders of greater and greater complexity, with the increasing certainty that they would go astray.

He decided to launch the invasion on 20 February 1804, when a winter's night gave the cover of twelve hours of darkness. Latouche-Tréville would sortie from Toulon on 11 January and lead Nelson's fleet away into the eastern Mediterranean, while the small French squadron at Rochefort decoyed Cornwallis in the direction of Ireland, leaving Ganteaume's Brest fleet free to sail up Channel. This operation was, however, aborted by a Royalist plot to kidnap Bonaparte. An alarmed First Consul decided that he must consolidate his personal authority by establishing an hereditary monarchy: on 18 May he proclaimed himself Emperor, with the title of Napoleon I.

After this distraction, Napoleon issued new invasion orders. This time Ganteaume was to keep Cornwallis occupied by staying in port, while Latouche-Tréville gave Nelson the slip, passed Gibraltar and headed for a rendezvous with the Rochefort squadron. 'If we are masters of the Channel for six hours, we shall be masters of the world. If you hoodwink Nelson, he will sail to Sicily, Egypt or Ferrol. You should leave by 29 July, sail round the north of Ireland and arrive off Boulogne in September.' But

Latouche-Tréville did not live to show whether he could evade Nelson as easily as his Emperor supposed.

In September Napoleon expounded a third plan to Decrès:

> We must send off three expeditions; from Rochefort to secure Martinique and Guadeloupe against enemy action and seize Dominica and St Lucia; from Toulon to capture Surinam and other Dutch [West Indian] colonies; from Brest [a small squadron] to capture St Helena. The Toulon squadron might sail on 10 October, the Rochefort one on 1 November and the Brest one on 22 November.

All this would allow Ganteaume to sortie, with Augerau's and Marmont's corps embarked, and head for Lough Swilly, while 'the *Grande Armée* of Boulogne will embark simultaneously and ... try to invade Kent'.

> The landing in Ireland is only the first act. [Ganteaume's] squadron must then enter the English Channel ... to get news of the Boulogne army. If, on arriving off Boulogne, it meets ... contrary winds, it must go on to the Texel, where it will find seven [*sic*] Dutch ships with 25,000 men embarked. It will convoy them to Ireland. One of the two operations must succeed. ... Whether I am in England or in Ireland, we shall have won the war.

But this elaborate scheme for an invasion in the winter of 1804–5 brought Napoleon no nearer to achievement. None of his fleets left their harbours.

So he issued another, more grandiose, plan. Villeneuve's fleet, with troops embarked, was to leave the Mediterranean and collect the *Aigle* from Cadiz. He was then to detach a squadron to relieve Sénégal, retake Gorée (surrendered to the British on 7 March 1804), ravage British settlements in West Africa and capture St Helena. He himself was to rendezvous at Cayenne with Rear-Admiral Missiessy's squadron out of Rochefort after this had landed reinforcements in Martinique and Guadaloupe *and* captured Dominica and St Lucia. These moves, Napoleon calculated, would draw not only Nelson's fleet but at least twenty other ships-of-the-line in pursuit, especially to save the rich sugar harvest which Britain gained from her West Indies possessions. Having secured Surinam (captured by Commodore Hood's Windward and Leeward Islands squadron on 5 May 1804) and other Dutch colonies, *and* the other British islands in the Caribbean, *and* having evaded action with any substantial British force, Villeneuve's fleet, now numbering fifteen sail-of-the-line, would return across the Atlantic, lift the British blockade of Ferrol and, thus further augmented to twenty sail, appear off Rochefort. Here he would receive orders as to how he should combine with Ganteaume's twenty ships-of-the-line, reinforced by ten of Spain's out of Cadiz, to gain command of the Channel for the *Grande Armée* to cross in safety in the spring or early summer of 1805.

Missiessy was the first to sail. Leaving Rochefort on 11 January 1805 with five sail-of-the-line and three frigates, with 3,500 troops embarked, he eluded Rear-Admiral Sir Thomas Graves' blockading squadron, and headed for the West Indies. He was pursued by Rear-Admiral the Hon. Alexander Cochrane who for this purpose did not hesitate to leave his assigned station off Ferrol. The Admiralty could more speedily assign further ships-of-the-line to the latter task than they could send another squadron after Missiessy: indeed Cornwallis was soon ordered to detach Vice-Admiral Sir Robert Calder to continue the watch on Ferrol. When communications were so slow, commanders *had* to act on their own initiative; and, as will shortly be seen, it was their readiness – above all Nelson's – to shoulder this responsibility, coupled with their experience and understanding of war at sea, that played such a large part in setting Napoleon's plans at nought. Throughout a year of baffling French moves, a large number of British admirals and captains in more or less independent commands, with no method of communication except by letter, and no organization for gathering and disseminating intelligence, made vital decisions on their own, as if by instinct. (In sharp contrast, less than a century and a half later, the *Bismarck* was more speedily found and sunk by widespread forces whose movements were directly controlled, almost from minute to minute, by radio from Whitehall.) But if it be said of Nelson and his contemporaries that they were giants who never put a foot wrong, it is well to remember that they were not almighty. The French defeat in the campaign of 1805 was as much due to their own errors, as to the consummate skill and courage of their British opponents.

Villeneuve sortied six days later: seeing no British sail off Toulon, he ordered his eleven ships-of-the-line, accompanied by seven frigates, to leave harbour on 17 January. But the *Active* and *Seahorse* were only just over the horizon: as soon as 6.30 pm their captains sighted the French on a southerly course and shadowed them until early on the 19th, before bearing up for the Maddalenas to signal the *Victory* in Agincourt Bay. The news was a tonic to their Admiral's flagging spirits. In little more than two hours his fleet was under way. He was in no doubt of the course to steer: since the French were headed for the southern end of Sardinia, they must be going to Naples, to Sicily or into the eastern Mediterranean.

By 7.0 pm Nelson's ships were under all plain sail in a brisk breeze down Sardinia's east coast. But on leaving the island's lee they met the full force of a southerly gale against which they could make no headway for the next three days, during which they gained no news of the enemy fleet.

Then, on the 26th, Nelson was able to communicate with Cagliari: no landing had been attempted in Sardinia. Later that day the frigate *Phoebe* reported that the French 80-gun *Indomtable* had been dismasted by the storm and lay crippled in Ajaccio. What could Nelson infer from this? 'I considered the character of Bonaparte; and that [his] orders . . . would not take into consideration winds or weather; nor indeed could [an] accident [to] three or four ships alter . . . [a] destination of importance.' With no news of the French to the south of Sardinia, which might portend an attack on Sicily, they must be going to Egypt. Since Napoleon's first invasion plans envisaged using the Toulon fleet to draw the British into the eastern Mediterranean, Nelson is not to be faulted for this reasoning. On 31 January he took his fleet through the Straits of Messina.

As soon as 7 February he was in touch with the British Consul at Alexandria; but, as before the Nile, he gained no news of his opponent there. So he returned to the west, arriving twelve days later off Malta where he received the disheartening report that all the excitement and anxiety of the chase had been for nothing. Villeneuve's fleet was back in Toulon.

Encountering a gale in the Gulf of Lions shortly after leaving port, the French ships had soon suffered enough damage to their masts and rigging for their captains to decide to run for safety. Except for four, including the *Indomtable* which sought refuge elsewhere, all returned to Toulon by 20 January. Though the Emperor could not know it, this early disruption of his complicated plan to gain command of the Channel was the beginning of the end of his ambition to invade England. For the moment he could only write: 'What is to be done with admirals who . . . hasten home at the first damage they receive? . . . The damage should have been repaired *en route*. . . . A few topmasts carried away . . . [are] everyday occurrences.' But, since Nelson's fleet had been doing as much for the past eighteen months, the truth lay in Napoleon's further words: 'The great evil of our Navy is that the men who command it are unused to all the risks of command.'

There being now no prospect of Villeneuve reaching the West Indies before the time limit of thirty-five days set for Missiessy's stay, Napoleon changed his plans again. On 14 March 1805, after assaulting but failing to

capture Dominica, St Kitts and Montserrat, Missiessy received orders
to return at once to Rochefort, where he arrived on 20 May, to be relieved
of his command because, wrote Napoleon to Decrès: 'I choked with indig-
nation when I read that he had not taken the Diamond Rock', which had
been seized and fortified by Hood in January 1804, to facilitate the British
blockade of Fort Royal, capital of the French West Indies. On the same
date, 14 March, Villeneuve was ordered to sail for Cadiz, collect such
Spanish ships as might be ready, and then head for Martinique. Augereau's
invasion of Ireland was cancelled: Ganteaume was to leave Brest with
twenty-one sail-of-the-line, collect such French and Spanish ships as
could escape from Rochefort and Ferrol, and likewise head for Martinique.
Having evaded any substantial British force, the combined fleets, numbering some forty sail, were to return from the West Indies, under Ganteaume's command, in time to defeat Cornwallis' force and appear off
Boulogne between 10 June and 10 July.

'Had [the French] not been crippled nothing could have hindered our
meeting them on 21 January off the south end of Sardinia', wrote Nelson.
As it was he had to encourage Villeneuve to make a fresh sortie by
allowing him to know that the British were to the westward of Toulon.
Having appeared off Barcelona, he returned to his old cruising ground off
Cape San Sebastian. Thence he proceeded to rendezvous with his storeships in the Gulf of Palmas at the southern end of Sardinia on 26 March,
where he was joined by Campbell's relief, and an old friend, Rear-Admiral
Thomas Louis who had commanded the *Minotaur* at the Nile. His ruse
succeeded: Villeneuve left Toulon for the second time on the 30th, as
before steering his ten ships-of-the-line to pass between the Balearics and
Sardinia, and five days elapsed before the *Phoebe* brought the news to
Nelson on 4 April.

Again he supposed the French to be destined for Naples, Sicily or
Egypt, but he did not this time press another vain chase to Alexandria:
declaring that 'I shall neither go to the eastward of Sicily, or to the
westward of Sardinia, until I know something positive', he cruised midway
between Sardinia and the Barbary Coast in the hope of intercepting the
enemy there. The wisdom of this decision was soon confirmed. On 9
April he decided to close Toulon to make sure that Villeneuve had not
again returned, only to be seriously delayed by head winds; so he was still
to the south of Sardinia on the 18th when a passing vessel reported seeing
the French off Cape de Gata ten days before. He knew immediately what
this must mean: 'I am going out of the Mediterranean. It may be thought
that I have protected too well Sardinia, Naples, Sicily, the Morea and

Egypt; but I feel I have done right, and am, therefore, easy about any fate which may await me for having missed the French fleet.'

Villeneuve had had the good fortune to learn as soon as 1 April that the British were to the south of Sardinia instead of, as he had been tricked into believing, off the Costa Brava. He immediately changed course to pass down the Spanish coast instead of to the east of the Balearics. On the 6th he was off Cartagena, to find that not one of Rear-Admiral Salcedo's six ships-of-the-line was ready for sea. Rather than wait for reinforcements of doubtful value, he pressed on to pass Gibraltar on the 8th.

This news reached Nelson the day after he had decided that the French must be leaving the Mediterranean. Although his opponent had gained a ten days start, he was determined that his long watch should not be in vain. But where was Villeneuve bound: whither should he pursue him? Some six months before, on 6 September 1804, Nelson had written: 'Suppose the Toulon fleet ... gets out of the Straits, I rather think I should bend my course to the westward; for if they carry 7,000 men ... St Lucia, Grenada, St Vincent, Antigua and St Kitts would fall, and ... England would be ... clamorous for peace.' But now he reverted to his earlier belief that Villeneuve would head north to join Ganteaume off the entrance to the Channel. He told the Admiralty, where the seventy-eight-year-old Admiral Lord Barham (who as Sir Charles Middleton had been Controller of the Navy Board from 1778 to 1790) had recently succeeded Melville as First Lord: 'If I receive no intelligence to do away with my proud belief, I shall proceed from Cape St Vincent and take my position 50 leagues west from [the] Scillies. ... My reason is that it is equally easy to get ... off Brest or to go to Ireland, should [my] fleet be wanted at either station.' But contrary winds delayed his progress towards Gibraltar; not until 20 April did he sight the Rock and learn that Villeneuve had passed Cadiz on 9 April when his fleet had been reinforced by the *Aigle* and by Vice-Admiral Don Federico Gravina's six ships-of-the-line – and that, to Nelson's anger, his *bête noire*, Orde, had taken his squadron north to reinforce Cornwallis's guard on the Channel approaches instead of keeping track of Villeneuve's fleet.

On 5 May Nelson anchored off Gibraltar to replenish his ships with water and victuals, when rumours reached him from Cadiz that Villeneuve's combined fleets were heading for the Caribbean. This almost decided him: as he sailed for Lagos Bay, after detaching Bickerton with the *Royal Sovereign* and a squadron of frigates for operations in the Mediterranean, he wrote: 'If I hear nothing [more], I shall proceed to the West Indies.'

Nelson did not, however, have to depend on rumours alone. *En route* to Lagos Rear-Admiral Donald Campbell, of the Portuguese Navy, gave him the sure news that Villeneuve was indeed crossing the Atlantic (for which unneutral act Campbell was subsequently dismissed his command at the instigation of the French Ambassador in Lisbon). Villeneuve had, moreover, now gained as much as a month's start. But Nelson was no more deterred by this from following him than by the reflection that his fleet of nine sail-of-the-line, was only half the strength of his enemy's. 'Although I am late,' he told Ball, 'yet chance may have given them a bad passage, and me a good one.' His optimism received no support. Three days after his fleet left Lagos on 11 May under all sail to the west,* Villeneuve reached Martinique having crossed the Atlantic in thirty-four days, after nothing more eventful than a brisk cannonade with the Diamond Rock.

So the French were already in the West Indies by the time the British sighted Madeira on the 15th. Nelson sent a frigate to warn Cochrane of his impending arrival in the Windward and Leeward Islands, which he had first visited as a midshipman of only thirteen summers, which he had come to know so well as a young frigate captain, but which he had not seen again since 1787. He hoped that on reaching Barbados, he would be reinforced by the Rear-Admiral's six ships-of-the-line. But when he anchored off Georgetown on 4 June he found only two; the others had been held at Jamaica. If only he could have countered this disappointment by reading Napoleon's estimate of his whereabouts: 'I am ... of opinion that Nelson is still in European waters. . . . He must have gone back to England to revictual, and to turn over his crews to other ships; for his vessels require docking, and his squadron may be supposed to be in a very bad condition.' So, indeed, it was; yet with captains of the quality of Nelson's, and manned by British seamen, it had crossed the Atlantic in twenty-four days, ten less than Villeneuve, having averaged five knots with studding sails set and 'the little *Superb* ... lagging all the way'.

> I am fearful that you think [wrote Nelson to Captain Richard Keats] the *Superb* does not go as fast as I could wish. However that may be (for if we all went ten knots I should not think it fast enough), yet I would have you assured that I know and feel that the *Superb* does all that which is possible for a ship to accomplish; and I desire that you will not fret upon the occasion.

Such words epitomize Nelson's greatness as a leader: commendation is so much more effective than condemnation.

*See rear endpapers for a map illustrating Nelson's pursuit of Villeneuve across the Atlantic.

From the date of their arrival at Fort Royal, 14 May 1805, Villeneuve and Gravina were instructed to wait up to forty days for Ganteaume to join them. During this period Villeneuve 'did not propose to go in search of the enemy. I . . . wish to avoid him in order to arrive at my destination [Boulogne].' He was, however, to do as much harm as possible to British interests. Wiser than Missiessy, he began with the Diamond Rock; a three-day bombardment, from 31 May to 2 June, exhausted Commander James Maurice's ammunition and compelled him to surrender. But no sooner had this success been achieved than a frigate arrived with fresh order from France. Ganteaume had not yet managed to leave Brest without contravening Napoleon's explicit instructions, comparable with Villeneuve's, to 'go to sea without fighting'. For all his greatness as a military commander, the Emperor's concept of naval strategy, coupled with his poor opinion of most of his admirals, was *evasion*, even when his fleets were stronger than the enemy's. Had he required them to *attack*, they might have so weakened the British Fleet that his plans for seizing Egypt, for conquering India and for invading England would have ended differently.

Villeneuve was now to stay in the West Indies for thirty-five days, seizing Antigua, St Vincent and Grenada before returning to Ferrol. Either there or earlier, he and Gravina would be joined by Ganteaume. Accordingly, on 4 June 1805, Villeneuve's combined fleets stood south to attack Antigua, after collecting at Guadaloupe Rear-Admiral Magon de Médine's two ships of-the-line which had managed to slip out of Rochefort. But on nearing his destination four days later the French Commander-in-Chief learned from a passing American schooner of a British convoy homeward bound to the NNE. He immediately gave chase, with significant consequences; before nightfall he had not only captured fifteen prizes (burnt by their escort before they could reach the safety of Guadaloupe to prevent them being retaken by the British) but learned of Nelson's arrival.

Since this exaggerated the size of the British fleet, Villeneuve decided to abandon all further attacks on the West Indies. He had achieved his chief purpose, that of drawing a substantial enemy force away from Europe. He had no confidence in the Brest fleet escaping in time to join him within the stipulated period – a just belief since Ganteaume made only one half-hearted attempt on 4 April before, on 20 May, Napoleon ordered him to await Villeneuve's return before trying again. Rather than risk an encounter with Nelson so far from home, he would best serve his Emperor's object, the invasion of England, if he returned at once. As soon as 30 June Villeneuve and Gravina, with their eighteen sail-of-the-line, passed north of the Azores on their way back to European waters.

Nelson's intentions were very different: if he could find Villeneuve's fleet he would attack it, overcoming the considerable disparity in numbers by the tactics that had won him the Nile and Copenhagen, by concentrating his eleven ships-of-the-line against one part of the enemy's; and when this had been crushed, dealing with the disorganized and demoralized remainder.

All his instinct told him to seek the enemy at Martinique, but when, at Barbados, he received substantial intelligence from General Brereton, commanding the troops at St Lucia, that 'it was *apparently* clear that the enemy had gone south' to attack Trinidad and Tobago, he felt compelled to pursue them there. Not until he arrived off Trinidad on 7 June did he learn that he had been misled, and so turn north again to hear from Dominica on the 9th that Villeneuve's fleet had passed by only three days before. 'But for false information,' he wrote, 'I should have been off Fort Royal as they were putting to sea; and our battle, most probably, would have been fought on the spot where the brave Rodney beat de Grasse.' As it was he reached Antigua just three days after Villeneuve's attack on the sugar convoy. 'O General Brereton! General Brereton!' he wrote to the First Secretary of the Admiralty; and to Davison: 'But for his damned information Nelson would have been, living or dead, the greatest man in his profession that England ever saw.'

If this be vanity, who shall criticize for it the man who then so swiftly, and with such uncanny strategic insight decided his next move. Where had Villeneuve now gone? Back to Fort Royal? To attack some other British island? From all the information available to him, and not least the fact that in the three weeks since his arrival in the Caribbean his opponent had attempted so little, Nelson believed that he was more likely to be returning to Europe than planning further operations in the West Indies. 'So far from being infallible, like the Pope, I believe my opinions to be very fallible, and therefore I may be mistaken that the enemy's fleet has gone to Europe; but I cannot bring myself to think otherwise.' And to Addington: 'My opinion is firm as a rock, that some cause, *orders*, or *inability* to perform any service in these seas, has made them resolve to proceed direct for Europe.' This news he sent post haste by the brig *Curieux* to Plymouth and Whitehall; then, with undaunted tenacity, steered his ships-of-the-line to the eastward in pursuit of an elusive foe whom he had been so near to catching in the Caribbean, and who now had only five days' start of him. And, 'if we meet them . . . *we won't part without a battle*'.

But was Villeneuve on a course for Ireland? For the Channel? For Ferrol? Or for Cadiz? Since the first three of these were adequately guarded by Cornwallis, Nelson's clear duty was to cover Cadiz and the possibility that the Toulon fleet might re-enter the Mediterranean. So he steered to pass *through* the Azores, with the consequence that as one disappointing day succeeded another, he saw no enemy sail. Nor after he sighted Cape St Vincent on 17 July, could his old friend Collingwood, now a vice-admiral of the blue, who with six sail-of-the-line had taken Orde's place off Cadiz, give him any news. And, when he called at Gibraltar for provisions and 'went on shore for the first time since 16 June 1803; and from having my foot out of the *Victory*, two years wanting ten days', he could only confirm that Villeneuve had neither entered Cadiz nor passed through the Straits.

Where then was the French fleet? He must have outpaced it as he had once outpaced Brueys. As soon as his ships were ready, on 24 July, Nelson bore away to the westward to renew his search in the Atlantic. Ten days later, on 3 August, an American merchantman provided him with positive evidence that Villeneuve had steered for a more northerly destination. Swinging round to the north, Nelson fell in with the Channel fleet off Ushant on the 15th. Then and there Cornwallis told him of all that had happened since the *Curieux* arrived at Plymouth bearing not only Nelson's despatch reporting that Villeneuve must be returning to Europe but, from a chance sighting *en route*, the news that he *was* doing so.

Barham and his Senior Naval Lord recognized the vital importance of this report as soon as they received it; the former might be near to his eightieth birthday but he had lost none of his capacity for speedy and decisive action. Urgent orders were hurried to Cornwallis requiring the five ships-of-the-line off Rochefort to join the ten with which Calder was watching Ferrol. Thus strengthened to fifteen sail-of-the-line, Calder was to intercept Villeneuve 100 miles west of Cape Finisterre, while Cornwallis continued his watch on Brest.

This redeployment should have paid a rich dividend. As soon as 11.0 am on 22 July Calder located Villeneuve's fleet on course for Ferrol; and although outnumbered, he did not hesitate to attack the enemy. But the wind was light, which delayed a general engagement until 6 pm, and the weather so misty that the result was a confused *mêlée*. However, by the time darkness compelled a cease-fire, Calder had gained a tactical victory with an inferior force; though several British ships had suffered considerable damage to their masts and yards, two Spaniards had struck their colours. But Calder made no attempt to follow up this success. When dawn next day revealed the two fleets scattered but still in sight of each other, with their centres some seventeen miles apart, he was chiefly concerned to succour his partially crippled ships and to save his prizes from an enemy who might at any time be reinforced from Rochefort and Ferrol. As Villeneuve headed his fleet away to the south-south-east, Calder did no more than keep in touch until, at 6.0 pm on the 24th Villeneuve had drawn so far ahead that the two fleets lost sight of each other (a feat which earned him this verdict from Napoleon: 'I consider that Villeneuve has not the courage to command even a frigate. He is a man without resolution or moral courage.')

Calder, after sending his two worst damaged ships and his prizes to Plymouth, then made for Ferrol where he resumed his blockade on the 29th; where, too, he learned that Villeneuve had taken his fleet into Vigo on the 28th, whence he had slipped round to Ferrol on 1 August. Cornwallis then required Calder to detach five of his remaining thirteen ships-of-the-line to resume the blockade of Rochefort. And when this was followed by the news that as many as twenty-nine French and Spanish ships-of-the-line were ready for sea in and near Ferrol – more than thrice his own strength – Calder decided to lift his blockade and rejoin Cornwallis on 14 August.

All this Nelson learned twenty-four hours later. Since both enemy fleets were now in the area for which Cornwallis was responsible, his superior agreed that the *Victory* and the *Superb* should be detached to Spithead. There, wearied, dispirited, and in sore need of rest, Nelson struck his flag on 19 August 1805 and proceeded on the leave which the Admiralty had approved more than nine months before. Next day at Merton, after a separation that had lasted for two years and three months, he was reunited with Emma, and the four-year-old Horatia who, since Hamilton's death, had been able to live with her mother.

He had already written from Gibraltar: 'I have brought home no honour for my Country, only a most faithful servant; nor any riches . . . but . . . a faithful and honourable heart.' But others saw his achievements in a different light. Elliot, writing from his post at Naples, was one:

Either the distances between the different quarters of the globe are diminished, or you have extended the powers of human action. After an unremitting cruise of two long years in the stormy Gulf of Lions, to have proceeded without going into port to Alexandria, from Alexandria to the West Indies, from the West Indies back again to Gibraltar; to have kept your ships afloat, your rigging standing, and your crews in health and spirits – is an effort such as never was realized in former times, nor, I doubt, will ever again be repeated by any other admiral. You have protected us for two long years, and you have saved the West Indies.

In sum, and to conclude this chapter, even if Nelson had never fought a battle, his unbroken watch on Toulon followed immediately by his relentless pursuit of Villeneuve across the Atlantic and back again, would rank him among the ablest of Britain's naval commanders.

CHRONOLOGICAL SUMMARY FOR CHAPTER X

EVENTS IN NELSON'S LIFE	DATE	RELATED EVENTS
	1801 *May*	Barbary States declare war on USA.
Appointed Commander-in-Chief Mediterranean.	**1803** *16 May*	Britain declares war on France.
Joins fleet off Toulon, flag in frigate *Amphion*, and begins his long wait for French to sortie.	*6 July*	
Rehoists flag in *Victory*, 100.	*30 July*	
	23 August	Main camps for Bonaparte's *Grande Armée* formed at St Omer and Bruges, with invasion flotillas concentrating at Boulogne and other Channel ports.
	9 October	Spain signs treaty of alliance with France.
	1804 *January*	Hood seizes Diamond Rock.
Birth and death of Nelson's and Emma's second daughter.	*February?*	
	7 March	British take Gorée.
Promoted Vice-Admiral of the White.	*23 April*	

EVENTS IN NELSON'S LIFE	DATE	RELATED EVENTS
	May	Pitt succeeds Addington as Prime Minister: Melville succeeds St Vincent as First Lord.
	5 May	Hood takes Surinam.
	18 May	Bonaparte proclaimed Emperor Napoleon I.
Entices Latouche-Tréville out of Toulon, but is unable to persuade him to fight.	*14–15 June*	
	20 August	Death of Latouche-Tréville.
	October	Orde's squadron arrives to watch Cadiz.
	November	Villeneuve assumes command of Toulon fleet.
	2 December	Napoleon's coronation.
	14 December	Spain declares war on Britain.
	1805	
	11 January	Missiessy's squadron leaves Rochefort for West Indies.
	17 January	Villeneuve's fleet leaves Toulon.
Leaves Maddalena Is. in search of Villeneuve.	*19 January*	
	20 January	Villeneuve returns to Toulon.
Passes through Straits of Messina.	*31 January*	
Off Alexandria.	*7 February*	
Off Malta: learns that Villeneuve has returned to Toulon.	*19 February*	
	30 March	Villeneuve again leaves Toulon.
Learns that Villeneuve is out.	*4 April*	
	8 April	Villeneuve passes Gibraltar.
	9 April	Combined French and Spanish fleets leave Cadiz for West Indies.
	11 April	Russia declares war on France.

EVENTS IN NELSON'S LIFE	DATE	RELATED EVENTS
Learns that Villeneuve has passed Gibraltar.	*19 April*	
	2 May	Barham succeeds Melville as First Lord.
Arrives in Lagos Bay after learning that Villeneuve is heading for West Indies.	*10 May*	
	14 May	Villeneuve arrives Martinique.
	20 May	Missiessy's squadron returns to Rochefort.
	26 May	Napoleon crowned King of Italy.
	2 June	Villeneuve retakes Diamond Rock.
Arrives Barbados.	*4 June*	
	8 June	Villeneuve captures British convoy off Antigua, learns of Nelson's arrival in West Indies, and decides to return to Europe.
	9 July	Villeneuve nears Cape Finisterre. Admiralty receives Nelson's dispatch reporting Villeneuve's departure from West Indies.
	11 July	Cornwallis orders Calder to intercept Villeneuve.
Meets Collingwood off Cape St Vincent.	*18 July*	
At Gibraltar.	*19–24 July*	
	22 July	Calder engages Villeneuve off Cape Finisterre.
	26 July	Villeneuve arrives Vigo.
	August	End of hostilities between USA and Barbary States.
	14 August	Calder rejoins Cornwallis.
Meets Cornwallis off Ushant.	*15 August*	
Arrives Spithead, strikes flag and proceeds to Merton on leave.	*18 August*	

XI

*Cape Trafalgar**
1805

Merton was all that Nelson expected. Lord Minto –

> went [there] on Saturday [24 August 1805] and found [him] just sitting
> down to dinner, surrounded by a family party, of his [elder] brother, . . .
> [and his wife], their children, and the children of a sister. Lady Hamilton
> at the head of the table, and Mother Cadogan [Emma's mother] at the
> bottom. I had a hearty welcome. He looks remarkably well and full of
> spirits. His conversation is a cordial in these low times. Lady Hamilton
> has improved and added to the house and the place extremely well. . . .
> She is a clever woman after all: the passion is as hot as ever.

This reveals much, but more telling in the context of this book is the
future Duke of Wellington's account of this chance meeting on 13
September:

> Lord Nelson was, in different circumstances, two quite different men
> as I myself can vouch, though I only saw him once in my life . . . for
> perhaps an hour. It was soon after my return from India. I went to the
> Colonial Office . . . and there I was shown into the little waiting room
> . . . where I found, also waiting to see the Secretary of State, a gentle-
> man whom, from his likeness to his pictures and the loss of an arm, I
> immediately recognized. . . . He could not know who I was, but he
> entered at once into conversation with me . . . all about himself, and
> in . . . a style so vain and so silly as to surprise and almost disgust me.

---

*Which should be pronounced Traffle-*gar*. Tra*fal*gar is the Anglicized form.

I suppose something that I happened to say may have made him guess that I was *somebody*, and he went out of the room for a moment . . . no doubt to ask the office-keeper who I was, for when he came back he was altogether a different man. . . . All that I had thought a charlatan style had vanished, and he talked of this country and . . . of affairs on the Continent with a good sense, and a knowledge of subjects both at home and abroad that surprised me equally and more agreeably than the first part of our interview . . . he talked like an officer and a statesman. . . . I don't know that I ever had a conversation that interested me more.

Now, if the Secretary of State had been punctual, and admitted Lord Nelson in the first quarter of an hour, I should have had the same impression of a light and trivial character that other people have had; but luckily I saw enough to be satisfied that he was really a very superior man.

Nelson hoped that he would be allowed to stay at Merton for several months before returning to his command: he needed time to restore his health and strength. But he was under no illusions about the critical situation across the Channel: 'I hold myself ready,' he wrote after only a fortnight in England, 'to go forth whenever I am desired. . . . God knows I want rest; but self is entirely out of the question.' Though 'the passion was as hot as ever', it had not since his return from the Mediterranean in 1801, been unrestrained, nor had it distorted his judgement. As significant, and again since 1801, he no longer sought honour and glory: conscious that he had gained a pre-eminent reputation, that both the Establishment (although they condemned his treatment of Fanny and his life with Emma) and the People (who were little concerned with his private life), believed him to be the only man who could thwart Napoleon's pretensions at sea, he now had but one ambition, to do his duty. Southey's story (in his *Life of Nelson*) that Emma had to plead with him to leave her when, in the event, the summons came early in September, has no substance: the truth is contained in a letter which she wrote to Lady Bolton when his stay at Merton was curtailed to only twenty-four days: 'I am again broken-hearted, as our dear Nelson is immediately going. . . . But what can I do? His powerful arm is of so much consequence to his Country.'

On 2 August Napoleon was sufficiently sure of a favourable opportunity for his invasion of England to join his *Grande Armée* at Boulogne. One week later he heard that Villeneuve had sought refuge from Calder in Ferrol. Even so, he expected him to sail again, northward for the Channel, as soon as his combined fleets had been watered: on the 29th, Ganteaume was ordered out to effect a junction with him. But the sight of Cornwallis's ships bearing down on the Brest fleet as soon as it cleared harbour on the 21st, followed by a brief exchange of shots, was enough to persuade the French to return to port. That the British numbered only seventeen ships-of-the-line when they had twenty-one counted for nothing against Napoleon's reiterated orders to *evade* action.

Cornwallis had so reduced his fleet on 17 August. Three days after Calder rejoined him off Ferrol, the Commander-in-Chief sent him back with eighteen sail-of-the-line to resume the blockade of Villeneuve, whose force now numbered thirty-five. For thus dividing his fleet Cornwallis has been much criticized on the score that it exposed him to defeat by a considerably larger force: if Ganteaume and Villeneuve had effected a junction, the former would have had more than fifty ships-of-the-line under his supreme command. But the point is no more than academic. Villeneuve was quick to leave Ferrol as soon as Calder lifted his blockade on 9 August; he hoped to meet Rear-Admiral Allemand's five ships-of-the-line that had slipped out of Rochefort. But when he failed to find them he remembered the last order he had received from Napoleon, when still in the West Indies; if, on returning to Europe, he was 'for any reason' unable to join Ganteaume, he was to go to Cadiz, seize Gibraltar and the Straits, and collect the Spanish squadron from Cartagena – which would give him a sufficient force to seize command of the Channel even if, on heading north again, Ganteaume failed to meet him. And, 'for any reason', was a fatal loophole to a man of Villeneuve's mentality: it was enough for him to choose Napoleon's alternative course of action. Heading south before Calder could again be off Ferrol, he rounded Cape St Vincent, and on the 20th entered Cadiz, after chasing away Collingwood's watching patrol of only three ships-of-the-line. Calder followed him, but could not arrive off this Spanish port until the 30th, when he provided Collingwood with a total of twenty-six ships-of-the-line with which to establish an effective blockade.

For this collapse of the elaborate scaffolding of plans for invading England which Napoleon had been erecting for more than two years, the Emperor laid the blame on Villeneuve. 'Where,' he complained, 'did my admirals learn that they can make war without taking risks?' But the truth is very different. Before any word of Villeneuve's decision to go south could reach Boulogne, Napoleon received news of much graver import: Austria and Russia had decided to join Britain in a Third Coalition against France. [As when he was in Egypt, Napoleon could not resist the trumpet call; '*La Patrie en danger*'.] He must strike before the Austrian and Russian armies could join forces against him. On 24 August he ordered the generals commanding the several divisions of his *Grande Armée* to break camp and 'march for Mainz. I want to be in the heart of Germany with 300,000 men before anybody knows about it.'

On 2 September Captain Blackwood, who had played a large part in the capture of the *Guillaume Tell* off Malta, and now held command of the frigate *Euryalus*, brought to London, and Nelson, the news that Villeneuve was in Cadiz. Pitt and Barham were in no doubt that the enemy's combined fleets must be held there and prevented from either threatening the Channel or entering the Mediterranean. The port must be blockaded until Villeneuve chose to sortie, which might well be soon because the place was known to be short of food; then, in Nelson's words, 'it is . . . annihilation that the Country wants, and not merely a splendid victory . . . honourable to all parties concerned, but absolutely useless . . . to bring Bonaparte to his marrow-bones'.

This task was clearly his: as soon as the *Victory* could be made ready, at half-past ten on the night of 13 September, and a fortnight before his forty-seventh birthday, he

> drove from dear, dear Merton, where I left all which I hold dear in this world, to go to serve my King and Country. May the great God whom I adore enable me to fulfil the expectation of my Country; and if it is His good pleasure that I should return, my thanks will never cease being offered up to the Throne of His Mercy. If it is His good Providence to cut short my days upon earth, I bow with the greatest submission, relying that He will protect those so dear to me, that I may leave behind. His Will be done: Amen, Amen, Amen.

There was nothing new in such religious fervour: Nelson was not only a clergymen's son but held the strong belief in God that is characteristic of those who follow the sea profession, despite his (and their) neglect of the seventh commandment. There was, too, no special premonition in such words: he had expressed similar sentiments before the Nile and Copenhagen – and many officers and men wrote in such terms before going into action in the First and Second World Wars. As he told Davison: 'I hope my absence will not be long, and that I shall soon meet the combined fleets with a force sufficient to do the job well; for half a victory would but half content me. . . . I will do my best. . . . I have much to lose, but little to gain; and I go because it is right, and I will serve the Country faithfully.'

On the Portsmouth Road Nelson stopped for refreshment at the Royal Anchor Hotel, Liphook (still a flourishing hostelry), and next morning breakfasted at Portsmouth's George Hotel (unhappily destroyed in a Second World War *blitz*). Thence he walked to Southsea beach (near where the Clarence Pier now stands: not as is often said, to the Sally Port at the end of the High Street). 'A crowd collected in his train, pressing forward to obtain sight of his face; many were in tears, and many knelt down before him and blessed him as he passed. England has had many heroes but never one who so entirely possessed the love of his fellow-countrymen. . . . They pressed upon the parapet to gaze after him when his barge pushed off, and he was returning their cheers by waving his hat.'* 'I had their huzzas before', he told Hardy as they rowed out to the *Victory*. 'I have their hearts now.'

Next morning, hearing that the *Royal Sovereign*, *Agamemnon* and *Defiance* were not yet ready, Nelson sent orders to their captains to follow as soon as they could. He would not delay an hour in getting to Cadiz: as he told Blackwood, whose frigate was to accompany him, 'I am convinced . . . [of] the importance of not letting the rogues escape us without a fair fight which I pant for by day and dream of by night.' But though the *Victory* sailed that afternoon the wind was dead foul: not until the 17th was she off Plymouth where the *Thunderer* and *Ajax* joined Nelson's flag. South-west of the Scillies he met his erstwhile second-in-command, Bickerton, a sick man on his way home. By the 25th his small force was off Lisbon, from where he sped the *Euryalus* to warn Collingwood of his coming. Three days later Nelson sighted his fleet. But, much more pleasing, he also saw the masts and yards of the combined fleets lying at their moorings in Cadiz. He had caught up with Villeneuve at last!

Nelson's first task on reassuming command of a Mediterranean station which was again extended out into the Atlantic, was a distasteful one. Calder, when first captain to Jervis in 1797, had severely criticized his decision to wear the *Captain* out of the line during the battle of Cape St Vincent. Yet, when Nelson heard the details of Calder's engagement with Villeneuve off Cape Finisterre, he wrote these sympathetic words:

> Who can, my dear Fremantle, command all the success which our Country may wish? We have fought together. . . . I have the best disposed fleet of friends, but who can say what will be the event of a

*Southey in his *Life of Nelson*.

battle? . . . I should have fought the enemy, so did my friend Calder; but who can say that he will be more successful than another?

But others were not so generous: he was required to tell Calder that the Government was dissatisfied with his conduct and that he was to return forthwith to England to stand trial by court martial. He felt so much for Calder's predicament that he had not the heart to reject his plea to return in his own flagship, rather than in a frigate, although this would deprive the fleet of a ship-of-the-line when it already numbered fewer than the enemy. Two months later Calder was acquitted of cowardice but severely reprimanded for not renewing the action on 23 or 24 July.

This episode excepted, 'the reception I [Nelson] met with on joining the fleet caused the sweetest sensation in my life. The officers who came on board to welcome my return forgot my rank . . . in the enthusiasm with which they greeted me.' This was not mere vanity: in the immediately following days, by frequent invitations to his flag officers and captains to visit him, Nelson quickly inspired them by his sympathetic understanding of their problems, his explanations of how he intended to carry out his task and, above all, by his magnetic personality. As George Duff of the *Mars* told his wife: 'He certainly is the pleasantest admiral I ever served under.'

With 'my dear Coll. as perfect as could be expected', as his second-in-command, and with Louis and the Earl of Northesk as his rear-admirals, Nelson's fleet was soon reinforced to as many as thirty-three ships-of-the-line, a figure much nearer to the forty with which he credited Villeneuve. Collingwood's strategy had been a *close* blockade, investing Cadiz with an inshore squadron of five ships-of-the-line under Louis, and holding the rest in support to seaward. Nelson changed this to the more enterprising one that he had adopted off Toulon: Villeneuve must be encouraged to come out before the winter gales set in. Louis was recalled from his inshore watch and the whole British battle fleet withdrew some fifty miles to the west, leaving the task of reporting any movement by the combined fleets to the *Euryalus* and three other frigates.

By 8 October Nelson had enough intelligence to be confident that Napoleon had issued new orders to Villeneuve. (Written on 14 September, shortly before the Emperor left Paris to lead his *Grande Armée* against Austria, Villeneuve received them on the 29th, the day after Nelson's arrival off Cadiz.) The combined fleets were to sail into the Mediterranean: no longer required to cover the discarded invasion of England, they were to land reinforcements at Naples to forestall the attack which

Pitt had ordered General Sir James Craig to stage from Malta, in conjunction with the Russians, on the 'soft under-belly' of Napoleon's empire. 'Should the enemy move,' he told Collingwood, 'it is probable that I shall make a signal to bear up and steer for the entrance to the Straits . . . to intercept them.'

Villeneuve had one distinct advantage; he and Gravina could sail on the day of their choice with thirty-three ships-of-the-line (not Nelson's over-estimate of forty), including the mighty *Santísima Trinidad* of 140 guns, the *Principe de Asturias* and *Santa Ana* with 112, and the *Rayo* with 100. Nelson could never have such a number: though his fleet totalled as many ships as the enemy, including seven of 98 or 100 guns, he must send detachments in turn to Gibraltar for victuals and water. More important, he had to provide battleships to escort convoys eastward from the Straits against attack by the Spanish squadron in Cartagena. So his force off Cadiz seldom numbered more than twenty-seven ships-of-the-line, six fewer than the enemy. Nelson had, however, an advantage of another kind, an abundant faith in the superiority of his officers and men as fighters and as seamen. 'Choose yourself, my Lord,' he had said to Barham, when offered a list from which to select his officers, 'the same spirit actuates the whole profession: you cannot choose wrong.' For contrast, though Villeneuve might trust his own ships, he had little faith in Gravina's: the Spaniards were not only incompetent but lacked interest in the war. Indeed, the French Commander-in-Chief so far distrusted them that, in his order of sailing, he mingled the Spanish ships with his own, so that it would be difficult for them to desert him in a crisis, instead of keeping them in one squadron under Gravina's command.

Two pieces of intelligence precipitated Villeneuve's departure. On 18 October he learned that Vice-Admiral François Rosily had arrived at Madrid. Knowing that Napoleon held him in contempt for his failure to make the Channel, Villeneuve surmised (correctly) that he was about to be superseded. The same day brought a report that a British convoy had sailed eastwards from Gibraltar escorted by four ships-of-the-line, leaving two more anchored in the Bay. With Nelson's strength thus reduced, here was an opportunity for him to salvage his honour, before Rosily could complete his difficult journey. To the masthead of his flagship, the *Bucentaure*, went the signal, 'Prepare to weigh'.

The wisdom of Nelson's strategy was soon apparent. At 6.0 am on 19 October the *Sirius*, which was the closest inshore of Blackwood's frigates, flew the group from Popham's code: 'Enemy have their topsails hoisted'. Three hours later Nelson responded with the signal, 'General chase south-east', so that he might place his fleet between the enemy and the Straits.

My dearest beloved Emma. . . . The signal has been made that the enemy's combined fleets are coming out of port. We have very little wind, so that I have no hope of seeing them before tomorrow. May the God of Battles crown my endeavours with success. I will take care that my name shall ever be most dear to you and Horatia, both of whom I love as much as my own life. And as my last writing before the battle will be to you, so I hope in God that I shall live to finish my letter after the battle.*

The wind being light from south-by-west, backing in the afternoon to south-east-by-east, Nelson did not sight the Rock until 1.0 am on the 20th, when he hove-to midway between Cape Trafalgar and Cape Spartel. And dawn brought two disappointments. There was no sign of Louis's six battleships: the sloop carrying Nelson's orders to them to rejoin him did not reach Gibraltar until after Louis had sailed with four into the Mediterranean escorting an eastbound convoy, leaving two to take in supplies. Secondly, as Collingwood wrote to his wife:

All our gay hopes are fled, and instead of being under all sail in a very light breeze and fine weather, expecting to bring the enemy to battle, we are under close-reefed topsails in a very stormy wind [from the south-south-west] with thick rainy weather, *and the dastardly French returned to Cadiz.*

Or, as Nelson continued his letter to Emma:

In the morning we were close to . . . the Straits, but the wind had not come far enough to the westward to allow the combined fleets to weather the shoals off Trafalgar. . . . A group of them was seen off the lighthouse of Cadiz this morning; but it blows so very fresh and thick weather that I rather believe they will go into the harbour before night. May God Almighty give us success over these fellows, and enable us to get a Peace.

Fortunately, Nelson's and Collingwood's appreciation of the enemy's movements was soon proved wrong. After writing to Barham: 'I must guard against being caught with a westerly wind near Cadiz, as a fleet

*Hardy found this letter, to which Nelson added more that is quoted below, lying unsealed on his Admiral's desk after the action and took it to England where Emma added the poignant words: 'O miserable, wretched Emma! O glorious and happy Nelson!'

of so many three-deckers would be forced into the Straits', and setting course to the north-west to regain his station fifty miles west of the Spanish port, one of Blackwood's frigates hove in sight with the news that the enemy was, after all, at sea to the north. The light winds of the previous day had prevented many of the French and Spanish ships clearing Cadiz before sundown. Indeed, the combined fleets were not finally at sea until noon on 20 October. And since another four hours elapsed before they were formed up in a *corps de bataille* of three divisions under Villeneuve's immediate command, with the remaining twelve French and Spanish ships-of-the-line as an *escadre d'observation* in reserve under Gravina, it was not until 4 pm that, after an initial move south-west, Villeneuve began to steer south to make a good offing for entering the Straits.

Nelson rejected Collingwood's advice in favour of an attack that day, because this would mean beginning the action too late to be sure of a decisive result. Nor was this an occasion for an attack in the dark, which was always more hazardous against a fleet at sea than, as against Brueys in Aboukir Bay, a fleet in harbour. He continued, instead, to the north-west under easy sail until his fleet was twenty miles south-west of Cadiz, a movement designed to encourage Villeneuve to pass inshore of him, whilst Blackwood's frigates, covered by three ships-of-the-line, kept the combined fleets under close observation. From them Nelson learned at 2.0 pm that Villeneuve was heading westwards. 'But that,' he wrote in his diary, 'they shall not do, if in the power of Nelson and Brontë to prevent them' – and steered to intercept. By nightfall, however, Blackwood had reported Villeneuve's true course. Since the combined fleets were then too far from the Straits to reach them before the morning, Nelson instructed Blackwood to continue shadowing whilst his battle fleet maintained its windward position. If the wind should shift round to the east, so as to place it to leeward, it would be of no great consequence because Villeneuve woudl then be unable to steer for the Straits.

At 4.0 am Nelson reversed course, and daylight on 21 October not only promised fairer weather but brought the reassuring sight of the combined fleets only nine miles to the north-east, though with the small disappointment that Henry Digby's 64-gun *Africa* had lost touch to the north during the night. But though the odds had lengthened to thirty-three against twenty-six, Nelson did not hesitate: at 5.40 am with the favourable omen that this was the forty-sixth anniversary of the action that had inspired him as a boy to join the Navy, Uncle Maurice Suckling's defeat of de Kersaint, Nelson signalled his fleet to, 'Form the order of sailing in two columns', followed twenty minutes later by, 'Prepare for battle'.

If Nelson's unorthodox strategy was so effective in enabling him to bring a reluctant enemy to battle, what of his tactics? Those which he conceived for the small fleet with which he had hoped to fight Villeneuve in the Caribbean were outlined in the previous chapter. For use against a much larger force, the combined fleets which he believed might number as many as forty-six ships-of-the-line when he could expect his own to be reinforced to no more than forty, he devised a fresh plan which, when he explained it to his flag officers and captains soon after arriving off Cadiz, 'was like an electric shock. Some shed tears, all approved. "It was new: it was singular: it was simple!" And from admirals downwards it was repeated, "It must succeed." '

Since this 'Nelson touch', as he called his plan, is of such importance to what followed, we are fortunate that it has survived in his own hand. On 9 October he wrote a secret memorandum of which this is the essence.

Thinking it almost impossible to bring 40 sail-of-the-line into a line of battle in variable winds, thick weather and other circumstances which must occur, without such a loss of time that the opportunity would probably be lost of bringing the enemy to battle, I have made up my mind that the order of sailing is to be the order of battle, in two lines of 16 ships each, with an advanced squadron of eight of the fastest, which will always make, if wanted, one line of 24 sail on whichever one the Commander-in-Chief may direct. The Second-in-Command will have the entire direction of his line.

If the enemy should be seen to *windward*, [i.e. the British would be required, contrary to their usual practice, to attack from to leeward], the enemy line of battle will probably be so extended that their van could not succour their rear. I should therefore signal the Second-in-Command to lead through, about the twelfth ship from their rear; my line would lead through about their centre, and the advanced squadron cut through two or three ships ahead of their centre, so as to ensure getting at their Commander-in-Chief. It must be some time before their untouched van of 20 sail can manoeuvre to attack any part of the British fleet, or to succour their own engaged ships.

For an attack *from* to windward, the British fleet will be brought nearly within gunshot of the enemy's centre. The signal will then be made for the lee line; under the Second-in-Command, to bear up together, setting all their sails in order to cut through the enemy's line as quickly as possible, beginning from the twelfth ship from the enemy's rear. Should the enemy wear together, the 12 ships first composing his

[handwritten facsimile of Nelson's Trafalgar Memorandum]

'The Nelson Touch': part of Nelson's Trafalgar Memorandum

rear are still to be attacked by the lee line. The remainder of the enemy's fleet are to be left to the Commander-in-Chief.

Something must be left to chance; nothing is sure in a sea fight. Shot will carry away the masts and yards of friends as well as foes; but I look with confidence to a victory before the van of the enemy can succour their rear, and then that most of the British fleet would be ready to receive them, or to pursue them should they endeavour to make off. Captains are to look to their particular line as their rallying point. But in case signals can neither be seen or perfectly understood, no captain can do very wrong if he places his ship alongside that of an enemy.

This memorandum included a line sketch making clear how Nelson intended to attack Villeneuve's fleet from the windward position, from which the diagrams on p. 262 are derived. In short, for the first action in which he would command a fleet against an enemy *under way at sea*, Nelson wholly rejected the dogma of a gun duel in line ahead on parallel courses. Instead, as he had told Lord Sidmouth (the erstwhile Addington) before leaving England: 'Rodney [at The Saints] broke the enemy's line in one place, I will break it in two' – which would not only cut it into three parts but enable him to concentrate his whole strength on little more than half the enemy's in 'a pell-mell battle . . . that is what I want', leaving the remainder powerless to intervene until too late. And to achieve this he could rely on Collingwood, just as half a century later, General Robert E. Lee trusted 'Stonewall' Jackson: 'I [Lee] have but to show him my design and I know that if it can be done it will be done. No need for me . . . to watch him.'

Notwithstanding the smaller number of ships (twenty-seven instead of forty) available to him when Villeneuve decided to sortie (with thirty-three instead of the expected forty-six) Nelson at first conformed to this plan. For much of 20 October Duff in the *Mars* led an Advanced Squadron of eight two-deckers: the rest of the fleet sailed in two columns, one including the *Victory*, the other Collingwood's *Royal Sovereign*. But during the manoeuvring of that day in search of the enemy in variable winds, the British fleet was unable to preserve this disposition: by the evening Nelson had absorbed Duff's ships into his main body. Villeneuve was in similar difficulties; though his fleet endeavoured to form up in accordance with his plan – a main body of twenty in three divisions under his own command, with the rest in reserve under Gravina – his captains laboured in vain to achieve this.

The night did nothing to improve matters: when dawn on 21 October revealed the two fleets in sight of each other, Nelson's being about nine miles to the west of his opponents, neither was in any regular formation. In the words of Able Seaman J. Brown: 'The French and Spanish fleets were like a great wood on our lee bow, which cheered the hearts of any

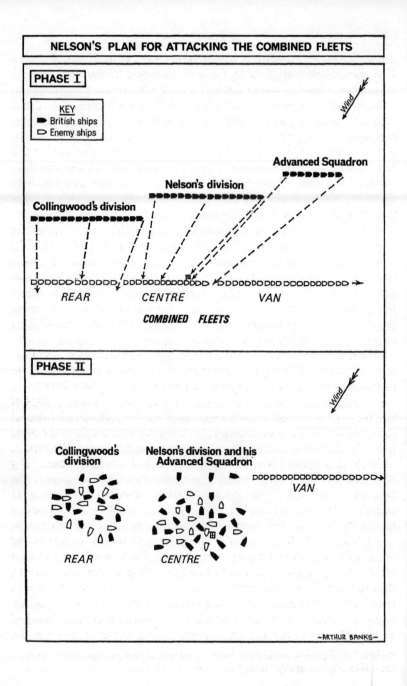

NELSON'S PLAN FOR ATTACKING THE COMBINED FLEETS

PHASE I

KEY
■▶ British ships
▷ Enemy ships

Advanced Squadron

Nelson's division

Collingwood's division

REAR *CENTRE* *VAN*

COMBINED FLEETS

PHASE II

Collingwood's division

Nelson's division and his Advanced Squadron

VAN

REAR *CENTRE*

~ARTHUR BANKS~

British tar in the *Victory* like lions anxious to be at it.' Nor did Nelson disappoint them: despite the lightness of the breeze from the west-north-west, his one thought was to close with the enemy before they could run through the Straits, or return to Cadiz; then to attack them in accordance with the essence of his plan – cutting their line in two places and concentrating all his ships against their centre and rear. He had taken particular care to ensure that his new Band of Brothers understood this, so that any departure from his memorandum, such as abandoning the concept of an advanced squadron, would be of no consequence. As soon as 6.0 am* he signalled, 'Form the order of sailing in two columns' – and all knew that the order of sailing was also the order of battle – followed at 6.10 by, 'Bear up and sail large [i.e. with the wind from abaft the quarter] on the course east-north-east', which at 6.45 was amended to east – with the need for speed repeatedly emphasized by, 'Make more sail', until, for the first time a British fleet was going into action with studding sails set, and with bands playing *Heart of Oak*, *Rule Britannia*, and *Britons Strike Home*, so that Midshipman John Franklin (later the famous Arctic explorer) of the *Bellerophon* wrote: 'One would have thought that the people were preparing for a festival rather than a combat.'

Villeneuve knew enough about Nelson to have perceived his plan: according to his fighting instructions: 'The enemy will not trouble to form line parallel to ours and fight it out gun for gun. . . . He will try to . . . cut through the line, and bring against our ships thus isolated, groups of his own to surround and capture them.' Nevertheless, the French Admiral did nothing to counter such tactics; he ordered his fleet to form the usual line of battle, a long single line on a southerly course towards the Straits, with Gravina taking his squadron into station immediately ahead. But only until 8.0 am: at that hour Villeneuve had a change of heart. If he held on he would be committed to passing Gibraltar with Nelson in pursuit, and to finding Louis's squadron waiting for him ahead. Supposing that he would do better to keep Cadiz under his lee, so that if needs be he could seek safety there, he ordered his ships to reverse course to the north, placing Gravina's squadron in the rear. But this was a manoeuvre which, in such a light wind, and in a swell rolling in from the Atlantic, took so much time that it was 10.0 am before the combined fleets were round, in far from good order. They had been thrown into what Collingwood described as 'a crescent convexing to leeward', with many bunched up two and three deep and only approximating to the sequence in the

*In what follows all times are necessarily approximate because there are considerable discrepancies between the various ships' logs.

table facing p. 268. Since the British fleet was now bearing down upon them less than five miles away, Captain Churruca of the *San Juan Nepomuceno* was moved to comment to his first lieutenant: 'The fleet is doomed. The French Admiral does not understand his business. He has compromised us all.'

Since the *Royal Sovereign* was already to leeward, Collingwood's division had little difficulty in moving to its allotted place on the *Victory*'s starboard hand. But it was otherwise with the rest of Nelson's plan. Had he wished to adhere closely to it, he must have held back his faster ships to allow both columns to form in line abreast in the sequence, from left to right, in the table facing p. 268 before turning north parallel with the enemy, and then bearing down to cut his line as in the diagram on p. 262. But he had always intended the plan to be a flexible one to fit any situation which might arise; hence the wide discretion given to his second-in-command. And in such a light wind there was no time for precision; if the enemy was not to escape he must be brought to action at the earliest possible moment. To this end Nelson pressed his fastest ships so hard that by 11.30 am neither column had achieved more than a line of bearing which, by the time the battle began, was no better than quarterline.

This formation needs to be stressed because, for more than a century afterwards, until in 1912 the matter was fully investigated by a committee of experts, it was generally believed that the two columns sailed into action in *line ahead* at near to right angles to the enemy line (as is shown in the contemporary painting reproduced as plate 41).* Had this been so, Nelson would have been open to the serious criticism of not only ignoring his carefully conceived plan, but of hazarding his fleet by reckless tactics equivalent to those which were later to be known as allowing the enemy to 'cross the T' – exposing his ships to enemy broadsides when they could not return them, and which, exactly a century later when gun range had increased from a mile to four or five, proved suicidal for Rozhéstvensky's fleet at Tsushima.

Nelson and Collingwood led their respective columns. When the faster *Téméraire* gained on the *Victory*, Nelson called across the inter-

---

*Collingwood's column is also shown flying his *blue* ensign although, as at the Nile, Nelson ordered his whole fleet to fly the *white* ensign because this was more readily distinguishable from the French *tricolor*. But in making such mistakes the artist is in good company. Turner painted the *Victory* flying 'England expects . . .' long after the battle had begun: moreover, subsequent research has shown that not all his signal flags are correct. And the Paris Musée de la Marine has a painting by Mayer in which the *Redoutable* is surrendering to a British three-decker which is not only flying the *red* ensign, but bears across her stern the name *Sandwich*, when no such ship took part in the battle.

vening water: 'I'll thank you, Captain Harvey, to keep in your proper station which is astern of the *Victory*.' He was determined to set the same example to his division as Collingwood was doing to his. But others, realizing that the *Victory* would bear the brunt of the action in the centre of the enemy's line before the rest of her division could come to her support, were concerned for their Commander-in-Chief's safety. He was advised to cover his uniform coat, with its several stars,* so that he would not be readily identifiable to the enemy when the fleets came within musket range. He rejected the suggestion on the just score that, by being clearly recognizable, his own officers and men would be greatly encouraged. (More than a century later, in 1943, Vice-Admiral Sir Algernon Willis made a practice of hoisting a very large silk flag in HMS *Nelson* when leading Force H into action, the importance of this inspiring sight – and that it *was* inspiring the author can testify from his own experience – overriding any possibility that it would more easily identify the flagship to the enemy.)

Likewise for a good reason Nelson rejected Hardy's suggestion that he should shift his flag to one of Blackwood's frigates which were lying to the north of his column. Rodney had tried this in his action against de Guichen on 12 May 1780 and found that, from a position out of the line of battle, he was unable to control it.† Both points give the lie to the suggestion that Nelson courted death at Trafalgar: he no more did so than in his previous actions, as any man devoid of fear must seem to do. So, too, with Blackwood's description of his visit to the *Victory* during the morning of 21 October in which he noted that Nelson's last words to him were: 'God bless you, Blackwood, I shall never speak to you again.' To see in this a 'death-wish' is to assume that Blackwood's recollections were accurate. A man so deeply affected by Nelson's death is as likely to have thus remembered nothing more ominous than: 'I shall not speak to you again until after the battle' – for there is ample evidence, notably the letter quoted on p. 257, that, subject to doing his duty, annihilating Villeneuve, Nelson wanted to live, for Emma and Horatia.

---

*The coat can be seen in the Nelson collection in the National Maritime Museum, Greenwich. The emblems of orders were then worn with *undress* uniform on all ordinary occasions, and so sewn on, just as medal ribbons now are. It was not until a later date that stars were restricted to *full dress* uniform and ceremonial occasions.

†For details of Rodney's experiment, see this author's article "The Fleet Flagship" in the *Journal of the Royal United Service Institution* for August 1936. Howe also hoisted his flag in a frigate on 8 August 1778, when he failed to bring the French to action in Narragansett Bay. So did Suffren in one of his actions against Hughes from which he learned this lesson: '*ce sera la première et dernière fois*'.

During the long six hours in which they closed the enemy at a speed that never exceeded a couple of knots in the light west-north-westerly wind which prevailed throughout the day, Nelson had no need to stay continuously on deck. Around 11.0 am he retired to the privacy of his cabin, to write in his diary these memorable words:

> May the Great God, whom I worship, grant to my Country, and for the benefit of Europe in general, a great and glorious victory; and may no misconduct in any one tarnish it; and may humanity after victory be the predominant feature in the British fleet. For myself, individually, I commend my life to Him who made me, and may His blessing light upon my endeavours for serving my Country faithfully. To Him I resign myself and the just cause which is entrusted to me to defend. Amen, Amen, Amen.

Then, remembering how he had failed to persuade the Government to give any tangible recognition for what he believed to be Emma's eminent services at the Neapolitan Court, and how little money he had managed to save, he added this codicil to his will:

> Could I have rewarded these services, I would not now call upon my Country; but as it is not in my power, I leave Emma Hamilton . . . a legacy to my King and Country, that they will give her ample provision to maintain her rank in life. I also leave to the beneficence of my Country my adopted [sic] daughter, Horatia. . . . These are the only favours I ask of my King and Country at this moment when I am going into battle.

As he finished writing, his signal officer, Lieutenant Pasco, came into the cabin. In all the hours since daybreak, Nelson had made only five general signals to his fleet, plus a dozen to individual ships. Now he ordered Pasco to hoist two more. First, to telegraph a final clarifying phrase to Collingwood, using Popham's recently issued vocabulary code: 'I intend to push or go through the end of the enemy's line to prevent them getting into Cadiz.' Then, for all his single-minded concern with the imminent battle, he was reminded that the growing swell which again and again lifted the *Victory*'s stern, presaged a storm, when the British fleet would be threatened with a lee shore that would be especially dangerous for damaged ships, particularly those of the enemy which he expected to take in prize. By anchoring on the night of 20 November 1759 Hawke had saved his fleet from the disaster that overwhelmed the French in Quiberon Bay. So, now, Nelson warned: 'Prepare to anchor after the close of the day.' Only after this did he 'amuse the fleet' with: 'England expects ...'* which for all its subsequent immortality, prompted Collingwood to growl: 'I wish Nelson would stop signalling, as we all know well enough what we have to do.'

'Old Coll' was heading for Vice-Admiral Alava's 112-gun *Santa Ana*. She might be the sixteenth ship from the rear of the enemy's line, counting Gravina's squadron, but she was the proper opponent for the 100-gun *Royal Sovereign*, and fifteen British ships were a match for sixteen of the enemy. Nelson, whose division numbered only eleven until the *Africa* rejoined later in the day, because of the absence of Louis with six on convoy duty and replenishing at Gibraltar, was heading for the 140-gun *Santísima Trinidad* in the centre of the enemy's line.

> It was a beautiful sight [wrote Midshipman Babcock of the *Neptune*] when their line was completed, their broadsides turned towards us, showing their iron teeth, and now and then trying the range of a shot ... that they might, the moment we came within point blank, open their fire upon our van ships. ... Some of the enemy's ships were painted like ourselves, with double yellow sides, some with a broad red or yellow streak, others all black, and the noble *Santísima Trinidad*, with four distinct lines of red, with a white ribbon between them, made her seem a superb man-of-war ... her head splendidly ornamented with a colossal group of figures ... representing the Holy Trinity from which she took her name.

At noon, the *Victory* flew Nelson's last signal: 'Engage the enemy more closely.' 'Now,' he said, 'I can do no more. We must trust to the great Disposer of all events, and to the justice of our cause. I thank God for this great opportunity of doing my duty.' A few minutes later the *Royal Sovereign* came within range of the enemy and Captain Baudoin's 74-gun *Fougueux* fired the broadside that began the battle of Trafalgar. And though it was Nelson's intention that his lee column should be the first in action, such was Collingwood's enthusiasm, and his understanding of his Commander-in-Chief, that he called to his flag captain: 'Rotherham, what would Nelson give to be here!'

Nelson was to be in the thick of the fight soon enough, but clarity requires this account to follow the further progress of Collingwood's division first. (Here the reader is referred to the diagrams on pp. 272 and 273.) Unperturbed by enemy fire, Edward Rotherham sailed the *Royal*

*See above p. 85.

Sovereign under the *Santa Ana*'s stern into which she discharged double-shotted broadsides, the while her starboard guns raked the *Fougueux*'s bow. He then turned north, so close under the *Santa Ana*'s lee that their yard-arms locked, and continued a furious duel muzzle to muzzle. The *Belleisle* was next in action, William Hargood holding his fire until he could engage the *Indomtable* at point-blank range. The remainder of Collingwood's captains likewise sailed their ships in succession into the grouped mass of the enemy's rear. By 1.0 pm most were shrouded in the smoke of a general engagement with seventeen of the combined fleet, which were not only thrown into confusion but partly separated from Villeneuve's centre.

At 2.15 pm the *Santa Ana*, having lost all her masts and with Alava severely wounded, struck to the *Royal Sovereign*, after the latter had herself suffered heavy damage. HMS *Belleisle* was not so fortunate, being reduced to a wreck by the *Fougueux*, and only being saved from destruction by the intervention of the *Polyphemus*, *Defiance* and *Swiftsure*, when Hargood had the deserved satisfaction of taking the surrender of the *Argonauta*. The *Mars* was seriously mauled in actions with the *Pluton*, *Monarca* and *Fougueux* in which Duff was killed. Charles Tyler's *Tonnant* then engaged the *Monarca* yard-arm to yard-arm until Captain Argumosa struck his colours, before turning his guns on the *Algésiras* which (according to one of the *Tonnant*'s lieutenants),

> locked her bowsprit in our starboard main shrouds and attempted to board us. . . . She had riflemen in her tops who did great execution. Our poop was soon cleared, and our gallant captain shot through the left thigh. . . . [But] we were not idle. We gave it her most gloriously with the starboard maindeckers, and turned the forecastle gun [carronade], loaded with grape, on the gentleman who wished to give us a fraternal hug. The marines kept up a warm destructive fire on the boarders, only one [of whom] made good his footing on our quarterdeck. . . . At length we had the satisfaction of seeing her three lower masts go by the board. . . . The crew were then ordered . . . to board her. They cheered, and in a short time carried her. They found the gallant Admiral Magon [de Médine] killed, and the captain dangerously wounded.

Despite Tyler's wound, the *Tonnant* then dealt likewise with the *San Juan Nepomuceno*. However, Captain Churruca rehoisted his colours before he could be boarded. Argumosa likewise rehoisted the *Monarca*'s and joined with the *Aigle* in engaging HMS *Bellerophon* in an action in which the French *Swiftsure* and the *Bahama* were also involved, the British ship losing not only her main- and mizen-topmasts but her Captain, John Cooke. With the help of Robert Moorsom's *Revenge*, she was nonetheless able to compel Argumosa to haul down his ensign for the second time.

James Morris's *Colossus* was first locked broadside to broadside with the *Argonauta*, then in action with the French *Swiftsure* and with the *Bahama*, suffering more casualties than any other British ship before compelling the *Bahama* to surrender, followed by the submission of the *Swiftsure*. Richard King in the *Achille* engaged the *Montañez*, then the *Argonauta* which struck in time for King also to take the *Berwick* in prize. Conn's *Dreadnought* captured the already damaged *San Juan Nepomuceno*, after a fight lasting only a quarter-of-an-hour. Robert Redmill's *Polyphemus* engaged the French *Neptune* and *Achille*. Robert Moorsom's *Revenge*, after being in action with the *Aigle* at such close range as to foul her jib-boom, was in a hot action with the *Principe d'Asturias*. William Rutherford's *Swiftsure* set the *Achille* on fire. Philip Durham's *Defiance* ran alongside and lashed herself to the *Aigle* which only surrendered after Captain Gourrége had put up a most gallant defence. In the *Thunderer*, Lieutenant John Stockham raked Gravina's flagship in a duel, mortally wounding the Spanish Admiral who later paid his victor this generous tribute: 'I am a dying man, but I hope I am going to join Nelson.' George Hope's *Defiance* compelled the *San Ildefonso* to strike. Finally, at 4.30 pm Richard Grindall's *Prince*, last in Collingwood's line, added her fire to the blazing *Achille* which blew up at 5.45 pm, with the loss of most of her crew.

Turning back the clock to the exploits of Nelson's own column, at 12.15 pm Villeneuve realized the need for the ships in the van of his line to tack to his support. But, instead of ordering Rear-Admiral Dumanoir Le Pelley's division to do this, he made only a general signal directing ships not engaged with the enemy to take whatever steps were necessary to get into action, on which Dumanoir did nothing. Five minutes after this the *Victory*, heading for the *Bucentaure*, was in action. Heavily engaged by the *Santísima Trinidad*, *Neptune* and *Redoutable* as well as by Villeneuve's flagship, one shot cut her mizen topmast in two, another shattered her wheel, others tore her sails to shreds. 'This is too warm work to last long', was Nelson's comment as, very slowly in the light breeze, the *Victory* continued to forge ahead.

By 12.30 the French *Neptune* and the *Redoutable* were so close astern of the *Bucentaure* that Hardy could see no gap through which to steer the *Victory*. 'I cannot help it', Nelson said. 'It does not signify which we run on board. Take your choice.' Hardy chose the *Redoutable*: but as he steered

THE OPPOSING FLEETS AT THE BATTLE OF TRAFALGAR, 21 OCTOBER 1805

BRITISH (in order of sailing)

Ship	Guns	Commander
Weather Column:		
Victory‡	100	Capt. T. Hardy / Flagship of Vice-Admiral Lord Nelson
Téméraire‡	98	Capt. E. Harvey
Neptune	98	Capt. T. Fremantle
Leviathan†	74	Capt. H. Bayntun
Britannia†	100	Capt. C. Bullen / Flagship of Rear-Admiral the Earl of Northesk
Conqueror	74	Capt. I. Pellew
Africa†	64	Capt. H. Digby
Agamemnon	64	Capt. Sir E. Berry
Ajax	74	Lieut. J. Pilfold*
Orion	74	Capt. E. Codrington
Minotaur	74	Capt. C. Mansfield
Spartiate	74	Capt. Sir F. Laforey, Bt.
Lee Column:		
Royal Sovereign‡	100	Capt. E. Rotherham / Flagship of Vice-Admiral C. Collingwood
Belleisle‡	74	Capt. W. Hargood
Mars†	74	Capt. G. Duff
Tonnant†	80	Capt. C. Tyler
Bellerophon‡	74	Capt. J. Cooke
Colossus‡	74	Capt. J. Morris
Achille‡	74	Capt. R. King
Dreadnought	98	Capt. J. Conn
Polyphemus	64	Capt. R. Redmill
Revenge†	74	Capt. R. Moorsom

FRENCH (F) AND SPANISH (S) (in order of sailing)

Ship	Guns	Commander	Fate (on 21 Oct. 1805)	Subsequent fate
Rear (became van):				
(S) Neptuno‡	80	Capt. Don H. C. Valdés	Taken	Retaken on 23 Oct.
(F) Scipion	74	Capt. C. Bellanger	Escaped	Taken by Strachan on 3 Nov.
(F) Intrépide‡	74	Capt. L. Infernet	Taken	Burnt on 26 Oct.
(S) Rayo	100	Capt. Don E. Macdonel	Escaped	Taken on 24 Oct., wrecked on 26 Oct.
(F) Formidable†	80	Capt. J. Letellier / Flagship of Rear-Admiral Dumanoir Le Pelley	Escaped	Taken by Strachan on 3 Nov.
(F) Duguay Trouin†	74	Capt. C. Touffet	Escaped	Taken by Strachan on 3 Nov.
(S) San Francisco de Asis	74	Capt. Don L. de Flores	Escaped	Wrecked on 24 Nov.
(F) Mont Blanc	74	Capt. J. La Villegris	Escaped	Taken by Strachan on 3 Nov.
Centre:				
(S) San Augustin‡	74	Capt. Don F. Cagigal	Taken	Burnt on 26 Oct.
(F) Héros	74	Capt. J. Poulain	Escaped	Sunk on 26 Oct.
(S) Santísima Trinidad‡	140	Commodore Don F. de Uriate / Flagship of Rear-Admiral Don B. de Cisneros	Taken	Sunk on 26 Oct.
(F) Bucentaure‡	80	Capt. J. Magendie / Flagship of Vice-Admiral P. Villeneuve	Taken	Retaken and wrecked on 23 Oct.
(F) Neptune	84	Commodore E. Maistral	Escaped	
(S) San Leandro	64	Capt. Don J. Quevedo	Escaped	
(F) Redoutable‡	74	Capt. J. Lucas	Taken	Sunk on 22 Oct.
Van (became rear):				
(S) San Just	74	Capt. Don M. Gaston	Escaped	
(F) Indomtable†	80	Capt. J. Hubert	Escaped	Wrecked on 24 Oct.
(S) Santa Ana‡	112	Capt. Don J. Gardoqui / Flagship of Vice-Admiral Don I. de Alava	Taken	Retaken on 23 Oct.

Ship	Rate	Commander		Status	Fate
Swiftsure	74	Capt. W. Rutherford			
Defiance†	74	Capt. P. Durham			
Thunderer	74	Lieut. J. Stockham*			
Defence	74	Capt. G. Hope			
Prince	98	Capt. R. Grindall			

Ship	Rate	Commander		Status	Fate
(F) Fougueux‡	74	Capt. L. Baudoin		Taken	Wrecked on 23 Oct.
(S) Monarca‡	74	Capt. Don T. Argumosa		Taken	Sunk on 26 Oct.
(F) Pluton‡	74	Commodore J. Casmao-Kerjulien		Escaped	

Escadre d'Observation (Reserve) which prolonged the rear:

Ship	Rate	Commander		Status	Fate
(F) Algésiras‡	74	Capt. Le Tourneur / Flagship of Rear-Admiral M. de Médine		Taken	Retaken on 23 Oct.
(S) Bahama†	74	Commodore Don D. Galiano		Taken	
(F) Aigle†	74	Capt. P. Gourrège		Taken	Wrecked on 26 Oct.
(F) Swiftsure†	74	Capt. C. l'Hôpitalier-Villemadrin		Taken	
(F) Argonaute†	74	Capt. J. Epron		Escaped	
(S) Montañez	74	Capt. Don J. Alcedo		Escaped	
(S) Argonauta†	80	Capt. Don A. Parejo		Taken	
(F) Berwick‡	74	Capt. J. Filhol-Camas		Taken	
(S) San Juan Nepomuceno‡	74	Commodore Don C. Churruca		Taken	
(S) San Ildefonso‡	74	Commodore Don J. de Varga		Taken	
(S) Achille‡	74	Capt. G. Deniéport		Destroyed by fire and explosion	
(S) Principe de Asturias‡	112	Rear-Admiral Don A. Escaño / Flagship of Admiral Don F. Gravina		Escaped	

Frigates:

Ship	Rate	Commander	Status
(F) Rhin	40	Capt. Chesneau	Escaped
(F) Hortense	40	Capt. La Marre La Meillerie	Escaped
(F) Cornélie	40	Capt. de Martinenq	Escaped
(F) Thémis	40	Capt. Jugan	Escaped
(F) Hermione	40	Capt. Mahé	Escaped

Frigates:

Ship	Rate	Commander
Euryalus	36	Capt. Hon. H. Blackwood
Naiad	38	Capt. T. Dundas
Phoebe	36	Capt. Hon. T. Capell
Sirius	36	Capt. W. Prowse

Notes
*Both ships were under the command of their first lieutenants because their captains had accompanied Calder to England to give evidence on his behalf.
†Indicates ships with more than 50 casualties.
‡Indicates ships with more than 100 casualties.

for her the French *Neptune* veered to starboard, so that the *Victory* cut under the *Bucentaure*'s stern after all. Firing double and treble shotted guns into her great cabin windows as she passed so close that, as the two ships rolled, the *Victory*'s main yard arm touched the *Bucentaure*'s gaff, Hardy's port broadsides wrecked the latter's stern, killing and wounding nearly 400 of her crew, and dismounting twenty of her guns. But the *Victory* did not escape unscathed, being raked and mauled from ahead by the French *Neptune*.

Having chosen the *Redoutable* as his opponent, Hardy turned towards her at about 1.10 pm, fouled her and dropped alongside, one of the *Victory*'s studding sail booms hooking into the French ship's rigging, carrying both to leeward as they continued to fire their main batteries into each other. The *Victory* also used her starboard carronades to clear the *Bucentaure*'s gangways when Captain Lucas ordered a boarding party aboard the *Victory*. But no one countered the Tyrolean sharpshooters in the *Redoutable*'s tops, until too late. At 1.15

Nelson was walking on the quarterdeck with Hardy when the fatal musket ball was fired, penetrating his chest and felling him to the deck. When Hardy expressed a hope that he was not severely wounded, he replied [much as he had done at the Nile]: 'They have done for me at last. My back-bone is shot through.' Hardy ordered seamen to carry the Admiral down the ladders to the cockpit with his face and stars covered so that he would not be seen by the crew. Laid upon a bed and stripped of his clothes, he was examined by the surgeon, Mr Beatty, who soon found that the ball had penetrated deep into the chest and had probably lodged in the spine. Other symptoms indicated the hopeless situation of the case but the true nature of the wound was kept from all except Hardy.*

Shortly before this Elias Harvey's *Téméraire* had come through the enemy's line by the gap which the *Victory* had carved astern of the *Bucentaure*. In a hot action with the *Neptune* Harvey's ship was so damaged that at 1.40 she drifted across the *Redoutable*'s bows, the latter's bowsprit passing through her rigging, from which position she was able to bring the raking fire of her port battery to the *Victory*'s support. The *Fougueux*, having managed to haul off from action with the *Belleisle* and *Mars* of Collingwood's column then approached the *Téméraire*. The British ship being badly damaged aloft, and her colours shot away, looked an easy prey. But Harvey's gunners had not yet discharged their starboard

*Abridged from *The Authentic Narrative of Dr William Beatty*, Surgeon to the *Victory*.

broadside; holding this until Baudoin's ship was as close as 100 yards, they poured the whole of it into her with such crushing effect that at 2.0 pm she ran foul of the *Téméraire*. Four ships were now locked together: *Victory*, *Redoutable*, *Téméraire*, *Fougueux*. Of these the *Fougueux* had suffered so much damage that Baudoin offered no resistance when boarded by men from the *Téméraire*. Lucas's ship was in little better straits; in his own words:

It would be difficult to describe the horrible carnage caused by [the *Téméraire*'s] murderous broadside. More than 200 of our brave lads were killed or wounded. . . . In less than half an hour our ship was so riddled that she seemed to be no more than a mass of wreckage. In this state the *Téméraire* hailed us to strike. . . . I ordered several soldiers to answer this summons with musket and shots. At the very same moment the mainmast fell on board the *Redoutable*. All the stern was absolutely stove in. . . . All the guns were shattered or dismounted. . . . An 18-pounder gun on the maindeck and a 36-pounder carronade on the forecastle having burst, killed and wounded many of our people. The two sides of the ship . . . were utterly cut to pieces. Four of our six pumps were shattered. . . . All our decks were covered with dead. . . . Out of the ship's company of 643 men we had . . . 300 killed and 222 wounded. . . . In the midst of this carnage the brave lads who had not yet succumbed . . . still cried, '*Vive l'Empéreur!* We're not taken yet.'

The *Redoutable* was, nonetheless, in such dire straits that at 2.20 pm Lucas 'ordered the colours to be hauled down. They came down themselves with the fall of the mizenmast.'

Half an hour before this, HMS *Neptune*, *Leviathan* and *Conqueror* had cut through the combined fleets astern of the *Bucentaure*, raking her with their broadsides. Thomas Fremantle then turned the *Neptune* to fight the mammoth *Santísima Trinidad* – 98 guns against 140 – whilst Henry Baynton headed the *Leviathan* for the *San Augustín*. Both enemy ships were soon reduced to a shambles by British gunfire and compelled to surrender, though Baynton subsequently came near to losing his ship to the *Intrépide* before Digby's *Africa* and Edward Codrington's *Orion* came to his rescue, and compelled Captain Infernet to haul down his colours at 5.0 pm. Meantime, Israel Pellew's *Conqueror* tackled the *Bucentaure*, where, at 1.30, Villeneuve realized Dumanoir's failure to uspport him and signalled his van to wear together. The flags had no sooner been hauled down than the last of the *Bucentaure*'s masts fell.

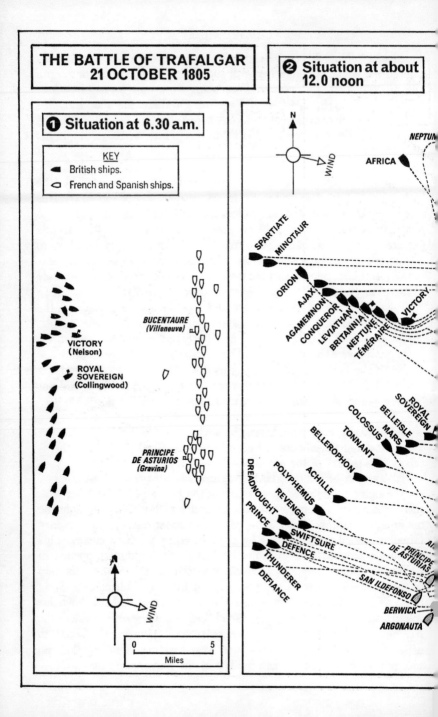

THE BATTLE OF TRAFALGAR
21 OCTOBER 1805

❷ Situation at about 12.0 noon

❶ Situation at 6.30 a.m.

KEY
◀ British ships.
◁ French and Spanish ships.

VICTORY
(Nelson)

ROYAL
SOVEREIGN
(Collingwood)

BUCENTAURE
(Villeneuve)

PRINCIPE
DE ASTURIOS
(Gravina)

N

WIND

0   5
Miles

NEPTUN

AFRICA

SPARTIATE
MINOTAUR
ORION
AJAX
AGAMEMNON
CONQUEROR
LEVIATHAN
BRITANNIA
NEPTUNE
TÉMÉRAIRE
VICTORY

ROYAL
SOVEREIGN
BELLEISLE
COLOSSUS
MARS
TONNANT
BELLEROPHON
ACHILLE
POLYPHEMUS
REVENGE
DREADNOUGHT
PRINCE
SWIFTSURE
DEFENCE
THUNDERER
DEFIANCE

PRINCIPE
DE ASTURIAS

SAN ILDEFONSO

BERWICK
ARGONAUTA

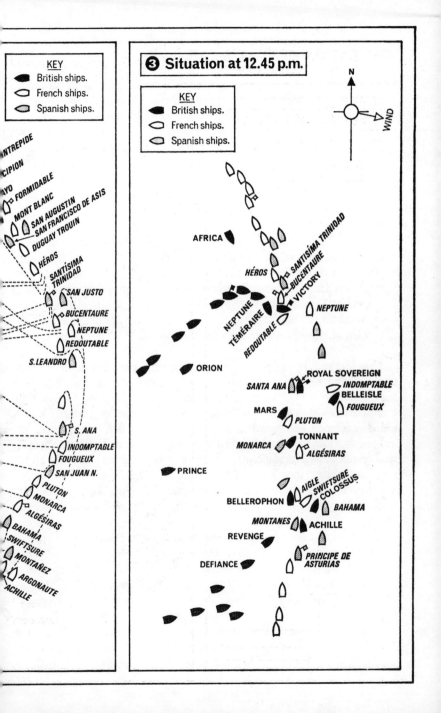

KEY
British ships.
French ships.
Spanish ships.

INTREPIDE
CIPION
AYO
FORMIDABLE
MONT BLANC
SAN AUGUSTIN
SAN FRANCISCO DE ASIS
DUGUAY TROUIN
HÉROS
SANTISIMA TRINIDAD
SAN JUSTO
BUCENTAURE
NEPTUNE
REDOUTABLE
S.LEANDRO
S. ANA
INDOMPTABLE
FOUGUEUX
SAN JUAN N.
PLUTON
MONARCA
ALGÉSIRAS
BAHAMA
SWIFTSURE
MONTAÑEZ
ARGONAUTE
ACHILLE

❸ Situation at 12.45 p.m.

N

WIND

KEY
British ships.
French ships.
Spanish ships.

AFRICA
SANTISIMA TRINIDAD
HÉROS
BUCENTAURE
VICTORY
NEPTUNE
NEPTUNE
TÉMÉRAIRE
REDOUTABLE
ORION
ROYAL SOVEREIGN
SANTA ANA
INDOMPTABLE
BELLEISLE
MARS
FOUGUEUX
PLUTON
MONARCA
TONNANT
ALGÉSIRAS
PRINCE
AIGLE
SWIFTSURE
BELLEROPHON
COLOSSUS
BAHAMA
MONTANES
ACHILLE
REVENGE
PRINCIPE DE ASTURIAS
DEFIANCE

In the words of an officer who was there: her

upper decks and gangways, heaped with dead and ... wreckage ...
presented an appalling spectacle. Amid this scene of disaster Admiral
Villeneuve, who from the first had displayed the calmest courage,
continued ... pacing up and down the quarterdeck. At length ... with
bitter sorrow he exclaimed: 'The *Bucentaure* has played her part: mine
is not yet over.' He gave orders for a boat to ... take him with his flag
on board one of the ships of the van squadron. He still cherished the
hope that he might ... yet snatch victory from the enemy. But ...
[this] illusion did not last long. Word was soon brought that his barge ...
and every single one of the ship's other boats had ... been destroyed.
Bitterly did Admiral Villeneuve realize his desperate position ...
imprisoned on board a ship that was unable to defend herself, while a
great part of his fleet was ... fighting hard. ... All he could do now
was to see after the lives of the handful of brave men fighting with him.
Humanity forbade him to allow them to be shot down without means
of defending themselves. Villeneuve looked away, and allowed the
captain of the *Bucentaure* to lower the colours.

This was at 1.45 pm. A few minutes later the French Commander-in-
Chief offered his sword to Israel Pellew's captain of marines. 'To whom
have I the honour of surrendering?' he asked in English. 'To Captain
Pellew of the *Conqueror*.' 'I am glad to have struck to Sir Edward Pellew.'
(All Frenchmen had heard of Sir Edward who, when commanding the
44-gun *Indefatigable*, had fought the 74-gun *Droits de l'Homme* until she
was driven ashore on the coast of Brittany where she was lost with all her
crew in January 1797.) 'It is his brother, sir.' 'His brother!' exclaimed
Villeneuve. 'Are there two of them? *Hélas!*' '*Fortune de la guerre*', was
Captain Magendie's comment as, for the third time, he became a prisoner-
of-war.

The wind was so light that Dumanoir's ships had difficulty in obeying
Villeneuve's signal. Eventually ten got round, but only five under
Dumanoir himself steered for the centre; the others kept away as if to
join Gravina in the rear. The first group were engaged by Codrington's
Orion, Lieutenant Pilford's *Ajax*, Berry's *Agamemnon* and by Northesk's
flagship, the *Britannia*, but to no great effect. Charles Mansfield's *Minotaur* and Sir France Laforey's *Spartiate*, which had been at the rear of
Nelson's column, had more success between 2.0 and 4.0 pm when they
captured the *Neptuno*. This, and a subsequent short action with the

Victory, were sufficient to deter Dumanoir from trying to recover any of the ships which the British had taken in prize: at 4.30 he took his four ships-of-the-line off to the south-west.

Meanwhile, at 2.15 pm Hardy managed to cut the *Victory* clear of the *Redoutable* and head northward. But without her mizen topmast, with her fore- and mainmasts badly damaged, her rigging much cut, and her hull severely holed, he was unable to take any further part in the battle. Instead he visited Nelson in the cockpit, to be asked:

'Well, Hardy, how goes the battle? How goes the day for us?'

'Very well, my Lord. We have taken twelve or fourteen of the enemy's ships; but five of their van have tacked and show an intention of bearing down upon the *Victory*. I have no doubt of giving them a drubbing.'

Nelson then said: 'I am a dead man, Hardy, I am going fast. It will be all over with me soon.' Then he told Beatty to tend the other wounded 'for you can do nothing for me'.

Hardy came down to the cockpit again after an interval of about fifty minutes, to shake hands with Nelson and congratulate him on his brilliant victory which, he said, was complete. Though he did not know how many of the enemy were captured he was certain of fourteen or fifteen.

Nelson answered: 'That is well, but I bargained for twenty', and then emphatically, '*Anchor, Hardy, anchor.*'

'Shall we make the signal, sir?'

'Yes, *for if I live, I'll anchor.*'

Nelson then told Hardy that in a few minutes he should be no more. 'Take care of my dear Lady Hamilton. . . . Kiss me, Hardy.'

The Captain knelt and kissed his cheek.* 'Now,' said Nelson, 'I am satisfied. Thank God I have done my duty. God bless you, Hardy.'

After this affecting scene Hardy withdrew, when Nelson's thirst increased and he called, 'Drink, drink', 'Fan, fan', and 'Rub, rub', in a very rapid manner, but with every now and then, with evident increase of pain, '*Thank God I have done my duty.*'

He became speechless about fifteen minutes after Hardy left him.

---

*It was then customary for men to embrace and kiss. Jervis embraced Nelson on the evening of the battle of Cape St Vincent; Nelson kissed Captain Thompson of the *Leander* after the battle of the Nile. But there is a further point: the author has had the painful experience of hearing a sick adult of fifty cry out in the delirium of a distressed mind, in the voice of a child: 'Kiss me, Mummy.' So, for two reasons, the suggestion that Nelson must have said, '*Kismet* [Fate], Hardy', has no substance.

K

And when Beatty took up his hand, it was cold and the pulse had gone from the wrist.*

'Partial firing continued until 4.30 pm,' says the *Victory*'s log, 'when a victory having been reported to the Right Hon. Lord Nelson, K.B., and Commander-in-Chief, he died of his wounds.' Hardy carried the sad news to Collingwood who was so overwhelmed that he wrote in his dispatch:

> I have not only to lament . . . the loss of a hero whose name will be immortal, and his memory ever dear to his Country; but my heart is rent with the most poignant grief for the death of a friend to whom, by many years' intimacy and a perfect knowledge of his mind, which inspired ideas superior to the common race of men, I was bound by the strongest ties of affection; a grief which even the glorious occasion in which he fell does not bring the consolation which perhaps it ought.

But when told of Nelson's earnest injunction that the fleet should anchor before it was hazarded on the lee shore of Cape Trafalgar, which was now distant only eight miles to the south-east, he exclaimed: 'Anchor the fleet! Why, it is the last thing I should have thought of.' Instead, he shifted his flag to the *Euryalus*, took the much damaged *Royal Sovereign* in tow, and stood off shore.

Dumanoir in the *Formidable*, with the *Duguay Trouin*, *Mont Blanc* and *Scipion*, had run to the southward; four other ships from the van and four from the centre had joined the survivors from Gravina's division, the *Principe d'Asturias*, *Montañez* and *Argonaute*, and were escaping to the north-west. But of the seventeen French and Spanish ships engaged by Collingwood's division, eleven had been taken in prize, and one had blown up; whilst of Villeneuve's ships engaged by Nelson's division, six had been taken in prize – making a total of eighteen taken or destroyed, only two less than Nelson's ambition for twenty. All the prizes had been extensively damaged, eight being entirely dismasted and nine partially dismasted. The combined fleets had, moreover, suffered casualties totalling 5,860 killed and wounded, and 20,000 taken prisoner.

The British fleet, though it had not lost a single vessel, had also suffered: in addition to the crippled *Victory* and *Royal Sovereign*, the *Belleisle* had been dismasted, the *Tonnant* had lost all three topmasts, eleven others had important parts of their masts and rigging shot away, and their casualties totalled 1,690 killed and wounded. So, although the measure of the British

*Abridged from *The Authentic Narrative of Dr William Beatty*, Surgeon to the *Victory*.

victory was abundantly clear, Collingwood had on his hands forty-four ships-of-the-line, of which all but twelve were unseaworthy to a greater or lesser extent. That he made no attempt to pursue the escaping enemy detachments is therefore understandable; he lacked the resources to prevent eleven of the combined fleets reaching the safety of Cadiz during the night. But his aversion to anchoring can only be described as an unhappy error of judgement which cost him dear, despite the handicap of a handful of ships which would be unable to comply because they had lost both anchors in the battle. At 9 pm, when the wind had freshened considerably and backed to west-south-west, accompanied by a heavy swell – dead on to the shoals of Trafalgar – he went so far as to signal: 'Prepare to anchor' which sufficed for four ships, HMS *Defence* and the prizes *San Ildefonso*, *Bahama* and the French *Swiftsure*, to drop anchor on their own initiative. But the rest obeyed his subsequent signal, to wear and head to the west, when at midnight the wind veered again to the south-south-west.

Next day the British fleet and its prizes, many in tow, held this course without incident in a fresh and squally southerly wind until 5.0 pm when the *Redoutable*, in tow of HMS *Swiftsure*, made signals of distress; and at 10.30, after many of her crew had been taken off, she had to be abandoned, to sink during the night. But this was only a presage of worse to come. By the morning of the 23rd, the full gale that Nelson had foreseen, was blowing from the north-west. This drove the *Fougueux* ashore with the loss of most of her company, and allowed the crews of the *Algésiras* and *Bucentaure* to retake their vessels, to carry the former into the safety of Cadiz, but to wreck the latter.

Much to his credit in the disheartening aftermath of such a defeat, this gale induced the senior French officer in Cadiz, Commodore de Cosmao-Kerjulien (who had played a major part in retaking the Diamond Rock), to put to sea with five ships-of-the-line in a brave attempt to recover some of the prizes. But when no less than ten of Collingwood's formed up to meet him, he thought it best to avoid action. Nonetheless, his frigates retook the *Neptuno* and *Santa Ana*. Against this, however, he had to set the loss of three of his own ships next day; the *Indomtable* and *San Francisco de Asis* were both wrecked when trying to re-enter Cadiz; the *Rayo*, after anchoring to avoid running ashore, surrendered to Pulteney Malcolm's *Donegal* which had just rejoined from Gibraltar – but only to be stranded and lost on the 26th. By that time the gale had cost Collingwood more of his prizes: the *Santísima Trinidad* and *Argonauta* had to be scuttled; the *Monarca* sank; the *Aigle* and *Berwick* were wrecked; the

Intrépide and *San Augustín* were burnt as useless. In sum, of the eighteen French and Spanish ships-of-the-line taken by Nelson's fleet on 21 October, only the *San Juan Nepomuceno* survived in addition to the three which had wisely anchored off Cape Trafalgar in company with HMS *Defence*. Against so many losses, Collingwood could only set the three ships that had emerged from Cadiz on the 24th and never returned.

On 30 October Louis rejoined from Gibraltar with five ships-of-the-line, when Collingwood shifted his flag to the undamaged *Queen* and resumed a close blockade of Cadiz – though the enemy which he contained, now under Rosily's command, were not destined to make another sortie. To complete the triumphant story of Trafalgar it remains, therefore, to tell only of what befell Dumanoir's detachment. Knowing that on 21 October Louis had several sail-of-the-line near Gibraltar, he decided against trying to make for Toulon and determined instead to reach one of the French Atlantic ports. But on 2 November he had the mischance to be sighted by a squadron of five British ships-of-the-line under Captain Sir Richard Strachan, which was searching for Allemand's squadron, still out of Rochefort and doing a good deal of damage to British trade. Strachan gave chase, and two days later brought Dumanoir's ships to action off Ferrol, compelling all four to surrender. Nelson's achievement, eighteen ships-of-the-line taken or destroyed, on 21 October, was thus capped in the two following weeks by three more out of Cadiz and all of Dumanoir's – the magnificent total of twenty-five out of a force that had a numerical superiority of thirty-three against twenty-seven.

Why was Villeneuve so heavily defeated?

The English fought us at every point with superior forces; 23 vessels only, of the 33 which formed the combined fleets, were in action. To whom are we to attribute the inaction of our van? Dumanoir did not consider Villeneuve's signal, ordering any ship which was not engaged to get into action, made at 12.15, to be addressed to his division. Not until 1.15, when it was too late, did Villeneuve signal his van to put about and get into action. By that time our centre was no longer offering any serious resistance.

It is the business of the Commander-in-Chief to direct the movements of his fleet so long as he can make signals. Villeneuve may therefore be reasonably held responsible for the inaction of the 10 ships ahead of the *Santisima Trinidad*. But what are we to make of the behaviour of a commander of the van who, when the fate of the action was in the balance, waited for orders? Ought he not to have recollected that Villeneuve, in his instructions dated 20 December 1804, said: 'Any captain who is not in action will not be in his station; and the signal that recalls him to his station will be a stain upon his character?' Dumanoir committed a serious error in not, on his own responsibility, leading his division to the assistance of the *Bucentaure*. The calm, he declared, prevented the van putting about earlier than it did. But the 16 vessels which followed the *Royal Sovereign*, and the 9 in the wake of the *Victory*, found enough wind to bring them into action. Moreover, the *Africa* was able to pass to windward of the entire van and join the vessels engaging the *Santísima Trinidad*. How is it that, while the English found the thing possible, we did not find it so?

It would appear that fatality clung to the movements of our van. When it did turn towards the fighting it split up. As a compact force it might have done something; as a divided one it invited the enemy's blows. These ten vessels joining the battle might not have changed the issue, but would have inflicted serious losses on the enemy. Dumanoir's inaction was seriously condemned in Paris. Seeing himself in disgrace, he asked for an inquiry. When this was held in 1809, he was exonerated.

Of Gravina Decrès wrote: 'His squadron, instead of making its way where events called for its presence, placed itself in the rear and rendered none of the services for which it had been designed. It allowed itself to be attacked, and fled.' The Dumanoir enquiry blamed Gravina's behaviour; his squadron ought to have kept its station to windward of the line where it would have covered the centre instead of prolonging the rear without being signalled to do so. Just blame may be given to Gravina for his behaviour on 21 October.

Such is a French verdict.* And clearly, Villeneuve, Gravina and Dumanoir, of whom the last deserved more criticism than the inquiry bestowed on the Spanish Admiral, made serious mistakes which contributed to the British victory. But how few are the battles in which a beaten foe has *not* made mistakes? And for the vanquished to determine these mistakes and apportion blame is understandable, even inevitable. Britain has done both: the escape of the *Scharnhorst*, *Gneisenau* and *Prinz Eugen* up Channel in 1942 is a recent example; of earlier ones the best remembered is the action off Minorca in 1756, for which Admiral Byng suffered death '*pour encourager les autres*'. But in how few, if any, battles is the result to be attributed *only* to the mistakes made by the vanquished, in which the victor deserves *no* credit?

*E. Chevalier in *Histoire de la Marine Française sous le Consulat et l'Empire* (abridged).

That the Royal Navy deserves credit in abundance for Trafalgar is not
to be disputed. That twenty-seven ships-of-the-line divided into two
columns, the ships in each coming into action in succession against
twenty-three, compelled all but five to strike, is clear evidence of superior
seamanship and gunnery. The British ships were better sailed and
manoeuvred in the light wind that prevailed throughout the day; and
their guns crews were better trained, both to hold their fire until within
point-blank range, and to discharge their broadsides, three to every one
of the enemy's, with devastating accuracy. Moreover, all, from captain to
powder monkey were imbued not only with dauntless courage, but a rock-
like belief in the justice of their cause, the need to defeat an enemy,
personified in Napoleon, who had for so long threatened to invade their
homeland.

In sharp contrast, the French, whose bravery is not in question, were
handicapped by an Emperor who had deprived them of the revolutionary
cause they had once so fervently espoused, and who had imposed on them
the concept of evading action with all but forces of marked inferiority,
so that many of their admirals and captains lacked the *will to win*. Even
more so did their Spanish allies, who were so little interested in the war
that several of their ships had to be fired on by the French to keep them
in the line, with the consequence that, when taken prisoner, their crews
volunteered to help their British captors fight their guns!

Even so, there would have been no such victory for the Royal Navy
if the British Mediterranean fleet had not been under Nelson's command.
His was the strategy which allowed the combined fleets to come out and
be brought to battle, not Collingwood's orthodox close blockade of
Cadiz. His was the magnetic personality and the understanding of the
whole art of leadership that inspired Collingwood and all the British
captains and their crews to fight as they did. His was the tactical plan,
based on the vital principle of concentration of force, and in disregard of
all dogma, that enabled the British fleet to engage and vanquish a
numerically superior enemy. And to him goes the credit for carrying out
that plan in a modified form to suit the situation which faced him on 21
October 1805, with a determination that crushed the enemy's centre and
rear. Nor, from the number of enemy ships that struck their colours
without the loss of a British vessel, is it difficult to believe that he would
have achieved victory if Villeneuve had directed his fleet more ably, and
Dumanoir and Gravina had possessed the qualities required of divisional
commanders, such as Nelson had shown when in command of the *Captain*
off Cape St Vincent nine years before.

For all the success of Nelson's strategy and tactics, coupled with his personality and leadership, there was, however, another reason why the Royal Navy won Trafalgar. Nelson himself expressed it again and again. As he had been obsessed with Emma, he was fervently determined to gain not just 'victory or Westminster Abbey' but to come near to *annihilating* an enemy whom he hated, on whom he had maintained such a long and arduous watch off Toulon, and after whom he had chased all the way to the Caribbean and back again. It is easy to say that Nelson was vain; but none can argue that, when Fate in the form of a ball from a French musket ended his life, he was more than justified in his dying words: *'Thank God I have done my duty.'*

CHRONOLOGICAL SUMMARY FOR CHAPTER XI

EVENTS IN NELSON'S LIFE	DATE	RELATED EVENTS
	1805	
	3 August	Napoleon with *Grande Armée* at Boulogne.
	9 August	Calder raises blockade of Ferrol: Villeneuve and Gravina's combined fleets sail. Austria and Russia join Britain in Third Coalition.
Meets Cornwallis off Ushant.	*15 August*	
	17 August	Calder ordered to re-establish blockade of Ferrol.
Arrives Spithead.	*18 August*	
Strikes flag and proceeds on leave.	*19 August*	
Joins Emma and Horatia at Merton.	*20 August*	Combined fleets arrive Cadiz.
	21 August	Ganteaume attempts sortie from Brest.
	24 August	Napoleon abandons invasion of England. *Grande Armée* ordered to march against Austria.
	30 August	Calder joins Collingwood, who establishes blockade of Cadiz.
Learns that combined fleets have arrived Cadiz.	*2 September*	

EVENTS IN NELSON'S LIFE	DATE	RELATED EVENTS
Rehoists flag in *Victory*.	*14 September*	
Sails from Spithead.	*15 September*	
	25 September	*Grande Armée* crosses Rhine.
Rejoins fleet off Cadiz.	*28 September*	
	8 October	French defeat Austrians at Wertingen.
	14 October	And at Elchingen.
Learns that combined fleets are at sea.	*19 October*	
	20 October	Austrians surrender at Ulm.
Destroys combined fleets in battle fought off Cape Trafalgar, in which killed.	*21 October*	
Collingwood loses many Trafalgar prizes in storm.	*23 October*	
	4 November	Strachan captures four French ships which escaped Trafalgar off Ferrol.

XII

Legacy

The rest is soon told. . . .

The crippled *Victory* anchored in Gibraltar Bay on 28 October 1805, where Hardy landed his dead for burial in the little Trafalgar cemetery which to this day remains hallowed ground. There, too, Hardy disembarked his wounded before effecting the repairs needed to make his ship seaworthy. One week later the *Victory* carried Nelson home. His body, 'after the hair had been cut off . . . [and] stripped of the clothes except the shirt' had been put into 'a cask . . . of the largest size on ship-board', by Dr Beattie, and 'then filled with brandy' (not the rum of legend, for all that this liquor has since been called Nelson's blood), which was replaced at Gibraltar by a better preservative, spirit of wine.

The voyage, at first in tow of Redmill's *Polyphemus* and later of Fremantle's *Neptune*, took more than a month: not until December did the *Victory* reach Spithead, then proceed to the Nore, where, on the 23rd Nelson's body was placed in a coffin, of which the inner shell was the one that Hallowell had caused to be made from the *Orient*'s mainmast, to be carried up the Thames and lie in state in the Painted Hall of Greenwich Hospital (now the Royal Naval College, Greenwich).

The news of Trafalgar had reached England long before this. Penzance heard it first (as a plaque in the Union Hotel, formerly the Assembly Rooms, commemorates) from a Mounts Bay lugger which chanced to fall in with the schooner *Pickle* off the Lizard, with her ensign at half-mast. From Falmouth her commander, Lieutenant Le Ponetière, posted through the night to deliver Collingwood's despatches to the Admiralty. Old Lord Barham sped the news to the King at Windsor where it stunned that most loquacious of monarchs into silence for a full five minutes. Pitt, in residence at 10 Downing Street, was awakened at 3.0 am, to be so shocked by the news that he was unable to resume his sleep. To Francis Lady Nelson, the First Lord began a letter: 'It is with the utmost concern that in the midst of victory I have to inform Your Ladyship of the death of your illustrious partner....' The task of writing to Merton was left to the Controller of the Navy Board. Emma was prostrate with grief: on 29 November she was still in 'my bed where I have been ever since the fatal sixth of this month.... I do not see anyone but the family of my dear Nelson.... His letters are in bed with me.... My heart is broken. Life to me now is not worth having. I lived but for him.... I am very, very ill.'

The Times published Collingwood's despatches on 7 November, 'the most afflicting intelligence which has ever elated or depressed the British nation'. (In sharp contrast, the French press made no allusion to their catastrophic defeat until after the New Year when the *Moniteur* published this classic understatement: 'A storm has caused us the loss of a few ships after an imprudently delivered battle.') Collingwood's grief (quoted on p. 276) was shared by the Fleet. Fremantle told his wife: 'The loss of Nelson is a death blow.... I shall never cease to lament his loss while I live.' A seaman in the *Royal Sovereign* wrote:

> Our dear Admiral Nelson is killed!... All the men in our ship ... are such soft toads, they have done nothing but blast their eyes and cry ever since he was killed.... Chaps that fought like the devil, sit down and cry like a wench.

The Times gave this verdict:

> The triumph, great and glorious as it is, has been dearly bought.... There was not a man who did not think that the life of the Hero of the Nile was too great a price for the capture and destruction of twenty sail of French and Spanish men-of-war.... No demonstrations of public joy marked this great and important event.... The people ... felt an inward satisfaction at the triumph of their favourite arms; they mourned with all the sincerity and poignancy of domestic grief their HERO slain.... If ever there was a man who deserved to be 'praised, wept and honoured' by his Country, it is Lord Nelson. His three great naval achievements have eclipsed the brilliancy of the most dazzling victories in the annals of English daring.... [His] death has plunged a whole nation into the deepest grief.

The leader writer did not exaggerate. On the previous evening the performance at Covent Garden Theatre ended with 'a superb naval scene . . . of columns . . . decorated with medallions of the naval heroes of Britain. In the distance a number of ships were seen. . . . The principal singers . . . with their eyes turned towards the clouds, from whence . . . a portrait of Lord Nelson descended . . . sang *Rule Britannia* with the following additional verse. . . .

> *Again the loud ton'd trump of fame*
> *Proclaims Britannia rules the main*
> *Whilst sorrow whispers Nelson's name,*
> *And mourns the gallant Victor slain,*
> *Rule, brave Britons, rule the main;*
> *Revenge the God-like Hero slain.'*

The reaction was the same throughout Britain: on 10 November, in distant Cumberland, the poet Wordsworth noted in his diary: 'At the breakfast table tidings reached us of the death of Lord Nelson and of the victory at Trafalgar. We were shocked to hear that the bells had been ringing joyously at Penrith', where they knew only of the triumph.

The first Trafalgar honours were announced on 9 November, other awards later; for Nelson a posthumous earldom, an estate and a hereditary pension of £5,000 ($12,000) per annum bestowed upon his elder brother; to each of his sisters £19,000 ($45,600); to Lady Nelson an annuity of £2,000 ($4,800); for Collingwood a barony; for Northesk a K.B.; for Hardy a baronetcy. Many officers were promoted. For every officer and man there was a medal. But there was nothing then, nor later, for Emma Hamilton: though Hardy fulfilled his task of delivering Nelson's last letter, and the codicil to his will leaving her 'a legacy to my King and Country, that they will give her ample provision to maintain her rank in life', it was not to be expected that the Government would show such generosity to any man's mistress: that was a Sovereign's prerogative – for his.

Nelson was carried up the Thames from Greenwich to Whitehall on 8 January 1806, to lie that night in the Captains' Room in the Admiralty. Next day he received a state funeral in St Paul's Cathedral. Thirty-one admirals, of whom the senior was Admiral of the Fleet Sir Peter Parker, he who had promoted Nelson to post-captain in 1779, and 100 captains followed the body. The Prince of Wales and the Duke of Clarence were there. Lady Hamilton was not: she waited at home to hear from Dr Scott that 'the very beggars left their stands, neglected the passing crowd, and seemed to pay tribute to his memory by a look. Many did I see, tattered and on crutches, shaking their heads with plain signs of sorrow. This must be truly unbought affection of the heart.' Garter King of Arms, after formally reciting Nelson's many honours, was moved to add in breach of all precedent: 'The Hero who in the moment of Victory fell covered with Immortal glory.'

And in St Paul's Nelson was accorded the much rarer honour of burial in the Crypt, beneath a great marble sarcophagus inscribed only with his name and the dates of his birth and death, whilst beside him sleep three of his last Band of Brothers, the two captains who were killed at Trafalgar, Duff of the *Mars* and Cooke of the *Bellerophon*, and 'Old Coll' who later joined him there.

This story would be incomplete if it did not tell of what befell certain of the other players in the drama of Nelson's life after his funeral. Collingwood stayed on as Commander-in-Chief Mediterranean until, worn out by more than five years of continuous sea service, he died on 7 March 1810 at the age of sixty-one. Codrington of the *Orion* was destined to be Commander-in-Chief of the combined British, French and Russian fleets at the victory of Navarino on 2 October 1827.

Villeneuve was repatriated to France on 22 April 1806. According to Napoleon, 'upon his arrival I ordered him to remain at Rennes, and not to come to Paris. . . . Fearing to be convicted by a council of war of having disobeyed my orders, and of having lost the fleet in consequence . . . [he] determined to put an end to himself', after writing these last poignant words to his wife: '*Quel honheur que je n'ais aucun enfant pour recueillir mon horrible héritage et qui soit chargé du poids de mon nom.*' Next morning (Napoleon speaks again), 'when they opened his room they found him dead, [a long] pin being in his breast [and through his heart]. He should not have acted in that way. He was a gallant man, although he had no talent.' He was buried without honours.

Lady Nelson, the bird-like Fanny whom Nelson treated so cruelly, lived in quiet retirement until her death on 6 May 1831. Her detestable son, Josiah, had already died of pleurisy at the age of fifty, 'successful proprietor of a yacht . . . a full nursery and a solid fortune, but perhaps never quite so proud a man as when he had commanded HMS *Thalia*, aged nineteen, according to Nelson, "a seaman every inch of him." '*

With £800 ($1,920) a year from Hamilton and a like sum from Nelson, in addition to Merton Place, Emma was left well enough provided for had

*Carola Oman in her *Nelson*.

she lived a prudent life. But in her distress she was recklessly extravagant and gambled so heavily that in 1813 she was gaoled for debt. A year later, after a second term in prison, she fled to France, taking Horatia with her, to live at No. 111, Rue Française, Calais. There she fell into 'the baneful habit . . . of taking wine and spirits to a fearful degree', and in the year of Waterloo contracted jaundice from which she died. But Horatia was not left to starve: adopted by the Matchams (Nelson's sister Catherine and her husband), she married the eminently respectable Rev. Philip Ward in 1822. Curiously, though she always acknowledged Nelson as her father (to the extent of adopting the married name of Nelson-Ward), right down to her death at the age of eighty-one she never agreed that Emma had been more than a guardian who

> with all [her faults] – and she had many – had many fine qualities, which, had [she] been placed in better hands, would have made her a very superior woman. It is but justice . . . to say that through all her difficulties, she invariably till the last few months, expended on my education, etc. the whole of the interest of the sum left to me by Lord Nelson,* and which was entirely at her control.

Collingwood writing 'whose name will be immortal': the Past Overseers of St Margaret and St John, Westminster raising their glasses to 'the Immortal Memory': Garter King of Arms proclaiming 'the Hero who . . . fell covered with Immortal glory'. These were the spontaneous reactions of those to whom Nelson's death deprived Britain of a victorious hero amidst the stress of a great war, when the dark shadow of invasion across the Channel had only recently been lifted. But time has long since proved the immortality of Nelson's name, not only by the erection of so many memorials, the most noteworthy being the great column guarded by Landseer's lions in London's Trafalgar Square, but by this eloquent tribute paid by Captain Alfred T. Mahan of the United States Navy:

> The words, 'I have done my duty', sealed the closed book of Nelson's story with a truth broader and deeper than he himself could suspect. . . . Other men have died in the hour of victory, but for no other has victory so singular and so signal graced the fulfilment and ending of a great life's work. . . . There were, indeed, consequences momentous and stupendous yet to flow from the decisive supremacy of Great Britain's sea power, the establishment of which, beyond all question or competition, was Nelson's great achievement; but his part was done when

*An annuity of £200 ($480).

Trafalgar was fought. The coincidence of his death with the moment of completed success has impressed upon that superb battle a stamp of finality, an immortality of fame. . . . He needed and he left, no successor. To use again St Vincent's words, 'There is but one Nelson.'*

But this book cannot leave the matter there: it must in its closing pages answer three questions. First, the consequences momentous and stupendous that flowed from Trafalgar. Second, the qualities that lifted Nelson to such pre-eminence among the world's naval commanders. Third, to what use for good or ill, did the Royal Navy put the legacy that Nelson bequeathed to it in the century and a half after his death?

Trafalgar did not destroy Napoleon's Navy; his Brest fleet remained, and he created a new fleet in Toulon. But in the ten years that elapsed before his final defeat at Waterloo, the Emperor only once contemplated a serious challenge to the Royal Navy's control of the sea. His armies having vanquished Austria at Austerlitz on 2 December 1805, and secured the greater part of Italy in 1806, he invaded Prussia on 7 October of that year, followed by Russia in December with such success that these two countries signed the Treaty of Tilsit in July 1807. To the 62 French, Spanish and Dutch ships-of-the-line already at Napoleon's disposal, plus (he hoped) nine Portuguese, this added 25 Russian. He had only to secure Sweden's 11 and Denmark's 18 to have as many as 125, enough, surely, to break the stranglehold of Britain's maritime power. But, as in 1801, the British Government was swift to sense the danger. Early in September, after Copenhagen had been bombarded intermittently for five days by twenty-five ships-of-the line under Admiral James Gambier, the Danes surrendered their entire Fleet.

Thus thwarted of one dream, Napoleon conceived another: he would 'conquer the sea by the power of the land'. By his Continental System he required all the countries of Europe to treat Britain as a pariah dog; their ports were to be closed to British trade, their ships would no longer supply Britain's needs. But Portugal refused to enforce this form of blockade; she had been Britain's ally for too long, and was averse to suffering the economic consequences, especially those involved in closing the great port of Lisbon. And to Lisbon the Royal Navy, using its unchallenged control of the sea, brought an expeditionary force to Portugal's support on 1 August 1808. As safely did it carry the greater part of this force away from Corunna when it was cornered there at the end of the year after General Sir John Moore's ill fated attempt to invade

*Mahan in his *Life of Nelson*.

Spain, when that country rebelled against the Continental System and her harsh occupation by a French army. As securely the British Navy landed a new expeditionary force under the future Duke of Wellington at Lisbon in April 1809. And so did Britain's ships keep his men supplied for the three years that they held the lines of Torres Vedras against the French until, in 1811, Wellington had a sufficient force to defeat Masséna's occupying army and drive it back into Spain.

During these years the French Navy was not idle. Its *guerre de course*, conducted by such men as Robert Surcouf, from which merchantmen sailing as close to home as the English Channel were not exempt, was a continuing embarrassment; but its battleships made few sorties of any significance. As soon as December 1805, Rear-Admiral Willaumez slipped out of Brest and was at large in the West Indies and South Atlantic with six sail-of-the-line for as many months, but Rear-Admiral Leissègues, who likewise slipped out with five sail-of-the-line, was caught off San Domingo by Duckworth, now a vice-admiral, on 6 February 1806. And with St Vincent reappointed to command the Channel fleet and to impose his own rigorous blockade of Brest, there were no further excursions until after his final retirement. Not until January 1808 did Allemand escape from Aix Roads with six ships-of-the-line, of which all but one succeeded in joining Ganteaume in Toulon. And because Collingwood considered it more important to blockade Cadiz, as many as ten French ships-of-the-line were able to slip out of Toulon to bring succour to Corfu. But Ganteaume achieved no more than this before, eluding all Collingwood's attempts to intercept him, he returned to Toulon on 10 April. Lastly, in February 1809, Willaumez again slipped out of Brest, this time with eight sail-of-the-line, but only to be driven into Aix Roads by Gambier's watching British force. There, after he had been superseded by Allemand, this squadron was attacked by fireships under Captain Lord Thomas Cochrane on 11 April, and many of its ships destroyed.

But none of these episodes, nor the activities of smaller French squadrons in the West Indies and in the Indian Ocean, notably Charles Decéan's tenacious defence of Mauritius, were a serious challenge to the Royal Navy's grip on the seas. This enabled Popham to capture the Cape of Good Hope (1806), and foolishly, to attempt to do likewise with Buenos Aires; Duckworth to force the Dardanelles (1807); Vice-Admiral James Dacres to capture Curaçoa (1807); Rear-Admiral Sir Edward Pellew (who was to gain renown and the title of Lord Exmouth for his bombardment of Algiers in 1816) to attack Java (1807); Saumarez, by this time a

vice-admiral, to gain command of the Baltic (1808); Strachan with troops
under Lieutenant-General the Earl of Chatham (brother of Pitt) to
bungle an attempt to destroy Missiessy's fleet at its moorings off Flushing
(1809); Hallowell to frustrate Rear-Admiral Baudoin's attempt to relieve
Barcelona (1809); Rear-Admiral the Hon. Alexander Cochrane to capture
Martinique, Sénégal and Cayenne (all in 1809); and Rear-Admiral
William Drury to take Amboyna in the Moluccas (1810).

Nor did Britain, whose trade and industry now flourished as it had
never done before, fight only Napoleon and his allies. In 1812 she became
embroiled in war with the USA, as much over the latter's ambition to
obtain possession of Canada as the former's insistence on the right of
search and impressment. The erstwhile Colonies had no battle fleet to
draw away across the Atlantic more than a tithe of the hard core of the
Royal Navy's strength. But Britain's frigates, whose captains had become
over-confident from their ability to beat the French, suffered much at
the hands of a mere sixteen which were better built and more heavily
armed, as well as ably fought by such officers as Commodore John
Rodgers and Captain Stephen Decatur. And her maritime trade and
fisheries were badly mauled by Yankee privateers before, in 1813, she
spared ten sail-of-the-line to impose an effective blockade of America's
Atlantic seaboard, and Captain Philip Broke of the *Shannon* did much to
re-establish the Royal Navy's supremacy by his lightning defeat and
capture of Captain James Lawrence's *Chesapeake* off Cape Cod. This,
coupled with the failure of the United States' attempt to invade Canada,
followed by the capture and destruction of the centre of Washington, DC,
and other operations by a British expeditionary force – not all of them so
successful – persuaded both powers to negotiate peace in 1814.

All these world-wide operations, and many more, were possible because
in the shadow of the overwhelming disaster of Trafalgar, Napoleon and
Decrès would not again allow the French battle fleet to risk destruction
by the British Navy. Moreover, when he wearied of his inability to sub-
jugate Spain, Napoleon made the fatal mistake of opening a second front;
because the Tsar proved an intransigient ally, to the extent of withdrawing from the Continental System, he ordered his *Grande Armée* to
march on Moscow – and to its destruction. And whilst the Emperor was
thus engaged, Wellington not only drove into Spain with 80,000 troops
plus numerous Spanish guerilla forces, against 250,000 under Masséna,
Marmont and Soult, but, much assisted by the Royal Navy's support for
his advance along that country's Biscay shore, in October 1813 crossed
the Pyrenees and invaded southern France.

The sequel to both these campaigns was the Allied occupation of Paris on 31 March 1814, followed by Napoleon's abdication and exile to Elba. His escape and his last journey to St Helena onboard HMS *Northumberland* after Wellington's triumph at Waterloo, followed in 1815. This humiliating end to one of the greatest of military commander's ambition to gain dominion over all Europe – he died in 1821 – was the awesome consequence that flowed from the decisive supremacy of British sea power, which Nelson, above all, did so much to establish – as Napoleon himself admitted: 'In all my plans I have always been thwarted by the British Fleet.'

The second point raised by Mahan's eulogy recalls words from our first chapter: 'A naval commander's greatness is measured by more than the number and extent of his victories: one must assess the inborn qualities and acquired skills that enabled him to achieve results of such consequence to this country.' And these were listed as ambition, leadership, an understanding of strategy, tactical skill, and diplomatic ability, plus star quality. 'There is but one Nelson': St Vincent voiced the phrase as a tribute to his unique qualities as a *naval commander*. Both as a commander-in-chief, and later as a First Lord who knew how much Britain depended upon her Navy to protect her from conquest by Napoleon, St Vincent was only marginally concerned with Nelson the *man*, for all that he deplored his callous treatment of Fanny and his liaison with Emma. And, if it is to be true to its title, so should this book judge him.

The two years from September 1798, when Nelson reached Naples wearing the laurels of the Nile, until his return to England in November 1800, were an aberration. His ambition was dormant, his leadership faulty, his grasp of strategy inept, his diplomacy both naive and intolerant, and he had only one minor opportunity to display his tactical skill. They were scarred by such episodes as the fiasco of the Neapolitan advance on Rome; by the many months which he spent in 'silken dalliance' at Palermo, leaving the active prosecution of the war at sea in the area under his command, such as the siege of Malta and the Levant blockade, to his subordinates, and to his ally, Ushakóv; by his inhuman treatment of Caracciolo and the Neapolitan rebels; and by his flagrant disobedience of Keith's orders.

'The reason why' is abundantly clear. Love is a many-splendoured thing but, as Shakespeare warns us, 'Keep you out of the shot and danger of desire'; or, as Pascal expressed it, *'le coeur a ses raisons que le raison ne connâit point'*. The historian cannot disregard this, nor pretend other than

L

that it disfigures Nelson's reputation – for all that many turn 'a blind eye' to it. If he had continued to allow Emma to govern him, he would never have gained immortality. But from the time that they severed their link with the Neapolitan Court, he was again true to himself. So, as Tolstoy is acclaimed for *War and Peace* and *Anna Karénina* despite his cruelty to his wife and family, and as Wagner is lauded for *The Ring* and *Tristan and Isolde* despite his shameless seduction of Cosima Liszt, Nelson is to be judged as a naval commander primarily by his achievements in the four years before (i.e. from the time that Hood first gave him command of a squadron of frigates in 1793 up to and including the Nile), and the five years after his enslavement at Naples and Palermo (i.e. from Copenhagen to Trafalgar).

The driving force which enabled him to scale the heights is very clear. Ambition for honour and glory inspired him to wear out of the line at Cape St Vincent, and to descend like the Assyrian wolf on Brueys' fleet in Aboukir Bay. Then, having achieved fame, he was driven on – in the Baltic, off Toulon, across the Atlantic and back again to Cape Trafalgar – by ambition of a purer kind, to do his duty. The vanity of his later years was not only an inevitable by-product of his initial ambition, but is not to be taken too seriously. It was always more evident to strangers and in his prolific correspondence than when in the company of his friends and brother officers. And how much better this than the *folie de grandeur* which afflicted Napoleon who, for all his undoubted greatness, not only as a military commander but as a ruler who effected so many reforms including the legal code that survives to this day, drove him over the abyss to Moscow, Elba, Waterloo and St Helena.

The evidence that Nelson was not only an outstanding leader but had star quality – that, indeed, no star has yet shone brighter – is so overwhelming that it needs no pointing, except only to stress that his leadership was of that uncommon kind by which his officers and men loved him instead of, as with Wellington and Napoleon, being dominated by fear of his wrath. Certain apparent defects must however be mentioned; his mercurial, self-critical nature, his tendency to dramatize events and to indulge in flights of fantasy, his pessimism and his hypochondria. But these were the price he paid for his creative talent: he suffered the tortures of the artistic temperament when denied the opportunity to exercise this. Moreover, as with his vanity, his faults were revealed chiefly in his letters which were as much a safety valve for his emotions as other men's diaries. (Lord Alanbrooke's are a notable example from the Second World War.) He was seldom *seen* to be vain, either by those who served with him or by those who met him ashore: on the contrary, he was the best of mess-mates and stimulating company.

Nelson's pursuit of Brueys, his urge to press on to Reval, his chase after Villeneuve, and his blockades of Toulon and of Cadiz – both designed to encourage the enemy to sortie and so be brought to action – plus the importance which he attached to *annihilating* the enemy, all these are abundant evidence of an exceptional understanding of naval strategy. The restraint which he showed towards the Tsar's negotiators, in sharp con-trast with his firm handling of the Danes after Copenhagen, are but two examples among many of his skilful diplomacy. Nor should it be forgotten that, though Nelson did not live to show how well – or ill – he might have filled the office of First Lord, he displayed during his long watch off Toulon a gift for administration such as is seldom possessed by men of imagination, a combination which did much to enable such commanders as Caesar and Napoleon to achieve immortal fame.

All this would entitle Nelson to be ranked among Britain's more distinguished admirals, just as Lord Fisher was to be for his great reforms a century later. But it is not enough to rank him among Britain's sea kings. A commander's prime task in war is to defeat the enemy in battle. By this, above all, is Nelson to be judged; and of the verdict there can be 'no manner of doubt whatever'. By his single-minded determination, not just to defeat the enemy to the limited extent that other admirals, even Jervis at Cape St Vincent, had been content to do, but 'to annihilate', coupled with the use of novel tactics of his own devising instead of those formulated by others in the *Fighting Instructions*, and a clear comprehen-sion of the value of time – 'Five minutes may make the difference between victory and defeat'* – by these he scored not one but three overwhelming triumphs. And no other naval commander before or since has achieved so much.

But what of the other side of the coin, his defeats at Santa Cruz and Boulogne? Is his rashness on both these occasions to be counted against him? On the contrary, he was the victim of a vital quality without which he would not have worn the *Captain* out of the line at Cape St Vincent, nor surprised Brueys by a night attack in Aboukir Bay; he would have hesitated, as Hyde Parker did, to tackle the hazards of the approaches to Copenhagen, and to engage Villeneuve's superior force off Cape Trafalgar without allowing his fleet time to form up in accordance with his Trafalgar memorandum. As Field-Marshal Montgomery has expressed it:

There are three types of commanders in the higher grades:

Cf. Napoleon's dictum: 'Ask me for anything but time.'

1. Those who have faith and inspiration, but who lack the infinite capacity for taking pains and preparing for every foreseeable contingency which is the foundation of all success in war. These fail.

2. Those who possess the last-named quality to a degree amounting to genius. Of this type I would name Wellington as the perfect example.

3. Those who, possessing this quality, are inspired by a faith and conviction which enables them, when they have done everything possible in the way of preparation, and when the situation favours boldness, *to throw their bonnet over the moon.**

There are moments in war when to win all, one has to do this. . . . Nelson was the perfect example. No commander ever took greater care . . . to prepare against every possible contingency. But no one was ever so well able to recognize the moment when, everything having been done that reason can dictate, something must be left to chance – to faith.†

The third point from Mahan's tribute is that with which this final chapter is titled; Nelson left a legacy not only to the British Navy but to the Fleets of all nations.

The lessons to be learned from his career being so clear, nothing is more extraordinary than the extent to which they were distorted or, worse, rejected in the century that followed his death. The Napoleonic wars were no sooner over than the Admiralty issued new *Fighting Instructions* which, instead of recognizing the value of the Nelson Touch, re-imposed the old rigid tactics. Future battles were to be fought as a gun duel in a single line ahead parallel to that of the enemy, despite all the experience which had so clearly shown that this was unlikely to achieve more than a marginal victory. It was safer that way. And with the exception of Admiral Sir William May who, when Commander-in-Chief Home Fleet in 1910–11, exercised 'divided tactics', which were comparable with Nelson's two columns at Trafalgar, no British admiral departed from this dogma despite the flexibility gained from the introduction of steam.

As important, through the century of the *pax Britannica*, in which the Royal Navy was required to do little more than police the oceans of the world and help to establish the rule of law throughout the British Empire, the spirit of initiative which Nelson encouraged in his subordinates was transmuted to the baser metal of unthinking obedience, as was disastrously exemplified when Admiral Tryon met his death in the collision between

---

*Author's italics.
†In a lecture to the Royal United Service Institution, printed in its *Journal* for August 1970.

the *Victoria* and the *Camperdown* in 1893. Thirdly, in the years that he was First Sea Lord and engaged in the task of transforming the Royal Navy's somnolent Victorian fleet into the fighting machine needed to meet Germany's threat to seize Britannia's trident, Fisher split its Band of Brothers into two rival camps by his vicious campaign against Lord Charles Beresford.

Nor was this Fisher's only mistake. To his First Lord, Winston Churchill, he wrote in 1911:

> I hope you have seen Jellicoe. . . . *He has all the Nelson attributes :* 1. Self-reliance, 2. Fearlessness of Responsibility, 3. Fertility of Resource, 4. Power of Initiative. . . . He will win the battle of Armageddon on 21 October 1914 (*Make a note of that date!*). . . . It won't be victory . . . that Jellicoe will accomplish! It will be annihilation.

On two counts he was very wrong. His belief that Germany's High Seas Fleet would seek an early action with Britain's Grand Fleet was founded on the dramatic attack on Port Arthur which opened the Russo–Japanese war, and the more extravagant statements of Grand Admiral von Tirpitz; though fond of citing Nelson's maxims, he overlooked the two years which it took him to bring Villeneuve to action at Trafalgar. Secondly, he gravely misjudged his *protégé*: though Jellicoe might be the best man available to command the Grand Fleet in 1914, he lacked Nelson's imagination and creative qualities as a tactician. He did not treat his flag officers and captains as a Band of Brothers; he controlled their every action. Above all he was cautious to a fault in the face of a threat that Nelson never faced, the underwater mine and torpedo.

The result was Jutland; although this cannot be paralleled with Trafalgar, in that Jellicoe's command included almost all of Great Britain's dreadnoughts whereas Nelson's counted only a quarter of her ships-of-the-line, so that a defeat for the former must have had more disastrous consequences than one for the latter, Jellicoe failed to defeat Scheer (tactically that is; subsequent events proved it to have been a strategic victory) because he adhered to the dogma of a gun duel fought in single line ahead, because all initiative was stifled in his flag officers and captains (with honourable exceptions), and because he could not 'throw his bonnet over the moon'.

The spirit of Nelson was not, however, dead in British naval commanders of this era. Beatty typified it at the battle of Heligoland Bight; the pity is that his great qualities did not gain him the victory that he deserved in subsequent clashes with the enemy. At the Dogger Bank, his second-in-command failed him; and at Jutland he suffered the loss of three of his nine battle-cruisers for a reason beyond his control, serious faults in their design. Nelson's spirit lived on, too, in Commodore Reginald Tyrwhitt's leadership of the Harwich Force; in Rear-Admiral Roger Keyes' assault on Zeebrugge, for all that this came near to being another Santa Cruz; and in Commodore Walter Cowan, though his successful raid on Kronstadt is now largely forgotten because it occurred after the Armistice.

As important was another aspect of Nelson's legacy. Because he personified the Royal Navy's great years of victory, his memory inspired the sure will to win in every officer and man in the British Fleet of 1914–18. The Kaiser feared this spirit so much that he refused to allow von Tirpitz to risk the High Seas Fleet in action. And because of it the Grand Fleet's morale remained unshaken by four long years of maintaining a blockade from the monotonous wastes of Scapa Flow, whilst that of the High Seas Fleet collapsed in the greater comforts of Kiel and Wilhelmshaven, despite the near success of its U-boats because Britain was so slow to recognize that the only way to defeat this new form of *guerre de course* was the old way, by convoy.

So, although there was no Trafalgar, the Royal Navy's very real achievements during the First World War are not to be denied. It was the blockade relentlessly maintained by the British Grand Fleet – with its power augmented during the last year by an American battle squadron – which by 1918 so weakened Germany's will to resist that the Allied armies were able to end the stalemate in Flanders. How much Nelson, watching from another world, must have envied Beatty that day in November 1918 when the High Seas Fleet surrendered and ceased to exist: this was annihilation beyond his dreams.

The Second World War is, perhaps, too recent for any historian to give a definitive judgement on its naval commanders. But that the Royal Navy had not lost the Nelson Touch was clearly shown as early as December 1939, when Commodore Henry Harwood's three cruisers set the pretensions of the German pocket-battleship *Graf Spee* at nought. The Nelson spirit animated Admiral Sir John Tovey and those under him who sank the *Bismarck*, Admiral Sir Bruce Fraser and those who dealt with the *Scharnhorst*, Admiral Sir Philip Vian of *Cossack* fame, Captain B. A. Warburton-Lee at Narvik, and many others. Above all, Nelson lived again in Admiral Sir Andrew B. Cunningham, especially at Taranto and Matapan. Nor was the Royal Navy alone in remembering Nelson; his spirit animated the Navy of the United States in its many actions against the Japanese and, to name just one of its commanders, Nelson would surely have seen much of his own image in Admiral W. F. Halsey. Above all, these two great Navies, together with those of their allies, achieved Nelson's enduring ambition, 'annihilation'; the total surrender of the Italian Fleet in 1943, and of all that remained of the German and Japanese Navies in 1945.

Since then the United States, which in the nineteenth century grew to greatness behind the sure shield of the Royal Navy, has grasped Neptune's trident. The USSR also aims to do so. Great Britain, as always 'very small among the nations', no longer boasts the largest Navy in the world, although it has spawned a number of not insignificant Fleets among such countries as Australia, Canada, India, Pakistan and New Zealand which were once under her dominion but now form part of that free association, the British Commonwealth of Nations. And among all these, the Royal Navy's history, reputation and traditions remain. Nelson long served his country by his exertions; he has served her and her friends for longer still by his example – and, one trusts, will always do so. In peace or war the Navy that is true to Nelson *cannot fail*.

The man and the ships he knew how to lead have passed away, but Nelson's uplifting touch remains. The hazardous difficulties of handling a fleet under canvas have passed beyond our conception. The difference in the character of the ships is so enormous that the modern naval man must feel that the time has come for the great sea officers of the past to be laid in the temple of august memories. But Nelson's conviction and audacity, sustained by an unbounded trust in the men he led, stand out from his Trafalgar Memorandum. Those who from the heat of Trafalgar sank together in the cool depths of the ocean would gaze with amazed eyes at the engines of our strife. All passes, all changes: the animosity of peoples, the handling of fleets, the forms of ships; even the sea itself seems to wear a different and diminished aspect from the sea of Nelson's day. We must turn to the national spirit which, in its continuity to good and evil fortune, can alone give us the feeling of an enduring existence and of an invincible power against the fates. In its incorruptible flow it preserves the greatness of our great men, amongst them the passionate and gentle greatness of Nelson, the nature of whose genius was such as to 'Exalt the glory of our nation'.*

So let 'Finis' be written in the words of Richard Brinsley Sheridan† – Dublin born be it noted by those who are still as critical of Nelson as the

*Abridged from *The Mirror of the Sea*, by Joseph Conrad.
†Here abridged.

two Irishmen quoted in the first chapter of this book – which are inscribed on James Smith's monument, erected in London's Guildhall as early as 1810 (nearly forty years before the completion of Railton's column in Trafalgar Square: the Alderman and Common Councilmen must have remembered how they had failed to do justice to Nelson's victory at Copenhagen):

A Man amongst the few, who promoted the grandeur, and added to the security of Nations. Providence implanted in his breast an ardent passion for deserved renown, and bounteously endowed him with transcendent talents. Rising to command, he infused into those he led the valorous ardour and enthusiastic zeal for the service of his King and Country with which he himself was animated; and while he acquired the love of all, he inspired universal confidence in the never-failing resources of his capacious mind. History will relate the many great exploits through which he became the glory of his profession; but in his illustrious career he commanded and conquered at the battles of the Nile and Copenhagen, victories never before equalled, yet afterwards surpassed by his own last achievement, the battle of Trafalgar. On that day he fell mortally wounded; but the sources of life and sense failed not until he knew the destruction of the enemy to be completed, and the glory of his Country, and his own, had attained their summit.

'This monument has been erected to manifest our estimation of the Man, and as admiration of his deeds. This testimony of our gratitude will, we trust, remain as long as our own renowned City shall exist. *The period to Nelson's fame can only be the end of time.*'

CHRONOLOGICAL SUMMARY FOR CHAPTER XII

EVENTS IN NELSON'S LIFE	DATE	RELATED EVENTS
	1805	
Destroys combined fleets in battle fought off Cape Trafalgar, in which killed.	*21 October*	
	2 December	Austrians vanquished at Austerlitz and sue for peace.
Victory arrives Spithead with Nelson's body.	*5 December*	
Body landed at The Nore, to lie in state at Greenwich.	*23 December*	

EVENTS IN NELSON'S LIFE	DATE	RELATED EVENTS
	1806	
Funeral in St Paul's Cathedral.	*9 January*	
	23 January	Death of (younger) Pitt.
	16 May	Britain declares blockade of French ports.
	7 October	Napoleon invades Prussia.
	26 December	Napoleon defeats Russians near Warsaw.
	1807	
	7–9 July	Treaty of Tilsit signed between France, Russia and Prussia.
		Napoleon enforces Continental System.
	7 September	Danish Fleet surrenders to Gambier at Copenhagen.
	1808	
	17 January	Allemand escapes from Aix Roads to Toulon.
	7 February	Ganteaume leaves Toulon to succour Corfu.
	10 April	Ganteaume returns to Toulon.
	Summer	Saumarez gains ascendancy over Russian and Swedish fleets in Baltic.
	1 August	Wellington's expeditionary force lands in Portugal.
	30 August	French evacuate Portugal.
	27 October	Moore invades Spain.
	1809	
	January	Royal Navy evacuates Moore's army from Corunna.
	21 February	Willaumez sorties from Brest and seeks refuge in Aix Roads.
	11 April	Lord Cochrane's attack on Aix Roads.
	26 April	Wellington's new army lands at Lisbon.

EVENTS IN NELSON'S LIFE	DATE	RELATED EVENTS
	1810	
	7 March	Collingwood dies.
	27 August	French invade Portugal.
	10 October	French halted by Wellington's lines of Torres Vedras.
	1811	
	March	French retreat from Portugal.
	1812	
	18 June	War between Britain and USA.
	24 June	Napoleon invades Russia.
	19 October	Napoleon begins retreat from Moscow.
	1813	
	7 October	Wellington invades France.
	1814	
	31 March	Allies enter Paris.
	4 May	Napoleon begins exile in Elba.
	24 December	Treaty of Ghent ends war between Britain and USA.
	1815	
Death of Emma Hamilton.	*15 January*	
	26 February	Napoleon escapes from Elba.
	18 June	Battle of Waterloo.
	17 October	Napoleon reaches St Helena in *Northumberland*.
	20 November	Treaty of Paris ends Napoleonic Wars.
	1821	
	5 May	Napoleon dies in St Helena.
	1831	
Death of Lady Nelson	*6 May*	
	1881	
Death of Mrs Nelson-Ward (*née* Horatia Nelson Thompson).	*6 March*	

NOTES ON THE PLATES

1 *Horatio Nelson, Vice-Admiral of the White, Knight of the Bath, Baron and Viscount of the Nile and of Burnham Thorpe and Hilborough in the County of Norfolk, Duke of Brontë* (1758–1805). A photograph of part of the wax effigy in the Norman Undercroft of Westminster Abbey, modelled by Catherine Andreas to whom Nelson sat. Georgiona, Duchess of Devonshire, who knew him well, said that it 'is as if he was standing there'. The undress uniform is Nelson's own. The stars are those of the Bath (as also the crimson sash), St Ferdinand (of the Two Sicilies), the Crescent (of Turkey), and St Joachim. The medal on the blue and white riband was awarded for the battle of the Nile.

2 *The old parsonage house (or rectory) at Burnham Thorpe in the County of Norfolk in which Nelson was born on 29 September 1758*. A print from the painting by F. Pocock in the National Maritime Museum, Greenwich. The house was demolished in 1802.

3 *Nelson's baptism recorded in the register of Burnham Thorpe Church.*

4 *The Church at Burnham Thorpe, of which Nelson's father was Rector.* A recent photograph. The Church flies the white ensign of pre-1801 design, *i.e.* without the cross of St Patrick which was added to the upper canton next the halyards after the Union with Ireland. Burnham thus pays its own tribute to its hero with the white ensign that was used by the Royal Navy for all but the last four years of his life.

5 *Midshipman Nelson's first fight* – with a polar bear, the incident reputed to have taken place during the 15 year-old Nelson's service with an Arctic expedition in 1773. The painting by Richard Westall (1765–1836) in the National Maritime Museum, Greenwich.

6 *Nelson's Dockyard, English Harbour, Antigua.* This recent picture shows the dockyard, with from left to right its careening capstans, officers' quarters, seamen's barracks, capstan, mast and boat houses, as restored to serve as a yacht marina. Note also the ruined forts which once protected the harbour.

7 *Captain Horatio Nelson at the age of 23.* Nelson gave the artist, John Rigaud, RA (1742–1810), sittings for this portrait in 1777 when he was a lieutenant. Still unfinished when he returned from the West Indies as a post-captain at the end of 1780, Nelson gave it to his friend, Captain William Locker, with the comment: 'It will not be the least like what I am now, that is certain, but you may tell Mr Rigaud to add beauty to it'. When completed, Rigaud inscribed it, *Captain Horatio Nelson, 1781*. In background Fort San Juan. Now in the National Maritime Museum, Greenwich.

8 Five of Nelson's ships: in left background, HMS *Agamemnon*, (64 guns); to the left, beam on, HMS *Vanguard* (74 guns); in left foreground, HMS *Elephant*

(74 guns); in right background, HMS *Captain* (74 guns); in right foreground, HMS *Victory* (100 guns); all anchored at Spithead (Portsmouth can be seen in the right distance) with sails loosed for drying. Painted by Nicholas Pocock (1741?–1821) in 1808 to illustrate Clarke and McArthur's *Life and Services of Admiral Lord Nelson*. Now in the National Maritime Museum, Greenwich.

9 HMS *'Victory' today (1970)*. Soon after the Napoleonic wars Nelson's flagship was secured to a buoy in Portsmouth harbour and somewhat altered to serve as an accommodation vessel, and to fly the flag of the Commander-in-Chief Portsmouth. There she remained until after the First World War when, in order to preserve her for posterity, she was moved into a dry dock whose caisson was replaced by a concrete wall, and the blocks on which the ship rested raised so that she was up to the level at which she once floated. She was subsequently restored to her Trafalgar appearance, her decayed timbers replaced, most of her guns replaced by wooden replicas to lighten the load on her hull, and her tall masts firmly stayed out to the dock side. She still flies an admiral's flag, that of the Commander-in-Chief Home who uses Nelson's cabin to receive and entertain important visitors. And on 21 October each year she flies Nelson's Trafalgar signal, 'England expects . . .', a wreath being laid on the spot where he fell mortally wounded. Otherwise she is open daily to the public, receiving many thousands of visitors every year.

10 *One of the 'Victory's gun decks.* A recent photograph. Note the centre gun on its elm truck carriage, with breeching rope, train tackle, quoin and (overhead) rod sponge, rod rammer, rope sponge and rammer (used when gun not fully run in) and crew's hammocks.

11 *The Admiralty building, Whitehall.* An early nineteenth-century print showing the Whitehall façade designed by Thomas Ripley in 1722, and still in use as Government offices, and the screen fronting the courtyard added by Robert Adam in 1760. Note, on the roof, the new semaphore telegraph which replaced Murray's in 1816, and the wind vane operating the dial in the Board Room (carved by Grinling Gibbons) by which the First Lord judged whether the fleet could sail from Spithead, etc.

12 *Murray's semaphore telegraph*; one of the stations used from 1796 for rapid communication between the Admiralty in London and ships in the Downs, at the Nore, at Portsmouth and Spithead, in Torbay, and in Plymouth Sound. This part of a contemporary print, shows how the letters of the alphabet were signalled by different arrangements of the six shutters.

13 *The battle of Cape St Vincent, fought on 14 February 1797.* This painting by William Dolphus Knell (1800?–1875), which hangs in the Peer's Corridor in the House of Lords, shows the action at about 3.15 p.m. Nelson's *Captain* (centre foreground) is engaged with the Spanish four-decker *Santísima Trinidad*

to starboard, and with the *San Nicolas* and *San José* to port. The *Blenheim*, *Culloden*, *Excellent*, *Irresistible*, *Orion*, *Prince George* and *Victory* are also shown.

14 *Nelson's Commander-in-Chief in the Mediterranean, 1793–94: Admiral Lord Hood, KB (1724–1803).* Detail from a three-quarter length portrait by Lemuel Abbott (1760–1803) in the National Portrait Gallery, London.

15 *Nelson's Commander-in-Chief in the Mediterranean, 1795–99: John Jervis, Admiral of the Fleet, KB, 1st Earl St Vincent (1734–1823).* Detail from a full length portrait by John Hoppner, RA, (1758–1810) in The Queen's collection.

16 *The abortive attack on Santa Cruz, Teneriffe, during the night of 24 July 1797.* Nelson with drawn sword, about to step ashore from one of the *Theseus*' boats, falls seriously wounded in the right arm into the arms of his stepson, Midshipman Josiah Nisbet. The painting by Richard Westall (1765–1836) in the National Maritime Museum, Greenwich.

17 *The battle of the Nile, fought on 1 August 1798.* This painting by Nicolas Pocock (1741?–1821) in the National Maritime Museum, Greenwich, shows the scene in Aboukir Bay, viewed from the south, at about 6.0 p.m. Note from left to right, the fortified town of Aboukir (in background), the four French frigates, Brueys' battle fleet at anchor with HMS *Zealous* rounding his van, and the rest of Nelson's fleet bearing down on the French ships-of-the-line lying head to wind.

18 '*The burning of the "Orient" at the battle of the Nile*', was the title given by Joseph Cartwright (1789?–1829) to this painting of the scene in Aboukir Bay at about 9.30 p.m., in The Queen's collection. Ahead of the *Orient*, which will shortly blow up, is the *Franklin* in action with HMS *Leander*. To the right are HM ships *Swiftsure*, *Defence* and *Minotaur*. Note how easily the British ships can be distinguished from the French by the broad black and yellow bands with which their sides were painted.

19 *A cartoonist's verdict on the Nile.* The cartoon by James Gillray (1757–1815) captioned, *Extirpation of the Plagues of Egypt; Destruction of Revolutionary Crocodiles, or, The British Hero cleansing ye Mouth of ye Nile.* 'The valiant Admiral is dispersing the French fleet, portrayed as crocodiles. He has destroyed many with his cudgel of British oak; he is beating down others; a whole bevy, with hooks through their noses, are attached by strings to the iron hook which he is here supposed to have had fixed to the stump of his right arm. In the distance one crocodile is blowing up, an allusion to the destruction of the *Orient*.'

20 *Lady Nelson*, a portrait by an unknown artist, now in the National Maritime Museum, Greenwich.

21 *Nelson out of uniform.* This painting by H. Füger for which Nelson sat in

1800, is the only contemporary picture of him not wearing uniform. Now in the National Portrait Gallery, London.

22 *Emma, Lady Hamilton*, painted by George Romney (1734–1802) when she was about 18. One of many portraits by the same artist. Now in the National Portrait Gallery, London.

23 *Emma Hamilton* née *Emily Lyon*, cartooned by James Gillray (1757–1815) in 1801. The title makes cruel use of Emma's name before her marriage.

24 *Spoils of victory*. This print, published in 1802, illustrates the twenty-six ships-of-the-line in whose capture or destruction Nelson took part between 1795 and 1801, viz: *Ça Ira* and *Censeur* at the battle of Genoa, 14 March 1795; *Alcide* at the battle of Hyères, 12 August 1795; *San José, San Nicolas, Salvador del Mundo* and *San Ysidro* at the battle of Cape St Vincent, 14 February 1797; *Orient, Guerrier, Conquérant, Spartiate, Aquilon, Peuple Souverain, Franklin, Tonnant, Heureux, Mercure* and *Timoléon* at the battle of the Nile, 1 August 1798; *Généreux* on 18 February 1800; *Prövestenen, Wagrien, Jylland, Dannebrog, Sjaelland, Holsteen* and *Infödsretten* at the battle of Copenhagen, 2 April 1801

25 *The battle of Copenhagen fought on 2 April 1801*. Painted by Nicolas Pocock (1741?–1821) in 1805, now in the National Maritime Museum, Greenwich, this panoramic view from the north-east shows the British bombs in left foreground, and behind them Nelson's battle fleet in hot action with (beyond) the Danish ships and floating batteries. In right background the Trekoner fort and, behind it, the city of Copenhagen.

26 *Captain (later Rear-Admiral Sir) Alexander Ball* (1759–1809), in command of HMS *Alexander* at the Nile. Detail from three-quarter length portrait by Henry Pickersgill, RA (1782–1875) in the National Maritime Museum, Greenwich.

27 *Captain Sir James (later Admiral Lord de, KB) Saumarez, Bart.* (1757–1836), Nelson's second-in-command at the Nile. Detail from full-length portrait by Thomas Phillips, RA (1770–1845) in the National Maritime Museum, Greenwich.

28 *Captain (later Rear-Admiral Sir) Edward Berry* (1766–1831), Nelson's flag captain in the *Vanguard* at the Nile. Detail from three-quarter length portrait by the American painter John Copley (1737–1815) in the National Maritime Museum, Greenwich.

29 *Captain (later Rear-Admiral Sir) Thomas Troubridge, Bart.* (1758–1807), in command of HMS *Culloden* at the Nile. Detail from full-length portrait by Samuel Drummond, ARA (1765–1844) in the United Service and Royal Aero Club, London.

30 *Commander of the Russian fleet in the Mediterranean, 1798–1800; Admiral Feodór Feodórovich Ushakóv* (1744–1817).

31 *Nelson's only meeting with the future 1st Duke of Wellington, then Lieutenant-General Sir Arthur Wellesley (1796–1852), in the Colonial Office on 13 September 1805.* Engraving by S. W. Reynolds from the painting (whose whereabouts cannot now be traced) done by J. P. Knight, RA (1803–1881) titled *The Army and the Navy*. To depict Nelson and Wellington wearing uniform rather than civilian dress on this occasion may well be artistic licence.

32 *Vice-Admiral François Paul Brueys* (1753–1798), detail from full length engraving of the French Commander-in-Chief defeated by Nelson and killed at the Nile.

33 *Commodore Johan Olfert Fischer*, the only known portrait of the Danish Commander-in-Chief defeated by Nelson at Copenhagen.

34 *Vice-Admiral Pierre Charles Villeneuve* (1763–1806), Commander-in-Chief of the combined fleets vanquished by Nelson at Trafalgar.

35 *Admiral Don Federico Gravina* (1756–1806), commander of the Spanish force at Trafalgar.

36 *Vice-Admiral Lord Nelson* (1758–1805) at the age of 43. Nelson sat for this painting by John Hoppner, RA (1758–1810) in 1802. In background the battle of Copenhagen. Now in The Queen's collection.

37 *Admiral Sir Hyde Parker* (1739–1807), Nelson's Commander-in-Chief in the Baltic, 1801. Detail from three-quarter length portrait by George Romney, (1734–1802) in the National Maritime Museum, Greenwich.

38 *Vice-Admiral (later Admiral Viscount) 1st Baron Keith, KB* (1746–1823). Nelson's Commander-in-Chief in the Mediterranean, 1799–1800. Detail from three-quarter length portrait by John Hoppner, RA (1758–1810) in The Queen's collection.

39 *Vice-Admiral Cuthbert (later Admiral Lord) Collingwood* (1750–1810), Nelson's second-in-command at Trafalgar. Detail from the full-length portrait by Colvin Smith, RSA (1795–1875) after William Owen, RA (1769–1825) in the United Service and Royal Aero Club, London.

40 *Captain (later Vice-Admiral Sir) Thomas Masterman Hardy* (1769–1839), Nelson's flag captain at Trafalgar. Detail from three-quarter length portrait by Richard Evans (1784–1871) in the National Maritime Museum, Greenwich.

41–2 *The battle of Trafalgar*, fought on 21 October 1805, painted by Thomas Luny (1759–1837) shortly after the news reached England, now in a private collection. Both pictures are of interest more for showing how the battle was generally supposed to have been fought than for their accuracy. In the first, titled '*The Approach*', Nelson's division appears in orthodox line ahead with the leading ships just beginning to engage the centre of the combined fleets, which are spread in an exaggerated concave line. Collingwood's division would be 'off stage' to the right. The second picture, titled '*The Engrace*', portrays the scene at about 1.30 p.m. but, except for the *Victory* (third from left), and the *Redoutable* with which she is in close action to starboard, and (on fire to the right) the unfortunate *Achille*, it is difficult to name the ships.

HMS 'Victory' breaking the line at Trafalgar, painted by George Chambers (1803–1840) after Clarkson Stansfield, now in Admiralty House, Whitehall. A vivid impression of the scene at about 1.30 p.m. with HMS *Victory* (right of centre) engaged to starboard with the *Redoutable* and, on the latter's starboard hand HMS *Téméraire*.

44 *HMS 'Victory' at Trafalgar* (looking forward along the main deck from the break of the poop): Nelson mortally wounded. The painting by Denis Dighton (1792–1827) in the National Maritime Museum, Greenwich. In foreground, a midshipman returning the *Redoutable*'s sharpshooter's fire; also right foreground Captain Hardy going to Nelson's aid. Other points of interest: the captain of the gun in left foreground tending the flint lock; the captain of the gun beyond pulling the firing lanyard of his weapon; and the red-coated marines clearing the enemy decks with musket fire.

45 *Humanity after victory*. This recent painting by Leslie Wilcox, RI, RSMA, (1920–   ), depicts Jeanette, wife of a French *matelot*, about to be rescued by a British boat after jumping overboard from the burning *Achille* (left background) in which she stowed away in order to be with her husband. Fortunately, he also survived this disaster and they were reunited, as prisoners-of-war, five days later.

Bibliography*

Anderson, R. C., *Naval Wars in the Levant, 1559–1853* (1952)
Archibald, E. H. H., *Wooden Fighting Ship* (1968)
Beatty, W., *Authentic Narrative of Death of Lord Nelson* (1807)
Berckman, E., *Nelson's Dear Lord* (1962)
Beresford, Captain Lord Charles and Wilson, W. H., *Nelson and his Times* (1897)
Berry, Sir E., *Authentic Narrative of Proceedings of H.M. Squadron under Command of Sir H. Nelson* (1798)
Brenton, E., *Naval History of Great Britain* (1823)
    Life and Correspondence of Earl St Vincent (1838)
Broadley, A. M. and Bartelot, R. G., *Three Dorset Captains at Trafalgar* (1906)
    Nelson's Hardy: his Life, Letters and Friends (1909)
Bryant, Sir A., *Years of Endurance* (1942)
    Years of Victory (1944)
Bundesen, R. C., *Mindeskrift om Slaget paa Redan København* (Copenhagen, 1901)
Callender, Sir G., *Story of H.M.S. Victory* (1929)
Chevalier, E., *Histoire de la Marine Française sous le Consulat et l'Empire* (Paris, 1886)
Clarke, J. and McArthur, J., *Life and Services of Horatio, Viscount Nelson* (1809)

*Most of the documents relevant to Nelson's life and career have now been published in one or other of these books. I have not, therefore, listed the various collections, etc. in which these are preserved. Exceptionally, however, this is indicated, *e.g.* in footnotes to the text, where RA denotes the Royal Archives at Windsor.

Clowes, Sir W. L. and others, *The Royal Navy, a History* (Vols III, IV and V) (1898–1900)

Collingwood, G. N., *Correspondence and Memoirs of Vice-Admiral Lord Collingwood* (1829)

Corbett, Sir J. S., *Campaign of Trafalgar* (1910)

Creswell, Captain J., *Some Principles of Maritime Strategy* (1911)
Naval Warfare (2nd ed. 1942)

Dancer, T., *Brief History of the Late Expedition against Fort St Juan* (1792)

Desbrières, E. (Ed. Eastwick, C. L.), *Trafalgar Campaign* (1933)

Drinkwater-Bethune, Colonel K., *Narrative of Action off Cape St Vincent with Anecdotes of Nelson* (1797 and 1840)

Douglas, Sir H., *Naval Gunnery* (1821 and 1860)

Duro, C. F., *Armada Espanola*, Vol. VIII (Madrid, 1902)

Edinger, G. and Neep, C. J., *Horatio Nelson* (1930)

Farrere, C., *Histoire de la Marine* (Paris)

Fothergill, B., *Sir William Hamilton* (1969)

Fraser, E., *The Enemy at Trafalgar* (1906)

Fremantle, A. (Ed.), *Wynne Diaries, 1789–1820* (in 3 vols. 1935, 1937 and 1940. Also a single volume selection with additional material, 1952)

Gérin, W., *Horatia Nelson* (1970)

Government, H.M., *Report of Admiralty Commission to Inquire into Tactics of Trafalgar*, Cd. 7120 (1913)

Graviere, J. de la, *Guerres Maritimes de la France sous la République et l'Empire* (Paris, 1883)

Grenfell, Captain R., *Horatio Nelson* (1962)

Guérin, L., *Marins Illustres de la France* (Paris)

Hardman, W., *French Occupation of Malta and Early British Rule* (1909)

Hardwick, M., *Emma, Lady Hamilton* (1969)

Harrison, J., *Life of Viscount Nelson* (1806)
Letters of Lord Nelson to Lady Hamilton (1814)

Howarth, D., *Trafalgar, The Nelson Touch* (1969)

James, W., *Naval History of Great Britain 1793–1820* (1837)

James, Admiral Sir W. M., *The Durable Monument, Horatio Nelson* (1948)
Old Oak, the Life of John Jervis, Earl St Vincent (1950)

Jeaffreson, J. C., *Lady Hamilton and Lord Nelson* (1888)
Queen of Naples and Lord Nelson (1889)

Jonquiere, C. de la, *L'Expedition d'Egypt* (Paris, 1899–1907)

Joubert, Admiral, *La Marine Française* (Paris, 1946)

Kennedy, L., *Nelson's Band of Brothers* (1967)

Kerr, Captain M., *Sailor's Nelson* (1932)

Laughton, Sir J. K., *Nelson Memorial* (1896)

Lecene, P., *Les Marins de la République et de l'Empire, 1793–1815* (Paris, 1884)

Lewis, M., *Navy of Britain* (1948)
Social History of Royal Navy, 1793–1815 (1960)

Lloyd, C., *St Vincent and Camperdown* (1963)
The British Seaman (1969)

Longridge, N., *Anatomy of Nelson's Ships* (1955)

Mackenzie, Colonel R. H., *Trafalgar Roll* (1913)

Mackesy, P., *War in the Mediterranean, 1803–1810* (1957)

Mahan, Captain A. T., *Influence of Sea Power upon History* (1890)
Influence of Sea Power upon French Revolution and Empire (1892)
Life of Nelson (1897)

Marcus, G. J., *Naval History of England*, Vol. II: *Age of Nelson* (1971)

Marshall-Cornwall, J., *Napoleon as Military Commander* (1968)

Masefield, J., *Sea Life in Nelson's Time* (1905)

Matcham, M. E., *Nelsons of Burnham Thorpe* (1911)

Miles, J. M., *Vindication of Lord Nelson's Proceedings in Bay of Naples* (1843)

Minto, Nina Countess of (Ed.), *Life and Letters of Sir Gilbert Elliot, first Earl of Minto* (1874)

Mordal, J., *Vingt-Cinq Siècles de Guerre sur Mer* (Paris, translated and published in London as *Twenty-five centuries of Sea Warfare*)

Mórdvinov, R. N. (Ed.), *Letters and Papers of Admiral Ushakóv* (in Russian), Vols. I–III (Moscow 1951, 1952 and 1956)

Morrison, A., *Hamilton and Nelson Papers* (1893–94)

Murray, G., *Life of Lord Collingwood* (1936)

Navy Records Society:
  Vol. XVI, *Logs of Great Sea Fights*, Vol. I
  Vol. XVIII, Ditto, Vol. II
  Vol. XX, *Naval Miscellany*, Vol. I
  Vol. XL, Ditto, Vol. II
  Vol. LXVIII, Ditto, Vol. III
  Vol. XCII, Ditto, Vol. IV
  Vol. XXIV, *Journals and Letters of Admiral-of-the-Fleet, Sir Thomas Byam Martin*, Vol. I
  Vol. XXV, *Nelson and the Neapolitan Jacobins*
  Vol. XXIX, *Fighting Instructions*
  Vol. XXXV, *Signals and Instructions*

Navy Records Society (contd)
   Vol. XXXIX, *Letters and Papers of Charles, Lord Barham*, Vol. III
   Vol. XLVI, *Private Papers of George, second Earl Spencer*, Vol. I
   Vol. XLVIII, Ditto, Vol. II
   Vol. LVIII, Ditto, Vol. III
   Vol. LIX, Ditto, Vol. IV
   Vol. LV, *Letters of Lord St Vincent*, Vol. I
   Vol. LXI, Ditto, Vol. II
   Vol. LXXIV, *Tomlinson Papers*
   Vol. XC, *Letters and Papers of Admiral Viscount Keith*, Vol. II
   Vol. XCVI, Ditto, Vol. III
   Vol. XCI, *Five Naval Journals*
   Vol. XCIII, *Sir William Dillon's Narrative of Professional Adventures*,
     Vol. I
   Vol. XCVII, Ditto, Vol. II
   Vol. XCVIII, *Private Correspondence of Admiral Lord Collingwood*
   Vol. C, *Nelson's Letters to his Wife and other Documents*
   Vol. CI, *Memoirs of James Trevenen*
Newbolt, Sir H., *Year of Trafalgar* (1905)
Nicolas, Sir N. H., *Despatches and Letters of Vice-Admiral Lord Viscount Nelson* (1844–46)
Oman, C., *Nelson* (1947)
Pettigrew, T. J., *Memoir of Life of Vice-Admiral Lord Viscount Nelson* (1849)
Phipps, C., *Voyage Towards the North Pole* (1773)
Plunkett, Captain the Hon. E., *Sketches of the last Naval War* (1848)
Pocock, T., *Nelson and his World* (1968)
Pope, D., *England Expects* (1960)
   Guns (1965)
Rawson, G. (Ed.), *Nelson's Letters from the Leeward Islands* (1953)
Richmond, Admiral Sir H. W., *Statesmen and Sea Power* (1946)
Robertson, F. L., *Evolution of Naval Armament* (1921)
Roncière, de la, *La Marine Française* (Paris)
Rose, J. H., *Life of Napoleon I* (1934)
Roskill, Captain S. W., *Art of Leadership* (1964)
   Strategy of Sea Power (1965)
Russell, J., *Nelson and the Hamiltons* (1969)
Russell, W. C., *Life of Admiral Lord Collingwood* (1891)
Sherrard, O. A., *Life of Lord St Vincent* (1933)
Sichel, W., *Emma, Lady Hamilton* (1905)

Skalóvoskvo, R., *Life of Admiral Fedór Fedórovich Ushakóv* (in Russian)
    (St Petersburg, 1856)
Southey, R., *Life of Nelson* (1813) (An edition published in 1922 contains
    notes by Sir G. Callender pointing out Southey's inaccuracies)
Thursfield, Rear-Admiral J. R., *Nelson and other Naval Studies* (1932)
Tours, E., *Life and Letters of Emma Hamilton* (1963)
Tramond, J., *Manuel d'Histoire Maritime de la France* (Paris)
Tucker, J. S., *Memoirs of Earl St Vincent* (1844)
Warner, O., *Portrait of Lord Nelson* (1958)
    Battle of the Nile (1960)
    Emma Hamilton and Sir William (1960)
    Trafalgar (1960)
    Nelson's Battles (1965)
    Life and Letters of Vice-Admiral Lord Collingwood (1969)
Wilkinson, C., *Life of Nelson* (1931)

Index

The numerals in **heavy type** refer to the figure numbers of the illustrations. The italicised numerals *268–9* refer to the table of the opposing fleets at Trafalgar to be found between these two pages.

People are given their most senior rank, title, etc. mentioned in this book. Those who changed their name (*e.g.* on elevation to the peerage) are cross-referenced (*e.g.* Jervis, Admiral Sir John, *see* St. Vincent).

Ships are listed under 'Ships, American', 'British', etc. N. is used as an abbreviation for Nelson.